THE POLITICS OF AMERICAN CITIES

Private Power and Public Policy

Third Edition

DENNIS R. JUDD

University of Missouri-St. Louis

 HarperCollins*Publishers*

Library of Congress Cataloging-in-Publication Data

Judd, Dennis R.
  The politics of American cities.

  Includes bibliographies and index.
  1. Municipal government—United States.   2. Urban
policy—United States.   I. Title.
JS331.J8   1988   320.8'0973   87-17942
ISBN 0-673-39730-0

          6 7 8 9 10 - PAT - 93

Printed in the United States of America

Acknowledgments

Table 7-4 General Government Expenditures
     From Alexander Ganz, "Where Has the Urban Crisis Gone? How Boston and Other
Large Cities Have Stemmed Economic Decline," *Urban Affairs Quarterly,* Vol. 20, No. 4
(June 1985), p. 460. Copyright © 1985 by Sage Publications, Inc. Reprinted by permission
of Sage Publications, Inc.

Table 12-1 Change in Earned Income
     From Alexander Ganz, "Where Has the Urban Crisis Gone? How Boston and Other
Large Cities Have Stemmed Economic Decline," *Urban Affairs Quarterly,* Vol. 20, No. 4
(June 1985), p. 454. Copyright © 1985 by Sage Publications, Inc. Reprinted by permission
of Sage Publications, Inc.

Table 12-2 Changing Occupational Structure of New York City
     Adapted from Norman I. Fainstein and Susan S. Fainstein, "Restructuring the City: A
Comparative Perspective," in *Urban Policy Under Capitalism,* ed. N. Fainstein and S.
Fainstein. Urban Affairs Annual Reviews, Vol. 22, p. 179. Copyright © 1982 by Sage Publi-
cations Inc. Reprinted by permission of Sage Publications, Inc.

This book is dedicated to my parents, Willard and Ethel, and to Lou Gold

PREFACE

National political and economic changes are amplified in the metropolitan context. Changes in the national economic structure—especially, in the 1980s, the continuing loss of manufacturing employment in favor of service sector jobs—have been felt by both urban communities trying to cope with declining local economies and those attempting to provide services and build the infrastructure to cope with rapid population growth. Differences in regional economic development are a national issue. In general, it has taken the form of a Sunbelt versus Frostbelt conflict, although with the drop in oil prices in 1985, several Sunbelt cities have begun to experience the problems normally associated with older industrial cities.

Changes in national governmental policy likewise reverberate within cities and metropolitan areas. The federal government has continued to cut federal urban and social service programs; in fact, by 1986 the national government had basically stopped trying to implement policies overtly designed to address urban problems. Changes in national policy interacted with transformations in the economy. Reductions in urban and social programs, combined with the replacement of higher-wage industrial sector with minimum-wage service sector jobs, created a circumstance in which healthy local economies benefitted only some occupational and social groups. The economic upturn beginning in 1983 increased investment in older industrial cities; new office towers, convention centers, and shopping malls sprang up in cities that had almost been written off as obsolescent and permanently depressed. At the same time, however, the numbers of the homeless roaming the streets increased dramatically, crime escalated, racial segregation and incidents of racial conflict continued, and poverty increased.

In some cities, new electoral movements came together behind populist programs based on the premise that the benefits of economic growth should be more widely distributed. City officials—especially minority mayors put into office by these coalitions—found themselves trying to deliver on promises of economic growth *and* better municipal services and social programs at the same time. Some of these issues found expression in Jesse Jackson's presidential campaign of 1984.

In this third edition, I have attempted to highlight some of the new issues that have surfaced since the 1984 election. Chapters 10 and 11 have been completely reorganized and rewritten to highlight the struggle over national urban and social welfare policy since 1960, so that the recent debates can be better understood. Chapter 13 contains entirely new material about the urban electoral coalitions of the 1980s and their likely impact on city politics. Relevant statistics have been updated throughout.

I have tried to cover all these developments and issues within the structure and themes of the previous edition. As before, it is my hope that this book will stand as a scholarly contribution in its own right. A textbook should derive its strength from original scholarship and insight. A textbook must also thoroughly synthesize the literature that defines a field of study. The two enterprises are not mutually exclusive, and I hope I have managed to make this book useful both to advanced scholars and to students taking their first course.

My thanks to Jeffrey Stonecash of Syracuse University and M. Elliot Vittes of the University of Central Florida for reviewing the manuscript.

Brad Dudding, an undergraduate student at the University of Missouri-St. Louis, provided invaluable assistance in updating tables and data throughout the book. I am very grateful for his help.

Sandy Overton-Springer did a magnificent job of typing (and finding errors) in the manuscript.

Dennis R. Judd

CONTENTS

CHAPTER 11
The Struggle over Urban Policy: 1968 to 1988   331

CHAPTER 12
The Politics of Redevelopment   371

Chapter 1

PUBLIC POLICY AND
PRIVATE RESOURCES

An Introduction
to the Themes of This Book

Public and Private Resources

Historically, city politics has evolved as an interplay between governmental power and private investment. In national politics and in local communities as well, governments in the twentieth century have vastly increased their responsibilities. But the growth of the public sector has not eclipsed the authority of private institutions to make critical political decisions involving jobs, land use, and investment. In summarizing the politics of San Francisco in the 1970s, one author wrote that:

> The . . . oligopoly of private resources acts as a major force on the community. . . . The diffusion of banks, retail stores, and industry from the core city to the outland is a basic quality of post–World War II land uses . . . the injection of . . . outside capital sources does affect such major decisions in local institutions of the economy and polity as: who shall work and for what returns; how such returns will be spent locally; what will be an available . . . tax source to support local public services; how traffic will move; and what public services will be needed. . . . The decision to insert or withdraw business resources, then, is a

1

decision certainly as important in scope and consequence as many others treated by students of community power.[1]

Despite the expansion of governmental responsibilities, the private sector has retained control over critical social and economic resources. This has been a fundamental fact throughout our national history, and in the politics of American cities.

The Underlying Values for Urban Politics in America

In nineteenth-century America, cities were regarded almost purely as economic entities. The constant process of territorial expansion, which lasted until the 1880s, placed new towns[2] at the leading face of economic exploitation and territorial claims. The abundance of land and raw materials in the frontier made expansion into new territory the principal measure of national progress. National economic growth was promoted through penetration into unsettled land, and exploitation of the new resources found there was made possible by the constantly expanding network of towns. The promise of success made capitalism—defined as unfettered entrepreneurial activity—unassailable as the mode of economic organization. No other system seemed appropriate in the face of seemingly boundless opportunities for individual enrichment. And capitalism also seemed to fit the fragmented, localized nation of small communities spread over a vast territory. Each town was its own capitalist system in miniature, held together by the independent actions of its local entrepreneurs, who were motivated by the search for profit and fortune.

If entrepreneurial activity alone defined city life, then the cities' politics and values would reflect the needs and outlooks of entrepreneurs. Local politics could be defined as the enterprise of protecting and promoting economic vitality. The political needs of entrepreneurs in America's towns and cities dictated that privatism—defined as the network of private economic transactions—would be the bedrock value in American culture: "the tradition of privatism is . . . the most important element in our culture for understanding the development of cities . . . (the) local politics of American cities have depended for their actors, and for a good deal of their subject matter, on the changing focus of men's private economic activities."[3]

And yet an understanding of the governmental role in urban areas must be anchored in some awareness of the expansion of the public agenda over time. As cities grew in the nineteenth century, governments assumed increasingly complex responsibilities—to supply water, curb disease, fight fire and crime, and provide streets and sewers. The expansion of the public sector was fueled by necessity, not by social theory. Problems of social order and organization tempered the capitalist impulse and influenced government activity throughout the nineteenth century. The periodic and recurring crises that threatened city residents also threatened entrepreneurs and their activities. In response to such threats, business leaders often promoted the expansion of local government. Riots, plagues, fires, and other calamities were problems to be solved by public authority, mostly because individual entrepreneurs were not motivated to supply the services adequate for addressing collective problems.

Public institutions were used to address the problems of social order because only government manifested the symbols of social cohesion— democratic decision making, representation, public taxes to support public services—in short, legitimacy. Business owners and managers in nineteenth-century cities frequently formed committees to build waterworks or to organize fire or health departments, but they claimed the legitimacy to do so by making these committees a part of local public, that is, governmental, authority.

The enlargement of government activity from the nineteenth century to the present can be traced invariably to a perceived threat to the social or economic order. In the twentieth century, three periods of crisis, and corresponding governmental expansion, can be identified.

The first great expansion occurred during the Progressive era, from about 1900 to 1920. Much of the reform impulse was motivated by a reaction to the terrible social conditions created by industrialization.

In the half-century following the Civil War, the American economy underwent a fundamental transformation. A railroad and telegraph network facilitated centralization of economic institutions. Large corporations grew to dominate the nation's economy and politics. A new hierarchy of industrial cities evolved, each controlling a hinterland, reducing smaller towns to economic satellites of the corporations located in the large cities.

Industrialization entailed a new level of exploitation of human beings. The factory, mine, and mill worked men, women, and children for long hours at low pay. By the turn of the century, ostentatious wealth contrasted with the poverty of immigrants crowded into festering city slums. Reformers began to demand that cities be humane as well as productive.

But even reformers who held grave doubts about the industrial economy believed that capitalism was a better system than any other, but that it had been subverted temporarily by corruption and greed. The socialist critique of capitalism as being inherently evil captured some followers, but for the most part it fell on deaf ears. What social reformers wanted was a return to the "golden age" before industrialization, when the world was, they thought, simpler, a time when individual enterprise and hard work were rewarded.

The reform impulse of the Progressives was multifaceted, but two important features stood out. One reform faction sought to moderate the worst effects of industrialization by providing protections for workers and their families through legislation regulating occupational safety, child labor, working hours, and the like. Another group of reformers attempted to curb the power of the large corporations through antitrust laws, corruption investigations, and utilities regulation. Lincoln Steffens, in his exposé of machine politics, blamed business leaders as much as politicians for municipal corruption: "The commercial spirit is the spirit of profit, not patriotism; of credit, not honor; of individual gain, not national prosperity; of trade and dickering, not principle."[4] In counseling reformers to separate business from politics, Steffens was not attacking capitalism but what he saw as its corruption.

The reform impulse reaffirmed, and was derived from, values extolling individualism and free enterprise. In fact, the attack on industrialism and "modernism" reflected a tenacious attachment to these values. The reformers' confusion, which at once worshiped individual competition and feared its consequences, resulted in a paralyzing impotence. Their own fear of government intrusion into the economic realm, defined as regulation of business, left government largely in the hands of conservatives, who kept government spending and responsibility as minimal as possible. Until the New Deal, national government institutions would reflect the concerns of large corporations.[5]

Local governmental institutions developed significantly during the first thirty years of the twentieth century, and especially during the 1920s. Reformers who pushed for state and national efforts to build parks, control monopolies, and regulate child labor also focused their efforts in the cities. New election regulations and campaign finance laws sought to impose honesty in the conduct of municipal elections. Housing reformers fought for tenement laws. Planners promoted park expansion. Health professionals wrote health and sanitation codes. In the 1920s, the automobile stimulated local efforts to improve streets and bridges, install traffic signals, and build parking lots.

The National Government's Role

The Great Depression of the 1930s was the first genuinely national crisis after the Civil War. When economic institutions collapsed, unemployment and destitution reached unprecedented levels. These conditions prompted a response from the national government. For the most part, this response took the form of regulating the economy and stabilizing economic institutions. The attempt to protect the economic system from collapse resulted in a "policy model" that persists to the present day. The "model" has two components: (1) to implement national policies through grants-in-aid to state and local governments, and (2) to implement government policies through the institutions of the marketplace. The American pattern has been to regulate and promote business enterprise as a way to accomplish social goals. This can be seen, for example, in the policies of the federal Economic Development Agency in the early 1970s:

> Both the legislation and the information leaflets of EDA (Economic Development Agency) claim that private enterprise is the key to remedying unemployment in depressed regions. A message from the assistant secretary of commerce in an information folder says, "The federal government, through EDA, can help with this task, but only private enterprise can get the unemployed off the relief roll and onto a payroll." In the United States Senate, following introduction of the public works and economic development bill, Senator Proxmire explained that he liked the bill because it stressed "private enterprise and private development," did not provide for a "gigantic federally controlled and directed public works program" and "basic investment decisions [would] be left up to the private sector of our economy."[6]

An indication of the extent of government reliance on private institutions to solve major public problems can be found in the testimony of New York Mayor Fiorello La Guardia before the Senate Committee on Banking and Currency just after World War II. In response to a question from one of the senators about the behavior of the "leaders of finance and industry" during the Depression, Mayor La Guardia replied:

> They had their program. "Just leave us alone. Don't interfere with business. The government doesn't know." Well, they were left alone. They were left alone more than at any time in the history of the country, and when they were left alone they crashed, and the whole thing came down.[7]

In La Guardia's view, business and financial interests were unable to correct the problems that brought on the Depression. Even so,

> "They were the first to get the relief," said the Mayor, "I remember," he continued, "in the closing days of the Congress of 1932–33 when the very crude, primitive RFC (Reconstruction Finance Corporation) bill came through. The argument was then, Oh yes; you must give assistance from the top. It will trickle down. It will create employment."[8]

The trickle-down assumption that business growth and investment would create jobs and incomes, thus reducing poverty and its related social problems, guided government programs then, as now. That the plight of the cities in such areas as housing deterioration, shrinking tax bases, increasing unemployment and poverty among minorities, and explosive leaps in public welfare expenditures might have other than economic origins was not discernible in government policies.

Housing and urban renewal legislation illustrates the singular emphasis on economic solutions. The several amendments to the Housing Act of 1949 sought to push urban renewal

> in the direction of utilizing renewal for urban economic rehabilitation and tax-base revitalization and for improving job opportunities. . . . From 1954 forward . . . there has been a gradual shift toward increasing emphasis on the economic consequences of urban renewal and an attendant growth in concern for the overall effects of renewal activities on the community.[9]

This tendency reflected a preference frequently expressed during the New Deal for reviving the economy *and* solving social problems by providing financial assistance to private sector institutions. For example, although housing legislation had social purposes, economic recovery was consistently the first priority, as was pointed out in a presidential committee report:

> . . . the Home Owner's Loan Act of 1933 . . . was enacted to protect both mortgagers and mortgagees from losing their interest in real property because of the Depression. The National Housing Act of 1932, while ostensibly designed to promote homeownership through the establishment of the FHA, in reality was developed because of the general collapse of economic activity in the 1930's and the assumption that stimulation of the residential construction industry would stimulate the entire economy. . . . The motivation was not to evolve a coherent housing policy . . . but to use housing as a means of aiding in the elimination of the Depression.[10]

The urban renewal programs of the 1950s and 1960s continued to reflect the federal government's concern about the national economy and the private institutions of the housing industry. By statute, publicly subsidized housing could be built only where it was demonstrated that the private sector could not fill the need.[11] Construction and redevelopment were accomplished through private contractors and developers, with government using eminent domain to acquire property, adjust taxes, and write down the cost of land to purchasers. Most projects were designed to renew or protect Central Business Districts.[12]

The third crisis to bring forth a national response occurred during the 1960s. Three components of this "urban crisis," as it was popularly called, prompted the Kennedy and Johnson administrations to extend the federal government into new areas of social policy. First, the civil rights movement, with its direct action strategies, threatened social disorder unless government solutions to racial inequality were forthcoming. Second was the crisis of slums, poverty, and especially racial violence. Third, the financial crisis of the central cities—the inability of cities to raise the revenue necessary to treat the social problems of the ghetto—caused difficulties for mayors and other public officials. These conditions motivated liberals in the Democratic party to sponsor the social legislation of the 1960s.

During the 1960s, the national government addressed the problems of inequality, poverty, urban decay, and local government organization. The legacy of American politics dictated that private institutions retain a large role in solving these problems. Even the most militant of the "social welfare" liberals clung tightly to this heritage. "To rely exclusively, even primarily, on government efforts," wrote Robert F. Kennedy,

> is to ignore the shaping traditions of American life and politics. To ignore the potential contribution of private enterprise is to fight the war on poverty with a single platoon, while great armies are left to stand aside.[13]

Reliance on the private sector in implementing government policies continued during the Carter administration. "We're trying to work out a scheme to get the benefits of the private sector but still keep a public purpose," announced a member of the Carter transition team.[14] And Ronald Reagan interpreted his presidential victory in 1980 as a mandate to cut government spending and regulation. Believing that government programs were the problem rather than the solution, Reagan began to reduce social and urban spending. Thus, for the first time since 1946, federal grants to cities and states dropped in 1982 to $86.8 billion, from $95.9 billion in 1981. Cities and states absorbed $13 billion (37 percent) of the $35.2 billion in budget cuts voted for fiscal year 1982. For a long time, government policy had been designed to use private institutions to achieve social goals. Under the Reagan administration, a new course was charted, at least in rhetoric: the purpose of public policy was to get government to step out of the way.

Politicians and Entrepreneurs: The Mutual Concern

Urban politics does not take place in a vacuum, dissociated from and unrelated to national politics. The political culture and traditions of the nation prevail in local communities. But the *consequences* of national politics are magnified at the local level.

The distribution of political and economic resources in American society is clearly visible on the urban landscape. Unequal incomes and other material resources are spatially distributed, and segregation adds to the problems already created by income inequality. Additionally, the segregation of social problems creates a politics of turf. Downtown business interests, for example, want to protect Central Business Districts from slums. Affluent white suburbanites try to exclude minorities and poor people from their neighborhoods. The fact that private institutions hold most of the valuable resources in urban areas and also have a vested interest in segregating land uses means that private resources are frequently used to actively maintain and promote inequality and spatial segregation.

Of course, public officials also frequently promote segregation. This is partly because they are products of a political culture that promotes individualism, competition, and secular progress. They have succeeded, and they wish to defend what they have. Second, they, like others who have "made it," benefit from segregation. By excluding the poor, keeping taxes low, and opposing programs that disproportionately benefit people below them, they enhance their own incomes and social class status. Third, public officials must answer to constituencies. Probably the most important groups in these constituencies represent the business and corporate realm. From the perspective of government officials, the answer to their problems of taxation, jobs, and adequate services is economic growth and investment. Only the wealthiest suburban communities can forgo industrial and commercial activity. Officials have little alternative, therefore, but to promote a favorable environment for private investment. "I never heard of a mayor who thought he could run a successful city without the private sector," remarked an official of the United States Conference of Mayors.[15] The public budget of any city is too small to accomplish community goals on its own. And that budget becomes smaller if business leaves for other environs.

Urban politics, then, is not the exclusive province of government institutions. It is the interaction of all institutions and individuals in the urban environment who have political stakes to defend. In the history of urban growth in the United States, these stakes have been principally economic. Analysis of strategies of leadership (public) and of investment (private) reveals much about the distribution of power in urban politics.

At times this book may seem to drift away from the central thesis concerning the nexus between private and public power. There are, for example, discussions of transportation technologies and demographic changes in nineteenth-century cities, foreign immigration to the cities, the movement of blacks from the South to northern urban areas, and the suburbanization of affluent whites. These events are examined in order to provide a setting for understanding the behavior of private and public institutions in allocating political and economic resources in urban areas.

This book is divided into three parts. In the first, the evolution of urban institutions is traced, from pre–Civil War cities to the New Deal. Particular emphasis is given to the impact of the economic and social changes brought about by industrialization. The political consequences of these changes are discussed in Chapters 3 through 5.

The second part treats the various elements of the "urban crisis." These elements include the political isolation of the central cities, the financial problems that resulted from their isolation, and the development of slums populated by minorities. These crises, which are widely associated with old northeastern and midwestern cities, are discussed in Chapters 6 through 8.

The third part of the book focuses on the governmental responses to the urban crisis. The interplay between private and public, federal and local, and economic and political institutions is especially important. Chapters 9 through 11 discuss the national government's attempts to resolve the various crises examined in Part II. Chapters 12 and 13 focus on the policies being pursued today by central city governments, and on the way these policies are intended to address the continuing "urban problem."

References

1. Frederick M. Wirt, *Power in the City: Decision-Making in San Francisco* (Berkeley: University of California Press, 1974), p. 329.

2. The U.S. Bureau of the Census defines "urban place" as an incorporated settlement of 2,500 people or more. With the 1910 Census, the concept of "metropolitan district" was introduced. This term went through several changes until 1950, when Standard Metropolitan Statistical Area (SMSA) entered the lexicon. SMSA is defined as a central city of 50,000 or more (or twin cities totaling that population) and surrounding counties that meet criteria of economic dependency (shown by journey-to-work research) and population density. Suburban population consists of SMSA population beyond central city boundaries. For a full discussion of these definitions, see U.S. Bureau of the Census, *The Growth of Metropolitan Districts in the United States: 1900–1940*, by Warren S. Thompson (Washington, D.C.: U.S. Government Printing Office, 1947). The prefaces to the Population Censuses for 1950, 1960, 1970, and 1980 include a discussion of definitions to date.

3. Sam Bass Warner, Jr., *The Private City: Philadelphia in Three Periods of Its Growth* (Philadelphia: University of Pennsylvania Press, 1968), p. 4.

4. Lincoln Steffens, *The Shame of the Cities*, introduction by Louis Joughlin, American Century Series (New York: Sagamore Press, 1957 [first published 1904]), pp. 4–5.

5. See appropriate sections of Chapter 4 for discussions of this point.

6. Jeffrey L. Pressman and Aaron B. Wildavsky, *Implementation: How Great Expectations in Washington Are Dashed in Oakland; or, Why It's Amazing That Federal Programs Work at All, This Being a Saga of the Economic Development Administration As*

Told by Two Sympathetic Observers Who Seek to Build Morals on a Foundation of Ruined Hopes (Berkeley: University of California Press, 1973), p. 71.

7. Quoted in Helen Ginsburg, ed., *Poverty, Economics and Society* (Boston: Little, Brown, 1972), p. 123.

8. Quoted in Ginsburg, p. 123.

9. Roscoe C. Martin, *The Cities and the Federal System* (New York: Atherton, 1965), p. 122.

10. President's Committee on Urban Housing, *A Decent Home: Report of the President's Committee on Urban Housing* (Washington, D.C.: U.S. Government Printing Office, 1968), p. 54.

11. Leonard Freedman, *Public Housing: The Politics of Poverty* (New York: Holt, Rinehart and Winston, 1969).

12. See, e.g., Scott Greer, *Urban Renewal and American Cities: The Dilemma of Democratic Intervention* (Indianapolis: Bobbs-Merrill, 1965); and James Q. Wilson, "Planning and Politics: Citizen Participation in Urban Renewal," and other readings in *Urban Renewal: The Record and the Controversy*, ed. James Q. Wilson, (Cambridge, Mass., and London: MIT Press, 1966).

13. Robert F. Kennedy, *To Seek a Newer World* (Garden City, N.Y.: Doubleday, 1967), p. 41.

14. Bruce Kirschenbaum, Carter transition team member in charge of intergovernmental relations, cited in Rochelle L. Stansfield, "Federalism Report: Is the Man from Georgia Ready to Help the States and Cities?" *National Journal: The Weekly on Politics and Government,* January 22, 1977, p. 130.

15. John J. Gunther, Executive Director of the United States Conference of Mayors, quoted in Stansfield, p. 130.

Part I

THE EVOLUTION OF CITY POLITICS IN AMERICA

Chapter 2

THE POLITICAL LEGACY OF THE NINETEENTH CENTURY

The Evolution of City Politics

The political problems that exist in contemporary American cities have evolved from social and economic transformations that occurred in the nineteenth century. There are three principal components of that legacy.

First. The United States was transformed by urbanization of such an unprecedented scale that it created nearly irresolvable political and social tensions. In considerably less than a century, cities mushroomed into large, complex social and economic entities that virtually overwhelmed the rest of the society. Cities and towns first claimed the wilderness and the frontier, then subjected them to the needs of urban society. The dominance of cities in American society—and what they became—spawned a distrust and sometimes a hatred for cities that influenced American culture well into the 1980s.

Second. What did cities do? They concentrated the wealth, ingenuity, and labor necessary for economic expansion. Transportation improvements and industrialization made them particularly efficient at this. After the 1850s, the railroad network spread from the cities into the hinterland, extracting ores, wood, and foodstuffs.

Industrialization involved a twin process of technological and organizational change. Handicrafts and artisan skills gave way to machine processes, which required rigidly enforced work habits. These processes in turn required greater concentrations of wealth and organizational complexity in business firms. The symbols and the reality of the industrial age were found in the cities, and thus the cities and the people who lived in them were blamed for the changes occurring in society. Everyone who resented the new economics—farmers who felt threatened by the new industrialism, American-born workers displaced by cheap immigrant labor—all vented their rage at the city.

Third. Industrial growth brought with it massive immigration; the search for cheap labor was insatiable. The cities became maelstroms of ethnic groups and ghettos. Tensions between immigrants and earlier settlers, between rich and poor, and between nationality groups often resulted in violence. The miserable condition of the newcomers—their poverty, illiteracy, and unfamiliarity with city life—bred social squalor. Cities seemed to be, literally, foreign invasions of American rural life.

These developments and the responses to them are important for an understanding of contemporary cities, largely because they are different in degree but not in kind from current political conflicts: the developments described in this chapter have contemporary parallels. Social class, ethnic, and racial conflicts continue to dominate politics in urban areas. The basic issues in today's urban areas are remarkably similar to those of 100 years ago.

The Urbanization of America

During the nineteenth century, the Western world underwent urbanization on a scale unprecedented in history. The size of cities and the proportion of people living in towns and cities exceeded anything previously experienced. In 1800, only London approached the 1 million population mark,[1] while Paris stood second among European cities at 547,000. By 1900, eleven cities contained more than 1 million people—London had 6,586,000; Paris, 2,714,000[2]; and New York, 3,437,000. In England and Wales the percentage living in towns[3] and cities increased from 1 in 4 to 77 percent; in Germany more than half the population was urban by 1910, compared with more than 40 percent in France.[4] The *Atlantic Monthly* (1895) summed up a century of urbanization: "The great fact in . . . social development . . . at the close of the nineteenth century is the tendency all over the world to concentrate in great cities. This tendency is seen everywhere."[5]

In the United States, urban population also soared. As the data in Table 2-1 show, urban population increased at approximately double the rate of growth of the entire United States population in every decade except the 1810s and 1870s. Between 1810 and 1820, a surge of westward movement increased the proportion of rural dwellers. In the 1870s, urban growth was slowed by a six-year economic depression.

The two decades preceding the Civil War signaled the first big movement to cities and towns. In 1840, nearly 90 percent of the nation was still rural, but at the outbreak of the Civil War, 19.8 percent of Americans were urban. This proportion doubled in the next forty years, to 39.6 percent. When the 1920 Census was taken, more than half of the American people lived in urban places with populations of 2,500 or more.

A startling increase occurred in the size and number of cities. New York, Philadelphia, and Boston, all colonial seaport cities, had reached a population of 100,000 or more by 1850. Six more cities joined the list by 1860, and at the turn of the century, there were twenty-three. In 1870, five cities exceeded a population of 250,000. Nine cities were this large by 1900.[6]

Smaller urban settlements dotted the rural landscape between the large cities. In 1820, 8 cities contained 10,000 or more people. This number increased to 25 by 1840, 58 by 1860, and 280 by the turn of the century. Twenty years later, 465 cities with more than 10,000 people were recorded in the Census.[7]

It is difficult to appreciate how fast individual cities changed in size and social complexity. In 1840, New York was the nation's largest city at population 369,000. Philadelphia, the second in size, had not yet attained 100,000 inhabitants. By the Civil War, New York had surpassed 1 million and Philadelphia 500,000 people. Since 1840, St. Louis had increased tenfold, while Chicago had been transformed from a village of just over 4,000 to a city of 112,000 people. At the turn of the century 1 million people lived in Chicago, and another 1 million streamed in during the next twenty years. More than 5.5 million people lived in New York City by 1920 (see Table 2-2).

Urbanization was a more complex process than these numbers alone might suggest. Social and economic transformations challenged the traditional relationships in society:

After several thousand years of relatively stable levels of urbanization, the past two or three centuries have witnessed an unprecedented increase in both rates and levels of urbanization with repercussions and ramifications that mark the changes of the period c.a.d. 1750–1850 as one of the crucial disjunctions in the

TABLE 2-1 The Pace of Urbanization in the United States, 1790–1920

Year	Total population	% increase over preceding census	Urban population	% increase over preceding population	% of total population Urban	% of total population Rural
1790	3,929,214	—	201,655	—	5.1	94.9
1800	5,308,483	35.1	322,371	59.9	6.1	93.9
1810	7,239,881	36.4	525,459	63.0	7.3	92.7
1820	9,638,453	33.1	693,255	31.9	7.2	92.8
1830	12,866,020	33.5	1,127,247	62.6	8.8	91.2
1840	17,069,453	32.7	1,845,055	63.7	10.8	89.2
1850	23,191,876	35.9	3,543,716	92.1	15.3	84.7
1860	31,443,321	35.6	6,216,518	75.4	19.8	80.2
1870	39,818,449	26.6	9,902,361	59.3	25.7	74.3
1880	50,155,783	26.0	14,129,735	42.7	28.2	71.8
1890	62,947,714	25.5	22,106,265	56.5	35.1	64.9
1900	75,994,575	20.7	30,214,832	36.7	39.6	60.4
1910	91,972,266	21.0	42,064,001	39.2	45.6	54.4
1920	105,710,620	14.9	54,253,280	29.0	51.2	48.8

Source: U.S. Department of Commerce, Bureau of the Census, *Historical Statistics of the United States, Colonial Times to 1970*, pt. 1, Bicentennial ed. (Washington, D.C.: U.S. Government Printing Office, 1975), p. 8; and U.S. Department of Commerce, Bureau of the Census, *1970 Census of Population*, vol. 1, *Characteristics of the Population*, pt. 1 (Washington, D.C.: U.S. Government Printing Office, 1973), p. 42.

TABLE 2-2 Population and Rate of Growth in Five Large Cities, 1820-1920*

	New York City**	% increase	Chicago	% increase	Phila-delphia	% increase	St. Louis	% increase	Boston	% increase	% increase in U.S. population
1820	137,388		—		63,802		4,598		43,298		
1830	220,471	60.5	—		80,462	26.1	5,847	27.1	61,392	41.8	33.5
1840	369,305	67.5	4,470		93,665	16.4	16,469	181.7	93,383	52.1	32.7
1850	660,803	78.9	29,963	570.3	121,376	29.6	77,860	372.8	136,881	46.6	35.9
1860	1,183,148	79.1	112,172	274.4	565,529	365.9	160,773	106.5	177,840	29.9	35.6
1870	1,546,293	30.7	298,977	166.5	674,022	19.2	310,864	93.4	250,526	40.9	26.6
1880	2,061,191	33.3	503,185	68.3	847,170	25.7	350,522	12.8	362,839	44.8	26.0
1890	2,507,474	21.7	1,099,850	118.6	1,046,964	23.6	451,770	28.9	448,477	23.6	25.5
1900	3,437,202	37.1	1,698,575	54.4	1,293,697	23.6	575,000	27.3	560,892	25.1	20.7
1910	4,766,883	38.7	2,185,283	28.7	1,549,008	19.7	687,029	19.5	670,585	19.6	21.0
1920	5,620,048	17.9	2,701,705	23.6	1,823,779	17.7	772,897	12.5	748,060	11.6	14.9

Source: Glen E. Holt, personal files; U.S. Department of Commerce, Bureau of the Census, *The Growth of Metropolitan Districts in the United States: 1900–1940,* by Warren S. Thompson (Washington, D.C.: U.S. Government Printing Office, 1947); and Blake McKelvey, *American Urbanization: A Comparative History* (Glenview, Ill.: Scott, Foresman, 1973), pp. 24, 37, 73.

*These five cities were ranked as the five largest in the 1910 Census.

**Using the consolidated borough boundaries of 1898.

history of human society. Whatever constraints had hitherto checked or moderated the growth and re-distribution of population were suddenly relaxed.[8]

In the United States, urbanization entailed (1) *fundamental economic change* from a mercantile to an industrial economic system; (2) *technological transformations* bringing higher productivity and transportation improvements; and (3) *social complexity* in cities, including social stratification, segregation, and high rates of mobility.

The Mercantile Cities

The complexity of modern cities can be put into perspective against the background of the mercantile cities of the preindustrial period. Before the century of massive urbanization, American cities were few in number, small in scale, relatively isolated from one another, and not very complex. Urban life was the exception rather than the rule. In 1800, only 322,000 of 5.3 million Americans—6.1 percent—lived in urban places of 2,500 people or more. Of this number, 168,000 lived in five seaboard cities: New York (60,515), Philadelphia (41,220), Baltimore (26,514), Boston (24,937), and Charleston, South Carolina (18,924).[9] No other cities contained as many as 10,000 residents.

The waterfront was the lifeblood of the merchant cities. Dock facilities, warehouses, clerks' offices, banks, bakeries, printing establishments, taverns, and private homes all clustered within walking distance of the harbor. The merchant city was a walking city, the area of urban settlement extending perhaps four to eight blocks deep and as wide as usable dock facilities would allow. Overland transportation was expensive, slow, and inconvenient: " . . . during the century's first decade, the cost incurred in hauling a ton of goods nine miles on inland roads was equivalent to that of importing the identical weight from Europe."[10]

Merchants and shopkeepers dominated the social and economic life of the preindustrial city. Business establishments usually employed one or two people. Those with as many as twenty workers were extremely rare. Large-scale assembly line production was unknown and inherently impossible. Nonspecialized modes of production, extensive hand labor, the difficulty of assembling a large work force within walking distance of a single establishment, and the snail's pace of transportation[11] placed strict limits on the size of businesses. Individual artisans, craftsmen, and shopkeepers ran businesses in their homes or in adjoining buildings.

Occupational and social class segregation existed, but it was a *proximate* segregation. Workers clustered together but still lived within shouting distance of wealthy merchants and dock facilities. Sam Bass Warner, in his study of Philadelphia, found a high degree of occupational segregation in the Philadelphia of 1774, but nevertheless concluded, "It was the unity of everyday life, from tavern, to street, to workplace, to housing which held the town together in the eighteenth century."[12] The small scale of the entire community fostered "a sense of community identification similar to that of traditional societies—an allegiance to a particular place where collective progress also meant individual enrichment."[13] Class and occupational diversity existed within the context of community—a social entity derived from frequent communication and close physical proximity.

Though there existed a profusion of occupational specialties, by modern standards the occupational structure was neither complex nor rigid. Until the Civil War, American cities were chiefly mercantile, not industrial. The movement of European goods into the cities, the organizing of farmers' markets, the financing and insuring of these kinds of activities, and the printing of accounting ledgers, handbills, and newspapers were major activities. Importers, bankers, wholesalers, shopkeepers, tavernkeepers, and innkeepers were the city's most prominent businesspersons. Another economic stratum was composed of service industries, comprising brewery and distillery workers, shoemakers, hatters, bakers, carpenters, blacksmiths, potters, and butchers. Most manufacturing was tailored to meet the needs of merchant activities, such as making containers and conveyances, or moving goods through the streets from dock to warehouse, creating the need for cordwainers, coopers, saddle makers, harness makers, wheelwrights, boatwrights, and carters.

Government was controlled primarily by wealthy aristocrats or prominent merchants. Among the members of this elite, there was a basic mistrust of what Thomas Jefferson had called "mobocracy," rule by the masses. Local politics was run through a government-by-committee system, an arrangement in which local notables served on committees formed to build public wharves, distribute money to the poor, organize town watches, and build and maintain public streets. Such an informal governmental structure fit the pace and organization of social life in small communities.

Like the eastern seaboard cities, western cities were dominated by merchants, who financed and controlled libraries, art and music societies, social activities, and politics. All these aspects of town life were closely tied to one principal purpose: making money. As the towns grew in size and complexity, entrepreneurial promotion, which had generally concentrated on the local commercial or industrial climate, began to extol cultural qualities as well. "'Lexington has taken on the tone of literary place,' claiming to be the 'Athens of the West,' while Cincinnati was 'struggling to become its Corinth.' 'Our advances in learning as in every kind of improvement, are altogether astonishing.' exulted a Pittsburgh editor in 1813, speaking for the whole West."[14]

Successful urban settlements served as trading and distribution centers for an expanding territory. This process is illustrated in the growth of cities in the West. St. Louis began as a fur-trading center, grew when it became the "gateway" to the West, outfitting explorers and wagon trains, and became larger and more complex with the changeover to an industrial base. Pittsburgh grew rapidly from village to town to city because of its location at the intersection of three rivers and its access to iron deposits and agricultural goods. By 1830, the entire inland iron industry had located in Pittsburgh. Chicago, through the Great Lakes and (after 1860) the railroads, had access to a variety of raw materials, ranging from the iron ore of Minnesota to the lead and coal of Illinois and Wisconsin, to the livestock and agricultural commodities of the plains.

Entrepreneurs in cities staked their fortunes on future growth. They were keenly aware that they were involved in a sweepstakes in which some cities would succeed in expanding and making money while others would die. The entrepreneurial motive for city-building in the West set off a "struggle for primacy and power" in which, "Like imperial states, cities carved out extensive dependencies, extended their influence over the economic and political life of the hinterland, and fought with contending places over strategic trade routes."[15] When improved transportation and new modes of production and manufacture allowed it, urban entrepreneurs extended their financial reach ever farther. In 1815, when the first steamboat made its run from New Orleans to Pittsburgh, the cities along the great rivers dramatically expanded their trade territories. Later, the cities would fight for railroad connections.

The transformations that allowed urbanization to occur on a large scale (transportation technologies, industrialization) were financed by entrepreneurs who held a vested interest in urban expansion.

Transportation Changes the City

Several transportation improvements during the nineteenth century allowed the cities to expand the outward boundaries of settlement and to achieve greater internal complexity. In the late eighteenth century, the population radius of New York, Philadelphia, and Boston varied from one to two miles. By the 1860s, New York had achieved a radius of about eight miles, and Philadelphia and Boston extended five miles from the center. Over the last half of the nineteenth century, many cities grew to between five and ten miles in radius.[16]

The first mass transportation breakthrough came in 1828, when the omnibus was introduced to the streets of New York City. From the 1830s until the Civil War, dozens of omnibuses careened down the streets of all major cities. The omnibus was pulled by two to four horses and carried about twelve people. Basically, it was a compromise between the hackney coach (which can still be seen in New York City's Central Park) and the long-distance stagecoach. Usually crowded, always uncomfortable, cold in winter and hot in summer, it invited unremitting complaints from its customers. A newspaper of the time complained that, "During certain periods of the day or evening and always during inclement weather, passengers are packed in these vehicles, without regard to comfort or even decency."[17]

Nevertheless, the middle class who could afford the fares—merchants, traders, lawyers, skilled artisans, managers, junior partners—crowded into the omnibuses. The omnibus ran on a fixed schedule and route, picking up and dropping passengers at frequent intervals, and thus it was more convenient and less expensive than any alternative method of traveling. A fixed fare, about a nickel, made the ride cheap compared with the cost of renting a hackney coach.

Omnibuses allowed the upper and upper-middle classes to expand their choice of residential location. For the first time the work place could be located at some distance from residential neighborhoods. American cities soon began to take on their present form, the center being abandoned by affluent urban residents. The omnibus, the first mass transportation device used in American cities, facilitated a process of spatial segregation and differentiation that is still occurring in the nation's urban areas.

Other transportation innovations followed. Steam railroad lines, for example, were constructed in Boston during the late 1830s and in several other large cities over the next twenty years. Steam engines were suited for constant speed rather than for frequent stops and starts, and they were expensive to build and operate. They did not, therefore, compete with omnibuses on crowded urban streets, but rather facilitated commuting from the area of dense settlement in large cities to smaller towns and villages eight to ten miles away. Only the wealthy could afford the high fares of 40 to 75 cents (the average laborer made about $1.00 a day; sometimes skilled workers made as much as $2.00).[18] But by 1848, 20 percent of Boston's businessmen commuted daily by steam railway.[19]

Between the mid-1840s and 1860, horse-drawn trolley cars gradually replaced the omnibus and further facilitated the spatial differentiation of cities. Trolley cars were vastly better than the omnibuses. The cars were pulled on rails, which reduced friction and leveled the street surface. The coaches could carry more than twice as many passengers, and fares were reduced. The horsecars traveled considerably faster, too, averaging six to eight miles per hour. As a result, an expanding proportion of the middle class rode the trolleys. Now artisans and craftsmen, shopkeepers, bank clerks, and some skilled laborers could regularly afford to ride to work.[20]

As residential settlements spread farther away from the city center, affluent populations segregated themselves in an outer zone. The horsecar lines sometimes extended well beyond built-up areas, serving hospitals, parks, cemeteries, and independent villages.[21] Residential subdivisions sprang up along these lines.

Richmond, Virginia, installed the first electric streetcar system in 1888.[22] Within a year, overhead electric wires were being strung in most of the big cities. In 1890, 60 percent of the streetcars were still horse drawn; twelve years later that figure was less than 1 percent.[23]

Electric streetcars were infinitely cleaner than the horsecars they replaced: city residents had always complained about "An atmosphere heavy with the odors of death and decay and animal filth and steaming nastiness."[24] And they traveled almost twice as fast as horsecars. Areas six to eight miles from the center could now be reached in a half hour. Horsecars in Chicago reached four miles from the downtown Loop in 1890, but electric streetcars soon reached out as far as ten miles.[25]

Like the earlier improvements in transportation, the electric streetcar facilitated social and economic segregation. The rich moved farther away from the middle class, who in turn moved away from the poor. Poor people increasingly were segregated in old neighborhoods in the center of the city.

Transportation improvements also led to the segregation of economic activities. Until about 1870, multifunctional warehouses dominated downtown areas, with small financial and retailing districts close by, and even mixed with, wholesaling and storage facilities.[26] From about 1870 to 1900, downtown business districts developed as self-contained shopping and financial centers separated from industries and warehouses. The middle class developed a distinctive shopping habit, taking streetcars downtown to shop in the new chain and department stores. The first chain retail company, the Great Atlantic & Pacific Tea Company, organized in 1864; in the 1870s, A & P stores expanded to several cities. Frank W. Woolworth opened his five-and-dime store in Lancaster, Pennsylvania, in 1879, and during the 1880s, Woolworth's became a familiar marquee in downtown areas.[27] Mail-order firms such as Sears Roebuck appeared in the 1870s, and catalogue sales boomed within the decade.

While distinct residential and business zones developed within the cities, suburban communities proliferated just beyond city boundaries. Between 1890 and 1910, the United States experienced its first suburban boom. In most large metropolitan areas, suburbs grew almost as fast as the central cities in the 1890s and often faster after 1900. The nation's central cities grew by 37 percent in the decade between 1900 and 1910,[28] but the largest cities were already beginning to lag behind their suburbs in population growth. Chicago added 29 percent to its population in the first decade of the twentieth century, but its suburbs increased by 88 percent. In St. Louis, Philadelphia, Boston, Pittsburgh, and New York, the suburbs grew at a faster pace than the central cities.[29]

Throughout the nineteenth century, city residents had sought to escape the noise, congestion, and filth of the waterfront. Improvements in transportation allowed them to develop separate social and ethnic communities. When affluent urban dwellers moved to the periphery, low-income city residents inherited the housing stock left behind.

The *opportunity* presented to urban dwellers to segregate themselves soon translated into *preference* as well.

> Well defined districts within cities assumed a symbolic status in the value systems of particular social groups; consequently, the prestige or ethnic identity of an area provided enduring attractions.[30]

These preferences became expressed on the landscape in the cities and in the suburbs. Like the residential and business districts within the cities, suburban communities became clearly differentiated from one another on the basis of ethnicity, social class, and economic function.

Cities and Railroads

Transportation developments not only changed the complexion of urban areas, they enhanced urban dominance over the nation's culture and economy. At least since the Revolutionary War, cities had exerted a disproportionate influence, but rural areas had retained a measure of autonomy and independence in proportion to the slow pace of communication and transportation. After the Civil War, the telegraph and the railroad undermined rural independence.

Railroads made it possible to transport heavy raw materials and finished products in bulk over long distances, allowing cities to expand their economic dominance. With the railroads, American cities thoroughly subordinated rural production to urban needs. The countryside became the supplier of raw materials—food, lumber, iron ore, coal, gold and silver—to the cities. At the same time the cities expanded their consumer markets to embrace rural hinterlands. Cities with railroad links grew rapidly; those that were passed by faded into obscurity.

The railroad network expanded at astonishing speed. In 1840, only 2,800 miles of tracks existed, most of them in the urban East. No connection existed even as far west as Pittsburgh. Each railway company used its own peculiar gauge, so that continuous rail networks did not exist: at the end of each line, goods had to be unloaded from one company's cars and reloaded onto the next. But an integrated rail system soon came into being. Each succeeding decade witnessed an explosion in railway building: 9,021 miles by 1850; 30,626 miles by 1860; 52,922 miles by 1870; and 258,784 miles by the turn of the century.[31]

In 1857, the newly consolidated Pennsylvania Railroad connected Pittsburgh with Chicago. Three years later, Chicago tied together the nation's largest railway network, where eleven trunk lines ended and twenty branch and feeder lines passed through. By 1869, the Golden Spike was driven at Promontory Point, Utah, completing the first intercontinental rail line. Within another decade, the outline of the modern railroad system was completed, with a cobweb of lines connecting the East with the Midwest and with lines reaching every important region in the West.

Urban entrepreneurs attempting to promote local economic growth fed the railroad-building fever. Federal, state, and local governments helped finance railroad construction. On the frontier, for St. Louis, Pittsburgh, Cincinnati, and New Orleans, the steamboat had been "an enchanter's wand transforming an almost raw countryside of scattered farms and towns into a settled region of cultivated landscapes and burgeoning cities."[32] Now the railroads held the enchantment—the promise of economic prosperity and entrepreneurial success: " . . . the pioneer railroads in a very real sense were built by the cities, represented an extension of their commercial enterprise, and spread their urban influences throughout their hinterlands."[33]

If railroads catalyzed urban growth, interurban rivalries in turn fueled railroad construction. Local business leaders tried to outbid one another to secure rail connections. Cities gave land to the railroads, bought their bonds, and even financed construction. In the 1860s, Kansas City gave away land, sold bond issues to private investors, and secured a federal grant in an attempt to secure a railroad connection. As a result of its success in this venture, Kansas City prospered while its rival, Leavenworth, stagnated.[34] Denver's board of trade raised $280,000 to finance a spur line to obtain access to intercontinental railroad in Cheyenne, Wyoming.[35] These efforts made Denver the urban center of a vast region of the West. No city benefited as much as Chicago, however, whose phenomenal growth was founded on the regional and national domination of resources and consumers made possible by the rails—corn and grain, slaughtering and meatpacking, iron and steel, foundries and machine shops. Chicago's eclipse of St. Louis as the great inland city has often been explained by reference to St. Louis's overreliance on river traffic and its failure to compete vigorously for rail service.

Like the contemporary automobile industry, railroads in the second half of the nineteenth century became economic giants. After the Civil War, rail construction became the most important stimulant to industrial production, accounting for more than half the demand for iron in the United States in 1875.[36] "Railroads . . . both lowered the cost of transportation and stimulated the economy directly by their use of labor, capital, and iron," and created "mass markets that made mass production possible."[37] It is not difficult to understand the Congressional motivation in providing land grants to the railroads in the Pacific Railways Acts of 1862 and 1864. Frontier settlement and national economic prosperity depended upon railroad construction (in addition, congressmen and senators received railroad stock in exchange for their favorable votes).

The Industrial Revolution in the Cities

The industrial revolution fundamentally changed the social composition and economic structure of cities. From about 1840 to 1860, large American cities began developing industrial economies. Following the Civil War, industrial production exceeded the commercial and agricultural sectors in value added to the economy. Industrial cities such as Chicago and Pittsburgh thrived; cities that failed to make the transition to industrial production fast enough, such as New Orleans, fell behind.

Industrialization altered social and economic relationships by removing economic production from small shops and homes to factories. Individual economic enterprises became vastly larger after 1860. Before the Civil War, manufacturing establishments rarely exceeded 50 employees, and in large cities they averaged between 8 and 20. In 1832, for example, manufacturing establishments in Boston averaged 8.5 workers.[38] Manufacturing concerns multiplied in size during the industrial age. In the agricultural implements and machinery field, the number of employees per establishment increased from 7.5 in 1860 to 79 in 1910. In malt liquor breweries, the number increased from 5 to 39. Iron and steel establishments increased their average number of employees from 54 to 426.[39]

Capital became concentrated in large firms. Limited-risk corporations[40] were relatively rare before the Civil War. By the turn of the century there were 40,000 such firms. They amounted to only one-tenth of all business establishments, but they produced 60 percent of value in manufacturing.[41] In 1896, twelve firms were valued at more than $10 million; by 1903 there were fifty worth more than $50 million.[42] The giant corporations that formed between 1896 and 1905 included (among others) U.S. Steel, (now USX), International Harvester, General Electric, and American Telephone & Telegraph.

In the small shop, the work atmosphere had been relatively informal.

Artisans and craftworkers often chose their working hours and manner of production. In contrast, factories utilized mass production techniques. Machine-tooled, standardized parts replaced handcrafted items. The changeover to standardization had begun with Eli Whitney's muskets, provided with standard interchangeable parts in 1798. Clocks, sewing machines, typewriters, and farm machinery were next. Huge military orders during the Civil War led to standardized shoe and clothing manufacturing. As a result of these developments, work became highly regimented and closely monitored. Skilled laborers replaced craftworkers and artisans. Additionally, factory methods of production required specialized, repetitive work and created a rigid distinction between management and workers.

The consequences of industrialization were magnified in the cities. Occupational specialization sharpened class and income differences. Concentration of economic resources in big corporations created a class of super-rich industrial magnates who flaunted their wealth by building mansions and estates, throwing lavish parties, and building monuments to their own wealth.[43] The number of poor people in the cities multiplied, prompting the rich to found charitable societies to deal with the "dangerous classes." And a new middle class took shape. Between 1870 and 1910, the number of people employed as clerical workers, salespersons, government employees, technicians, and salaried professionals ballooned from 756,000 to 5,609,000.[44] The well-defined class differences became replicated on the urban map in segregated residential patterns. Immigrant working-class tenement districts crowded around the central business district and were, in turn, surrounded by a middle-class ring. The wealthy claimed such exclusive urban areas as Park Avenue in New York and Beacon Hill in Boston or lived on estates beyond the middle-class sections.

Foreign immigration constituted the most visible effect of industrialization in the cities. The industrial economy depended upon a constantly expanding pool of labor. Millions of foreign workers were pulled to American shores to work on the railroads and in meatpacking, steel, coal, lead, and other industries. An unprecedented migration from farms to urban centers was simultaneously set in motion. Between 1830 and 1896, developments in farm machinery reduced by half the time and labor required to produce agricultural crops, and for wheat, the time was cut by one twentieth and the labor cost reduced one fifth.[45] Replacing farm labor with machinery also increased the capital investment required for farming. Unemployed farm laborers and young people fled in droves to the manufacturing and mining centers.

The story of post–Civil War nineteenth-century America revolves around the theme of massive population movement and restlessness. By 1910, more than one-third of city residents were of rural origin.[46]

Growth of the cities at the expense of the countryside generated new political alignments. State legislatures divided into rural versus urban factions. In the 1880s an antiurban Populist movement swept the prairie states. The resentment toward the cities intensified when foreign immigrants crowded into teeming ethnic ghettos in the big cities.

Immigration and the Social Composition of the Cities

Industrialization and immigration were entwined, perhaps most clearly in this respect: the immigrants visibly and unalterably changed conditions in the cities, thus becoming the scapegoats for the insecurities loosed by the new industrial order. American cities were never the same once the immigrant tide broke. The spectacular growth of the cities guaranteed that urban life would become a maelstrom of antagonistic groups. Cities were soon characterized by overcrowding, inadequate housing, public disorder and violence, and poor public services.

Between 1820 and 1920, 33.5 million immigrants arrived on American shores, most of them settling into a few big cities (see Table 2–3). Many of them were destitute and lacked labor skills; the majority were unfamiliar with American culture and unable to speak or read English. Approximately 24 million settled in the cities. By 1870, more than half the population of at least twenty American cities were foreign-born or were children of foreign parents.[47]

Each of these cities possessed at least one of three features that drew immigrants. Ports of arrival had heavy immigrant populations, with New York City leading the list. Industrial cities in the Midwest also attracted immigrants: St. Louis, Chicago, Milwaukee, and Pittsburgh employed the newcomers in steelmaking, meatpacking, brewing, and foundry and machinery plants. Smaller cities built around specialized manufacturing and mining also lured immigrants.

By 1910, all eight cities with more than 500,000 people contained sizable immigrant populations. New York City was 40 percent foreign-born; Chicago, 36 percent. Boston's and Cleveland's populations were more than one-third first-generation immigrant. If the American-born ("second generation") sons and daughters of these immigrants are added to the totals, the foreign-stock populations in the cities often accounted for three-fourths or more of all residents. In 1910, 80 percent of New York's population was composed of first- or second-generation immigrants; in Chicago, the proportion was 77.5 percent.

Although immigrants were attracted disproportionately to the big cities, many smaller urban places also held sizable foreign populations. In 1910, the fifty largest cities *averaged* 29 percent first-generation

TABLE 2–3 Proportion Immigrant Population in Cities of 500,000 or More

		% foreign- born	% foreign-born or born of at least one foreign parent*
New York City	1870	44.4	80.0
	1910	40.4	78.6
Chicago	1870	48.3	87.0
	1910	35.7	77.5
Philadelphia	1870	28.4	51.1
	1910	24.7	56.8
St. Louis	1870	36.1	65.0
	1910	18.3	54.2
Boston	1870	35.1	63.2
	1910	35.9	74.2
Cleveland	1870	41.8	75.3
	1910	34.9	74.8
Baltimore	1870	21.1	38.0
	1910	13.8	37.9
Pittsburgh	1870	32.3	58.2
	1910	26.3	62.2
Mean for all 8 cities	1870	40.0	72.0
(each counted equally)	1910	32.0	72.3

Source: U.S. Department of the Interior, Superintendent of Census, *The Ninth Census* (June 1, 1870), vol. 1, *Population and Social Statistics* (Washington, D.C.: U.S. Government Printing Office, 1872), p. 386; and U.S. Department of Commerce, Bureau of the Census, *Thirteenth Census of the United Sates Taken in the Year 1910*, vol. 1, *Population 1910* (Washington, D.C.: U.S. Government Printing Office, 1913), p. 178.

*Native-born with foreign parents is unavailable in the 1870 Census. The figures for 1870 are estimated by adding 80 percent to the number of foreign-born. In all cases, this should yield a safely conservative estimate.

foreign-born (compared with 32 percent for the eight largest cities).[48] Without the huge volume of rural to urban migration that was occurring at the same time, most of the population of cities would have been composed of immigrants and their American-born children.

But numbers alone cannot describe the impact of the immigrant tide. Immigrants carried with them "strange" customs, languages, and, in the case of Catholics and Jews, "un-American" religions. Most foreign groups encountered some hostility, but none was more despised than the Irish, who, along with Germans and Scandinavians, made up the first massive immigrant movement.

A potato blight that swept Ireland in 1845 and for several years thereafter set off a surge of Irish immigration that lasted until the turn of the century. Crop failures and civil war in the German states during the 1840s and 1850s forced millions of Germans to migrate. As Table 2–4 shows, Irish and Germans made up 73 percent of all immigrants in the 1840s and more than 50 percent of all immigrants in the 1850s and 1860s.

Famine and disease pushed the Irish to American cities. Irish peasants subsisted on vegetables grown on tiny, rocky plots of ground not claimed by English landlords. Potatoes were their staple crop, because these could be hand-cultivated on small plots of thin pebbly soil and even in strips of land along the roads. When the potato blight wiped out the crop, its effects were felt even more severely in Ireland than in the rest of Europe. Between 1845 and the 1850s, perhaps one-fourth of Ireland's peasants died of starvation. Many of the survivors streamed into Liverpool and used the last of their resources to buy passage on ships heading for America. Passage was cheap because ship captains needed ballast to hold their ships in the water. On the way back, the ships would be loaded with cotton, tobacco, lumber, or raw materials needed for England's factories.

The Irish were met with intense antipathy from "native" Americans. Irish workmen could rarely read or claim a skilled occupation. For the most part, they had no previous city experience. They took menial, temporary, low-paying jobs—moving goods on the waterfront, building streets and roads, working in slaughterhouses and packinghouses. Partly because of their poverty, their religion, and their cultural habits, they were etched in the public mind as dangerous, alcoholic, criminal, and dirty. Organizations formed to attack "Papist" influence in the schools and to keep Catholics from taking desirable jobs. Protestant Yankees were in positions to hire, promote, and fire. Even as late as the 1920s, want ads in Boston frequently added the word "Protestant" as a qualification for employment.[49] The Irish clustered on the lower rungs of the social and economic ladder well into the twentieth century.

The schools sometimes evinced the most vicious anti-Catholic hostility. Nineteenth-century educators struggled against the dissolution that allegedly characterized Irish homes:

> Our chief difficulty is with the Irish. . . . So cheaply have they been held at home—so closely have they been pressed down in the social scale—that for the most part the simple virtues of industry, temperance, and frugality are unknown to them; and that wholesome pride which will induce a German, or a native American, to work hard from sun to sun for the smallest wages, rather than seek or accept charitable aid, has been literally crushed out of them. . . .

TABLE 2-4 Decennial Immigration to the United States, 1820–1919

	1820 to 1829	1830 to 1839	1840 to 1849	1850 to 1859	1860 to 1869	1870 to 1879	1880 to 1889	1890 to 1899	1900 to 1909	1910 to 1919
Total in Millions	0.1	0.5	1.4	2.7	2.1	2.7	5.2	3.7	8.2	6.3
Percentage of Total from:										
Ireland	40.2	31.7	46.0	36.9	24.4	15.4	12.8	11.0	4.2	2.6
Germany	4.5	23.2	27.0	34.8	35.2	27.4	27.5	15.7	4.0	2.7
United Kingdom	19.5	13.8	15.3	13.5	14.9	21.1	15.5	8.9	5.7	5.8
Scandinavia	0.2	0.4	0.9	0.9	5.5	7.6	12.7	10.5	5.9	3.8
Canada	1.8	2.2	2.4	2.2	4.9	11.8	9.4	0.1	1.5	11.2
Russia					0.2	1.3	3.5	12.2	18.3	17.4
Austria-Hungary					0.2	2.2	6.0	14.5	24.4	18.2
Italy					0.5	1.7	5.1	16.3	23.5	19.4

Source: From N. Carpenter, "Immigrants and Their Children," *U.S. Bureau of the Census Monograph,* No. 7 (Washington, D.C.: Government Printing Office, 1927), pp. 324–325.

The rising generation must be taught as our own children are taught. . . . In too many instances the parents are unfit guardians of their own children. If left to their direction the young will be brought up in idle, dissolute, vagrant habits, which will make them worse members of society than their parents are; instead of filling our public schools, they will find their way into our prisons, houses of correction, and almshouses . . . the children must be gathered up and forced into school, and those who resist or impede this plan, whether parents or *priests*, must be held accountable and punished.[50]

The schools were relatively peaceful means of Americanizing the Irish, compared with other methods that were employed. Anti-Catholic riots became a common occurrence in American cities. Irish churches, taverns, and houses were attacked by mobs incited by fears of "an invasion of venomous reptiles . . . , long-haired, wild-eyed, bad-smelling, atheistic, reckless foreign wretches."[51]

The Germans were thought to be less troublesome. The German immigrants were made up of a sizable middle class who brought with them cultural institutions that eased the transition to American life: music societies, gymnastic institutes, parochial school traditions. Although the Germans nominally faced a greater language barrier than the Irish, the Irish brogue—and even more, the widely used Gaelic—sounded just as foreign to Americans as the German language.

All immigrant groups were less economically and socially successful than native Yankee Protestants, but important variations existed among them. In late nineteenth-century Boston, an immigrant "pecking order" could be easily discerned.[52] Militant racial discrimination kept blacks in the most menial jobs. Irish and Italians competed for low-wage and low-skill jobs and held a slight advantage over blacks. German and recent British immigrants frequently entered middle-class occupations, and sometimes even moved into managerial positions. Russian and Eastern European Jews emphasized formal education and business careers and held precarious middle-class jobs as jobbers, middlemen, or small shopkeepers.

The ethnic makeup of the immigrant tide gradually became more complex as the nineteenth century progressed. As shown in Table 2–4, until the 1880s about 85 percent of immigrants came from Ireland, England, Germany, Canada, and Scandinavia. From 1890 to 1920, the composition changed radically. In the 1890s, Jews from Russia and Austria-Hungary and Catholics from Italy made up 42 percent of immigrants, and more than 60 percent from 1900 to 1920.

Immigration intensified social conflict in American cities. The immigrants clustered together into districts that sometimes developed such a characteristic social life that the dominant American culture was largely excluded. Ethnic clustering no doubt increased distrust of "foreigners."

Ethnic communities were crucially important, however, in assimilating recently arrived immigrants into city life. Such community institutions as the church, beer halls, and ethnic clubs offered a familiar language and culture, as well as financial aid. The ethnic communities also provided a buffer against the resentment and prejudice exhibited by other groups.

Immigrants were subjected to overcrowded and dilapidated housing, poverty, high disease rates, and other pathologies, but for some immigrant groups, community institutions and social and religious practices facilitated adjustment to city life. Thus, although the Lower East Side of Manhattan became the most densely crowded residential settlement in any American city during the 1890s, its disease, death, crime, and alcoholism rates remained extremely low. The customs and lifestyles of the Eastern European Jews who settled there accounted for this anomaly. Jewish families insisted on personal cleanliness and careful preparation of food. By 1897, more than half of New York's bathhouses were run and used by Jews.[53] Jewish children were imbued with the idea that education was the sure road to success. Orthodox Jews did not tolerate heavy drinking, and suicide and crime were nearly nonexistent among Jewish youth.

In contrast, the Irish were unusually susceptible to social disorders. Crime, alcoholism, and disease ran high in the Irish wards. Nowhere was this shown more graphically than in the yellow fever epidemics that swept Memphis in 1873 and 1878. The Irish population was virtually decimated. No other group was affected so much.[54]

Urban Crisis and the Expansion of City Services

All city residents, native-born as well as immigrant, were subjected to the dislocations arising from frenetic urban expansion. In the contest between deteriorating social conditions and city services, services generally proved inadequate to the challenge. In most cases, municipal services were provided only when city residents faced calamity.

In comparison with life in contemporary cities, conditions throughout the nineteenth century ranged from squalid to barely tolerable. Disease and infant mortality rates ran extraordinarily high. Cities ordinarily lacked adequate and sanitary water supplies, and city residents lived in constant fear of fire. Police protection was minimal and disorganized. Streets turned to seas of mud in winter and to dust bowls in summer; in any season they were littered with horse dung and refuse. Even the most ordinary services were inadequate. For example, 1,404 suits were pending against the city of Chicago in 1901 as a result of injuries attributed to unsafe sidewalks.[55] No aspect of city life escaped complaint.

The provision of urban services was limited strictly to addressing conditions that manifestly threatened public safety and social order. Cities were organized to promote individual economic activity; if they also accomplished any degree of social cohesion and community well-being, it was more by accident than by design. A Swedish novelist commented that Chicago in 1850 was "one of the most miserable and ugly cities," where people had come "to trade, to make money, and not to live."[56] Urban dwellers complained about social conditions, but "the desirability of the city as an institution for the promotion of economic activity was seldom questioned."[57]

Epidemics were feared in all cities. In the summer of 1793, 10 percent of Philadelphia's population died from yellow fever.[58] The city's economy came to a standstill, and one-third of its population fled. Outbreaks of yellow fever or cholera occurred in Philadelphia, Baltimore, and New Haven in 1793; in New York, Baltimore, and Norfolk in 1795; and in Newburyport, Boston, and Charleston the next year.[59] Nearly a dozen cities were hit in 1797; in Philadelphia, three-fourths of the population fled and 4,000 died (about 7 percent of the population).[60]

Disasters such as these prompted cities to invest in waterworks, drain swamps, regulate the keeping of animals, and organize refuse collection. Philadelphia was prompted by its epidemics to construct the first municipal waterworks in the nation's history. Begun in 1798 and operational by 1806, it piped water to the city from the upper Schyulkill River, several miles away. Although other cities used Philadelphia's system as their model, the systems were rarely adequate. Usually, water was supplied to residents through street hydrants and hand pumps. Only wealthy people had water piped into their homes. In 1860, about one-tenth of Boston's residents had access to a bathtub, and one-twentieth of the homes had indoor water closets.[61] Little was done in most cities to supply clean water until the 1850s. Because of this, there were frequent epidemics of smallpox, yellow fever, and cholera. Several water systems were built in the 1850s; by the Civil War, seventy towns had waterworks, owned by eighty different private companies.[62] However, these companies often neglected middle-class and, virtually always, poor neighborhoods.

In part, the water supply problem could be solved only through the development of adequate technology. Even Philadelphia's relatively sophisticated system delivered its water with only the heaviest silt filtered out.[63] Pumps frequently failed; in the winter, pipes froze. People found silt, insects, and even small fish in their water. During the first decade of the twentieth century, when modern filtration techniques were developed, death rates in New York, Boston, Philadelphia, and New Orleans were cut by one-fifth.[64]

Epidemics also prompted cities to provide sewer facilities. In 1823, Boston began installing the nation's first sanitary sewers. Other large cities followed suit, but slowly. By 1857, New York City provided sewers for only one-fourth of its streets, but most of these were open drainage sewers that ran between the sidewalk and the street. Underground sanitary sewers in continuous pipes came later.[65] Taxpayers resisted the high cost of laying underground pipe and installing costly pumps. Although most of the big cities had constructed sewers by 1870, the service only reached some neighborhoods, and the sewage was usually not drained away from the cities but collected in community cesspools, which had to be dug out frequently. Even when sewers drained waste away from the city, the benefits were somewhat doubtful. Serious typhoid epidemics occurred in the cities along the Merrimac River in Massachusetts during the 1880s because residents were drinking one another's sewage-polluted water. Boston Harbor was called "one vast cesspool" in 1877, because of Boston's habit of dumping wastes directly into the harbor.[66] Most other towns followed the same practice. Until the 1920s, crowded residential districts were dotted with outdoor privies, and water bearing a burden of horse manure and other refuse coursed along open street gutters.

Crime and disorder also beset nineteenth-century cities. Added to the high levels of everyday crime were outbursts of mob violence and rioting. No major city escaped destructive riots launched against and between ethnic groups or between political factions. Violence and criminality eventually forced cities to provide professional police forces, but only when these conditions reached emergency status.

Until at least midcentury, the law enforcement function in most cities was met irregularly with night watches and constables. Until 1845, the New York City Council appointed parttime police. Because the police were selected on the basis of political loyalty to councilmembers, they went entirely unsupervised.[67] Frequently, their only tools of law enforcement consisted of brutality and intimidation. Until late in the 1830s, Philadelphia relied on posses, militia, and night watchmen to enforce the law. Like New York City's forces, they were unsupervised, parttime, and did not wear uniforms.[68] Cities in the West provided law enforcement informally and irregularly. Observing a haphazard schedule, night watchmen and constables patrolled the streets.[69]

As cities grew in size and social complexity, the effectiveness of informal community norms in keeping crime and violence in check seriously deteriorated. During the 1830s and 1840s, rioting broke out regularly in Philadelphia. The fact that riots often accompanied election campaigns and were directed at Irish Catholics indicated the degree to which permanent factions divided groups in the city. A serious depression from 1837 to 1843 further eroded public order. Finally, racial hatred directed against blacks inflamed riots, with white workers burning blacks' homes and churches.

No large city escaped this kind of violence. In frontier cities, the connection between rapid population growth and social instability was particularly apparent. More than half the residents of early San Francisco, St. Louis, and New Orleans were transients. Rivermen, wagoners, and traders moved in and out of these cities and brought with them demands for liquor, gambling, and prostitution. Violent crimes became such a common occurrence in San Francisco during the 1850s that vigilante committees were organized by business leaders who found vigilantes cheaper than a police force. Soon, however, the vigilantes appeared to be almost as dangerous as the criminals they were supposed to suppress.[70]

When ward constables and night watches proved inadequate to the tasks of law enforcement, business leaders were forced to support the public financing of professional police forces. Following several riots, New York City hired its first full-time police officers in 1845. Eight years later, New York City police finally received uniforms and some formal training. Likewise, in the 1850s, Philadelphia organized a uniformed police force following recurrent disorders.

New York's police forces were in constant disarray for many years. After the 1857 mayoral election, the new mayor dismissed the entire force and appointed his own men. The former policemen refused to relinquish their jobs, and for several months the city had two competing police forces. In June of that year, a full-scale riot broke out between the two groups.[71] Such confusion repeated itself again in 1868, when the newly elected Democratic governor removed all the city's police commissioners, who were Republicans. The commissioners refused to vacate their offices. Finally, the legislature resolved the dispute by assuming the appointment powers. In 1870, when the Tweed Ring acquired complete control of patronage jobs in New York City, loyalty to the machine became a prerequisite for appointment to the force.

These events illustrate one reason it took so long to build modern police forces. Fear of the police arose from the possibility that an armed, quasi-military organization might be used by one political faction against another. Business leaders pressed for police forces only when it became apparent that disorder seriously threatened their interests in promoting economic growth and stability.

All municipal services were provided only in the face of imminent catastrophe or social crisis. In many cities, volunteer fire gangs were replaced by municipal fire departments following holocausts, such as Chicago's Great Fire in 1871. Urban schools were likewise organized in response to a perceived crisis. In colonial Philadelphia, "the whole public debate on educating the poor reflected the belief that the poor formed a dangerous class. The primary question was how best to keep them in check."[72] On this basis, almshouses and charity societies were formed for the immigrant parents, and schools were established for the children.

Publicly-financed municipal services were organized in response to the breakdown of informal community norms and the consequent chaos of urban life. Services were expanded out of practical necessity, not because there were theories about how or why they should be provided. The development of organized city government was a slow, painful process. When the urban community became too complex to be governed informally, urban leaders were forced to invent new institutions.

The preindustrial city was relatively simple and homogeneous. Informal governance was appropriate in the context of the small community. Newburyport, Massachusetts, for example,

> was a community in which every citizen was closely bound to other members of the community by familial, recreational, economic, and social ties. The social hierarchy was clear; a series of institutions supported that hierarchy; and the community was so compact that it was difficult to escape the vigilance of the dominant class.[73]

Business leaders provided leadership in all the preindustrial cities. Governance was basically provided through committees staffed by volunteers; merchants, landowners, and bankers took turns running the committees. Full-time specialization in politics was rare.

As urban social conditions deteriorated, government-by-committee became inadequate. Part-time politicians could not organize and supervise complex urban services. As the scope of municipal services broadened, the number of paid city employees multiplied. Where volunteers once joined firehouse gangs and even cleaned streets, salaried, full-time employees took their places.

In the 1850s, Milwaukee's volunteer fire department gave way to paid professionals when new steam pumps proved too complicated for volunteers to maintain and operate.[74] Public works employees were hired to maintain the streets when it became difficult to find volunteers for the task. In the same decade, the provision of health services became too complex for volunteers when the city council required vaccination for smallpox and when it provided funds to build a sewer system. Political leadership in cities was becoming a full-time job too demanding for volunteer business leaders. "As businessmen abandoned the city's affairs and its politics new specialists assumed their former roles. Politics became a full-time business and professionals moved in to make careers of public office."[75]

The business elites that ran cities opted for informal, minimal government. Crisis or catastrophe forced them to support the creation of water and sewer systems, health programs, and fire and police departments. But these municipal services were always inadequate, precisely because they were one step behind whatever crisis brought about their existence: " . . . municipal authorities, loath to increase taxes, usually shouldered new responsibilities only at the prod of grim necessity."[76]

The Evolution of Urban Government

Throughout the nineteenth century, the structure of municipal government became progressively more complicated. The various institutions of city government—boards of health, police departments, fire departments, street and maintenance departments, water and sewer services—each had their own peculiar history and reason for being. Municipal government had grown by bits and pieces, like a building constructed without any plan. Over time, crises had been met by the creation of special boards and commissions whose functions were quite specialized. New York City's situation, as described in 1876, was analogous to the chaotic state of affairs that existed in most large cities.

The mayor has been deprived of all controlling power. The Board of Aldermen, seventeen in number, the Board of twenty-four Councilmen, the twelve Supervisors, the twenty-one members of the Board of Education, are so many independent legislative bodies, elected by the people. The police are governed by four Commissioners, appointed by the Governor for eight years. The charitable and reformatory institutions of the city are in [the] charge of four Commissioners whom the City Comptroller appoints for five years. The Commissioners of the Central Park, eight in number, are appointed by the Governor for five years. Four Commissioners, appointed by the Governor for eight years, manage the Fire Department. There are also five Commissioners of Pilots, two appointed by the Board of Underwriters and three by the Chamber of Commerce. The finances of the city are in charge of the Comptroller, whom the *people* elect for four years. The street department has at its head one Commissioner, who is appointed by the Mayor for four years. Three Commissioners, appointed by the Mayor, manage the Croton Aqueduct department. The law officer of the city, called the Corporation Counsel is elected by the *people* for three years! Six commissioners, appointed by the Governor for six years, attend to the emigration from foreign countries. To these has been recently added a Board of Health, the members of which are appointed by the Governor.[77]

The result of such fragmentation of government authority was to weaken significantly the mayor's—or anyone else's—ability to assert overall public authority.

All cities offered variations on the same theme. Smaller cities successfully resisted the urge to "professionalize" city services and continued to be governed by parttime amateurs. All large cities, however, were forced to deal with the threat of disease, violence, and other conditions arising from overcrowding and growth. The decade of the 1850s marked a watershed. During this ten-year period, New York, Boston, Milwaukee, and several other cities provided police uniforms for the first time. Water services were expanded, public health authorities were organized, and professional fire companies replaced volunteers. But there was no consistent ideology suggesting how services should be provided. Private companies still supplied water, sewers, lights, and streetcar services in some cities, while in others these services were supplied by the municipality. As in New York, boards and commissions were appointed by different public officials, or elected, with little apparent logic. The governor made some appointments, the mayor others, the city council still more.

Government by crisis gave rise to a multitude of boards and commissions, each created to deal with a particular problem. The precedent for the board system can be found in the committee systems of the mercantile city, whereby the need for a water system prompted the organization of a committee to supply a waterworks, an epidemic prompted the creation of a health board, and so on.

The board system also arose from political factionalism. Within the cities, mayors fought with city councils over the right to appoint board members. Sometimes board memberships were elective posts. Just as frequently, boards were appointed by state legislative committees or governors who wished to control city governments in order to build an urban constituency.

> The result of the introduction of [the board] system was completely to disorganize the municipal administration. Each important branch of city government was attended by a board or officer practically independent of any other municipal authority.[78]

The lack of any central direction in city affairs contributed to the ineffectuality of government policy and kept the scope of municipal authority limited. Thus, government had little ability to arbitrate conflicts in city affairs. In fact, control of the various pieces of government provided the impetus for considerable conflict. The weakness of local government was effectively assured by the way it was organized. Cities were limited to supplying basic, "necessary" services. Both political tradition and state legislative restrictions kept municipal governmental authority in check.

Such restrictions had not always been imposed. Until the Revolutionary period, the municipal corporation was the most important governmental body in the colonies. This status derived from "the municipality's unique role as a center of trade and commerce."[79] Cities and towns, as trading centers sitting astride the transportation nexus for commercial goods, were easily distinguished from any other governmental unit. "The municipal corporation was a community of trade and industry, an organization molded by the distinctive needs of commercial life amid a world of subsistence agriculture."[80]

In England, municipal corporations traditionally had regulated and promoted commercial activities. During the sixteenth century, English boroughs fixed standard weights and measures, regulated the price of commodities, and passed ordinances against shoddy, unsafe, and adulterated goods. The boroughs set wages and controlled entry into occupations; for example, they set limits on the number of bakers, brewers, tanners, and other specialists who could work within the boroughs' confines. These communities also maintained public markets, wharves, fairs, and streets by taxing retailers and manufacturers.

Early American communities copied these practices, including not only the seaboard cities but also the towns of the West, especially St. Louis, Cincinnati, Pittsburgh, Lexington, and Louisville. In the early towns of the West, "authorization of public money for market houses and detailed regulations for their operation were among the earliest ordinances."[81] These towns adopted ordinances to prevent fraud, sales of spoiled goods, inaccurate scales, and hoarding by merchants.[82]

Municipal corporations in the colonies operated under broad royal charters granted by the king. Within these charters, municipal corporations enjoyed considerable latitude. Most of the municipal corporations were run by wealthy merchants. Voting was normally restricted to businessmen or property owners, and municipal offices were the exclusive property of the economic elite. Until the Revolutionary period, Boston's important public offices were controlled by men who had high commercial or family connections.[83] The same was true in other colonial cities, even though class tensions posed a constant threat to oligarchic control.[84]

The idea that city governments should regulate business activities came under attack in the late eighteenth century. Adam Smith, in his landmark book published in 1776, *The Wealth of Nations*, argued that any governmental restraint of private entrepreneurial activity interfered with personal liberties and reduced the material welfare of society. Smith specifically addressed the economic regulations imposed by English municipalities, and concluded that "the pretence that [municipal] corporations are necessary for the better government of . . . trade is without any foundation."[85] According to Smith, the law of supply and demand should govern all economic relations; if allowed to operate without interference, this "natural" law of economics would result in a constant material improvement in society. Entrepreneurs seeking to maximize their own profits would always supply the goods that brought the highest prices—and those would be the goods most demanded by consumers. Thus, in seeking to serve their own selfish interests, entrepreneurs were guided by an "invisible hand" to serve the interests of society.

The theories of classical economics helped justify a new definition of the purpose of cities. Cities existed not to regulate but to provide a favorable atmosphere for economic activities. The true function of cities was to provide business owners with the maximum freedom to pursue production and commerce. This limited definition of the city's role persists to the present day, and it is why individual cities cannot exert any control over their economic destinies.

The power of cities to decide their own fate was also withdrawn by state legislatures. The growth of cities, which seemed to require an increase in the authority of city governments to respond to social problems, brought about a backlash from rural populations, who would have agreed with a New York delegate to a state constitutional convention that "the average citizen in the rural district is superior in intelligence, superior in morality, superior in self-government to the average citizen of the great cities."[86]

State legislatures dominated by rural interests were convinced that cities would soon govern the states if allowed to do so. They foresaw mobs of immigrants, foreigners, Catholics, and poor people taking over the whole nation unless steps were taken to ensure that cities were kept in their place. Maine's constitutional convention of 1819 established a ceiling on the number of representatives who could represent towns in the state legislature. In 1845, the Louisiana legislature limited New Orleans to 12.5 percent of the state's senators and 10 percent of the state's assemblymen. (New Orleans's population was then 20 percent of the state's total.)[87] By the end of the century, every state had ensured that no matter how large the cities became, rural legislative districts would continue to hold a controlling majority in state legislatures.

Legislatures went even further to assert control over the cities. Beginning in the 1850s, state legislative committees or governors controlled the police departments of Detroit, Baltimore, Boston, St. Louis, Kansas City, and New York. Legislative committees sometimes governed every detail of municipal service and expenditures, from the construction, paving, and naming of streets and the buying of parks to the awarding of sewer contracts.

Sometimes cities tried to contest the control wielded by people beyond their borders. But state and federal court decisions consistently upheld the powers of the states. In 1819, in the *Dartmouth College* case, the U.S. Supreme Court held that cities were nothing but the creatures of the state, and that their charters could be amended or even rescinded at will.[88] In 1868, an Iowa magistrate, Judge John F. Dillon, made the doctrine of state supremacy more explicit:

Municipal corporations owe their origin to, and derive their powers and rights wholly from, the legislature. It breathes into them the breath of life without which they cannot exist. As it creates so it may destroy. If it may destroy, it may abridge and control. Unless there is some constitutional limitation on the right, the legislature might, by a single act, if we can suppose it capable of so great a folly and so great a wrong, sweep from existence all of the municipal corporations of the state, and the corporations could not prevent it. We know of no limitation on the right so far as the corporations themselves are concerned. They are, so to phrase it, the mere tenants at will of the legislature.[89]

This doctrine would later become known in municipal government textbooks as "Dillon's rule," for it became the basic legal fact of life for cities everywhere.

Horatio Alger and Urban Culture

The weakness of municipal authority in the nineteenth century was inevitable. The pace of urban growth overwhelmed attempts to solve the cities' problems. Added to this were the restrictions placed on municipalities by state legislatures.

In fact, however, all governments—federal, state, and local—were kept in check during this period. The explanations for the limited scope of public authority are to be found in the values embedded in American culture. Following the Civil War, a new conservative ideology was promoted that attempted to justify prevailing modes of production, defend private exploitation of the nation's resources, and discourage government interference in the economy. This ideology was built on the powerful idea that "the true and central concern of American democracy is the morally free individual, [and] the right of this individual to maintain his dignity and develop his moral capacities is at the apex of the democratic-value hierarchy."[90] In industrial America, these ideals tended to be expressed as property rights. The accumulation of wealth was seen as the measure of an individual's moral capacities. Thus, democracy became defined functionally as that system which interfered least with people's attempts to prove their worth or develop their capacities, that is, to secure wealth. Government, at least government when it proposed social reform, was interpreted as a danger to freedom. Insofar as advocates for this view were influential, they undermined the government provision of services that might have improved the lot of the least successful citizens:

Since most positive social programs in an industrial age necessarily involve some curtailment of economic freedom, the advocate of such programs finds himself at odds with an accepted postulate of democracy. The citizen who feels that something should be done to mitigate the power of industrial combinations over the lives and destinies of individuals is at the same time troubled by the suspicion that such a restraint on industry would outrage the democratic faith.[91]

The American political tradition has always been guided by the idea that the best government is that which governs least. The American Revolution guaranteed that government institutions would be distrusted for a long time. The ideal of limited government was founded on the assumption that individual freedoms would be preserved, not primarily through the intervention of government, but by its weakness.

For most of the nineteenth century, the political state of affairs in American cities and in the nation was heavily influenced by the fear of strong executive-centered government and by the Yankee-Protestant ideal of individual success. According to Richard Hofstadter, those Americans holding such ideals "wanted economic success to continue to be related to personal character, wanted the economic system not merely to be a system for the production of sufficient goods and services but to be an effectual system of incentives and rewards."[92] Government intrusion into this system was thought to be unhealthy and dangerous, since it would undermine the natural process whereby individuals could compete to prove their worth. William Graham Sumner expressed these values when he asserted that, "society needs first of all to be freed from . . . meddlers—that is, to be let alone. Here we are, once more back at the old doctrine—*Laissez faire.*" Earlier, he had written that it was necessary to "minimize to the utmost the relations of the state to industry."[93]

It would be difficult to overstate the strength of conservative doctrines after the Civil War. In part, the militant assertion of the sanctity of the marketplace was a logical extension of the Founding Father's fears about a strong government and a reaffirmation of the classical economists' *laissez faire* doctrines. In the second half of the century, however, these attitudes were expressed in particularly strident tones.

The need to promote conservative values was heightened by the class tensions created by industrialization. Labor violence, social unrest, and poverty endangered the new economic relationships. To economic elites, it was imperative that a persuasive rationale be articulated to explain and justify inequality.

Social Darwinism provided the language and the logic to defend industrial capitalism as an expression of democratic principles. Charles Darwin's *The Origin of Species*, published in 1859, revolutionized theories about the processes of nature. Before long, his ideas were adopted to explain social relationships. Darwin's idea was that the "struggle for existence" weeded out the weakest species, those unable to adapt to changing conditions in nature, and resulted in the "survival of the fittest." Social Darwinists suggested that society, like nature, provided a competitive environment in which the fittest survived *if no one intervened to save the weak.* The doctrine was seized upon by conservatives who wanted to minimize political constraints on economic activities. The Darwinist idea also provided a convenient justification for the adverse consequences of industrialization (unemployment, poverty, starvation), a rationale by which conservatives could "reconcile their fellows to some of the hardships of life and to prevail upon them not to support hasty and ill-considered reforms."[94] It was explained that reforms designed to mitigate the effects of competitive individualism could only upset the natural social processes that resulted in progress for the human species. The conservatives "suggested that all attempts to reform social processes were efforts to remedy the irremediable, that they interfered with the wisdom of nature, that they could lead only to degeneration."[95]

To the Social Darwinists, it was obvious that government interference in the social order would destroy the continual process of moral and material improvement. It was better to let the poor die, to let drunks lie in the gutter; assisting the weak individuals of society would endanger the welfare of all. "Let it be understood," wrote the influential American Social Darwinist William Graham Sumner, "that we cannot go outside of this alternative: liberty, inequality, survival of the fittest; not—liberty, equality, survival of the unfittest."[96]

Social Darwinism glorified the business leaders who accumulated large amounts of capital, for these were (it was clear by their success) the individuals who contributed most to societal progress.

> As the conservatives employed it, the Darwinian revelation supported all their traditional premises. In nature, the fittest rise to positions of dominance, the less fit are eliminated. Thus the species slowly improves through natural selection, so long as no extraneous influence interferes. "Fitness" was defined in terms of material success, because nature is incapable of recognizing another standard.[97]

According to Sumner, those who held great wealth had demonstrated by their success their superior ability to preside over economic institutions: "the aggregation of large amounts of capital in few hands is the first condition of the fulfillment of the most important tasks of civilization."[98]

One measure of the influence of the materialistic ethos was the great popularity of "success" literature between the 1860s and the turn of the century. Especially in the 1880s, following the worst depression after the Civil War, dozens of books extolled the virtues of hard work, thrift, moral habits, discipline, and cleanliness as the main ingredients in the attainment of wealth. The titles of some of the bestsellers are revealing. In 1882, P. T.

Barnum published *The Art of Money Getting*, and two years later followed it with *How I Made Millions. How to Succeed* (1882), *The Royal Road to Wealth* (1882), *The Secret of Success* (1881), *Success in Life* (1885), and *Danger Signals: The Enemies of Youth from the Business Man's Standpoint* (1885) were other popular books. Poverty was widely acclaimed as the greatest teacher of virtue; climbing out of poverty was a test of character. Andrew Carnegie, the self-made steel magnate, enthusiastically praised poverty: "Abolish luxury if you please, but leave us the soil upon which alone the virtues of all that is precious in human character grow; poverty—honest poverty."

Rural life was promoted as the teacher of moral habits and industry. By playing on the twin themes of poverty and rural beginnings, the literature offered hope of success to nearly everyone. The Unitarian minister, Horatio Alger, bound these themes together into a literary formula. Beginning with his first successful book, *Ragged Dick*, he was wildly popular, writing 106 rags-to-riches stories between 1868 and 1904 (the last books were written by others using his name). His stories invariably described a poor boy who, through perseverance, hard work, honesty, religious probity, and a little luck, achieves moderate financial success.

The literature flooded the schools, with the express purpose of teaching immigrant children proper "American" values and personal habits. *McGuffey's Readers*, which dominated the schools from the later 1830s through the 1890s, were full of stories and poems based on success motifs.

Such values exerted a powerful impact on political institutions and public policies. Social Darwinism and the success ethic provided a logical explanation for inequality and poverty and helped to create a favorable atmosphere for business expansion and freedom from government interference.

Municipal Government and Social Justice

American cultural values became increasingly divorced from social and economic realities as urbanization unfolded. Against the vast transformations taking place in industrial America, the idea of the city as a marketplace not only survived but became embellished and amplified. Cities became progressively more complex and chaotic, yet the task of municipal government was not redefined as an instrument to further social justice or to ameliorate the conditions brought about by industrialization and urbanization. At the same time that opportunities for upward mobility by the working class were being shut off, the success ethic promised rewards for those possessing the proper virtues of hard work, frugality, and self-denial. The Horatio Alger stories perfectly symbolized the discontinuity between myth and reality. The stories always set their heroes (Ragged Dick, Phil the Fiddler, Jed the Poorhouse Boy, and a hundred more) in a simple world of small business and small town, a world that certainly did not exist in the cities of the post–Civil War era.

The values of competitive individualism, when interpreted against a romantic background of small town America and rags-to-riches mythology, allowed elites to persuade their fellow Americans that the economic system was just and efficient. The need to create a sense of legitimacy helps to account for much of the published Social Darwinist and success literature.

Why was the success literature persuasive to those who had not succeeded already? There were just enough self-made millionaires, men like P. T. Barnum and Andrew Carnegie, that the success formula *seemed* to work, at least often enough. The logic of Social Darwinism, from which the success ethic borrowed heavily, seemed persuasive: no competing interpretation of society provided such an inclusive explanation for social conditions, or promised so much hope for improvement. The optimistic promise obscured the dark side of Social Darwinism—the poverty. It was an age of striking changes and dislocation, an atmosphere ripe for the founding of optimistic religions that held out the promise of a brighter future. This, as Richard Hofstadter has pointed out,[99] is why America provided such fertile ground for an idea that originated in Europe.

References

1. London proper had 957,000, but the greater London area contained 1,117,000.

2. Brian R. Mitchell, *European Historical Statistics, 1750–1970* (New York: Columbia University Press, 1975), p. 76 (population of major cities).

3. Defined as settlements with at least 5,000 population.

4. Emerys Jones, *Towns and Cities* (New York: Oxford University Press, 1966), p. 30.

5. "The Inevitability of City Growth," reprinted from *Atlantic Monthly,* April 1895, in *City Life, 1865–1900: Views of Urban America,* ed. Ann Cook, Marilyn Gittell, and Herb Mack (New York: Praeger, 1973), p. 17.

6. U.S. Bureau of the Census, *Historical Statistics of the United States, Colonial Times to 1970,* pt. 1, Bicentennial ed. (Washington, D.C.: U.S. Government Printing Office, 1975), p. 11.

7. Bureau of the Census, *Historical Statistics of the United States, Colonial Times to 1970,* pt. 1, p. 11.

8. Eric Lampard, "Historical Aspects of Urbanization," *The Study of Urbanization,* ed. Philip M. Hauser and Leo F. Schnore (New York: John Wiley, 1965), p. 523.

9. From Table 2, "Populations of Principal U.S. Cities, 1790 to 1839," in Blake McKelvey, *American Urbanization: A Comparative History* (Glenview, Ill.: Scott, Foresman, 1973), p. 24.

10. Allan R. Pred, *The Spatial Dynamics of Urban-Industrial Growth, 1800–1914* (Cambridge, Mass.: MIT Press, 1966), p. 103.

11. It was also difficult to accumulate large amounts of capital. The corporate form of business organization, which allowed the selling of shares to investors who were financially liable only for their direct investment, did not become common until the 1850s.

12. Sam Bass Warner, Jr., *The Private City: Philadelphia in Three Periods of Its Growth* (Philadelphia: University of Pennsylvania Press, 1968), p. 21.

13. Howard P. Chudacoff, *The Evolution of American Urban Society* (Englewood Cliffs, N.J.: Prentice-Hall, 1975), p. 26.

14. Richard C. Wade, *The Urban Frontier: Pioneer Life in Early Pittsburgh, Cincinnati, Lexington, Louisville, and St. Louis* (Chicago: University of Chicago Press, 1959), p. 103.

15. Wade, p. 336.

16. Glen E. Holt, "The Changing Perception of Urban Pathology: An Essay on the Development of Mass Transit in the United States," in *Cities in American History*, ed. Kenneth T. Jackson and Stanley K. Schultz (New York: Alfred A. Knopf, 1972), p. 331; and David Ward, *Cities and Immigrants: A Geography of Change in Nineteenth-Century America* (New York: Oxford University Press, 1971), p. 134.

17. George Rogers Taylor, "Building an Intra-Urban Transportation System," *The Urbanization of America: An Historical Anthology*, ed. Allen M. Wakstein (Boston: Houghton Mifflin, 1970), p. 137.

18. Taylor, p. 139.

19. C. G. Kennedy, "Commuter Services in the Boston Area, 1835 to 1860," *Business History Review* 26 (1962): 277–287.

20. Holt, "The Changing Perception of Urban Pathology," p. 327–328.

21. Ward, *Cities and Immigrants*, p. 4.

22. Holt, "The Changing Perception of Urban Pathology," p. 331.

23. Gary A. Tobin, "Suburbanization and the Development of Motor Transportation: Transportation Technology and the Suburbanization Process," *The Changing Face of the Suburbs*, ed. Barry Schwartz (Chicago: University of Chicago Press, 1976), p. 99.

24. "The Smell of Cincinnati," *Enquirer* (Richmond, Va.), November 15, 1874, cited in *City Life, 1865–1900*, ed. Cook, Gittell, and Mack, p. 143.

25. Ward, *Cities and Immigrants*, p. 134.

26. Ward, chap. 3.

27. Blake McKelvey, *The Urbanization of America 1860–1915* (New Brunswick, N.J.: Rutgers University Press, 1963), p. 54.

28. U.S. Bureau of the Census, *The Growth of Metropolitan Districts in the United States: 1900–1940*, by Warren S. Thompson (Washington, D.C.: U.S. Government Printing Office, 1947); and Bureau of the Census, *Population Trends in the*

United States: 1900 to 1960, by Irene S. Taeuber, Technical Paper no. 10 (Washington, D.C.: U.S. Government Printing Office, 1964).

29. U.S. Bureau of the Census, *The Growth of Metropolitan Districts.*

30. Ward, *Cities and Immigrants*, p. 128.

31. U.S. Bureau of the Census, *Historical Statistics of the United States, Colonial Times to 1970*, pt. 2, Bicentennial ed. (Washington, D.C.: U.S. Government Printing Office, 1975), pp. 728, 731.

32. Wade, *The Urban Frontier*, p. 70.

33. McKelvey, *American Urbanization*, p. 31.

34. McKelvey, *The Urbanization of America*, pp. 25–26.

35. Ibid., p. 26.

36. Samuel P. Hays, *The Response to Industrialism, 1885–1914* (Chicago: University of Chicago Press, 1957), p. 8.

37. Hays, p. 8.

38. Pred, *The Spatial Dynamics*, p. 170.

39. Pred, pp. 68–69.

40. Chartered by the states, limited-risk corporations allowed the selling of shares to investors whose liability in case of corporate failure was limited to their direct investment. In partnerships, the partners were liable for all debts incurred by the company, and these could easily exceed the partners' own assets. The corporate form of business organization thus made it easier to raise capital, for investors risked less than in other forms of business investment.

41. U.S. Department of the Interior, Census Office, *Census Reports of 1900*, vol. 7, *Manufacturers*, pt. 1: "United States by Industries" (Washington, D.C.: U.S. Government Printing Office, 1902), pp. 503–509.

42. William Miller, "American Historians and the Business Elite," *Journal of Economic History* 9 (1949):184–208.

43. The skyscraper boom on Fifth Avenue between 1900 and 1915 was largely fueled by the desire by rich individuals to outdo one another in pretentious architecture. Cf. Seymour I. Toll, *Zoned American* (New York: Grossman, 1969), chap. 2.

44. Hays, *The Response to Industrialism* p. 73.

45. Hays, p. 14.

46. Everett S. Lee and Anne S. Lee, "Internal Migration Statistics for the United States," *Journal of the American Statistical Association* 55, no. 292 (December 1960):664–697.

47. In addition to the cities in Table 2–3 in that category, cities with half or more of their populations of foreign stock (foreign-born or born of at least one foreign-born parent) include San Francisco, Detroit, Milwaukee, Scranton (Pa.), Lawrence and Fall River (Mass.), Cincinnati, Buffalo, Jersey City, Troy (N.Y.), Lowell (Mass.), Paterson (N.J.), Toledo, and probably a few more, mostly in upstate New York. Cf. U.S. Department of the Interior, Superintendent of the Census, *Ninth Census (June 1, 1870)* (Washington, D.C.: U.S. Government Printing Office, 1872). See Table 2–3 for explanation of how second-generation Americans were calculated for 1870.

48. U.S. Bureau of the Census, *Thirteenth Census of the United States Taken in the Year 1910* (Washington, D.C.: U.S. Government Printing Office, 1913).

49. Stephen Thernstrom, *The Other Bostonians: Poverty and Progress in the American Metropolis, 1880–1970* (Cambridge, Mass.: Harvard University Press, 1973), p. 160.

50. Michael Katz, ed., *School Reform: Past and Present* (Boston: Little, Brown, 1971), pp. 169–170.

51. John Higham, *Strangers in the Land: Patterns of American Nativism, 1860–1925* (New Brunswick, N.J.: Rutgers University Press, 1955), pp. 54–55.

52. Thernstrom, *The Other Bostonians.*

53. Moses Rischin, *The Promised City, New York's Jews 1870–1914* (Cambridge, Mass.: Harvard University Press, 1962), p. 87.

54. Gerald M. Caters, Jr., "Yellow Fever in Memphis in the 1870s," *The City in America Life, From Colonial Times to the Present*, ed. Paul Kramer and Frederick L. Holborn (New York: Capricorn Books, 1970), pp. 180–185.

55. "Tenement Conditions in Chicago," *City Life, 1865–1900*, ed. Cook, Gittell, and Mack, p. 149.

56. Charles N. Glaab and A. Theodore Brown, *A History of Urban America* (New York: Macmillan, 1967), p. 86.

57. Glaab and Brown, p. 55.

58. Nelson M. Blake, *Water for the Cities: A History of the Urban Water Supply Problem in the United States* (Syracuse, N.Y.: Syracuse University Press, 1956), p. 6. Also see Warner, *The Private City*, pp. 102–103.

59. Blake, p. 6.

60. Blake, p. 6.

61. Edgar W. Martin, *The Standard of Living in 1860* (Chicago: University of Chicago Press, 1942), pp. 44–47, 89–112.

62. McKelvey, *The Urbanization of America*, p. 13.

63. Ibid., p. 13.

64. Ibid., p. 90.

65. McKelvey, *American Urbanization*, p. 44.

66. McKelvey, *The Urbanization of America*, p. 90.

67. James F. Richardson, "To Control the City: The New York Police in Historical Perspective," in *Cities in American History*, ed. Jackson and Schultz, pp. 272–289.

68. Warner, *The Private City*, chap. 7.

69. Wade, *The Urban Frontier*, p. 89.

70. Fred M. Wirt, *Power in the City* (Berkeley: University of California Press, 1974), p. 110.

71. Richardson, "To Control the City," p. 278.

72. John K. Alexander, "The City of Brotherly Fear: The Poor in Late-Eighteenth-Century Philadelphia," in *Cities in American History*, ed. Jackson and Schultz, pp. 79–97.

73. Stephen Thernstrom, *Poverty and Progress: Social Mobility in a Nineteenth-Century City* (Cambridge, Mass.: Harvard University Press, 1964), p. 39.

74. Bayrd Still, *Milwaukee: The History of a City* (Madison: The State Historical Society of Wisconsin, 1984), chap. 10.
75. Warner, *The Private City*, p. 86.
76. Arthur N. Schlesinger, "A Panoramic View: The City in American History," in *The City in American Life*, ed. Kramer and Holborn, p. 23.
77. Seymour Mandelbaum, *Boss Tweed's New York* (New York: John Wiley, 1965), pp. 50–51.
78. Frank J. Goodnow, *City Government in the United States* (New York: Century, 1904), p. 63.
79. Jon Teaford, *The Municipal Revolution in America: Origins of Modern Urban Government, 1650–1825* (Chicago: University of Chicago Press, 1975), p. 3.
80. Teaford, p. 4. Most of the subsequent discussion of early municipal corporations relies on Teaford's excellent book.
81. Wade, *The Urban Frontier*, p. 79.
82. Wade, pp. 79–82.
83. James A. Henretta, "Economic Development and Social Structure in Colonial Boston," in *Cities in American History*, ed. Jackson and Schultz, p. 76.
84. Alexander, "The City of Brotherly Fear," in *Cities in American History*, ed. Jackson and Schultz.
85. Quoted in Teaford, *The Municipal Revolution*, p. 48.
86. Mark I. Gelfand, *A Nation of Cities: The Federal Government and Urban America, 1933–1965* (New York: Oxford University Press, 1975), p. 11.
87. Gelfand, p. 11.
88. See *Dartmouth College v. Woodward*, 4 Wheat. 518 (1819).
89. *City of Clinton v. Cedar Rapids and Missouri River Railroad Co.*, 24 Iowa 455, 475 (1868).
90. Robert Green McCloskey, *American Conservatism in the Age of Enterprise, 1865–1910* (New York: Harper and Row, 1951), p. 3.
91. McCloskey, pp. 18–19.
92. Richard Hofstadter, *The Age of Reform* (New York: Alfred A. Knopf, 1956), pp. 10–11.
93. McCloskey, *American Conservatism*, p. 61.
94. Richard Hofstadter, *Social Darwinism in American Thought*, rev. ed. (New York: George Braziller, 1955), p. 5.
95. Hofstadter, *Social Darwinism*, p. 7.
96. McCloskey, *American Conservatism*, p. 49.
97. McCloskey, p. 27.
98. Quoted in McCloskey, p. 50.
99. Hofstadter, *Social Darwinism*.

Chapter 3

THE POLITICIAN AS ENTREPRENEUR

Bosses, Machines,
and Urban Leadership

The Political Environment of the City Machines

By the late nineteenth century, municipal governments lacked the power to respond to the social and political disorder in American cities. There was no enduring solution to the problem. Only state militia or federal troops had the capacity to suppress serious disorders. The causes of class and ethnic tensions persisted.

The crisis in public order manifested itself in at least three ways. First, tension between workers and employers periodically broke out in violent strikes. Second, there were recurring confrontations between native-born Americans and immigrants. Finally, the ailments of the immigrant wards in the cities—overcrowding, ill health, poverty, bad housing, and crime—threatened the social and economic well-being of all urban residents.

Labor militance seemed to herald a frontal assault on existing political and economic relationships. A serious depression from 1873 to 1879 left hundreds of thousands unemployed; in several cities, workers went on strike and mobs rioted. Although the 1880s were more prosperous, the decade witnessed bloody confrontations between strikers, government authorities, and private security agents hired by employers. Another depression gripped the nation from 1893 to 1897.

The depression of the 1870s was the first of several to hit industrial America (by the time of the 1929 stock market crash, four more—about one each decade—had occurred). Small railroads and undercapitalized business concerns went bankrupt, while the larger firms reacted by cutting wages, extending work hours, and laying off workers. One fifth of the work force remained unemployed through the 1893–1897 depression, and incomes dropped drastically—for railroad workers and furniture carpenters 30 to 40 percent, for textile workers 45 percent.[1] About 1 million tramps wandered the streets, begging from door to door or living in railroad cars and often in jails, as well. By 1877, 100,000 workers were on strike, and 4 million were unemployed. The tensions exploded into violent confrontations between workers and authorities. In 1877, nonunionized railroad workers rioted in Chicago, St. Louis, Indianapolis, Pittsburgh, Buffalo, and other cities. Violence and property damage reached a peak in Pittsburgh, where track facilities and scores of railroad cars were wrecked and burned.

Following the depression of the 1870s, labor agitation continued. Between 1880 and 1900, there were almost 23,000 strikes.[2] Many of these were bloody and protracted confrontations that looked more like industrial warfare than conflict over wages and working conditions. Highlighting the tensions was Chicago's Haymarket Square riot and bombing on May 4, 1886.[3] For several weeks, union leaders in various parts of the country had been agitating for an eight-hour day (the normal work week was ten hours a day, six days a week, and sometimes much more). By May 1, 30,000 workers in Chicago were on strike. Several clashes between police and strikers led to a meeting in Haymarket Square, where someone threw a bomb at police lines, killing six policemen and two workers. The incident touched off a national campaign by politicians and the press against radical labor. In a sensationalized trial, nine labor leaders were tried, and eight were sentenced to be hanged. Four eventually were executed—even though none was ever shown to have anything to do with the bomb.

The Haymarket affair was less bloody than several other labor confrontations. In the mining and lumbering camps of the West, employers regularly hired "goon" squads to break strikes. In retaliation, workers armed themselves and destroyed property. In the East, company owners employed private security agents and often received the aid of state and federal troops in dealing with strikers. In the Homestead, Pennsylvania, strike of 1892, Pinkerton agents battled with strikers. Nine strikers and seven Pinkerton agents died. At one point, Andrew Carnegie in effect imprisoned workers in a steel mill and forced them to work. Two years later, during the Pullman railroad strike, state militias were mobilized in seven states, federal troops were sent to Chicago and Pullman, Illinois, and thirty-four strikers were killed in various confrontations. Such events made it look as though industrial warfare might destroy the national economic system.

A vicious reaction against immigrants further aggravated class, racial, and religious tensions. Immigrants were compared with the Goths and Vandals, who invaded Europe in the second century A.D. According to the Reverend Josiah Strong, immigrants defiled the Sabbath, spread illiteracy and crime, and corrupted American culture and morals, giving strength to the "great perils" threatening Anglo-Saxon Christians: Romanism, Mormonism, intemperance, socialism, mammonism, materialism, and luxuriousness.[4] Concentrated in the cities, the immigrants were accused of providing "a very paradise for demagogues" who ruled by manipulating the "appetites and prejudices" of the rabble.[5]

A social crisis also existed within the immigrant wards. Poverty and long working hours tore at the stability of family and community life. Every day new arrivals disembarked from ships, destitute and confused. The social pathologies in the immigrant ghettos were precariously contained within them. In cities there was an unmet need for *governance*, for urban institutions that could do more than supply minimal services. Obviously, the institutions of municipal government were unlikely to fill the void. The prevailing philosophy of limited government, the division of public authority among city agencies, and the restrictions imposed by state governments all guaranteed that city governments would remain weak.

However, political and social chaos presented opportunities as well as problems. Entrepreneurs who were denied access to the business world entered politics. After the 1870s, party organizations that fulfilled the need for governance arose in most big cities. They were able to barter among diverse groups by centralizing power and material resources in a few hands. But they exacted a price; like their counterparts in the business world, they were in it for profit.

Political party machines flourished in the cities by doing three things effectively. First, by mobilizing the immigrant electorate, they "delivered" the ethnic vote for selected candidates in the immigrant wards. Second, they distributed important material benefits. Some of these benefits, in the form of jobs and other favors, went to their electoral constituencies. The most valuable benefits went to the business community. By capturing important public offices, machine politicians held power over utility franchises, contracts, taxes, and business regulations. Astute machine politicians used these powers to raise money and to build personal political support. Third, by distributing patronage and material benefits resourcefully, machine politicians built centralized party organizations, with disciplined workers whose loyalty was guaranteed by the prospect of material rewards in exchange for work in the party. Thus, machines overcame the fragmentation of authority characteristic of the formal government structures of the time. The machines were brokers among contending political interests; they supplied material and symbolic rewards to poor immigrants, and by centralizing political authority, they brought a semblance of social and political order to the cities.

How Machines Were Organized

Machine organizations did not develop overnight. They were, rather, the final step in the slow process of building a network of social customs and political institutions within ethnic communities. The social and economic insecurities of the immigrant, coupled with the segregation of ethnic neighborhoods, encouraged the development of closed, protective social institutions and personal interactions.

In the Irish wards, the Roman Catholic church and the pubs were the most important social institutions outside the family. These social structures provided a leadership system in which priests and pub owners were sought out as reliable sources of information and advice. They often offered help in time of need. Irish pub owners not only occupied a nexus of communication and gossip but also dipped into the till to help with the rent or the groceries. Gestures like these sometimes translated into political leadership.

The decentralized nature of local politics facilitated the consolidation of ethnic political power. The basic electoral unit, the precinct, rarely included more than 600 to 800 voters. Aldermen sitting on city councils typically represented wards containing forty or fifty precincts. Patterns of ethnic segregation guaranteed that some wards would be dominated by lower-class Irish, others by Italians, and still others by native Protestants.

The decentralized structure of the urban political system, combined with mass suffrage and ethnic residential segregation, led to a style of politics in which social and political relationships became closely interconnected. Most large American cities went through a "friends and neighbors" or "local followings" style of politics, in which local leaders, often pub owners, came to dominate first a precinct and then a ward. Party machines linked these local leaders together into mutually supportive alliances.

Party machines combined two apparently contradictory elements: informality and hierarchy. Precinct captains knew each voter personally, often as a friend and neighbor. To secure a following at this level, a politician had to be regarded not only as a person involved in politics but as someone who participated in community life. Built on this foundation, the machine organization looked like a pyramid, as shown in Figure 3–1.

FIGURE 3–1   The Organization of Machine Politics

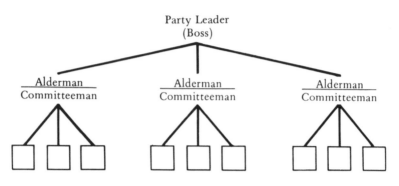

The alderman represents a ward in the City Council. He is sometimes also the ward committeeman.

Ward committeemen are in charge of several precinct captains. They chair the ward's party committees and are members of the city-wide party committee.

Each square represents several precincts, but one ethnic cluster. Precinct captains must deliver the vote in their precinct.

This structure once was described by Frank Hague, the Jersey city boss, to columnist Joseph Alsop:

> He [Hague] was talking in the dining room of one of the local hotels. He took the squares on the tablecloth to illustrate precincts and wards, tracing them out with his finger, and he explained the feudal system of American politics, whereby the precinct captain is governed by a ward lieutenant, the lieutenant by a ward leader, and each ward leader by the boss.[6]

The career of one machine politician, James Pendergast of Kansas City, illustrates the process and structure of machine politics.[7] In 1876, Pendergast moved into Kansas City's West Bottoms Ward, an industrial section nestled in the floodplain of the Missouri River. The residents of West Bottoms worked in the meatpacking houses, machine shops, railroad yards, factories, and warehouses of the area. Blacks, Irish, Germans, and rural migrants lived in crowded four- or five-story tenements and tiny shanties. Overlooking this squalid area of dirt streets and open sewers was Quality Hill, from which the wealthy elite literally presided over the town. Pendergast held jobs in the packinghouses and in an iron foundry until 1881, when he used racetrack winnings to buy a hotel and a saloon. He named the saloon Climax, after his lucky horse.

Three factors contributed to Pendergast's success in First Ward (West

Bottoms) politics. First, he was Irish, like the majority of his constituents. Second, gambling, prostitution, and liquor were important to the politicians of the First Ward, since most of them made their money from these three sources. Pendergast's new business made him a member of this group. Third, as a successful saloonkeeper, Pendergast was in a position to meet the people of his ward. By staying out of factional fights within the Democratic party in his ward while simultaneously making himself a trusted friend of politicians and ward residents, he soon found himself being promoted for an aldermanic seat, which he won in 1892.

During his first term as alderman, Pendergast established himself as a champion of the working class, successfully fighting against salary reductions for firemen, securing a city park in the West Bottoms, and opposing an attempt to move a fire station out of his ward. He won support from reform elements by favoring lower telephone rates and by proposing a better garbage collection system. Within his ward, he served his constituency. On payday, he cashed payroll checks and settled credit agreements. He posted bond for men who had been arrested for gambling. His generosity cost money, but his business flourished: "Men learned that he had an interest in humanity outside of business and that he could be trusted, and they returned the favor by patronizing his saloon and giving him their confidence."[8] Thus, Pendergast's politics and social life became one and the same. It even seemed that politics was merely an extension of his personality, rather than a calculated activity:

> He had a big heart, was charitable and liberal, . . . no deserving man, woman or child that appealed to "Jim" Pendergast went away empty handed, and this is saying a great deal, as he was continually giving aid and help to the poor and unfortunate. . . . Grocers, butchers, bakers and coal men had unlimited orders to see that there was no suffering among the poor of the West Bottoms, and to send the bills to "Jim" Pendergast.[9]

Building on his solid support in the West Bottoms, Pendergast extended his influence into other areas of the city. In 1892, he opened another saloon in the North End Second Ward. In that saloon he employed twenty-two men to operate gambling tables, and in his West Bottoms ward he continued to employ a large gambling staff. Gambling operated on a very large scale in Kansas City. Opening his own operations in the North End enabled Pendergast to form alliances with the politicians of that ward, and Pendergast soon became as influential in the Second Ward as he was in the First. By working with aldermen with similar interests, he was able to secure police protection for gambling and liquor operations, by paying off individual policemen and also by influencing the choice of a police chief in 1895.

Pendergast's political influence began to grow. The politicians and the people of the North End supported him. His "generosity" to his West Bottoms constituents was extended to the Second Ward:

> the North Siders went to Pendergast for more than jobs. They went to him when they were in trouble and needed someone to soften the stern hand of justice. Many of them got fuel and other supplies from his precinct captains when they were down and out. Others ate his turkey and trimmings at the free Christmas dinners . . . , beginning with fifty guests and growing into the hundreds as the number of drifters increased year after year.[10]

By delivering the voters of his two wards, Pendergast was able to forge alliances with other politicians in the city. In 1900, he dominated the city's Democratic convention and named the mayoral nominee. After his candidate won the election, Pendergast was given control of a large number of patronage jobs. He appointed his brother, Tom, to the position of superintendent of streets. More than 200 men and 30 teams of horses were employed by the streets department, and large orders for gravel and cement went to favored suppliers and contractors. Positions in the fire department also became available to Pendergast and his Democratic coalition. One of Pendergast's men was appointed as the city's deputy license inspector, an important job because saloons and other business establishments needed licenses to operate. Finally, and perhaps most important of all, by 1902 Pendergast had named 123 of the 173 patrolmen on the police force. Thus, he pyramided his ability to control politics in two wards into alliances with men who needed his support within the Democratic party or on the board of aldermen. He became Kansas City's most powerful politician.

The Pendergast machine, like the party machines in other cities during the period, operated on the basis of exchange relationships. The boss distributed material rewards as favors and expected loyal support in return. Some machine politicians made this relationship explicit, but the most effective ones never had to; after helping with the rent, they could advise their constituent to "vote your conscience." Pendergast expressed it in this way: "I've been called a boss. All there is to it is having friends, doing things for people, and then later on they'll do things for you."[11] Pendergast's ward always elected him by at least a 3 to 1 margin, and without discernible voter fraud. It never occurred to him that he would need to manipulate an election.

Like Pendergast, most of the bosses had backgrounds and personalities that offended silk-stocking elements. Schooled in rough-and-tumble political competition, they often were men of incredible energy, hot tempers, and inflated egos. At the least, they loved what they were doing and felt no alienation from it. Far from being a parttime avocation, politics was everything they knew and did—their social life, their profession, their first love. When the Louisiana boss, Huey Long, was dying from an assassin's bullet in 1935, he offered political advice—what else would there be to talk about?[12]

For the machine politicians, politics was an ongoing business; delivering the vote on election day was only one part, although a critical part, of it. Machine politicians expected and received material benefits in return for their political activities. A great many of the Irish politicians of Chicago, for example, were saloonkeepers, and when their saloons became the recreation and information centers of their neighborhoods, their business naturally prospered. But that kind of return was merely incidental. More important was that politics put them in places of power, where they could win elections, choose people for public office, and influence important public decisions. Politics was the ladder to success. Frank Skeffington, the Irish boss in Edwin O'Connor's novel *The Last Hurrah*, remarked, "I had no education to speak of, a good many roads were closed to our people, and politics seemed the easiest way out."[13]

Machine politicians were supreme pragmatists. They appealed to their constituents' material needs and self-interests. Some of them, like Pendergast, went out of their way to ascertain and fulfill their constituents' needs. Others delivered less. All of them, however, delivered something, for their stock-in-trade was the distribution of jobs and favors.

All the bosses had at their disposal patronage jobs in streets, police, fire, and sanitation departments and sometimes in private industry. Special construction projects, such as levee construction or road building, could give a boss control over hundreds of permanent and temporary jobs. The best jobs went to party workers who performed well. Precinct captains (the party officials in charge of delivering a precinct's vote) usually held low-level jobs arranged through the machine. Ward committeemen, who ran the party committee representing an entire ward, generally were rewarded with higher-paying positions. Aldermen or other elected officials often owned lucrative insurance companies, ran their own law firms, or owned saloons. The most menial jobs were reserved for the loyal voters who turned out faithfully on election day.

Important patronage positions required no more than a few hours of work a week, and sometimes no work at all. This situation allowed party regulars to attend to their machine duties. Without the machine, members of the working classes could never have found time for political participation.

An understanding of the patronage "ladder" can be gained by examining the machine of Richard J. Daley, mayor of Chicago from the mid-1950s to the mid-1970s. The Cook County Central Committee had about 30,000 positions available for distribution. Most of these jobs were unskilled; 8,000 were available through Chicago's departments and commissions, including street cleaners, park supervisors, and the like.[14] The jobs ranged from $300-a-month elevator operators and $500-a-month stenographers to $25,000-a-year department directors. Individual ward committeemen controlled as many as 2,000 jobs. (Richard Daley began his career as committeeman of his ward.) There were fifty wards in the City of Chicago, with an average of 500 to 600 jobs available in each of them.[15]

The number of jobs available for distribution by precinct captains and ward committee members was determined by the vote on election day. A precinct captain in Chicago was expected to know all the voters in the precinct, and to be known by them. "When a man is given a precinct, it is his to cover, and it is up to him to produce for the party. If he cannot produce for the party, he cannot expect to be rewarded by the party. 'Let's put it this way' [one alderman told political scientist Milton Rakove], 'If your boss has a salesman who can't deliver, who can't sell his product, wouldn't he put in someone else who can?'"[16]

The Chicago machine, like the party organizations at the turn of the century, was a political pyramid. It was rooted in the precincts, where the votes must be delivered. Ward committee members directed the captains of the precincts within their wards, and the committee members, in turn, reported to the Cook County Central Committee. Although most of the city machines at the turn of the century were similarly organized, some were directed from the top with an iron hand, as in Daley's Chicago, while others were little more than loose confederations of individual politicians who could deliver the vote in their own neighborhoods. However well-structured individual machines were, they all showed these qualities: they were rooted in neighborhoods, they were held together by material incentives, and they delivered the vote by manipulating these incentives.

The machines were held together by the glue of material rewards for their loyal workers. Tangible benefits also supplied the crucial link between machine politicians and voters. Pendergast was a typical machine politician. When he provided bail money and paid the rent, fuel, and food bills, he expected a vote in return. So did Dan O'Connell, boss of the long-lived Albany machine: "Every Saturday night, Dan walked from the Elks Club on State Street to Fourth Avenue and Pearl Street. On the way, people would buttonhole him. They would stop and ask him for five or ten dollars, or more. They usually never paid back his money, but Dan didn't mind, because they voted Democratic."[17]

Every week, Alderman Vito Marzullo of Chicago scheduled a formal audience with his constituents. Flanked on each side by a precinct captain, he heard their complaints.

> A precinct captain ushered in a black husband and wife. "We got a letter here from the city," the man said. "They want to charge us twenty dollars for rodent control in our building." "Give me the letter, I'll look into it," Marzullo replied.

The captain spoke up. "Your daughter didn't vote on November fifth. Look into it. The alderman is running again in February. Any help we can get, we can use."[18]

In the course of hearing his constituents, Marzullo exclaimed, "Some of those liberal independents in the city council, they can't get a dog out of a dog pound with a ten-dollar bill. Who's next?" Marzullo then arranged to have a traffic ticket fixed; agreed to recommend someone for a job at an electric company; refused to donate money to the Illinois Right to Life Committee ("Nothing doing. . . . I don't want to get into any of those controversies. People for it and people against it."); agreed to try to find a job for an unemployed truck driver; gave $50 to a welfare mother. Responding to several more requests, he offered to "see what I can do."[19]

The Authority to Make Decisions

The reward system that made the machines operate also made it possible for power to be centralized into a few hands. The only way that individual ethnic politicians could exert influence was to coordinate their efforts with other politicians representing the same ethnic stock or with politicians who shared their political interests. Machine politicians were constantly looking for ways to expand the size of their coalitions. The most successful machines welcomed all groups, ethnic or otherwise, so long as these groups were loyal on election day. Tom Pendergast (who succeeded his brother Jim) of Kansas City, Frank Hague of Jersey City, and Richard Daley of Chicago each sought and won a sizable middle-class following. Pendergast sponsored baseball leagues, scout troops, and civic organizations in middle-class neighborhoods. Hague supported reform causes and encouraged party workers to organize (Democratic) civic organizations. Daley always slated a sprinkling of middle-class candidates for election and gave the sons and daughters of middle-class parents summer jobs and college scholarships.

One of the secrets of the Daley organization's longevity was its willingness to make peace even with the reformers. To capture a share of middle- and upper-class support, Daley "learned the lesson of what retailers call the loss leader—that is, the item that may lose money for the storekeeper but which lures customers in and thereby leads to increases in purchases of profitable merchandise."[20]

Successful bosses learned to distribute material rewards adroitly and to consolidate decisions into their own hands. Under these bosses, government policy became quite centralized. The party machine managed to overcome the extreme fragmentation of city governments, because it controlled municipal jobs and nominations and appointments to public office. Pendergast controlled Kansas City's mayor, police force, fire and streets departments, and license inspector's office by choosing the individuals who presided over and worked in those agencies. Similar arrangements were worked out in other large cities. In each case, the boss had something to offer to lower-level politicians in exchange for their support. When asked the basis of Earl Long's power in Louisiana, a politician once remarked, "Earl's good at . . . knowing every local politician in the state and remembering where he itches. Then Earl knows where to scratch him."[21]

The methods employed by some bosses to accumulate power are illustrated by Abraham Reuf's rule in San Francisco, from October 1901 to March 1907.[22] Reuf skillfully exploited class divisions in San Francisco at the turn of the century. Traditionally, Republican businessmen had held the city's public offices and had always pursued probusiness, antilabor policies. In the 1890s, the Democrats won office on a reform agenda that promised legal restraints on dishonest election practices and a charter reform implementing a "strong mayor" form of government.

San Francisco's laborers were not represented by either of the parties, even though the union movement had been growing in membership and strength from the 1870s through the 1890s. The business community became increasingly alarmed about union activities, and in response to a drayman's strike in 1901, members of the new teamster's union were locked out of the warehouses. This action precipitated a waterfront strike involving more than 15,000 men. Seeing the opportunity to organize a workingman's party, Reuf deserted the Republicans and promoted a mayoral candidate under the Union Labor Party label. Reuf's choice, Eugene Schmitz, was a moderate businessman, and Reuf himself held extensive real estate holdings. In October, Schmitz won handily, winning the votes of both moderate businessmen and striking laborers.

During the machine era, the major types of graft in American cities involved the awarding of lucrative franchises and utility rates and control of police power (involving tavern and liquor regulations, gambling, and prostitution) and public works (road building and maintenance, construction, and public buildings and parks). Through his influence over Mayor Schmitz and his control over city departments that issued franchises, licenses, and jobs, Reuf centralized political power in San Francisco.

Control over the police force was a central feature of the Reuf regime. Early in Schmitz's administration, Reuf let it be known to the brothels in the city that the laws against prostitution would be strictly enforced. He pointed out to the brothel owners the wisdom of having an attorney who could effectively represent their interests. The owners promptly agreed to pay him one-fourth of their profits, half of which he shared with Mayor

Schmitz. This arrangement allowed the brothels to continue their operations without fear of prosecution. In his role as an attorney, Reuf also "advised" saloons in the red-light district to pay premium prices for a low-quality whiskey supplied by one of Reuf's clients. In return for police protection, the saloon owners followed Reuf's advice.

In 1905, Reuf agreed to become the attorney for the French Restaurant Keeper's Association of San Francisco, for an annual retainer of $5,000. The restaurant owners decided to retain Reuf after a decision by the city's policy commissioners to revoke the liquor license of one of their establishments. Reuf, on behalf of his new clients, persuaded the mayor to remove one of the commissioners and replace him with someone sympathetic to the owners, thus assuring renewal of the restaurants' liquor licenses.

Illicit businesses commonly forged alliances with political machines. The exchange relationship was mutually beneficial, for these kinds of operations flourished best under "enlightened" attitudes by police, and the machines needed funds for their operations. Sometimes, as in Chicago during the 1920s, the machine's main business seemed to be selling police protection.

But urban machines centralized decision making for legitimate enterprises, too. Government authorities routinely made important decisions affecting legitimate businesses and entrepreneurs. Reuf's largest attorney's fees came from businesses seeking franchises or favorable utility rates. Like other growing cities of the late nineteenth century, San Francisco invested heavily in new municipal services. Entrepreneurs were competing to install new streetlights, supply gas, install telephones, and build electric trolley lines. In the stroke of a pen, mayors, city councils, and utilities commissions could enrich or impoverish business owners by awarding monopoly contracts to supply the city. The temptation to make decisions in smoky rooms outside of public scrutiny was overwhelming. As the chairman of the public utilities committee of the San Francisco Board of Supervisors told a group of businessmen in January 1906:

> Mr. Green should bear in mind that we are the city fathers; that from the city fathers all blessings flow; that we, the city fathers, are moved in all our public acts by a desire to benefit the city, and that our motives are pure and unselfish. . . . But it must be borne in mind that without the city fathers there can be no public service corporations. The street cars cannot run, lights cannot be furnished, telephones cannot exist. And all the public service corporations want to understand that we, the city fathers, enjoy the best of health and that we are not in business for our health. The question at this banquet board is: "How much money is in it for us?"[23]

Actually, there was plenty of money for everyone. In a fight between two telephone companies to secure an exclusive franchise for service in San

Francisco, Reuf collected a $1,200 monthly "attorney's fee" from one company while secretly accepting $125,000 from the other. Of course, Reuf awarded the contract to the highest bidder. Keeping $63,000 for himself, he distributed the remainder to the board of supervisors, using a loyalty test: $6,000 each to those who had received no independent bribes (showing they were not trying to go outside Reuf's control), $3,500 to those voting correctly despite bribes to do the opposite, and nothing for those who would not cooperate.

Reuf's position as an important "adviser" to Mayor Schmitz ended when he was indicted and tried for corruption. His downfall was facilitated by too much success; through the Union Labor Party, he had been able to select most of the supervisors, who, after seeing that politics in the city could be very lucrative, struck out on their own in search of bribes. It became impossible to contain the corruption once individual supervisors began to compete.

Although most machines were less recklessly corrupt than Reuf's, virtually all of them took graft. The temptation was overwhelming. The machines governed the cities during a period of explosive growth in population, services, and construction. In many cases corruption was engineered from the top, by business tycoons eager to expand their companies. In the 1880s and 1890s, several financial syndicates made millions of dollars by gaining control of the street railway franchises in New York, Philadelphia, and scores of other cities. Though the machines in individual cities were local, the sources of corruption were not. The Bell Telephone Company launched its drive for monopoly in the early twentieth century by offering bribes to officials in city after city. It was an unusual city regime that failed to take advantage of the financial opportunities offered by Bell and other giant companies.

Corruption on this scale helped to centralize power in the hands of one boss. Only machines could reliably deliver votes. Machine politicians bought the vote with jobs and favors and were, in any case, closer to their constituents than anyone else. Because they controlled important public offices and governmental decisions, these politicians could exchange public power for a small portion of the financial resources of the business community. Corruption encouraged centralization of the machines at the top because it was in everyone's interest to "cooperate" with a boss who could divide the spoils.

The urban machines were centralized, extralegal governments superimposed on the official governmental structures. Urban government —with its proliferation of boards and commissions, its division of power among a multitude of elected officials, and its uncertain sources of revenue—had proved inadequate both for providing services and for governing. The machines were organized through a coherent party apparatus that captured public offices by manipulating the vote. Thus, a boss could control the behavior of public officials even though he lacked the constitutional and legal authority to do so. People from various walks of life found the centralization of power beneficial. That is why the machines prospered.

The Advantages of Machine Rule

The relationship between machine politicians and immigrant neighborhoods gave the urban machines a unique character. No other way of organizing politics held the advantage of combining social interactions with political self-interest. "The immigrant, a new kind of uprooted urban proletarian, was the disinherited of a new frontier, the frontier of the urban wilderness, untamed, exploitive, dingy. The quality of life left the urban immigrant vulnerable to the inducements of the boss."[24]

The "inducements" were valued commodities—jobs, loans, emergency food, shelter. The machines also supplied a structure of opportunity, a system in which ambitious young men without formal education or job experience could serve an apprenticeship and then work their way up, a path of upward mobility for those "otherwise excluded from the conventional avenues of personal 'advancement.'"[25] Most machine politicians regarded politics as a way to get ahead personally. Politics was a career like any other business, except that for someone of immigrant stock it promised more success than a job in the business world.

And the machines offered symbolic reassurance to immigrant communities. Machine politicians organized activities, picnics and patriotic gatherings (always Fourth of July celebrations), baseball teams, choirs, and youth clubs. Machines were important community social institutions, the Democratic Club being a place where a person could get up a card game, play checkers, or just talk.

The machine's political activities were invested with great symbolic significance. It was an organization that supplied its services with a personal touch.

> It [government] is an environment that in normal times is often impersonal, remote, and meaningless to the people themselves until a wide-awake division leader appears before them in the flesh. He is an individual who speaks their own language and knows their own wants. He often makes warm and personal that which had been cold and distant. He "knows everybody" at City Hall, or he knows someone who does. He bridges the gap between the unseen outer world and the inadequate citizen.[26]

Machine politicians characteristically were able to personalize services and know people through their aggressive and often colorful personalities.

Nearly all machine politicians had lower-class, immigrant origins. One study of twenty bosses found that fifteen were first- or second-generation immigrants, thirteen had never finished grammar school, and most had gone into politics at a young age, serving as message carriers or detail boys at rallies and meetings.[27]

Machine leaders were symbols of "making it." Immigrants may not have read the Horatio Alger stories, but in machine bosses they could see men who had risen out of poverty. Aspiring politicians often accepted this interpretation of themselves, too; such men were examples of what could be done with a little hard work and some luck along the way. The politicians helped assimilate the immigrants by providing them with a sense of belonging, not only to their community, but to America. They tended to be patriotic, and they believed America truly was a land of opportunity (and for them, it was). Patriotism fit the machine's style of camaraderie and community togetherness. Thus, a description by George Washington Plunkitt,* a Tammany Hall sachem:

> The very constitution of the Tammany Society requires that we must assemble at the wigwam on the Fourth, regardless of the weather, and listen to the readin' of the Declaration of Independence and patriotic speeches.
>
> You ought to attend one of these meetins. They're a liberal education in patriotism. The great hall upstairs is filled with five thousand people, suffocatin' from heat and smoke. Every man Jack of these five thousand knows that down in the basement there's a hundred cases of champagne and two hundred kegs of beer ready to flow when the signal is given. Yet that crowd stick to their seats without turnin' a hair while, for four solid hours, the Declaration of Independence is read, long-winded orators speak, and the glee club sings itself hoarse.
>
> Talk about heroism in the battlefield! That comes and passes away in a moment. You ain't got time to be anything but heroic. But just think of five thousand men sittin' in the hottest place on earth for four long hours, with parched lips and gnawin' stomachs, and knowin' all the time that the delights of the oasis in the desert were only two flights downstairs! Ah, that is the highest kind of patriotism, the patriotism of long sufferin' and endurance. What man wouldn't rather face a cannon for a minute or two than thirst for four hours, with champagne and beer almost under his nose?[28]

From the point of view of the immigrant, the machine bestowed many advantages, both material and symbolic. Immigrants were not the only beneficiaries, however. The bosses organized public power, a particularly important achievement for a portion of the business community. Illicit businesses were protected from blue-blooded reformers. Some legitimate

---

*From *Plunkitt of Tammany Hall* by William L. Riordan. Published by E. P. Dutton and reprinted with their permission.

businesses also benefited because centralization and the ability to bribe a few public officials stabilized the urban environment, reducing competition for public utilities franchises and regularizing policies on public works contracts, licenses, and permits.

The Disadvantages of Machine Rule

The machines partially overcame the chaos of urban life in the late nineteenth and early twentieth century. They also exerted important negative effects, however, and these must be balanced against their positive contributions to the governance of cities.

The machines' importance in integrating the immigrants into city life should not be overestimated. Many immigrant groups were not represented in party machines at all. In most cities the Irish controlled machine politics, and they defended their political and social organizations from infiltration by outsiders. The Irish also dominated the Roman Catholic church in the United States, with German and Italian Catholics accounting for a very small number of bishops. Until the turn of the century, Catholic parochial schools were almost exclusively Irish. Italians actually preferred the public schools to the Irish Catholic schools.[29] The Irish doggedly held onto their control in both religion and politics.

In Boston, New Haven, New York, and other cities, the Irish grabbed a disproportionate share of patronage jobs. Police forces, in particular, were long regarded as an Irish domain. In the 1930s, Italians secured representation in Boston and New York, and after World War II in Chicago. But in the era of the classic party machine, from the 1870s to 1930s, the Irish were sufficiently strong in large northeastern and midwestern cities that their power in politics was rarely challenged effectively.

Several important immigrant groups hardly participated in the machines at all, including the Scandinavians and Russian and European Jews. The Germans were important in machine politics in only a few cities, and not at all in others. Yet these groups were rapidly assimilated into the economic and social structures of the society, a fact that is especially remarkable in the case of the Jews, who faced persistent and virulent anti-Semitism. It is clear that other factors besides access to party politics assisted in assimilation.

As for the Irish, the machines failed to measurably accelerate their assimilation into economic and social institutions. Long after their success in politics, the Irish had still failed to achieve economic and status parity with other ethnic groups. In New Haven, for example, they were still "overrepresented in political positions and drastically underrepresented in the city's social and economic elites" in the 1960s.[30] Nationwide, however, the Irish finally achieved economic success (as a group) in the 1960s and 1970s.

Machine politics no doubt *increased* antagonism toward the Irish. White Anglo-Saxon Protestant natives looked on Irish politicians with disdain. Politics was thought to be a "dirty business," populated with criminals and rough-talking hooligans. Middle- and upper-class elements in many cities were horrified that immigrants had so much political influence, and in the early years of the twentieth century they launched crusades to "reform" politics, with machine politicians as their first targets and their immigrant supporters second in line.

All this would have mattered little if the bosses had distributed enough material resources to improve the immigrant communities. The fact is that politicians helped themselves tremendously and did not, in the end, deliver very much. Machines softened the harshness of the economic system, though not by much, through the small favors they bestowed. But the jobs distributed to loyal voters did not begin to meet the people's needs, and were in most cases menial, low-paying jobs with little or no future. By the turn of the century the labor-management division was sufficiently rigid that being a laborer was no way to rise through the ranks of business. The party machine did not change this simple fact.

The machines rarely attempted to reform the immigrant's economic and political environment. Few machine politicians offered any ideas about restructuring the social order. They were notoriously fearful of "radicals" and malcontents, for divisive issues would endanger the efficiency and discipline of their organizations.

> Instead of social welfare policies the machine politicians chose to offer the poor no more than a few twists on their old stock in trade, the petty favor. [In Chicago] one of these twists was the establishment of free lunch counters stocked with food "donated" to the ward politician by local grocers. Of course in return for this beneficence . . . , the fact that it was the regular practice of the merchants involved to use short weight scales in his everyday business was overlooked.[31]

Machine politicians were not overgenerous in exchanging material commodities for the vote. Most voters got little more than a little money and a free lunch at the bar on election day. It was a system with "monetary rewards for a few and symbolic gratification for the rest."[32]

In any case, machine politicians rarely relied solely on the appreciation of the voters to win elections. During the machine era city elections were notoriously corrupt. There were few legal constraints on the election process. Many cities did not adopt voter registration laws until the twentieth century. Fictitious or repeat voters, false counting, and stuffed ballot boxes were regular features of city elections.

A ruse commonly employed by the machines on election day was for "repeaters" to vote several times under various names. A Philadelphia politician once boasted that the signers of the Declaration of Independence were machine loyalists. "'These men,' he said, 'the fathers of American liberty, voted down here once. And,' he added with a sly grin, 'they vote here yet.'"[33]

Politicians sometimes completed the ballot for the voter or accompanied him into the voting booth. "Farmer Jones," a member of the Chicago machine in the 1890s, revealed to an inquiring reformer how he guaranteed voter loyalty.

> [The reformer asked] "When you got the polling stations in your hands, what did you do?"
> "Voted our men, of course."
> "And the negroes, how did they vote?"
> "They voted as they ought to have voted. They had to."
> "...how could you compel those people to vote against their will?"
> "They understood, and besides," said he, "there was not a man voted in that booth that I did not know how he voted before he put the paper in the judges' hands."[34]

A simple and effective means of securing electoral loyalty was to buy the vote. The 1896 election in the First Ward of Chicago was conducted thusly:

> The bars were open all night and the brothels were jammed. By ten o'clock the next morning, though, the saloons were shut down, not in concession to the reformers, but because many of the bartenders and owners were needed to staff the First Ward field organization. The Bath, Hinky Dink and their aides ran busily from polling place to polling place, silver bulging in their pockets into which they dug frequently and deeply.
> The effort was not in vain, and outcome was gratifying.[35]

When peaceful means of guaranteeing election results failed, machine politicians sometimes resorted to intimidation and violence. Tom Pendergast, who inherited his brother's Kansas City organization after Jim died, regularly used coercion to control elections. In the summer of 1914, Pendergast's organization used a mixture of bribes and violence to get out the vote for a proposed railway franchise. He "used money, repeat voters, and toughs to produce North Side majorities that pushed the franchise to victory."[36] In black and Italian neighborhoods, liquor and money were distributed to voters, and workers in his organization "paid men to vote under assumed names; and election judges who questioned some of those dragged off the streets and out of flop houses to vote were intimidated and abused, both verbally and physically."[37] Such practices became a staple of the Kansas City machine's methods. In 1934, four persons were killed by gangsters on election day. Two years later, an attempted assassination and massive voter fraud led to an intensive investigation that eventually resulted in 259 convictions for election fraud and criminal behavior.

Chicago ward boss John Powers intimidated voters and threatened landlords, merchants, and other business owners with loss of licenses unless they supported him in his 1898 campaign for alderman.[38] "Hinky Dink" Kenna and "Bathhouse John" Coughlin, of Chicago's First Ward, expressed loyalty to their loyal lower-class constituents and routinely harassed opponents. During the 1920s, organized crime and politics in Chicago became almost synonymous. Assassination and "hits" were visited upon politicians who stood outside the inner circle of men controlling and protecting illegal liquor, speakeasies, prostitution, and gambling.

Ed Crump, the boss of Memphis, Tennessee, won his first mayoral election in 1909 by watching the polls himself. He interfered personally with the use of marked ballots by a machine he was opposing, in one case by hitting a voter in the face.[39] In Pittsburgh's state and city elections of 1933, the Democrats and Republicans—both rightly fearing fraud by the other party—mobilized an army of poll watchers. The State Police were called in to keep the peace, and lawyers and judges stood by to provide quick court action.[40]

Machines have always been notorious for electoral corruption, which is one reason reformers of the period put election reform high on their agenda. Elections rarely were won solely on the basis of voter loyalty, and machines were not always responsive to their constituents. Some machine politicians governed through fear as much as through popularity. Machines were not as "democratic" as the bosses wanted to claim.

Business and the Machines

The business community generally found the machines convenient. Cooperation between business and machine bosses was a natural arrangement, arrived at when each side discerned its enlightened self-interest: "the special economic privileges sought by the wealthy elite in that materialistic and economically ruthless age [were] soon discovered to be purchasable more readily than they were to be obtained, if at all, through decisions brought about by free discussion in a participatory democracy—which perhaps had never really existed except in folklore."[41] Machine politicians sometimes discovered that the interests of their business clientele conflicted with the needs and desires of immigrant voters. Money often, perhaps usually, won out.

It might seem that the protection of liquor, gambling, and prostitution simultaneously satisfied business interests and the desires of poor immigrants. However, such a view oversimplifies the social values of the immigrants. There is little doubt that Irish family life was disrupted by the easy availability of illicit entertainment. Catholic priests and a large proportion of the immigrant population opposed vice activities.

Legitimate businesses that dealt with the machines asked for and received favors that assuredly victimized the immigrant poor. Under the aegis of machine politicians, the costs of public construction and utility rates soared, while the politicians and businessmen lined their pockets. Probably the most corrupt machine of the nineteenth century was led by William Marcy "Boss" Tweed, who ran the Tweed Ring in New York City from 1868 to 1871. In three years, Tweed diverted $30 to $100 million of public funds to the machine's private use. Under Tweed's regime, the machine's "take" of 10 percent on construction contracts quickly escalated. A courthouse construction project, with an original estimate of $250,000, ended up costing $14 million, of which at least 90 percent was the cost of corruption.[42] From 1869 to 1870, the city's debt increased from $36 to $97 million. Corruption reached everywhere. In 1869, Tweed paid $600,000 in bribes to state legislators to get a new city charter passed. Newspaper reporters were offered bribes, and *The New York Times* was offered $5 million to stop an investigation of corruption. By 1871, when Tweed was arrested, the city was bankrupt.[43]

The Tweed Ring was perhaps more corrupt than most, but by the turn of the century, business-machine "cooperation" was a fact of life nearly everywhere. Cities rushed to build and expand waterworks, natural gas lines, electric services, streetcars, telephones, sewers, and roads. From a business point of view, competition for city contracts and franchises was an unhealthy situation that limited prices and growth. In 1890, for example, there were thirty-nine street railway companies in Philadelphia, nineteen in New York City, twenty-four in Pittsburgh, nineteen in St. Louis, and sixteen in San Francisco.[44] National corporations struggled for monopolistic control of local franchises, and they generally succeeded. By the turn of the century, only one or two major street railway companies operated in most cities.

Because of the mutually beneficial arrangements between business owners and politicians, the bosses rarely questioned business practices and rarely sought an expanded public role. The machines did not expand the social welfare functions of government. Machine politicians did not seek to restructure the social, political, and economic institutions of the cities.

The Machines and the Political Culture

The party machines reaffirmed the culture within which they operated, a culture that extolled competitive individualism and entrepreneurial success. They were conservative organizations that responded to individual rather than to collective demands. Machine politicians did not represent the needs of poor immigrants *as a whole* but instead treated each constituent's request as a separate problem. Machine politicians avoided controversial issues. Personal favors were ther stock-in-trade. This approach confirmed, in effect, an ideology of conservative individualism:

> such a system . . . deals with all individual claimants in terms of their established resources. Those who had the resources to make major claims upon the machine politician (and to pay a major price for being served) could receive major benefits. Those who had only limited resources and consequently were able to pay only limited costs received only limited benefits. . . . Consequently such arrangements systematically benefitted those with considerable resources—specifically the business interests who controlled the resources of the private sector and the machine politicians who controlled the resources of the public sector. And for the poor, it let them eat turkey, at least at Christmas.[45]

The politicians' success in solving personal problems created a mystique. Constituents who received services, however small, felt grateful. Machine politicians became symbols of success and power, which "established a sort of political Horatio Alger myth, thus fulfilling one promise of the American dream."[46] A politics based on personal recognition and favors was far less dangerous than a politics of social class, for it encouraged ethnic populations to "cast their ballots on the basis of ethnicity rather than policy considerations."[47]

Successful machine politicians made it appear that their ethnic group as a whole was being recognized and integrated into American society. Tangible benefits for the group were given up for the gratification of individuals. In the American context, ethnic politics, rather than being a politics of the group, was turned into a politics of personal success. Machine politicians were thought to be, and also saw themselves as, successful practitioners of the American way of individual success.

Ethnic politics, therefore, was not necessarily a politics of collective self-interest. Immigrants gave their votes to party politicians, not as an act of consciousness about the group's goals, but because it was easy to do and there were no plausible alternatives. The vote was a minimal commitment by the immigrant, but a sufficient one for the machine. Commensurate with the level of commitment, constituents could hardly expect miracles in return.

Like business organizations, the machines did best under conditions of monopoly. City bosses suppressed, violently if necessary, organizations that attempted to compete for the loyalty of the immigrant voter. Thus the machines undercut not only reform groups but groups that attempted to address the collective aspirations of immigrant populations. Machines were actively antagonistic to organized labor, which threatened both the machines' electoral base and its business constituency. A heightened political awareness among the immigrant working class could not but threaten the machines' control of the vote, especially if labor parties were mobilized based on this awareness.

In the New York City mayoral campaign of 1886, a coalition of labor unions and socialists supported Henry George, a prominent proponent of the idea that undeveloped private property should be heavily taxed in order to encourage its conversion to public use. The Tammany Hall machine first offered bribes to George to persuade him to remove himself from the Labor ticket. Its next response was to label him a subversive whose followers were "Anarchists, Nihilists-Communists, and mere theorists."[48] Tammany's victory margin in the general election was surprisingly close, especially considering the number of votes manipulated by Tammany Hall.

In Lawrence, Massachusetts, Irish machine politicians opposed a lengthy strike initiated by the Industrial Workers of the World ("the Wobblies"). Lawrence's machine mayor ordered the police to attack the strikers and pickets.[49] Finally, the state militia was called in to attack the strikers. Martin Lomasney, an important boss in the Boston machine, shared control over the militia through his strong influence in state politics. He ordered the militia to launch a violent assault not only on the strikers, but on their wives and children as well.

In 1911, the Tammany-controlled New York police were ordered to put down a garment workers' strike. They systematically rounded up pickets and sent them to jail, often after beating them senseless. Peace was restored only when the Tammany Hall mayor fell ill and the president of the board of aldermen, who was independent of the machine, restrained the police. In Pittsburgh's 1919 steel strike, the Republican machine likewise ordered police to harass strikers.[50]

Some of the big city machines reached close accommodations with the moderate trade unions, especially after Franklin D. Roosevelt's presidential election victory in 1932. Radicals were still singled out for harassment, however. In the 1930s, Ed Crump, the famous Memphis boss, ordered his police to attack Congress of Industrial Organizations (CIO) organizers who were attempting to unionize the Ford and Fisher plants.[51] Chicago's Memorial Day Massacre of 1938 occurred when the city's machine-controlled police fired on laborers trying to form a picket line around the

Republic Steel Company plant. Ten strikers were killed.[52] Throughout the 1930s, Jersey City's Mayor Frank Hague held especial emnity for organized labor.

> In addition to outright physical violence, unions found their halls closed for violations of building codes; union leaders were deported from Jersey City, offered the choice of jail or exile; and signs, pamphlets, handbills, and other union property were seized.[53]

Hague allowed the CIO and other militant unions into Jersey City only after a court order in 1937.

When Mayor Daley ordered Chicago's police to crack heads at the 1968 Democratic convention, he was following a well-established tradition. Machine politicians have never been tolerant of radicals who try to mobilize the electorate. Surely it was inimical to machines to allow organizations promoting collective action to penetrate the immigrant wards. At a minimum, such organizations competed for the attention and loyalty of potential voters. Labor organizers sometimes attacked machines as corrupt and conservative. This no doubt helps to account for machine hostility to labor unions and political radicals.

The operating principles and the structure of the urban machines mandated that they be conservative organizations. To deal with constituent requests effectively, machine politicians had to learn the art of manipulating public and private institutions in the urban environment. The emphasis was on pragmatic "exchange," not on societal change. Additionally, machine politicians materially benefited from existing political arrangements. It made little sense for a ward committeeman who could deliver his ward to rock the political boat.

Still, there is evidence that machine politicians sometimes backed reform legislation proposed in state legislative bodies. Sometimes reforms were carried out, as well, within the cities they governed. In these cases, the machines seem less conservative than this analysis has suggested.

By the second decade of the twentieth century, machine politicians serving in the state legislatures began to support such reform measures as widows' pensions, factory legislation governing safety and conditions of work, maximum hours and minimum wages for women and children, and worker's compensation.[54] On some occasions, they also supported utilities regulation, legalization of boycotting and picketing by labor unions, and regulation of insurance companies. Even laws to equalize taxes were sometimes supported by machine representatives.

Nevertheless, support for reform measures did not transform machine politicians into crusading reformers. While they sometimes supported reforms in state laws, they rarely supported it within the confines of their own political arenas, the cities. Reform in state and national politics was not especially painful for local politicians, for the application of the state or federal reform laws was always uncertain and slow.

Machine legislators rarely sponsored a coherent reform agenda of their own. Rather, they backed individual reform items proposed by non-machine reformers who wanted to address a particular social problem. Machine politicians were willing to enter into temporary coalitions to support legislation, but they were never permanent partners in reform coalitions. They were not reformers in the sense of promoting a consistent program founded on principles of justice and equity. Their support for reform was piecemeal and circumstantial: if support for a particular reform bill fit their interests and seemed, on the whole, beneficial to their lower-class constituents, they might support the legislation simply because there was little reason for opposition. Machine politicians could be quite capricious, however, for immediate political circumstances often took precedence of principle. They were as likely to oppose as to support reform, and they often did oppose it.

Machine politicians rarely promoted programs of change. They lacked a reform "consciousness" about what needed redress. Machine politicians, in fact, generally regarded reformers as "goody-goodies" or "goo-goos" who were in politics for a few thrills. ("Goo-goo" also meant "good government," often the reformers' rallying cry.) Much of this bias was no doubt rooted in the social differences between upper-class reformers and lower-class immigrant politicians. There is little doubt that many reformers were thrill-seekers who were impossibly naive about political realities. Still, the politicians' excessive respect for pragmatic as opposed to idealistic motivation translated into an orientation toward the status quo, for important political changes usually entail an attack upon politics-as-usual.

It could be asserted that there was little alternative to the machines' individualist style of politics, that in the face of the vast economic and political resources held by corporations and wealthy elites, the machines milked the system on behalf of their constituents as effectively as they could. In fact, alternatives were available, and on occasion they were attempted. On some occasions, social reform was actively sought in American cities. These instances illustrate how little the machines actually delivered.

The Social Reform Alternative

What the urban machines failed to accomplish can be appreciated only by examining the social reform alternatives that were tried during the machine era. In several cities, political organizations arose that accomplished important social reforms that benefitted urban dwellers, including the poor and the immigrants.

Seth Low, mayor of New York City from 1901 to 1902, expanded the city parks and recreation budget, increased spending for public schools, and expanded mass transit and bridge construction. Health, charities, and tenement regulation also received higher appropriations.[55] Low's administration was defeated after only two years because he alienated many immigrants and workers with his hostile attitude toward Sunday drinking.

More stable electoral coalitions were built by men who campaigned for support from both immigrants and the middle classes. Mayors Tom L. Johnson, Cleveland, 1901–1909, Samuel "Golden Rule" Jones, Toledo, 1897–1903, and Brand Whitlock, Toledo, 1906–1913, all fought against high streetcar and utility rates and for fair taxation and better social services. They won some success, and their campaigns became models for likeminded reforms elsewhere.

Jersey City, Philadelphia, and Cincinnati elected mayors who led similar reform crusades. In each case, the new mayor attempted to raise more municipal revenue by equalizing taxes and negotiating new streetcar and utility leases. Machine politicians and the business community bitterly fought reform in these cities, as they had earlier in Cleveland and Toledo.[56]

Detroit provides the best example of social reform in an American city. From 1889 to 1897, Detroit's Mayor Hazen Pingree vaulted to national prominence as a reformer fighting the corporations.[57] He improved the public streets from the worst to the best in the nation, reconstructed the sewage system, expanded public schools and parks, built a public bath, and successfully fought for public access to the Detroit River. In a series of bitter and often protracted battles, he ended street tolls, forced down the ferry, gas, telephone, and streetcar rates, and established a municipal light plant. He successfully fought for public control of public utilities. Finally, during the national depression that began in 1893, he initiated a municipal public works program for the unemployed, forced the bakeries to lower bread prices, and established an eight-hour day for municipal employees. And despite (or because of) his controversial programs, he was elected mayor of Detroit four times and governor of Michigan twice.

Pingree's programs, and the strategies he used to implement them, reveal how much could have been accomplished in other cities. Hazen Pingree was picked as the Republican candidate for mayor in the fall election of 1889, largely because he was the only member of the exclusive Michigan Club who could be persuaded by its members to run. The conservative businessmen who controlled Republican politics trusted him, as a member of the club, to pursue a program of low taxes and municipal government economy. Pingree's success in running a profitable shoe factory was considered by his backers as ample preparation for public office.

Pingree turned out to be an astute campaigner. He attacked the Democratic machine for corruption, advocated an eight-hour work day for city employees, and appealed directly to German, Polish, and Irish voters. Unlike the typical reform-business candidate, he started his campaign drinking redeye whiskey in an Irish saloon and conducted a personal campaign in the ethnic wards. His willingness to seek the ethnic vote provided the broad foundation on which he built future electoral success.

Pingree inherited a city with one of the worst street systems in the nation. Many of the streets were made of wooden blocks, which would catch fire in the summer and sink into the mire in the winter. The paved streets were rutted and potholed. Pingree soon realized that collusion between the Democratic machine and paving contractors was at the heart of the street problem. He launched an aggressive campaign against this arrangement, appealing to his business supporters by pointing out that the prosperity of the city depended on good streets. His insistent efforts led the city council to adopt strict paving specifications for the city. As a result, by 1895 Detroit had one of the nation's best street systems.

Pingree's next target was corruption in the schools. He personally paid private detectives to gather evidence on payoff arrangements on the awarding of contracts for school furniture, land, and buildings. In August 1894, he secured indictments against four members of the school board.

Such campaigns as these fit well within the conventional reform agenda by focusing on corrupt ethnic politicians and government waste. Before long, however, the mayor's definition of reform called into question the relationship between public authority and private enterprise.

Three battles foreshadowed Pingree's new social reform orientation. In the first, he challenged what he thought was an unnecessarily high cost for the ferry ride across the Detroit River to Belle Isle Park. The company dropped its rate from 10 cents to 5 cents after the mayor threatened to revoke its franchise or to put into operation a municipal ferry service. In a related campaign, he found that private companies had located along the Detroit River waterfront, often on municipal property, choking off public access to water and recreation. He soon cleared away waterfront areas for public use.

Pingree became particularly angry over the existence of toll gates on two of the city's main thoroughfares. These gates were operated under old charters secured by road companies early in Detroit's history. Pingree saw the issue as fundamental, concerning whether the city had the right to control its public streets and property. After failing to secure legislative remedies, Pingree resorted to an "end run" by building a well-paved loop around one of the toll houses, leaving it stranded in the middle of the street. The toll companies saw the light and soon sold out to the city.

Pingree's concern about public control and municipal rights likewise led him to confront the Detroit City Railway Company, which operated most of the streetcar lines in the city. At a time when other street railways throughout the nation were converting from animal to electric power, the Detroit company refused to modernize. In April 1891, the company's employees went on strike, furnishing a perfect opportunity for Pingree to fight for modernization and lower fares.

The three-day strike culminated in a riot in which workers and citizens tore up the tracks, stoned the cars, and drove off the horses. Pingree not only refused to call in the state militia at the company's request but called privately-owned public services "the chief source of corruption in city governments."[58] Pingree's stance initiated a protracted, bitter fight to regulate the streetcars. This conflict vaulted him to national prominence.

Many business leaders had supported the 1890 strike, feeling that the street railway was so badly run that it was hurting local business. The business community mainly wanted better service, but Pingree pressed further, advocating lower fares and municipal ownership. Such a position ran afoul of business leaders when the company passed into the hands of a wealthy eastern entrepreneur. The new owner's first action was to pack the company's board of directors with prominent Detroit business leaders. The new company then demanded a franchise renewal on favorable terms. Pingree countered with a suit to terminate the existing company. At that point, his former colleagues took action to bring him around to their point of view. The new owners bought Pingree's own attorney away from him and then proceeded to offer bribes to city council members, including a $75,000 bribe to Pingree himself. The Preston National Bank dropped him from their board of directors. He lost his family pew in the Baptist church. He and his friends were ignored in public. For Pingree, the lesson he learned in all this was that business supported reform only on its own terms. He also began to form an analysis about what was wrong in city politics.

In 1891, Pingree began attacking the tax privileges of the city's corporations. The railroad, he observed, owned more than one-fifth of the property value in the city but paid no taxes at all because of tax-free status granted by the state legislature. Shipping companies, docks and warehouses, and other businesses escaped local taxation by claiming that their principal places of business existed outside the city. The city's biggest employer, the Michigan-Peninsula Car Company, paid only nominal taxes. In questioning these privileges, Pingree was confronting the combined wealth and power of the city's business elite. Although he was unsuccessful in equalizing the tax burden, Pingree was able to modify some of its worst features, especially the practice of assessing homes at far below the assessment rate for real estate and buildings owned by wealthy people. Pingree earned the special enmity of the city's elite by successfully campaigning for a personal property tax on home furnishings, art objects, and other luxury items.

What confrontation with wealth had failed to do in molding Pingree's social conscience, the depression of 1893–1897 completed. During the depression, social tensions rose to dangerous levels. Thousands of unemployed and destitute people clamored for jobs and relief. Competition for scarce jobs pitted Irish against Poles, and both against Germans. Native-born Americans intensified their hatred of immigrants. Throughout Michigan, a clamor arose for immigration restriction laws. In 1894, Michigan voters overwhelmingly approved a constitutional amendment to disenfranchise aliens. Many employers, including some of Detroit's city departments, refused to hire them. Anti-Catholic feelings ran high.

Pingree's first response to the depression was to apply pressure on city departments to expand public works programs. New sewer, paving, park renovation, and school construction projects were undertaken. The eight-hour day was enforced. People replaced machinery, pushing wheelbarrows at construction sites or hand-sweeping the streets. The mayor vigorously opposed efforts by some city administrators to save money by cutting jobs and pay, arguing that higher-paid employees should take salary reductions first.

Pingree even threatened to construct a municipal bakery if the city's bakeries did not cut bread prices in half. After winning this issue, he initiated a "potato patch plan" in which plots of city land were made available to poor people for gardens. Detroit's aristocracy and the newspapers poked fun at the idea. Pingree became more convinced than ever that wealthy people were irresponsible protectors of their narrow self-interest.

Programs to help the unemployed were but temporary additions to Pingree's ongoing social reform agenda. His guiding principle—the public's right to regulate public property and services—led him to tangle with light, gas, telephone, and streetcar companies. In all these fights, he appealed for support from immigrants and working-class people.

On April 1, 1895, Detroit began operating a municipal electric plant to supply power for its streetlights. This ended a five-year running battle between Pingree and the private lighting interests. Pingree had used two issues to win his battle. His main argument against the private control of electricity was that it cost too much. Pingree gathered voluminous information on the costs of power in other cities, and he established that Detroit's service was overly expensive and unreliable. His argument was persuasive but not sufficient. Corruption became the issue that tipped the scales in his favor. In April, 1892, Pingree walked into a city council meeting waving a roll of bills and dramatically accused the Detroit Electric Light and Power Company of bribing council members. As usual, the mayor had the room packed with his working-class supporters. With Pingree's followers whipped into a dangerous mood, the council members quickly cooperated.

Pingree used similar tactics in his fights with gas and telephone interests. To force lower gas prices, he first initiated a campaign to educate the public on the high price of Detroit's gas, which, he claimed, was more than one-third higher than the price charged by the same company in five other cities. When his attempt to force lower prices was stalled in the courts, he got the public works board to deny permits to excavate streets for the purpose of laying gas lines. The gas company attempted to excavate anyway, at which point Pingree had the owners arrested. "Possession is a great point," argued Pingree. "Let them get their gas systems connected and then they could float their $8,000,000 of stock in New York City and become too powerful for the city to control. Detroit would be helpless in the hands of corporations as never before in her history."[59]

Pingree continued his campaign, encouraging users not to pay their full gas bills. As public resistance against the Detroit Gas Company increased, investors' confidence in the company plummeted, initiating a plunge in the company's stock values. Even when Southern Pacific Railroad magnate Samuel Huntington became the company's principal investor, it was impossible to hold prices, and he negotiated an agreement to lower prices from $1.50 a cubic foot to $0.80.

In his fourth term as mayor, Pingree took on the Bell Telephone Company. Again, the issue was high prices and inadequate service. This time, he helped organize a competing phone company that charged less than half Bell's rate. The new company soon attracted twice as many customers as Bell. In response, Bell initiated a rate war and began to improve its equipment and service. By 1900, when Michigan Bell bought out the Detroit Telephone Company, Detroit had the lowest telephone rates and the most extensive residential use of any of the large United States cities.

Pingree's accomplishments in Detroit were unique. In no other American city was such a broad program of social reform accomplished. Unlike most other reformers, he keenly recognized the necessity of building a broad-based coalition of support. He so assiduously courted ethnic voters that, by his fourth term, he had even won the dependable Irish away from the Democrats. Unlike the Democratic politicians, who exploited ethnic hostilities to win votes in their wards, he appealed to the unity of interests of the working-class Poles, Germans, and Irish. On many occasions, he personally led boycotts or strikes.

Pingree shunned the narrow interests of the business community, especially when he learned the limited extent of its commitment to reform. He accepted the support of those upper- and middle-class individuals who shared his reform aspirations. During his last two terms, he traveled around the country making speeches and gathering information. He wrote prolifically. His national prominence inspired reformers elsewhere and also helped him win reform campaigns in his own city. In short, he was aware that to accomplish reform it was necessary to "recruit a coalition of power sufficient for his purpose."[60]

The Limited Government Ideal of Machine Politicians

The big city machines could have forged coalitions broad enough to implement social reform in the cities. As Pingree did, they could have sought to educate their constituents about working- and middle-class interests in modifying the practices of business and industry in the urban environment. Rather than passing out petty favors and low-paying jobs, they could have attacked monopolistic practices that inflated the cost of urban services while keeping corporate taxes low. They could have helped put together a labor program designed to modify dangerous working conditions, long hours, child labor, and low pay.

Instead, the machines reaffirmed a tradition whereby city growth would be decided by the individual decisions of private institutions. Public authority continued to be reactive rather than active. Even more important, the machines served as buffers between the corporations and the poor. In doing so, they exacted a modest price from corporate leaders. But the exchange was far from beneficial for their immigrant constituency.

Social reform was rare in American cities partly because party machines fought it bitterly. The political power of corporate business, in alliance with the machines, overwhelmed reform efforts. When reformers achieved victory, it was generally short-lived and partial.

The machines' main accomplishment was the achievement of social control. By acting as a buffer between the immigrants and the economic system, machines reduced the level of dissatisfaction. They were successful in this even though they delivered little.

> Though the reformers fumed and raved, the hated political bosses were in truth buffers between the rich and the poor, buffers that taxed the one to keep the other in good humor. . . . Naturally, there were brokers' charges on the collections but these were small as compared with the costs of riots and revolutions.[61]

It is inadequate to assert that the machines had no alternative. The truth is that the machines were instrumental in limiting the alternatives that were available. By manipulating immigrants and lower-class communities for their own narrow advantage, they materially contributed to a politics that disproportionately benefited a few.

References

1. Neil Betten, "Urban Workers and Labor Organization," *The Urban Experience: Themes in American History*, ed. Raymond A. Mohl and James F. Richardson (Belmont, Calif.: Wadsworth, 1973). The subsequent data in this paragraph are also derived from Betten's article.
2. Stuart D. Brandes, *American Welfare Capitalism, 1880–1940* (Chicago: University of Chicago Press, 1976), chap. 1. Two concise histories of labor conflict in the United States are Milton Meltzer, *Bread and Roses: The Struggle of American Labor, 1865–1914* (New York: Alfred A. Knopf, 1967), and Edward C. Kirkland, *Industry Comes of Age: Labor and Public Policy, 1860–1897* (New York: Holt, Rinehart and Winston, 1961). The sources on labor history are voluminous. A very good bibliography is James C. McBrearty, *American Labor History and Comparative Labor Movements: A Selected Bibliography* (Tucson: The University of Arizona Press, 1973).
3. See Bernard Kogan, ed., *The Chicago Haymarket Riot: Anarchy on Trial* (Boston: D.C. Heath, 1959).
4. Josiah Strong, *Our Country*, ed. Jurgen Herbst (Cambridge, Mass.: The Belknap Press of Harvard University Press, 1963 [first published 1886]).
5. Strong, p. 55.
6. Dayton McKean, *The Boss* (Boston: Houghton Mifflin, 1940), p. 132.
7. The information presented here on the Pendergast machine comes from Lyle W. Dorsett, *The Pendergast Machine* (New York: Oxford University Press, 1968). Only material quoted directly from the source is noted by page.
8. Dorsett, quoted at p. 14.
9. Dorsett, p. 21.
10. Dorsett, quoted at p. 41.
11. Dorsett, quoted at p. 26.
12. While dying, Long counseled one of his ambitious friends to be "more charitable" toward his political opponents. Adds journalist A. J. Leibling: "It reminded me of how an old friend of mine, Whitey Bimstein, described the death of Frankie Jerome, a boxer he was seconding in the Madison Square Garden ring. 'He died in my arms, slipping punches,' Whitey said. Huey, mortally shot, talked politics." A. J. Liebling, *The Earl of Louisiana* (New York: Simon and Schuster, 1967), p. 14.
13. Edwin O'Conner, *The Last Hurrah* (Boston: Little, Brown, 1956).
14. Milton Rakove, *Don't Make No Waves . . . Don't Back No Losers: An Insider's Analysis of the Daley Machine* (Bloomington: Indiana University Press, 1975).
15. Rakove, pp. 114–115.
16. Rakove, p. 115.
17. Noal Solomon, *When Bosses Were Leaders: An Inside Look at Political Machines and Politics* (Hicksville, N.Y.: Exposition Press, 1975), p. 7.

18. Rakove, *Don't Make No Waves*, p. 120.

19. Rakove, p. 122.

20. Wallace S. Sayre and Herbert Kaufman, *Governing New York City: Politics in the Metropolis* (New York: W. W. Norton, 1965), p. 155.

21. Liebling, *The Earl of Louisiana*, p. 120.

22. The information presented here on Abraham Reuf's machine is taken from Walton Bean, *Boss Reuf's San Francisco* (Berkeley: University of California Press, 1972 [first published 1952]). Only quoted material is subsequently cited.

23. Bean, quoted at pp. 93–94.

24. Alexander B. Callow, Jr., ed., *The City Boss in America* (New York: Oxford University Press, 1976), p. 91.

25. Robert K. Merton, *Social Structure and Social Theory* (New York: The Free Press, 1957), p. 72.

26. J. T. Salter, *Boss Rule: Portraits in City Politics* (New York: Whittlesey House, 1957).

27. Harold Zink, *City Bosses in the United States* (Durham, N.C.: Duke University Press, 1930).

28. William L. Riordan, *Plunkett of Tammany Hall* (New York: E. P. Dutton, 1963), pp. 69–70.

29. The Irish heavily dominated all aspects of the Roman Catholic church in the large cities. The following sources are especially helpful: Carl Wittke, *The Irish in America* (Baton Rouge: Louisiana State University Press, 1956); Nathan Glazer and Daniel Patrick Moynihan, *Beyond the Melting Pot: The Negroes, Puerto Ricans, Jews, Italians, and Irish of New York* (Cambridge, Mass.: MIT Press and Harvard University Press, 1963); William V. Shannon, *The American Irish* (New York: Macmillan, 1963); and Andrew M. Greeley, *The Catholic Experience: An Interpretation of the History of American Catholicism* (Garden City, N.Y.: Doubleday, 1967).

30. Raymond E. Wolfinger, *The Politics of Progress* (Englewood Cliffs, N.J.: Prentice-Hall, 1974), p. 67.

31. Allan Rosenbaum, "Machine Politics, Class Interest and the Urban Poor," paper delivered at the American Political Science Association meetings, September 4–8, 1973.

32. Wolfinger, *The Politics of Progress*, p. 69.

33. Callow, *The City Boss in America*, p. 158.

34. William T. Stead, *If Christ Came to Chicago* (Chicago: Laird and Lee, 1894), pp. 56–57.

35. Lloyd Wendt and Herman Kogan, *Bosses in Lusty Chicago* (Bloomington: Indiana University Press, 1967), p. 169.

36. Dorsett, *The Pendergast Machine*, p. 59.

37. Dorsett, p. 60.

38. Allan F. Davis, *Spearheads for Reform* (New York: Oxford University Press, 1967), pp. 156–162.

39. William D. Miller, *Mr. Crump of Memphis* (Baton Rouge: Louisiana State University Press, 1964), p. 74.

40. Bruce M. Stave, *The New Deal and the Last Hurrah: Pittsburgh Machine Politics* (Pittsburgh: University of Pittsburgh Press, 1970), p. 77.

41. Ernest S. Griffith, *A History of American City Government: The Conspicuous Failure, 1870–1900* (New York: Praeger, 1974), p. 68.

42. There are many sources of information on the Tweed Ring. The two books used for the data here are Alexander Callow, Jr., *The Tweed Ring* (New York: Oxford University Press, 1966), and Seymour J. Mandelbaum, *Boss Tweed's New York* (New York: John Wiley, 1965).

43. Both Callow, *City Boss in America*, and Mandelbaum, *Boss Tweed's New York* report these figures.

44. Griffith, *A History of American City Government*, p. 183.

45. Rosenbaum, "Machine Politics," p. 36.

46. Wolfinger, *The Politics of Progress*, p. 70.

47. Wolfinger, p. 70.

48. Rosenbaum, "Machine Politics," quoted at p. 29.

49. Rosenbaum, pp. 25–26.

50. Rosenbaum, p. 26.

51. Alfred Steinberg, *The Bosses* (New York: Macmillan, 1972), pp. 113–114. Also cited in Rosenbaum, "Machine Politics."

52. Barbara W. Newell, *Chicago and the Labor Movement* (Urbana: University of Illinois Press, 1961), pp. 138–143.

53. McKean, *The Boss*, p. 191.

54. John D. Buenker, *Urban Liberalism and Progressive Reform* (New York: Charles Scribner's Sons, 1973). In a 1962 article, Joseph Huthmacher also provided evidence of machine legislators' support for reform. See Joseph J. Huthmacher, "Urban Liberalism and the Age of Reform," *Mississippi Valley Historical Review* 44 (September 1962):231–241.

55. Martin J. Schiesl, *The Politics of Efficiency: Municipal Administration and Reform in America, 1880–1920* (Berkeley: University of California Press, 1977), p. 80.

56. Schiesl, pp. 80ff.

57. This discussion of Pingree's rule relies on Melvin Holli's *Reform in Detroit: Hazen S. Pingree and Urban Politics* (New York: Oxford University Press, 1969). An interesting account of Pingree's administration can be found in the quaint book by Stead, *If Christ Came to Chicago*, pp. 282–291.

58. Quoted in Holli, *Reform in Detroit*, p. 42.

59. Quoted in Holli, p. 92.

60. Peter Marris and Martin Rein, *Dilemmas of Social Reform* (New York: Atherton Press, 1967), p. 7.

61. James Bryce, *Modern Democracies*, vol. 2 (New York: Macmillan, 1921), pp. 209–210.

Chapter 4

THE REFORM LEGACY

The Reform Impulse

In 1902, George Washington Plunkitt of Tammany Hall pontificated that reformers "were mornin' glories—looked lovely in the mornin' and withered up in a short time, while the regular machines went on flourishin' forever, like fine old oaks."[1] At the time Plunkitt delivered himself of that poetic homily, he was essentially correct. Through the last quarter of the nineteenth century, reform movements sprang up in many cities, the reformers attempting to dismantle the party organizations that thrived on immigrant votes. These movements tended to be short-lived and sporadic, lacking an organizational base or sustaining cause, exactly as Plunkitt had observed. But in the period from about 1900 to 1920, a well-organized and powerful municipal reform movement swept the nation.

To many middle- and upper-class Americans the party machines symbolized a deepening political and social crisis. Cities seemed to be in the hands of criminals who plundered the public for their own personal gain. Although reformers in Cleveland, New York, Chicago, and other cities had temporarily overthrown boss rule, the machines had always made a comeback as soon as the reform fervor died down. Members of the upper and upper-middle classes generally shared Englishman James Bryce's view that "the government of cities is the one conspicuous failure of the United States."[2] Upper-class Anglo-Saxon Protestants regarded politics as untouchable and unclean.

> The privilege seeker has pervaded our political life. For his own profit he has willfully befouled the sources of political power. Politics, which should offer a career inspiring to the noblest thoughts and calling for the most patriotic efforts of which man is capable, he has . . . transformed into a series of sordid transactions between those who buy and those who sell governmental action.[3]

The reformers' concerns about political corruption were entwined with their fears about the corrupting moral influence of the "Great Unwashed." While upper-class Victorians covered piano legs and attended lectures and concerts in formal dress, they observed the Irish and German immigrants drinking beer on Sundays and they read newspaper accounts of prostitution, dance halls, gambling, and public drunkenness in the immigrant wards. Protestants secured city and state statutes abolishing prostitution, gambling, and Sunday liquor sales. Reformers passed laws requiring school attendance, and they raised the upper age limit for mandatory schooling, and built industrial schools and kindergartens to teach immigrant children middle-class versions of dress, speech, manners, and discipline. Later, upper-class women in the cities joined with rural prohibitionists in the campaign for the Eighteenth Amendment, which outlawed alcohol consumption. The attempts to impose moral standards, language, and religious conformity on the immigrants went hand in hand with the reformers' fears that American morals and politics were being adulterated by alien influences. Americans had been nurturing this fear for more than half a century. An 1851 issue of the *Massachusetts Teacher* asked:

> The constantly increasing influx of foreigners . . . continues to be a cause of serious alarm to the most intelligent of our people. What will be the ultimate effect of this vast and unexampled immigration. . . ? Will it, like the muddy Missouri, as it pours its waters into the clear Mississippi and contaminates the whole united mass, spread ignorance and vice, crime and disease, through our native population?[4]

By the early years of the twentieth century, the distrust of foreigners had developed into an often-expressed racism. During this period, "editors, novelists, and politicians competed with each other in singing the praises of the 'big-boned, blond, long haired' Anglo-Saxon with the blood of the berserkers in his veins, and in denigrating Jack London's 'dark pigmented things, the half castes, the mongrel bloods, and the dregs of long conquered races.'"[5] Novels, plays, and social science literature repeated the themes of Anglo-Saxon superiority. In the West, Orientals who had been imported to build the railroads now were chased out of small towns and forced into San Francisco's Chinatown, or deported. In 1900, under the terms of the "gentlemen's agreement," Japan agreed to halt emigration to the United States. At the same time, blacks in the South were subjected to their worst harassment since the Civil War. In 1897, 123 blacks were lynched in the Southern and border states, and the number of lynchings continued to exceed 100 a year for many years. Progressive reformers either applauded or remained silent about these events.

The spatial segregation of social classes within the cities exacerbated middle- and upper-class nervousness about the immigrants. By the turn of the century, all large cities contained overcrowded immigrant ghettos, with the middle classes occupying a ring buffering the center from the upper-class periphery. Economic activities were still concentrated in the core, so the more affluent city residents could hardly escape seeing, on their way to work, the drab tenements and the dirty streets and alleys where the immigrants lived.

The impulse toward municipal reform was rooted in class tensions. Most reformers were members of the upper class or exceptionally well-educated members of the middle class. The reforms they advocated were designed to enhance the influence of the "better classes" and to undercut the immigrants' influence in politics.

The Reform Environment

Though government corruption had provoked campaigns to "throw the rascals out" in a few cities during the 1870s and 1880s, the issues had usually been local and the remedies specific to the situation. Several developments during the 1890s altered this picture and transformed reform into a national movement promoting change in local government structures.

By the 1890s, industrialization and urban growth had created conditions that could no longer be ignored. In response to widespread government corruption and social and physical deterioration in the immigrant wards, citizens' groups had sprung up in most cities to agitate for improved public services and honesty in government. The problems faced by the reformers varied little from one city to another. Like-minded reformers from different cities soon began to exchange advice and information about their efforts. These informational networks subsequently led to the formation of national reform organizations.

In 1894, delegates to the First Annual Conference for Good City

Government met in Philadelphia to create the first national reform organization, the National Municipal League. Many of the delegates to the conference were disturbed that democratic institutions had been "corrupted"
in the "rabble-ruled cities."[6] Some argued that the vote should be denied to
those unqualified to exercise it responsibly.

The nationalization of reform proceeded quickly after the formation of
the National Municipal League. Within two years, 180 local organizations
had affiliated with it. By the turn of the century, all cities of consequential
size had member organizations. In the next twenty years, reform and professional organizations proliferated. Liberal business leaders organized
the National Civic Federation in 1900, mainly to reduce union agitation by
sponsoring worker's compensation and other minor social insurance
schemes.[7] The National Child Labor Committee organized in 1904 to
fight for child labor legislation. In 1910, the National Housing Association
brought together housing reform groups from many cities. Other important reform organizations included the National Association of Settlements (1911), the National Society for the Progress of Industrial Education (1906), and the National Short Ballot Organization (1909). And there
were many more.

Professional associations also organized during this period, and nearly
all of them contained reform programs. Most of the academic professions
now in existence formed associations between 1890 and 1910, as did doctors, lawyers, engineers, architects, planners, and members of other professions. The American Political Science Association, founded in 1903,
was very interested in municipal reform. Architects, engineers, and housing reformers organized the first planners' conference in 1909 and
formed the association now known as the American Institute of Planners.
Such organizations were interested, if not in reform per se, at least in
upgrading and regulating the training, licensing, or credentialing of their
members.

Likewise, public officials' associations and municipal research bureaus
came into existence. Groups with such titles as the National Association of
Port Authorities, the Municipal Finance Officers Association, the American Association of Park Superintendents, and the National Conference of
Mayors and Conference of City Managers multiplied in the first decade of
the twentieth century. New bureaus of municipal research in the major cities provided information and lobbying services to public officials and
municipal reformers.

These organizations created an institutional structure for promoting
reform. This characteristic is primarily what made the Progressive Era different from any previous reform period in American history. The Progressive reformers created a communications and lobbying network that

financed and organized reform on a national scale, using a complex network of specialized organizations to develop a coherent reform agenda.

At the same time, a newly developed mass media spread the reform gospel to upper-class and educated middle-class readers. By the turn of the century, falling paper prices and technical advances in printing made it possible to produce high-quality mass-circulation newspapers and magazines. Newspaper circulation doubled and then tripled within the 1890s, and a multitude of new periodicals appeared. All that was required to develop a reading habit in a mass audience was a way to popularize the press. "Muckraking" was such a technique. Crusading journalists investigated and reported "inside stories" on corruption in government, big business, organized vice, the stock market, and the drug and meatpacking industries.

Beginning with its September 1902 issue, *McClure's* magazine printed a series of seven articles by Lincoln Steffens, each detailing municipal corruption in the nation's big cities. In October, *McClure's* carried an article by Ida Tarbell exposing corporate corruption and profiteering by John D. Rockefeller's Standard Oil Company. The stories were an instant success, revealing in the public a nearly insatiable appetite for sensational exposures of wrongdoing in business and industry. A new mass circulation formula was discovered. In the next few years, *Munsey's*, *Everybody's*, *Success*, *Collier's*, *Saturday Evening Post*, *Ladies' Home Journal*, *Hampton's*, *Pearson's*, *Cosmopolitan*, and dozens of daily newspapers carried stories that appealed to the popular feeling that political, economic, and social institutions had become corrupted. Big business was accused of producing unsafe and shoddy goods, fixing prices, and crushing competition. Lurid articles exposed frauds in medicine and life insurance, detailed the hours and conditions of children's and women's labor, and documented urban poverty, prostitution, white slavery, and business-government collusion to protect vice.

An outpouring of popular books played on the same themes. Steffens collected his articles together into the best-selling *The Shame of the Cities*, published in 1904. Other popular titles included *The Greatest Trust in the World*, an exposé of the steel industry; *The Story of Life Insurance*; and *The Treason of the Senate*, which detailed big business bribery and corruption of the U.S. Senate. Several important novelists also entered the field. In *An American Tragedy*, Theodore Dreiser stood Horatio Alger on his head by describing the corrupting influence of greed on a self-made small-town boy. In *The Financier*, his theme was the ruthless drive for power and wealth, using the Chicago streetcar magnate Charles Yerkes as his model. Upton Sinclair's *The Jungle* dealt with a Lithuanian immigrant's fight to survive in corrupt and chaotic Chicago. In the story, the immigrant's wife becomes a prostitute, his children die, and he eventually becomes a socialist revolutionary. In telling the story, Sinclair vividly portrayed the nauseating conditions in Chicago's meatpacking industry. His book catalyzed a crusade that resulted in the creation of the U.S. Food and Drug Administration. Dreiser's *Sister Carrie* and David Graham Phillip's *Susan Lenox* both played on the theme of how the impersonal forces of urban life victimized young women.

Whether focusing on specific ills or on generalized conditions, the "muckrakers"—an epithet applied to them in 1906 by President Theodore Roosevelt, referring to a character in John Bunyan's 1645 book, *Pilgrim's Progress*, who was too busy raking muck to look up and see the stars—were a powerful force in building popular interest in reform. Although investigations by reform organizations were often dull and unexciting to the average citizen, the muckrakers conveyed a feeling of drama and urgency.

The Municipal Reform Agenda

It did not take long for municipal reformers to reach substantial agreement about the urban problems they wished to attack. At the first meeting of the Conference of Good City Government in 1894, it was obvious that there was no generally accepted theory of good municipal government. "We are not unlike patients assembled in a hospital," one of the participants put it, "examining together and describing to each other our sore places."[8] By its November 1899 meeting, however, the members of the National Municipal League had reached agreement on a model municipal charter.

To abolish the machines, the model charter recommended that ward elections be abandoned in favor of at-large elections, so that city councillors would represent the whole city rather than a single ethnic group. It sought also to abolish the party label on election ballots by instituting nonpartisan elections. It recommended that most administrative positions be placed under civil service so that party officials would not be able to use public jobs for patronage purposes. The League also thought that local elections should be held at different times than national and state elections so that national parties would have no influence on local affairs.[9]

All these measures sought to undercut the basic organizing feature of machine politics: the political party. Besides eliminating the machines, however, the reformers wanted to "streamline" local government operations to make them more efficient. The model charter recommended that a small, unicameral city council replace the bicameral councils then existing in most cities. It also encouraged reformers to implement strong-mayor governments, giving the mayor the power to appoint top administrators and to veto legislation. The purpose of this was to centralize governmental authority so that voters could hold accountable an official who was responsible for the city's overall governance. The League also encouraged city reformers to seek "home rule" charters from their state legislatures so cities could be governed without interference from state political factions.

The national municipal reform agenda drew from the same values that had inspired the early conferences organized by the city reformers. Throughout the period of reform, efforts were made to implement efficiency and cost accounting in municipal affairs. Corruption, both moral and political, was always a chief target. Petty vice, patronage, and favors were high on the list of political sins to be exorcized.

The municipal reformers shared a conviction that it was their responsibility to educate and instruct the lower classes about good government. These reformers placed their faith in rule by educated, upper-class Americans and, increasingly, in municipal experts. These tendencies underlie all the specific reforms advocated from the 1890s and after.

The Campaigns Against Machine Rule

The reformers' first targets were the party machines. For this reason, a great number of strategies designed to accomplish "good government" attempted to weaken and dismantle political party control over elections. Some upper-class reformers went so far as to question the wisdom of universal suffrage, arguing that illiterate immigrants in the cities hopelessly corrupted free suffrage. Semiofficial sanction even existed for this view. The Tilden Commission, appointed by the New York legislature to investigate the Tweed Ring scandals, recommended in 1878 that suffrage be restricted to those who owned property.[10] The commission's report was reprinted in an 1899 issue of the National Municipal League's magazine, *Municipal Affairs*, and was read with approval by those sharing the view that a debased, ignorant electorate accounted for the city's problems. The rationale for disenfranchising the unqualified masses was stated by the first president of Cornell University, who wrote in an 1890 issue of *Forum* magazine that:

> A city is a corporation; . . . as a city it has nothing whatever to do with general political interests. . . . the questions in a city are not political questions. . . . The work of a city being the creation and control of the city property, it should logically be managed as a piece of property by those who have created it, who have a title to it, or a real substantial part in it, . . . [and not by] a crowd of illiterate peasants, freshly raked in from the Irish bogs, or Bohemian mines, or Italian robber nests.[11]

Although taking the vote out of immigrant hands appealed to some reformers, late in the nineteenth century, it was hardly feasible to attempt such a drastic remedy. To wage an all-out campaign on this premise would surely have invited a strong counterattack from many groups, including those that supported reform causes. Other strategies designed to accomplish a similar result therefore became the principal components of the reform agenda.

Several of these strategies were designed to regulate elections and to make nomination and election procedures more accessible to public inspection and control. Municipal elections were chaotic and corrupt, partly because few election laws existed, and those that did exist were rarely enforced. Nominating procedures were not regulated at all. To select candidates for public office, political parties held city conventions or closed caucuses according to their own changeable rules. Although forty states regulated campaign finances by 1912, most of the laws contained numerous loopholes and were difficult to enforce.

Reformers everywhere launched campaigns to regulate elections and nominations. By 1905, voter registration laws had been placed on the books in most states.[12] From 1905 to 1920, states and localities set up election boards, made it illegal to vote more than once, and tried to define the legitimate uses of campaign funds. Although enforcement of all these laws was sporadic and inadequate—the machines continued to control prosecutors and the courts in many places—the existence of new laws provided the basis for investigations and prosecutions when the middle- and upper-class public became aroused about corruption.

In a further attempt to weaken party control of elections, many reformers backed devices designed to implement direct democracy. Wisconsin adopted the first statewide primary law in 1903, and twelve other states followed suit in the next ten years.[13] The popular nomination of senatorial candidates was an accomplished fact in twenty-nine of the states by 1909, forcing the Senate to propose the Seventeenth Amendment, which provided for popular election of senators in all states. A wave of state laws also implemented the initiative, the referendum, and the recall, all devices to allow the popular will to bypass public officials.

Within the cities, reformers focused more on the structure and operations of the party machines than on electoral reform. It was obvious that the machines derived their strength from the ethnic neighborhoods, and that the overall unity of the machines was furthered by the immigrants' ability to identify a party label on the election ballot. The reformers' two most popular strategies, the nonpartisan ballot and at-large elections, constituted frontal assaults on the structure of the urban party machines.

Municipal reformers felt that party labels encouraged bloc voting and organizational rather than civic loyalty. They wanted a more "rational," educated voter who could "accumulate and carry in his head the brief list of personal preferences and do without the guidance of party names and symbols on the ballot."[14] It was the responsibility of citizens to educate themselves and vote for the best candidates strictly on their merits, not on the basis of party loyalty.

The proposal to remove the party label from election ballots reflected the reformers' conviction that there was a singular public interest that overrode the interests of particular ethnic groups or political factions. Reformers generally agreed that the public interest required one thing— that public services be provided as cheaply and efficiently as possible. Party symbols created artificial political differences that allegedly blurred people's perceptions of their real interests. As Brand Whitlock, the famous reform mayor of Toledo, put it:

> It seems almost incredible now that men's minds were ever so clouded, strange that they did not earlier discover how absurd was a system which, in order to enable them the more readily to subjugate themselves, actually printed little woodcuts of birds—roosters and eagles—at the heads of the tickets, so that they might the more easily and readily recognize their masters and deliver their suffrages over to them.[15]

By removing the party symbol as an easy reference for lower-class voters, the nonpartisan ballot made it harder for immigrants to vote as a bloc. Working-class and immigrant candidates had few personal resources to expend in political activities. The party organization supplied campaign money and workers, and freed the working-class candidate from the necessity of holding a normal job, which of its own accord would have denied the candidate time for participation in politics. Few politicians in the machines could have started or stayed in politics without the organization's help. Without party organizations, people of wealth and social standing could dominate political campaigns. In fact, this was the objective of the nonpartisanship crusade—to make politics once again an "honest" calling appropriate to the educated and "cultured" classes.[16]

Another plank in the reform platform, the proposal to substitute at-large for ward elections, was designed to destroy the neighborhood base of the machine. Under the ward system, complained Andrew D. White, Cornell University's president, "Wards largely controlled by thieves and robbers can send thieves and robbers," to city hall, and "the vote of a single tenement house, managed by a professional politician, will neutralize the vote of an entire street of well-to-do citizens."[17] The remedy was to have each city council candidate campaign in one, at-large district, covering the entire city. Thus, candidates would be forced to compete for the votes of all the city's residents; none could be elected by a particular neighborhood or ethnic group. Gone would be the politics of tradeoff and compromise

among legislators representing different groups and wards. "Special interest" politics would allegedly give way to "public interest" politics. One
observer sympathetic to these reform ideas thought that "enlightened"
politics was virtually impossible so long as elections were held in wards:

> . . . for decades the election of councils by wards had superimposed a network
> of search for parochial favors, of units devoted to partisan spoils, and of cater-
> ing to ethnic groups that time and again had either defeated comprehensive
> city programs or loaded them with irrelevant spoils and ill-conceived ward
> projects. The ward and precinct were the heart of machine control, and the
> councils so elected were usually also infested with corruption, however accept-
> able the councilors may have been to the voters of their wards.[18]

Small wards virtually guaranteed that ethnic and racial groups could
exert electoral influence. For example, Lithuanians might be able to send
an alderman to the city council, even though they constituted a small proportion of the city's total population. Small wards multiplied the points of
access through which groups and individuals could influence public officials. This enhanced access was a result of the relatively large number of
officials and of the wide variety of interests they represented. Though a
"boss" might sit at the apex of the party organization, he was required to
strike bargains and make compromises with local politicians.

That citywide elections have an opposite effect is obvious. If the whole
city is one big electoral district, candidates representing ethnic and racial
groups clustered in specific neighborhoods are handicapped, for they are
forced to appeal to a complex array of political and social groups to be
elected. Organizations representing middle- and upper-class areas and
business groups have a campaign advantage in citywide elections, for they
are able to raise the funds required to reach a large and diverse audience.
Campaigns covering an entire city are costly and time-consuming for individual candidates. In such a system, wealth and social prominence are
important ingredients of political success.

These effects were well known to reformers, which explains why the
Municipal League's model city charter in 1899 recommended citywide
elections and nonpartisan ballots. Every subsequent model charter of the
League contained these two features, and the League carefully compiled
annual statistics to track the pace of reform.

There were other reforms intended to undercut machine rule. Civil
service was particularly important. Aimed at patronage, civil service was a
system that presumably provided "objective" standards for hiring municipal employees. Under civil service, written and oral examinations provided the basis for hiring, and a tenure system was designed to make
employees safe from political firings.

In the first two decades of the twentieth century, nonpartisanship, at-large elections and civil service were implemented in cities throughout the nation. Reformers were least successful in the big cities with complex electorates, where middle- and upper-class voters did not constitute an electoral majority. New cities, especially in the Midwest and the West, usually adopted reform items in their new charters. In these communities, lower-class ethnics were invariably outnumbered, and the rules of politics adopted in these communities tended to exclude them from any formal representation in government.

In large cities, nonpartisanship, at-large elections and civil service were nearly always coupled with antimachine, anticorruption campaigns. But in smaller towns and cities, these reforms were popular because they seemed to streamline government and put it on a "nonpolitical" footing. The residents of smaller urban settlements viewed government as, at best, a necessary evil that should provide such vital public services as water, sewage disposal, streets, and perhaps libraries and community centers. "Consensus" politics, which, of course, excluded the ethnic minorities that might be present, was a common feature of small towns.

Reform programs succeeded in some big cities. Nonpartisan, at-large elections were instituted in Los Angeles (1908), Boston (1909), Akron (1915), and Detroit (1918).[19] Several states required cities within their boundaries to use nonpartisan ballots. Civil service was adopted at least partially in most northern cities by the 1920s, mostly because it was such an appealing reform that it seemed necessary for efficient municipal administration.

The electoral rules preferred by municipal reformers are much in evidence in contemporary cities. Before 1910, nonpartisan elections were almost unknown. By 1929, they were standard in 57 percent of the cities over 30,000 in population.[20] By the 1960s, several states required their cities to use nonpartisan elections, including Minnesota, California, Alaska, and most of the western states. In ten more states, nonpartisan ballots were used in 90 percent or more of the cities. In the West, 94 percent of cities used nonpartisan elections. The Eastern Seaboard is the only region where partisan elections are used more often in cities than are nonpartisan elections. Among the nation's cities with more than 500,000 residents, 58 percent use nonpartisan ballots, but for cities below 5,000 in population, 85 percent use them. It is clear that the reformers have enjoyed substantial success in instituting this particular electoral rule.

Most cities with nonpartisan elections also have at-large rather than district or ward elections. Several of the cities listed in Table 4–1 have adopted one or both reforms.

TABLE 4–1   Electoral Systems in Cities over 500,000 Population,* 1983

	At-large	District	Combination
Partisan cities	Pittsburgh Jacksonville	Cleveland	Baltimore New York New Orleans Philadelphia St. Louis Indianapolis
Nonpartisan cities	Phoenix Columbus Dallas** Detroit San Antonio San Diego Seattle	Los Angeles Milwaukee Chicago*** San Francisco	Memphis Houston Denver Boston

Source: Municipal Yearbook, 1976. Due to certain omissions in the *Yearbook,* we would like to thank Ms. Joan Casey of the National Municipal League for her kind assistance in the preparation of this chart. Updated to 1983 by author.
*Excluding Washington, D.C.
**Councilors are nominated by districts but run at-large.
***Only mayoral elections are partisan.

We have seen that electoral systems that were originally designed to reduce electoral influence by ethnics and minorities have been widely adopted in American cities. There seems to be plenty of evidence that the reformer's intentions were generally realized. Where their electoral rules have been adopted, minorities have not been well represented. Before the adoption of new electoral rules, working-class candidates, many of them socialists, were elected to city offices in dozens of cities.[21] At-large elections made it much more difficult for these kinds of candidates to win. In the 1909 Dayton elections, socialists elected two aldermen and three assessors, even though these candidates received only 25 percent of the city vote. Before the 1913 election, Dayton implemented citywide elections and abolished ward boundaries. In 1913, the socialists received 35 percent of the popular vote, and in 1917, they polled 44 percent. In neither instance did they elect a single candidate. Similarly, Pittsburgh in 1911 changed to at-large elections, with the result that upper-class business leaders and professionals pushed lower- and middle-class groups out of their previous places on the city council and the school board.[22]

St. Louis provides an excellent example of these two electoral systems at work. The members of the city's board of aldermen are placed in office through partisan elections in each of twenty-eight wards (see Figure 4–1). Members of the St. Louis Board of Education, in contrast, are elected through a nonpartisan, at-large ballot, in the true spirit of reform politics.

In a city that in 1970 was 43 percent black and that has been largely abandoned by the middle class, race has effectively replaced ethnicity as the basis of neighborhood identification. The municipal wards yielded ten black aldermen, on the average, during the 1970s. Reflecting the neighborhood, and hence racial, basis of ward politics, all ten came from the heavily black wards of the north-central part of the city. Similarly, the other eighteen wards always returned white aldermen to city hall. The 1977 municipal elections were no exception to this rule.

The school board elections, on the other hand, yielded entirely different results. In the 1977 contest, all five seats went to white, middle-class candidates. In a city where 70 percent of the public school enrollment was black, not a single black candidate was able to win office in the racially tinged election. Not only were the three black candidates overpowered by the electoral power of the white majority, but three other black would-be candidates were excluded from the ballot through the enforcement of stringent filing rules.

The impact of nonpartisan, at-large elections was readily visible in St. Louis all through the 1970s. The highly concentrated black minority was excluded from effective participation in the governing of the local schools, even though more than two-thirds of the students were black. Under the ward representation used in the city government, however, blacks were assured representation. In this way the interests of the black minority, where they diverged from those of the white majority or the city as a whole, were articulated in the chambers of the board of aldermen.

"Efficiency and Economy" in Municipal Affairs

In their attempts to change the government of cities, reformers sought to institute new forms of government as well as to reduce the influence of the immigrants. Early in the municipal reform movement, the catchwords for good government became efficiency and economy. Theodore Roosevelt, addressing the delegates to the First Annual Conference for Good City Government in 1894, urged them to go beyond their moral outrage at the way things were being run to find ways of streamlining and improving government: "There are two gospels I always want to preach to reformers. . . . The first is the gospel of morality; the next is the gospel of efficiency. . . . I don't think I have to tell you to be upright, but I do think I have to tell you to be practical and efficient."[23]

**FIGURE 4–1   Racial Composition of Municipal Wards in the City of
St. Louis, 1977***

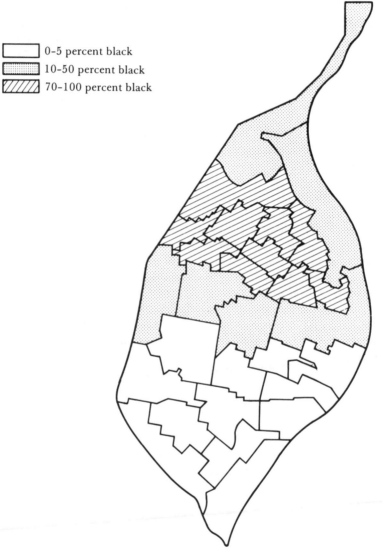

□ 0–5 percent black
▦ 10–50 percent black
▨ 70–100 percent black

*Racial composition of each
ward estimated on the basis
of 1970 Census data.

Actually, Roosevelt probably had to tell them neither. Municipal reformers were hard at work searching for a theory of good government that could unite them. They needed not only shared values but some strategies to implement those values. Once they had "kicked the rascals out" and installed better people in government, they needed to know what to do with their inheritance.

During the 1890s, municipal reformers developed a theory of good government that motivated subsequent reform. Four basic elements made up the theory. First, the reformers held that there was a public interest, which could be defined objectively and which, if implemented, would benefit all citizens equally. The main components of this defined public interest included careful budgetary controls, to see that public services were delivered at the lowest possible cost. Second, the theory held that democratic politics—elections and representation—should be strictly separate from day-to-day administration of services. If, after all, the public interest could be defined objectively, politics should have no part in satisfying it; it could best be implemented through efficient administrative procedures. The third component flowed logically from the second, namely, that experts with training, experience, and ability should run the public's business. Fourth, it was assumed that government should be run like a business and that the principles of scientific management then being applied in business organizations should also be applied to government. Implementing efficient government services was, in sum, a question of mechanics.

The reformers derived their ideas about how to run government from the scientific management movement that swept the country in the Progressive Era. In the last decades of the nineteenth century, accountants, engineers, and corporate managers were searching for ways to rationalize business organization. With the growing size and complexity of individual business enterprises, there was considerable interest in discovering ways to elicit the highest possible output from work forces by achieving coordination of work tasks, hierarchy, and discipline in the work place. If science could invent efficient machines, it was thought, then surely it could discover how to make workers more efficient.

The search for principles of scientific management became a fevered crusade. To some, it seemed an answer had been found for the periodic economic crises that had plagued the United States since the Civil War. To others, it held the potential for ending conflict between business and labor: proper wage levels could be calculated scientifically by reference to output and labor efficiency. Still others saw efficiency as the basis for productivity and social betterment. Efficiency societies sprang up in most major cities; expert speakers on efficiency were in demand.[24] The efficiency advocates maintained that inefficiency was the principal cause of poverty and other social problems. Morality was even redefined in the language of efficiency:

"Compared with what we ought to be we are only half awake. . . . We are making use of only a small part of our possible mental and physical resources."[25]

In 1911, Frederick Winslow Taylor became world famous when he published *The Principles of Scientific Management*.[26] Basically, Taylor wanted to apply military discipline and hierarchy to the factory and advocated that the movements of workers be studied meticulously in order to discover how work tasks could be organized to achieve maximum output with minimum expenditure of worker energy. Taylor's efficiency principles promised progress, prosperity, and happiness; in that respect, the efficiency movement became a religion with its own gospel. Efficiency management, Taylor said, could apply the lessons of science, encourage harmony and cooperation, achieve maximum output, and, finally, encourage "the development of each man to his greatest efficiency and prosperity."[27] The essence of the Taylor catechism was that, "In the past, the man has been first; in the future the system must be first."[28] Taylor's lectures against "soldiering" (slow work) and inefficiency were applied by him and his disciples not only to the work place but to the home as well. Popular magazines featured articles on efficient housework and child-rearing.

The efficiency ideal was appealing because it promised social betterment without a change in class relationships. It was the perfect revolution, a panacea for creating amicable employer-worker relations, ending disastrous economic panics, and abolishing poverty and want. Taylorites invaded the factories to implement the gospel of efficiency. They also applied their "scientific principles" to government operations. Efficiency and scientific management—"business methods"—soon became the model for municipal reform. In the reformers' language, the appropriateness of efficiency principles to government was unmistakable:

> The rising prestige of technicians in industry and the increasing demand for new public works and municipal services strengthened the desire for more technical efficiency in local government.[29]

In 1912, Henry Brueré, the first director of the New York Bureau of Municipal Research, published a popular book applying efficiency principles to municipal management.[30] Brueré took the position that much of the mismanagement in New York City "formerly attributed to official corruption and to popular indifference was really due to official and popular ignorance of . . . orderly and scientific procedures."[31] What these procedures amounted to were elaborate accounting and reporting devices designed to codify the responsibilities of city officials, the actions taken by them to carry out their duties, the costs of equipment and personnel, and other details. For example, Brueré constructed scores and ratings of the cities he studied to quantify everything from "number of disorderly persons" to "location of garbage dumps."[32] To construct the ratings, he asked such questions as: "Is a record kept of all city property?" "How often are the treasurer's books audited?" "Is location of houses of prostitution known and recorded?"[33] In all, cities were rated on 1,300 standardized questions, resulting in a list of cities, from the "worst governed" to the "best." Throughout the book, cities were advised to codify all aspects of their operations so that "inefficient" practices could be identified and eliminated.

In 1913, Brueré was given the opportunity to implement his efficiency ideals. In November of 1913, John Purroy Mitchell, one of Brueré's closest confidants, was elected the mayor of New York City. Mitchell appointed Brueré to the office of City Chamberlain (the mayor's policy adviser). One of Brueré's first tasks was to attack Tammany Hall's patronage system and to replace it with civil service. It was the nation's first large civil service system, and it was explicitly designed as a Taylorite approach to municipal reform.

Brueré assigned the task of designing a civil service system to Robert Moses, a young staff member of the New York Bureau of Municipal Research. Moses carried out his assignment with the enthusiasm of a Taylorite zealot. He proposed a system in which all municipal employees would be closely observed at work by efficiency experts. Their efficiency was to be determined with mathematical accuracy. Various functions and responsibilities of each employee would be codified and "given a precise mathematical grade. These grades would . . . be 'used as a basis for salary increase and promotion.'"[34] Moses thought that even personality must be rated mathematically. To implement his system, Moses had his assistants draw up forms to be used by supervisors in evaluating employees. Only by totally standardizing each job could ratings be objectively determined. Each employee would be handed a scorecard and be paid, promoted, or fired on the basis of the ratings on it.

Such a system, if implemented, would have fallen of its own weight. There was no way to ensure objective ratings. The amount of time required to rate employees would have resulted in an enormous civil service administrative staff. But Moses's scheme was never put into action, for Tammany Hall politicians and the 50,000 city employees steadfastly refused to use the reporting forms. Their main objection was not only that the system was time-consuming and unwieldy, but also that it was arbitrary and unjust. It tried to reduce human tasks to machinelike precision.

The civil service reform attempted during Mitchell's mayoral tenure illustrated the tendencies of the municipal reformers. Mayor Mitchell, while trying to reorganize city departments and implement civil service, also tried to reduce "unnecessary" programs and expenditures. He sought cutbacks in school expenditures, asked teachers to work without salaries in the summers, tried to close down special schools for the retarded, and reduced park and recreational expenditures.[35]

The efficiency gospel was so all-encompassing that inequality, poverty, and even poor health and bad education were considered the results of inefficiency in people's habits. Such an interpretation lacked an essential human element. As Taylor had put it, "The natural laziness in men is serious, but by far the greatest evil from which both workmen and employers are suffering is the systematic *soldiering* which is almost universal."[36] The problem of the reformer, therefore, was to reorganize work tasks so as to deliver maximum work for the tax (or the employer's) dollar, and thus raise the general level of societal prosperity.

Efficiency principles were adopted by reformers across the country. Not only the cities but the federal government and the states entered the field. President Taft appointed a Commission on Economy and Efficiency, and President Wilson later created the Bureau of Efficiency. Between 1911 and 1917, sixteen states established efficiency commissions. These commissions generally recommended more streamlined budgeting procedures, more centralized power in the governor, and consolidation of state agencies, as well as civil service reform.[37]

The Business Model

With efficiency and scientific management supplying the rationale, it was predictable that the organization of municipal government would be compared with private business. Reformers pointed out that municipal governments, unlike business firms, were not organized in such a way that decisions could be made efficiently. A sympathetic history of reform described the problem in these terms:

> The reformers, who tried to get good men into office, found . . . that, even if they elected a mayor or council, they were intolerably handicapped by the existing systems of municipal government. [Due to] the principles of separation of powers and of checks and balances . . . there was no single elective official or governing body that could be held responsible for effecting reform.[38]

Because so many officials were elected, and because ward systems resulted in councillors who were allegedly "party henchmen, careless of the needs of the city as a whole,"[39] it was impossible for local government to take concerted action.

Reformers claimed that the "weak mayor" form of government, which existed in most cities, dispersed authority so broadly that no one person could be held accountable for overall governmental policy. Organizational

FIGURE 4–2   Weak Mayor Government

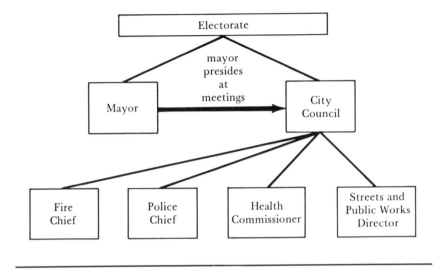

charts used by the reformers to demonstrate this fact looked like the one shown in Figure 4–2.

In contrast, it was supposed that businesses were organized to achieve efficiency, high output, and responsibility. The business model had a clear division of tasks and responsibilities. One feature of the model was a separation between policymaking by a board of directors and administration by executive officers. Applied to cities, public policy would still be made by elected officials representing their constituents, just as a board of directors in a business presumably made decisions in accordance with the wishes of stockholders. But policy would be implemented by administrators applying scientific principles of cost accounting and personnel management. To ensure that city management conformed more closely to business principles, uniform accounting systems were proposed, as well as debt limitations to force city officials to live within their budgets.

The business model required a strong executive with sufficient power to run the company—or the government. Reformers sought charter reforms to expand the mayor's power to appoint most city officials and to veto legislation passed by the council. The mayor would preside at the top of a hierarchical chain of command with clear lines of authority and accountability. The strong mayor form of government recommended by the National League of Cities did precisely that. The National Municipal

FIGURE 4–3   Strong Mayor Government

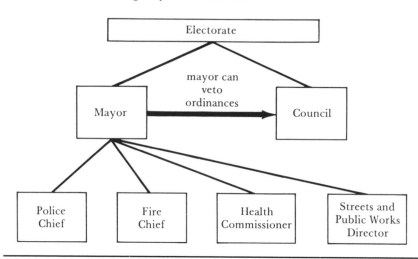

League's model city charter included a small city council and a strong mayor with broad appointive and veto powers. In the first decade of the twentieth century, municipal research bureaus began to design organization charts, which had previously been unknown, in order to promote government reorganization.

Principles of efficiency motivated reformers to fight for a loosening of state control over cities. One problem with such control was that people who knew nothing about cities were, in part, running them. The other problem was that city governments could not run services efficiently if they had no authority to set tax rates, decide where services were to be provided, or hire the best-trained administrators. At its state constitutional convention in 1875, Missouri became the first state to write a general "home rule" charter for its cities, although the legislature retained control of St. Louis's police budget. Ultimate legal power was still held by the state, but Missouri's cities would not have to seek approval for their every action, as long as they stayed within the charter powers. They could hire new sanitation workers and firefighters, for example, or build a new street without consulting the legislature. The general charter only spelled out the services to be provided, not such details as street location and number of personnel. The home rule movement, pushed hard by the National Municipal League and other organizations, was quite successful. By 1925 fourteen states had granted home rule charters to their cities. Today, virtually all cities have home rule charters.

Commission and Manager Governments

Galveston, Texas, ushered in the first municipal government copied explicitly from the business model. Beginning in 1894, Galveston's business and professional leaders initiated a campaign to elect business leaders to the city government. In 1895, a coalition of city council and business leaders secured a charter amendment from the Texas legislature to replace ward with at-large elections. Over the next few years, some businessmen were elected to the city council, but they continued to be outvoted by a nonbusiness faction.[40]

The press of emergency, rather than political victory, handed the government over to business and corporate leaders. On September 8, 1900, hurricane-driven waves breached the seawall protecting Galveston, and the inrushing sea flooded the town. By the next day, 6,000 of the town's 37,000 residents were dead. Half the city's property was destroyed. To rebuild the city, prominent businessmen organized the Deepwater Committee and set out to gain full control of the government.

If "a municipality is largely a business corporation,"[41] it follows that it should be run as such, with the voters being viewed as stockholders and the government as a board of directors responsible to the stockholders. On this principle, the Deepwater Committee drafted an outline of a commission form of government and asked the state legislature to approve it. It was promptly enacted.

The Galveston plan created a five-member commission, with each of the commissioners heading a department of government. Such concentration of authority seemed appropriate in an emergency. At first, the commission was even given full criminal and civil jurisdiction over law enforcement in the city, though this power was subsequently struck down by a state court. But even without that power, the commission's authority was considerable. Under the leadership of five aggressive businessmen, Galveston initiated a vigorous rebuilding program and, in the process, reduced its debts and restored and improved public services.

The success of the Galveston Commission in providing leadership for the rebuilding effort attracted the attention of reformers across the country. Commission government spread like wildfire. Its attraction was obvious: it seemed to streamline government, it was a governmental form that held the potential for attracting business leaders back into active government service, and it was a concrete organizational plan around which reformers could rally in challenging the urban party bosses. Commission government was generally accompanied by other reforms designed to rid government of "politics"—nonpartisan ballots and at-large elections, and frequently the initiative, the referendum, and the recall.

Galveston's performance impressed business leaders in other Texas cities who soon pressed for commission government. By 1907, seven major cities in the state had imitated Galveston's charter, including the large cities of Houston, Dallas, and Fort Worth. In 1908, Des Moines, Iowa, adopted a charter that became a model for reformers around the country. Besides a five-member commission, Des Moines adopted the initiative, the referendum and the recall, along with civil service, at-large elections, and a nonpartisan primary system. The Des Moines Plan, as it was labeled by reformers, caught on rapidly. There were twenty-three adoptions of commission government in 1909 and sixty-six in 1910.[42] In September 1915, there were at least 465 cities under the commission form. By 1920, about 20 percent of all cities with populations over 5,000 had adopted it.[43] During these years, a few states made commission government compulsory for their cities, and in most states it became an optional feature.

The commission idea was viewed as a cure-all by its promoters, who promised less taxation, more efficient public service, and "better men" in government. In city after city, it was promoted as a means of making government more like business in its organization and methods. Accordingly, chambers of commerce and other organized business groups became the strongest backers of commission government. The Commercial Club successfully pushed Des Moines's new charter in 1907, although, interestingly enough, the first commissioners voted into office represented a working-class slate, much to the dismay of the business group.[44] In Pennsylvania, the Pittsburgh Chamber of Commerce organized a statewide convention of business organizations to plan a lobbying campaign at the state legislature to require cities above a minimum size to adopt commission government. The coalition of bankers, merchants, and manufacturers secured the legislation in 1913.[45] The pattern was similar elsewhere: business leaders trying to change government into a business operation.

Commission government was not without its problems. Its worst feature was that it did not purely fit the business model. It was unlike a true board of directors, in that the commission combined policymaking and administration in the same hands. Because each of the commissioners was a separate executive who headed a department, leadership was often fragmented, with the commissioners refusing to cooperate with one another or to follow the mayor's lead. All the commissioners were "first among equals." This feature was, in fact, the chief complaint of the secretary of the Short Ballot Association, Richard S. Childs. Noting that commission government was "an accident, not a plan," he addressed the problem of having five coequal executives.

The theory that the commission as a whole controlled its members in their departmental activities became neglected—the commission could not discipline a recalcitrant member.[46]

Commonly, Childs asserted, commissioners would ignore one another's performance ("You attend to your department and quit criticizing mine") or exchange favors and support ("I'll vote for your appropriation if you'll vote for mine").[47]

Before long, other municipal theorists began to notice these problems. Their response was to promote another panacea. The new reform entailed placing all administrative power in the hands of an appointed, trained administrator, a city manager. According to this plan, the city council members were supposed to be policymakers, not administrators. "The reform leaders realized that technical ability could not be expected of elected officials, and they hoped that a strong mayor could appoint trained technicians and administrators as department heads."[48] Chief among these technicians would be the city manager. The city manager movement, because of its persuasive logic and "pure" business analogy, eclipsed the commission government reforms during the 1920s.

In 1913, the National Municipal League issued a report (written by Childs) recommending that commission government reforms include a professional city manager. A manager would bring to government administrative unity, expertise, clear accountability, and formal training in management.[49] Only six years later, in 1919, the League recommended the manager idea in its model charter.

Between 1908 and 1912, several midwestern cities hired city managers. The idea caught on in earnest when Dayton, Ohio, changed its city charter. As in Galveston, an emergency served as the catalyst for a new government form. In 1913, John H. Patterson, president of the National Cash Register Company, had persuaded the Dayton Chamber of Commerce to devise a new charter. The Chamber established the Bureau of Municipal Research to advertise its efforts. A business-dominated Committee of One Hundred subsequently ran a slate of candidates for city office who were pledged to charter reform. By organizing a well-run campaign ward by ward, the business slate elected some city councilmen, but they still constituted minority of the party-dominated city council. Two months later, a devastating flood from the Miami River poured into the town. The municipal government was slow in organizing emergency services. Patterson turned his factory into a shelter for flood victims. Overnight, he became the town's leading citizen. When requested by local business leaders, the state governor appointed Patterson to head a new charter reform commission. The charter commission sold the city manager idea to the voters.[50]

The results were spectacular. The new government improved public

services, retired most of the city debt, instituted new budget-making procedures, enforced a uniform eight-hour day for city employees, and established civil service. The Dayton Plan soon became the main reform
alternative to commission government. By 1920, more than 150 cities had
city managers, and in the 1920s and later it became the most popular
reform model for "good" municipal government. Though rarely instituted in the big cities, it became common in smaller cities around the
nation. In the five years before 1918, 87 cities adopted manager charters,
and 153 did so between 1918 and 1923. During the next five years, 84
more cities were added to the list.[51]

The commission and the manager plans each attained the status of final
solution to the organization of city government because they seemingly
fulfilled reformers' desires to find an objective, nonpolitical, efficient governmental structure. It is not surprising that the business world supplied
the model for reform. In many cities, reform crusades were led primarily
by business leaders. Reformers who were not members of the business
community sympathized with the business view of the purpose of government: to provide necessary public services at the lowest possible cost. The
business analogy almost always supplied the principal supporting logic for
structural reform. The *Dallas News* promoted the manager plan in 1930
by asking: "Why not run Dallas itself on a business schedule by business
methods under businessmen? . . . The city manager plan is after all only a
business management plan. . . . The city manager is the executive of a corporation under a board of directors. Dallas is the corporation. It is as simple as that. Vote for it."[52]

The Class Bias of Municipal Reform

The commission and manager movements elicited support from the
middle and upper classes, not only because they held forth the promise of
saving money, but also because they placed political handicaps in the way of
the Great Unwashed. Reform was inspired by class antagonisms. Changes
in electoral rules were designed to undercut the voting power of lower-class
groups, and so were the changes in governmental structure. As pointed
out in a sympathetic history of the city-manager movement, where the plan
was adopted in "machine-ridden" cities,

> there were differences in nationality or religion that intensified their social
> and political disagreements; . . . and each of them established the city manager
> plan through a concerted effort, organized by commercial or reform organiza-
> tions, to take the city government away from the politicians, to give it to busi-
> nessmen, and to make it conform to business ideals and standards.[53]

In "faction-ridden cities," the change to manager government resulted in "the election of men who had never before taken part in municipal affairs and who had promised to end politics in the business of city government."[54]

Analysis of the social class backgrounds of reformers reveals, especially in the big cities, a uniformly upper-class bias. Studies of the origins of reform movements show that business and upper-class elements normally championed reform while lower- and working-class groups usually opposed it. For example, the New York City Bureau of Municipal Research, founded in 1906, was initially financed by Andrew Carnegie and John D. Rockefeller.[55] The U.S. Chamber of Commerce provided office space and paid the executive secretary of the City Managers Association for several years.[56] Civic clubs and voters' leagues generally contained names from elite social directories. Professional people involved in reform tended to be the most prestigious members of their professions, and many of them had upper-class origins.

George Mowry has traced the backgrounds of more than 400 prominent Progressive reformers, and his data show that most were upper class.[57] Many of the prominent reformers were wealthy industrialists, including names like McCormack, du Pont, Pinchot, Morgenthau, and Dodge. Most of them had earned a college education in a day when a degree marked a select social stratum (less than 10 percent of the population held college degrees). Even more striking, most of the women and social workers had gone to college. In a sample of 400 reformers, a majority were lawyers, many of them politicians. Almost one-fifth were newspaper editors or publishers. Most of the remainder were engaged in business, medicine, real estate, or banking. Most of them were native-born Americans of British ancestry, Protestant, and urban.

Other studies confirmed these results. A California sample of forty-seven reformers found that fourteen were engaged in banking, real estate, or business, seventeen in law, and fourteen in journalism.[58] In Baltimore, the reform group was overwhelmingly WASP, university-graduated, and engaged in professional practice or business. Studies in Ohio, Chicago, Pittsburgh, and Kansas City reported similar evidence.[59]

The Progressive reformers whom these studies describe constituted a more complex group than the municipal reformers. The municipal groups contained a greater proportion of local business leaders, and in most cities commission and manager charters were advocated *primarily* by business organizations.[60] Samuel P. Hays has catalogued overwhelming business dominance over municipal reform in Dallas, Des Moines, Pittsburgh, and several other cities.[61]

These groups were keenly aware of their political interests. The expectation that new forms of government would result in the election of "better" class of citizens was usually fulfilled. Business leaders dominated politics after reform in Galveston and Austin, Texas; Dayton and Springfield, Ohio; Jackson, Michigan; Des Moines, Iowa; and other places.[62] This fact explains why business leaders organized reform movements. Opponents of the commission and manager plans were just as aware of their political interests. Machine politicians, socialists, and trade unionists opposed the plans because they rightly perceived that centralized electoral systems and decision-making processes would make it more difficult for working-class candidates to win public office.[63] In the big cities, these elements often successfully opposed reform, but in smaller cities, where they were a distinct minority of the electorate, they could not effectively resist reform. In Oakland, California, socialists polled nearly 50 percent of the vote in the 1911 city elections.[64] With the vociferous assistance of the *Oakland Tribune*, local business leaders then led a successful reform movement to secure commission, at-large, nonpartisan government. As a result, the socialists were decimated in the next city elections. The business community found, however, that it could not keep all the commissioners from labor influence, so in 1928 it replaced the commission with a council-manager government.[65] The manager was much easier to handle than the politically sensitive, elected commissioners. In 1938, Jackson, Michigan, under the leadership of the chamber of commerce, instituted the council-manager plan. The new mayor and councilmen were members of the chamber of commerce and of Protestant reform groups. The new officials celebrated with a reception in the Masonic hall and, once in power, dismissed most of the Roman Catholic city employees.[66]

Reformers were not apolitical. What municipal reformers wanted to reestablish, once and for all, was the idea of the city as a marketplace. They rejected the notion that city governments should broker among the many groups making up the urban social environment. If the city's singular purpose is to provide a climate for profit-making and profit-taking, the "efficient" public services are indeed a first priority. The danger that socialists and working-class people presented was a redefinition of the public interest to include social programs and city services aimed at improving the health, welfare, and living conditions of lower-income city residents. Obviously, this would require higher taxes from wealthier citizens and from the business community.

The contrast between the structural reformers and such social reformers as Hazen Pingree is striking. "Social reform" encompassed restructuring of tax burdens, attempts to secure favorable public utility rates, and efforts to expand housing, recreation, and public works programs for less privileged people. While structural reform mayors and city managers generally sought economy and efficiency, social reformers tried to devise programs founded on some conception of how government could improve the lives of citizens who suffered from poverty and unemployment. A delegate to the 1913 meeting of the League of Kansas Municipalities protested that "a city is more than a business corporation" and that "Good health is more important than a low tax rate."[67] The vast social distance between most municipal reformers and the rest of the urban populace, however, made such utterances anathema to most reformers.

The Consequences of Municipal Reform

Even when reformers achieved the structural changes they sought, the result was not necessarily what they had anticipated. In many cities the balance of power was weighted sufficiently against upper-class and business reformers that structural change did not always translate into political change. When the Des Moines Committee on One Hundred, representing the business community, succeeded in persuading the voters to adopt commission government in 1908, they were appalled when working-class candidates were elected as the first commissioners.[68] Chicago adopted nonpartisan primaries and elections for aldermanic candidates in the 1920s. But to this day, the Democratic organization easily communicates with loyal voters through year-round personal contacts and hard work on election day.

Structural reforms did, however, change politics in many cities, and this was especially true where reform elements could outvote ethnic and working-class neighborhoods. This was rarely the case in the large cities, for the party machines were supported by reliable electoral constituencies. But groups that lacked a stable political base, such as blacks, socialists, and labor candidates, were frequently denied formal electoral representation because of nonpartisan, at-large elections, civil service, and other reforms. Until the 1970s, for example, Los Angeles virtually excluded blacks from formal representation.[69] City councillors were selected by nonpartisan ballots from large districts that had been carefully drawn to ensure that blacks would remain a voting minority in all districts. Civil service was strictly enforced so that a political organization based on patronage could not be started. With "no city-wide organization with a need to attract all segments of the population," there was little incentive to try to represent the particular ethnic, racial, and religious groups in the city. As a result, officeholders were generally white Anglo-Saxon Protestants. Similar situations also existed for a long period in Detroit and Boston.

In contrast, blacks gained representation early in Chicago, because the fifty ward boundaries could not be easily drawn so as to exclude them. Before its downfall in the 1930s, the Republican machine tried to perpetuate its continued electoral strength in the black community.[70] As a consequence, the first black was elected to the Chicago city council in 1915. In 1920, a black became a ward committeeman in the Republican machine, a position that ensured a few patronage jobs. Chicago's Oscar de Priest became the first northern black representative elected to Congress in 1928. In contrast, Adam Clayton Powell of New York City was not elected until 1944, and Charles Diggs of Detroit was not elected until 1954. As of 1976, fifteen of fifty Chicago aldermen were blacks, two Congressmen were black, as were four state senators and several state representatives. Electoral rules do make an important difference for minorities.

Social Welfare as Private Philanthropy

While municipal reformers were attempting to change politics directly, many members of the upper class were seeking alternative methods for influencing community affairs. Politics was beneath them; direct political activity was viewed as demeaning and socially unacceptable, requiring contact with lower-class people. The functions of status allocation and recognition had once been fulfilled by public officeholding, in the "golden age" when patricians dominated city affairs. In the industrial city, new ways of fulfilling those functions had to be devised. Beginning about the turn of the century, there was a proliferation of private cultural and philanthropic institutions that provided upper-class people an opportunity to affirm their social status by giving money and running well-publicized activities. Through work "in behalf of the community," the upper-class could reinforce the pecking order within their own ranks, and thus philanthropic service became a useful adjunct to the social clubs, cotillions, and debutante balls.

Additionally, they provided an essential means of bypassing politics and government in dispensing social welfare benefits. If provided privately, social services could be financed and controlled by wealthy members of the community. Unlike government-financed social services, private associations remained outside public scrutiny and thus allocated their resources according to the preferences of rich contributors. Compromise, negotiation, and competition—the principal components of the political process—were therefore replaced by decision-making behind closed doors and in country clubs.

Philanthropic organizations assumed a large number of functions that might have been supplied through governments. Red Cross chapters specialized in disaster relief; family welfare services and charity organizations provided help to some of the poor. Many hospitals were privately financed. Museums, libraries, and symphonies were the responsibility of still other associations. Community chests, which ran well-organized, heavily publicized campaigns to raise money, became the most inclusive of these organizations. The money was distributed by community chest committees dominated by wealthy upper-class individuals. These patterns were repeated in communities across the nation. Often the philanthropic activities of the local social elite dominated local newspapers, competing for coverage with world and national news. The "Society Page" became an indispensable news feature.

In a study of a New England town they named Bay City, Peter and Alice Rossi found that by the 1950s private associations had taken over most functions of status allocation and recognition in the community.[71] Service on the boards of the community chest, Red Cross, and other associations had largely displaced public service in prestige. The voluntary associations had also developed into social screening devices. In Bay City, wealth alone did not guarantee appointment to a board. The proper credentials included wealth, occupational status, family background, and religion.

Within the voluntary association community, a complex network of hierarchy and rank ordering existed. Some boards and committees were more prestigious than others, and a variety of titles provided further clues regarding status. Old families normally occupied the best positions, followed by owners or managers of important businesses and corporations. Jews (and presumably blacks) were excluded.[72] As a result of the willingness of individuals to serve in this status-defining network, Bay City had a well-financed public library, art collection, and private hospital.

Robert Schulze found the same pattern in the big city he called Cibola.[73] As in Bay City, Cibola was governed during the nineteenth century by economic and social elites who participated directly in public affairs. In the twentieth century, these elites shifted their participation to voluntary associations. Politics came to be viewed as a controversial activity that could make corporate executives unpopular. Participation in private associations carried no risk and endeared corporations to the local community.

A study of a city the researchers called Bigtown discovered similar motivations for corporate managers to participate in civic committees.[74] Through these committees, "a conservative, business-oriented ideology" was promoted, and "undesirables" were screened out of important community affairs.

It frequently happens in the course of a meeting that someone will call attention to the heavy burden of civic responsibilities that is carried by a small proportion of the population. Someone will say, "My God, it's a shame that just a few of us have to do all the work. Why, this community is just full of talented people who could help a lot, if only they wouldn't shirk their civic duties."

At this point heads will nod vigorous assent, and comments along the same line will be made by several persons. Then someone else will say, "Yes, all of this is true, but we have to select people we can depend on." Everybody agrees emphatically with this too, so the idea of enlarging the circle of policymakers is dropped.[75]

In St. Louis, as in all cities, most United Way executive positions are held by the chief executive officers of the major corporations or, on rare occasion, by their wives. There is a complex network of social welfare agencies in St. Louis, but they are tightly interlocked.

Boards of voluntary agencies, like their corporate counterparts, have interlocking directorates. This fosters consensus . . . in decision-making and contributes to the domination of social policy by business influentials. Because boards of community agencies are self-perpetuating, executives from these corporations can nominate each other as they rotate off one board of directors on to the board of another agency. Many corporate executives hold multiple board memberships.[76]

An organization of prominent corporate leaders, Civic Progress, Inc., dominates private philanthropy in St. Louis. Not only does it screen charities through its control of the United Fund (now United Way), but it has created many of the private agencies in St. Louis that expend federal funds. For example, it created the United Fund, the Hospital Planning Commission, and the Regional Industrial Development Corporation. It influenced the Model Cities Agency and the Human Development Corporation (St. Louis's poverty agency) by having representatives in those organizations.[77] When St. Louis's Legal Services organization represented blacks who were protesting the all-white Veiled Prophet Ball, the premier annual event for debutantes in St. Louis, the United Way cut off funding, which seriously reduced legal services for the poor for many years.

The extent of overall influence exerted by private welfare institutions no doubt varies from city to city. In St. Louis it is considerable. In 1975, the United Way had 150 volunteer directors and 40,000 fund-raising volunteers. Every prominent private welfare agency in St. Louis relies to some extent on United Way funding; altogether, these number about 100. Additionally, the St. Louis Symphony and Art Museum are presided over by closed committees composed of social and corporate elite members of the community. In sum, a very large area of social policy is kept private in St. Louis.

The legacy left by the growth of the private welfare and philanthropic sector is an important one, for it was one of the developments during the era of reform that helped to trivialize city politics by reducing its status and functions. Private social welfare successfully kept important social welfare activities out of the public realm.

Reformers who chose to change rather than opt out of public service viewed "politics" as evil and unnecessary and tried to replace it with cost accounting and "expert" management. Thus government's proper role was not viewed as arbitrating the various demands made by political groups, but as providing low-cost municipal services.

The consequences of both of these developments was to institutionalize and legitimize business influence in local government and control of most resources by social and economic elites. The city was to be run not only as a business but *for* business. As in the nineteenth century, the city's main reason for being was to provide a hospitable environment for business operations. By throwing "undesirable" elements out of politics and by reducing the importance of politics, this objective was accomplished.

The Reform Legacy

In their campaigns for electoral and governmental reform, the municipal reformers sought to install governments that would be free of political conflict. They assumed that their own conceptions of the public interest were objectively true and beyond challenge. The answer to class tensions was not a redistribution of political and economic power. It was, rather, a brand of social reform that would perpetuate existing social, economic, and governmental institutions but *make them more efficient* and therefore allegedly more beneficial to all classes of people. Reformers viewed corruption and inefficiency as injurious to the poor as much as to themselves. They self-righteously viewed their attacks on the machines, and their campaigns for "better" government, as activities that saved the Great Unwashed from themselves.

Reformers were often disingenuous. They knew full well that the reforms they advocated were not very democratic. Centralized elections and government dominated by bureaucratic "experts" were not accessible to people without the advantages of education, status, and wealth; but above all, municipal reformers feared mass democracy. "Too much" democracy introduced potentially devisive conflict over the purposes and responsibilities of government.

It is often, and logically, assumed that the party machines died out because of the reformers' successes. During the 1930s, most of the machines withered away. After World War II, the surviving organizations were considered anachronisms of a bygone era. The only successful machine existed in Chicago, resurrected by Richard J. Daley in 1953 and finally losing its grip in the late 1970s, after Daley's death.

But the demise of the machines is probably *not* the main legacy of the municipal reform movement. In big cities the reformers usually lacked the electoral majorities necessary for achieving reform; and, in any case, powerful machines often could survive nonpartisan elections and civil service reform, Chicago's machine being the best example.

The machines died basically because they could not successfully adapt to fundamental national transformations affecting cities and their populations. Three developments especially stand out. First, foreign immigration was severely restricted in the early 1920s, a political development of immense national importance (discussed in Chapter 5). The immigrant base that gave the machines its bloc votes was bound, thereafter, to erode. Indeed, this happened rapidly after World War II. The second devastating blow to the machines occurred when immigrants began to improve their economic position. During and after World War II, people of immigrant stock joined the ranks of the middle class, and they joined the mass movement to the suburbs. Precinct captains saw their constituents moving (or they moved, too), being replaced by blacks or poor whites from Appalachia and elsewhere.

The final blow to the machines was delivered by the New Deal programs of the 1930s. Machines thrived on patronage jobs and handouts. When the federal government began hiring the unemployed during the Great Depression, and when federally assisted welfare programs became available to some of the poor, the machines were, for the first time, put in direct competition. Now the federal government provided material benefits, and the machines were allowed only in rare instances to distribute federal jobs and welfare benefits. The machines did not do well in a competitive environment.

In the 1930s and 1940s, reformers sometimes delivered the *coup de grace* to machine organizations already weakened by these developments. Their instrument was law enforcement more often than structural reform. Machines were notoriously corrupt. Thus, they became handy targets for sensational indictments and prosecutions.

What replaced the machines? Rarely, in big cities, were reformers able to realize their ideals of efficiency and good management. Many cities went through a period when nobody could make effective decisions. Stronger city governments came about when political leaders forged alliances with business groups that feared the loss of their investments in downtown property. The urban renewal coalitions of the 1950s and 1960s replaced the machines. They delivered material rewards, but now to downtown business and some of the middle class, and they married private resources with public power into a coalition with sufficient authority to govern. This story is told in Chapter 9.

References

1. William L. Riordon, *Plunkitt of Tammany Hall* (New York: E.P. Dutton, 1963), p. 17.

2. James Bryce, *The American Commonwealth*, 3d rev. ed., vol. 1 (New York: Macmillan, 1924), p. 642.

3. H. E. Deming, *The Government of American Cities: A Program of Democracy* (London and New York: G. P. Putnam's Sons, 1909), p. 194.

4. Michael B. Katz, *School Reform: Past and Present* (Boston: Little, Brown, 1971), p. 169, quoted from the *Massachusetts Teacher*, October 1851.

5. George E. Mowry, *The Era of Theodore Roosevelt, 1900–1912* (New York: Harper and Row, 1958), p. 92.

6. Josiah Strong, *Our Country*, ed. Jurgen Herbst (Cambridge, Mass.: The Belknap Press of Harvard University Press, 1963 [first published in 1886]), p. 55.

7. James Weinstein, *The Corporate Ideal in the Liberal State, 1900–1918* (Boston: Beacon Press, 1968).

8. Melvin G. Holli, "Urban Reform in the Progressive Era," in *The Progressive Era*, ed. Louis L. Gould (Syracuse, N.Y.: Syracuse University Press, 1974), p. 137.

9. Frank Mann Stewart, *A Half Century of Municipal Reform: The History of the National Municipal League* (Berkeley: University of California Press, 1950), chap. 1.

10. Samuel Haber, *Efficiency and Uplift: Scientific Management in the Progressive Era, 1890–1920* (Chicago: University of Chicago Press, 1964), pp. 99.

11. Edward C. Banfield, ed., *Urban Government: A Reader in Administration and Politics* (New York: The Free Press, 1969), pp. 271–272. Selection from Andrew D. White, "The Government of American Cities," *Forum*, December 1890.

12. Ernest S. Griffith, *A History of American City Government, 1900–1920* (New York: Praeger, 1974), p. 71.

13. Griffith, p. 71.

14. Richard S. Childs, *Civic Victories: The Story of an Unfinished Revolution* (New York: Harper and Brothers, 1952), p. 299. In this passage, Childs was also referring to the short ballot reform in conjunction with nonpartisanship.

15. Banfield, *Urban Government*, p. 275. Selection from Brand Whitlock, *Forty Years of It*, preface by Allen White (New York and London: Appleton, 1925 [first published 1914]).

16. Haber, *Efficiency and Uplift*, pp. 99–101.

17. Banfield, *Urban Government*, pp. 272 and 274. Selection from White "The Government of American Cities," *Forum*, December 1890.

18. Griffith, *A History of American City Government*, p. 130.

19. Griffith, p. 131.

20. Willis D. Hawley, *Nonpartisan Elections and the Case for Party Politics* (New York: John Wiley, 1973), p. 14. The subsequent material is drawn from Hawley, pp. 15–18.

21. Weinstein, *The Corporate Ideal*, p. 109. Subsequent information on the Dayton election is from Weinstein.

22. Samuel P. Hays, "The Politics of Reform in Municipal Government in the Progressive Era," *Social Change and Urban Politics: Readings*, ed. Daniel N. Gordon (Englewood Cliffs, N.J.: Prentice-Hall, 1973), pp. 107–127. In Pittsburgh, as in many other cities, the reformers were able to enact the reform by pushing through state legislation abolishing ward boundaries.

23. Holli, "Urban Reform in the Progressive Era," p. 144.

24. Haber, *Efficiency and Uplift*, p. 56.

25. William James, quoted in Haber, pp. 57–58.

26. Frederick Winslow Taylor, *The Principles of Scientific Management* (New York: Harper and Brothers, 1919 [first published 1911]).

27. Taylor, p. 140.

28. Taylor, p. 7.

29. Harold A. Stone, Don K. Price, and Kathryn H. Stone, *City Manager Government in the United States: A Review after Twenty-five Years* (Chicago: Public Administration Service, 1940), p. 5.

30. Henry Brueré, *The New City Government: A Discussion of Municipal Administration Based on a Survey of Ten Commission-governed Cities* (New York: Appleton, 1912).

31. Brueré, p. v.

32. Brueré, p. 23.

33. Brueré, pp. 27–29.

34. Robert A. Caro, *The Power Broker: Robert Moses and the Fall of New York* (New York: Alfred A. Knopf, 1974), p. 75.

35. Melvin B. Holli, *Reform in Detroit: Hazen S. Pingree and Urban Politics* (New York: Oxford University Press, 1969), p. 167.

36. Taylor, *The Principles of Scientific Management*, p. 20.

37. Haber, *Efficiency and Uplift*, p. 115.

38. Stone, Price, and Stone, *City Manager Government*, p. 4.

39. Stone, Price, and Stone, p. 4.

40. Martin J. Schiesl, *The Politics of Municipal Reform: Municipal Administration and Reform in America, 1880–1920* (Berkeley: University of California Press, 1977), pp. 134–135.

41. Quoted in Weinstein, *The Corporate Ideal*, p. 96.

42. Clinton R. Woodruff, ed., *City Government by Commission* (New York: Appleton, 1911), pp. 293–294.

43. Childs, *Civic Victories*, p. 138.

44. Hays, "The Politics of Reform," p. 116.

45. Weinstein, *The Corporate Ideal*, p. 99.

46. Childs, *Civic Victories*, p. 137.

47. Childs, p. 137.

48. Stone, Price and Stone, *City Manager Government*, p. 5.

49. Griffith, *A History of American City Government*, p. 167.

50. Griffith, p. 166; and Schiesl, *Politics of Municipal Reform*, pp. 175–176.

51. Weinstein, *The Corporate Ideal*, pp. 115–116.

52. Quoted in Stone, Price, and Stone, *City Manager Government*, p. 27.

53. Stone, Price, and Stone, p. 37.

54. Stone, Price, and Stone, p. 43.

55. Hays, "The Politics of Reform," p. 111.

56. Griffith, *A History of American City Government*.

57. Mowry, *The Era of Theodore Roosevelt*, p. 86. Mowry claims the reformers represented the "solid middle class," but his own data belie this classification.

58. Griffith, *A History of American City Government*, p. 21. The subsequent studies are reported in Griffith.

59. Though most historians have labeled the reformers as "middle class," empirical research uniformly documents upper-class occupations, incomes, and educational status. It defies common sense to think that middle-class people would have had the time or the personal resources to participate in politics as active reformers. Middle-class bank and store clerks, accountants, small business owners, sales clerks, schoolteachers, and small-town lawyers and college professors normally worked sixty-hour weeks, with perhaps Sunday off. Their salaries were little above those of working-class skilled laborers. If college-educated (most weren't), their degrees were usually granted by small, unprestigious private colleges or state schools. Then as now, only a very small percentage of the middle class participated in politics at any level. Much of the problem with the historians' research is that they have rarely provided careful definitions of social class. Often the term *middle class* seems to cover everyone except immigrant unskilled laborers.

60. Hays, "The Politics of Reform," p. 111.

61. Hays, p. 111; also Weinstein, *The Corporate Ideal*, pp. 99–103.

62. Weinstein, *The Corporate Ideal*, pp. 103–105; and Stone, Price and Stone, *City Manager Government*, pp. 32–50.

63. Weinstein, *The Corporate Ideal*, pp. 106–109.

64. Edward C. Hayes, *Power Structure and Urban Policy: Who Rules in Oakland?* (New York: McGraw-Hill, 1972), p. 11.

65. Hayes, pp. 13–14.

66. Stone, Price, and Stone, *City Manager Government*, pp. 35–36. Several other case studies in this book reveal a similar bias.

67. Quoted in Weinstein, *The Corporate Ideal*, pp. 106, 107.

68. Hays, "The Politics of Reform," p. 116.

69. James Q. Wilson, *Negro Politics: The Search for Leadership* (New York: The Free Press, 1960), p. 27. Subsequent material in this paragraph is drawn from Wilson, p. 27–32.

70. Wilson, p. 26.

71. Peter H. Rossi and Alice S. Rossi, "An Historical Perspective on the Functions of Local Politics," in *Social Change and Urban Politics*, ed. Gordon, pp. 49–60. Bay City is a fictitious name for a New England town.

72. Rossi and Rossi, p. 59.

73. Robert O. Schulze, "The Role of Economic Dominants in Community Power Structure," in *Social Change and Urban Politics*, ed. Gordon, pp. 40–48. Cibola is a fictitious name for a large city in the United States.

74. Roland J. Pellegrin and Charles E. Coates, "Absentee-Owned Corporations and Community Power Structure," *Social Change and Urban Politics*, ed. Gordon, pp. 65–74. Bigtown is a fictitious name for a large city in the United States.

75. Pellegrin and Coates, pp. 71–72.

76. Richard E. Edgar, *Urban Power and Social Welfare: Corporate Influence in an American City* (Beverly Hills, Calif.: Sage Publications, 1970), pp. 181–182.

77. Edgar, pp. 182–183.

Chapter 5

THE CITIES' RISE TO NATIONAL POWER

The Changing Political Balance

In 1912, a Harvard political scientist wrote that "before many years have passed, the urban population of the United States will have gained numerical mastery."[1] This judgment was based on a simple calculation of demographic change. Although a nascent suburbanization process could be discerned in the early years of the twentieth century, total population movement to the cities still far outweighed the suburban shift.[2] Until the Great Depression years, the cities continued to burgeon. This fact alone did not mean that the American tradition of small government and laissez faire individualism would be challenged. Rather, the danger that cities posed to traditional American values was rooted in the *composition* of city populations.

In the thirty years from 1890 to 1920, more than 18 million immigrants poured into America's cities. These new immigrants were more "foreign" than those who had arrived before, coming mainly from Italy, Poland, Russia, Greece, and Eastern Europe. Overwhelmingly Catholic or Jewish, they came to cities that were already industrialized and class conscious. They made up the preponderance of the working force in the iron and steel, meatpacking, mining, and textile industries. They shared no collective memories of the frontier or the Civil War, much less of the American Revolution. Few spoke English, and many were illiterate even in their native language. To "native" Americans, New York City seemed to be a foreign island, an alien land within, to be controlled and disciplined.

Politics in the states had been motivated by this perception of cities as "enemy country" throughout the nineteenth century. State legislatures had placed stringent limits on the powers of municipal officials and had frequently assumed control of police departments, utilities boards, and other city functions. In the twentieth century, the distrust of cities amplified into several national movements, all intent on keeping the "dangerous elements" within the cities in their place.

These movements failed in their objective. The same characteristic that made the cities seem so threatening, their ethnic composition, also held the potential for a more or less unified urban coalition. In the election of 1928, ethnic populations in the cities began to align with the national Democratic party, whose presidential candidate, New York Governor Al Smith, was the first Roman Catholic nominated by a major party. With the Roosevelt landslide of 1932, the fate of the Democratic party was linked to the cities. For the first time, the cities began to wield influence in national politics. The efforts to control the cities were doomed when the national political parties gained an "interest in creating and maintaining national party identifications in the major cities of the country."[3]

National Politics and the Cities

Neither of the major political parties had ever paid much attention to the cities. For the most part, this was a result of the cities' position in the federal system. Not only were cities at the bottom of the intergovernmental hierarchy, but it was generally assumed that the federal government had no legitimate interest in local affairs.

The cities were invisible in national politics because they did not fit into the coalitional structure of the national Republican and Democratic parties. Following the Civil War, each of the parties appealed to distinct sectional interests. The Republicans, the triumphant party of Lincoln, emerged from the war as the dominant national party controlling Congress and the presidency. Representing eastern finance, industry, and commerce, they enacted high tariffs on foreign imports, gave land to the railroads for western expansion, and financed canal and river improvements. Republicans opposed taxes on business, encouraged private exploitation (mining, grazing, homesteading) of federal lands in the West, used troops to quell strikes, and generally promoted a laissez faire ideology.

The Republican party appealed to other political interests, too. It was popular in the middle- and working-class electorates in the North because of the Civil War, and because it presided during a period of generalized economic expansion. In the prairie states and in the West, "cattle barons, lumber kings, the mineral exploiters, the land speculators, and the humble homesteaders"[4] identified their prospects with the Republican party. By identifying with the ideas of competitive individualism, the Republican party appealed to all those elements that hankered after the "main chance":

> Thanks to a deep-rooted American ideology of individual enterprise, even the small farmers generally remained faithful to the party. . . . They, too, were entrepreneurs, after a fashion.[5]

The Republicans fit well with the post–Civil War climate of exploitation of natural resources and glorification of unfettered business enterprise.

The Democrats became the party of protest. Southerners joined with a loose coalition of groups opposed to eastern banks and corporations, the railroads, and "big money." The worst problem with the Democrats' coalition was its instability, for its major issues played on midwestern small farmers' insecurities, southerners' resentments, and (occasionally) labor's opposition to business. During times of prosperity, the party suffered. Discontent over economic conditions constituted its strength. Its only secure base was in the South, where race remained the paramount political issue.

In 1896, Democrats campaigned on a platform that advocated government intervention to protect the common man against the "money interests," symbolized by Andrew Mellon, Andrew Carnegie, James Fisk, and J. P. Morgan. With William Jennings Bryan of Nebraska as its presidential candidate, the Democratic party advocated lower tariffs to force eastern businesses to compete with foreign producers. Bryan called for a paper currency backed by silver as well as by gold. Such a move would have led to inflation and currency instability, benefiting heavily indebted small business owners and farmers. The Democrats also proposed a graduated income tax, a government takeover of land grants previously given to the railroads, and public ownership of telegraphs and telephones. These positions failed to appeal to workers in the cities, who felt that tariffs and sound money protected their jobs. They did, however, help create a party with an alternative to laissez faire doctrines, and over the next three decades the Democrats slowly transformed into an organization with a distinct social class identity.

Several events between the elections of 1896 and 1932 changed the

Democratic party. In the 1900 election, which Bryan also lost, the potential appeal to urban voters became apparent. Bryan assailed trusts and monopolies, urged the direct election of senators, opposed government injunctions against strikes, and favored the creation of a Department of Labor. Although his audience was southern and western agrarian, his antibusiness positions clearly represented a class, not only a sectional concern.

Bryan saw the possibility of uniting western farmers and southerners with industrial labor in a generalized opposition to big business dominance of the nation's money supply and policies. Finding few friends among the Republicans, the American Federation of Labor (AFL) endorsed Bryan in his third campaign in 1908.

After the Democrats won the 1912 election, with New Jersey governor and former Princeton University president Woodrow Wilson leading the ticket, the coalitional nature of the party became apparent in new policies. The Underwood-Simmons Act of 1913 lowered tariffs for the first time since 1857 and put wool, lumber, paper, wood pulp, steel rails, and sugar on a free trade list. Prices soon declined. A graduated income tax was adopted, shifting taxes from excises and tariffs, which consumers had paid in higher prices, to direct taxation of earnings. The Federal Reserve Act of 1913 spread the money supply more evenly across the nation by establishing a dozen regional banks to receive federal deposits and to distribute the new federal reserve notes, which did not have to be backed by full value in gold reserves. The Clayton and Federal Trade Acts outlawed some unfair business practices (such as price fixing) and established boards for voluntary mediation between management and labor, created an eight-hour day for railroad workers, and provided federal administrative assistance to states and companies to set up workmen's compensation programs. The Federal Farm Loan Act extended limited credit to farmers. Additionally, the Wilson administration favored child labor and women's hours laws, exempted labor unions from anitrust legislation, and encouraged employers to negotiate with organized labor. Against this background, the Republican party continued to favor harsh action against unions and tariffs to protect business.

Nevertheless, urban ethnic voters did not identify strongly with the national Democratic party. Many of the urban party machines (as in Chicago until 1932) were Republican. Democratic machine politicians paid little attention to national politics. Neither the voters nor the politicians paid much attention to national candidates and issues. Machine politicians had learned their trade in their neighborhoods and wards—theirs was a politics of ethnicity and tradeoffs, not of issues. The machines were peculiarly local organizations, a product of the segregation of ethnic voters from the rest of American society. The city machines were distant from state and national political organizations.

There was little pay or respect for ethnic politicians who were elected to the state legislature or who took part in national electoral contests. Being elected to the state legislature meant living in a small, conservative upstate or downstate town like Albany, New York, or Springfield, Massachusetts away from friends, family, and "boodle." It could be the kiss of death to be sent "away" by the machine to Albany or Washington. When, at the age of thirty, Al Smith was sent by Tammany Hall to Albany, he felt exiled:

> Al Smith went to Albany unprepared to be a legislator—or even to sleep away from home . . . overcome by the intricacies of the legislative process, he sat day after day in the high-ceilinged chamber in silence.
>
> As he sat there staring down at the desk, a page boy would deposit another pile of bills on it. The wording was difficult enough for the expert. It might have been designed to mock a man whose schooling had ended in the eighth grade, who had never liked to read even the simple books of childhood, who, he had once said, had in his entire life read only one book cover to cover: *The Life of John L. Sullivan*.[6]

Before Al Smith, no Tammany politician had ever done much in Albany.

Voters, too, felt isolated from national political issues. Their political activity was motivated by their personal loyalties and by their pocketbooks. When precinct captains took them to the polls, they voted for a local party organization, not for a cause. What in their background would excite them about national issues and candidates—tariff policy, free silver, William Jennings Bryan, Woodrow Wilson? The upshot was that although many cities were dominated by powerful party organizations, the leaders of these organizations and their voters had only occasionally become important in gubernatorial contests and had never been noticed in presidential elections. The rise of the cities in national politics began only when nativist Protestant elements launched a national assault on the city machines and their immigrant constituency. In doing so, they created issues that an urban electorate could easily understand.

Although Wilson had adopted many programs in response to labor pressure (and Bryan had advocated a Labor Department and favored outlawing strike injunctions) the Democratic party had not transformed itself into anything resembling an urban party. Far from it. Its strength was still to be found in the country, not the city. When the urban wing of the party began to grow in strength, a potentially devastating split developed along urban-rural lines. The rural elements of the party had not minded the votes it could get in the cities, so long as the cities did not become dominant. By the 1920s, however, the party was bitterly divided.

A New Urban Consciousness

The cleavages within the Democratic party mirrored the urban-rural conflict in the nation. Rural Democrats feared that the urban wing of their party might someday command a majority. A similar concern preyed on the minds of native Protestants. What would happen to political and religious traditions if the barbarous hordes from Europe took over? The ever-present nineteenth century nervousness about the "strangers in the land" escalated into a national phobia in the twentieth century.

Prohibition was a direct assault on the cities. Proposed to the states by Congress in 1917 and ratified in 1919, the Eighteenth Amendment prohibited the sale, use, and distribution of alcoholic beverages. Small-town Methodists and Baptists, joined in their crusade by upper- and middle-class Protestants in the cities and in the new suburbs, hoped to reduce poverty, improve workers' efficiency and family life, and end immorality and crime by forcing abstinence on society's "derelicts." Prohibition became the compelling political issue of the 1920s, for it represented a frontal assault upon the cultural values and customs of the immigrants.

> [Drinking] was associated with the saloonkeepers who ran the city machines and who used the votes of the whiskey-loving immigrant . . . with the German brewers and their "disloyal" compatriots who drank beer and ale. . . . The cities, which resisted the idea that "thou shalt not" was the fundamental precept of living, were always hostile to prohibition. The prohibitionists, in turn, regarded the city as their chief enemy, and prohibitionism and a pervasive antiurbanism went hand-in-hand.[7]

To rural Americans and native-born urban dwellers, the sins of liquor were indistinguishable from the sins of the immigrants. Southern and western newspapers reflexively connected crime, national origin, and liquor. When it was not legitimate to attack foreigners directly, it was easy to do it through the surrogate liquor issue, allowing "prohibition partisans to talk about morality when in reality they were worried about cultural dominance and political supremacy."[8]

Prohibition was intimately connected to religious conflict. To Protestant Americans, the Roman Catholic church was the symbol of evil incarnate. It signified ostentatious authority, the robes, the ceremony, and the architecture bespeaking a menacing presence threatening the simplicity and informality of small-town life. Worse was the fear of papal imperialism. Like the right-wing groups of the 1950s that were haunted by the specter of an international Community conspiracy, poised to subvert American culture, fundamentalists of the early twentieth century were haunted by the fear of a Roman Catholic church intent on subverting civil authority around the world.

Feeding on these fears, the Ku Klux Klan attracted millions of members. Revived in Atlanta in 1915, the Klan enjoyed spectacular growth during the 1920s in both the North and South. Klan membership mushroomed in California, Oregon, Indiana, Illinois, Ohio, Oklahoma, Texas, Arkansas, and throughout the South. By 1924, 40 percent of the Klan's membership resided in Ohio, Indiana, and Illinois. Half its membership was located in cities of more than 50,000, with large chapters in such cities as Chicago, Detroit, Indianapolis, Pittsburgh, Baltimore, and Buffalo.[9] The Klan was a powerful political force until at least the mid-1920s. It helped elect a United States senator; governors in Georgia, Alabama, Oregon, and California; and seventy-five members of the House of Representatives.

While the Klan found its strongest support among lower-middle-class Americans, its basic message appealed to a wide audience. Nationalism and racism were further inflamed when the United States entered World War I. German-Americans and people of Italian descent were obvious targets, for their loyalty was suspected by Americans whose anti-immigrant passions were fanned by wartime propaganda. The popular press also kindled racist fears. In 1916, Madison Grant, curator of New York City's Museum of National History, published *The Passing of the Great Race*, which worried that Aryans were being threatened by dark-skinned races. His book was elevated to the status of a scientific work, along with Lothrop Stoddard's *The Rising Tide of Color Against the White World-Supremacy* (1921).

Congress responded to this national phobia with the Emergency Quota Act of 1921 and the National Origins Act of 1924. Both laws received support from intellectuals, labor, southerners, western farmers, and other major nonimmigrant groups. The Emergency Quota Act reaffirmed exclusion of Orientals and established a national origins quota of 3 percent of each nationality's proportion of the United States population recorded in the 1910 census. The law succeeded in cutting immigration from 805,228 in 1920 to 309,556 in 1921–1922.[10]

The National Origins Act of 1924 further reduced the origins quota to 2 percent and established the 1890 census as the basis for calculating the quota. These changes drastically reduced the number of Southern and Eastern European immigrants allowed into the country. Total immigration declined from 357,803 in 1923–1924 to 164,667 in 1924–1925. Italian immigration was reduced by 90 percent, British and Irish immigration by only 19 percent.[11]

In debates on the bills, members of Congress reviled the foreign-born of the cities in language not unlike that found in Ku Klux Klan pamphlets. This assault helped to create a new political consciousness among the immigrants. In the 1920s, the tensions between city and country and between native-born and foreign-born entered the national political arena.

The Urban Wing of the Democratic Party

The prosperity of the 1920s dealt the Democratic party a devastating blow. The Democrats' coalition could be held together only by shared grievances. The party was composed of an unlikely combination of eastern and northern urban ethnics, western farmers and Prohibitionists, and southern, dry, Klan-saturated fundamentalists. The 1924 Democratic convention showed the untidy nature of this coalition.

The Democrats treated the first radio audience of a national convention to a futile 103-ballot performance in 1924. After sixteen days, they finally nominated a presidential candidate neither the agrarians nor the city factions wanted.

At the convention in Madison Square Garden, New York City, the galleries booed the speeches of southerners and westerners, especially when William Jennings Bryan asked the convention not to condemn the Ku Klux Klan by name. The resolution to condemn the Klan brought forth such heated oratory that police were brought into the Garden in case a free-for-all broke out. Delegates shouted and cursed each other; when the final vote was taken, the resolution to condemn the Klan lost by 542 3/20 to 541 3/20. Demands for a recount were drowned out when the band struck up "Marching Through Georgia." All in all, it enraged the eastern delegates.

The southern and western delegates were no happier. They were disoriented and frightened by the crowds and the din of New York City. They found New Yorkers unfriendly and rude, and the city seemed frighteningly easy to get lost in. Delegates who "wandered downtown to Fourteenth Street to gawk at Tammany Hall with its ancient Indian above the door reacted as if they expected to see an ogre come popping out. Almost all delegates were dismayed by the New York traffic, the noise and hustle."[12] Their antagonisms toward the city were reaffirmed every day the convention dragged on. Western and southern reporters found much that was wrong as well and filled their hometown newspapers with vivid accounts of the horrors of the city.[13]

Despite these divisions, only four years later, in 1928, the Democrats nominated Al Smith, the four-term governor of New York. Smith represented everything that was anathema to the city haters. He was a self-made Catholic graduate of Tammany Hall. He said "foist" instead of "first" and wore a brown derby, which only accentuated his bulbous nose and ruddy complexion. He proudly reminisced about his past, swimming in the East River and working at the Fulton Fish Market as an errand boy. Considering the divisive conflicts within the party, how could he have been nominated? Once he was, why did the anticity faction not bolt the party?

The southern and western factions had little choice but to stay. First, the Republicans were controlled entirely by business and wealthy elites, and had few concerns outside the realm of protecting business from government regulation. Second, despite their differences, the Democrats shared, however crudely, a common class interest. They had symbolically become, mostly through default by the Republicans, the nonbusiness party, the "little man's" party. Third, the western and southern factions could never hope to have a voice in national presidential politics without aligning with one of the two national parties. The southern wing had long ago learned the cost of separation in the Civil War.

The time was ripe for compromise. Few Democrats thought that Smith could win, but no candidate was available who was capable of uniting the nonurban elements behind another candidate. In addition, Smith had broad political support. As the four-term governor of New York, he had gained national prominence as a progressive governor who had created state parks and beaches, sponsored factory legislation, and financed public improvements throughout the state. He had reorganized state government, making New York the model for progressives who believed in efficiency principles. Smith was admired by progressives for his record as governor and supported by Democratic organizations with ethnic constituencies. His nomination could be denied by antiurban elements, but only at the cost of another fiasco like that in 1924—multiple ballots and a guaranteed loss for the presidential nominee. There was reason to think that Smith might have a chance. When he ran for governor in 1924, he had received 100,000 more votes than the Democratic presidential ticket in New York.

In 1928, the Democrats gave the nomination to Al Smith. Although he lost the election, his candidacy marked the beginning of the Democratic party's political ascendency in the big cities.

> The election of 1928 marked a significant change in the attitude of the urban masses. Both in 1920 and 1924, the twelve largest cities in the United States had, taken together, given a decisive majority to the Republicans; now the tables were turned, and the Democrats came out ahead. This, as later elections were to prove, marked the beginning of a long-term urban trend.[14]

For the Roman Catholic ethnics in the cities, Smith's campaign sharpened their perception of the national issues of Prohibition, ethnicity, and religion. Smith campaigned with his brown derby and his theme song, "The Sidewalks of New York."

The campaign was exceptionally dirty. Protestants shuddered at the idea of a Catholic in the White House. Smith's equivocal stand on Prohibition made drink a main issue in the campaign. Blue-nosed upper-class Protestants found him beneath them. The campaign highlighted the issues of

TABLE 5-1   The Revolt of the City: Voting in the Largest 12 Cities

Year	Net party plurality
1920	1,540,000 Republican
1924	1,308,000 Republican
1928	210,000 Democratic
1932	1,791,000 Democratic
1936	3,479,000 Democratic
1940	2,112,000 Democratic
1944	2,230,000 Democratic
1948	1,481,000 Democratic

The cities in this table include: New York, Chicago, Philadelphia, Pittsburgh, Detroit, Cleveland, Baltimore, St. Louis, Boston, San Francisco, Milwaukee, Los Angeles.

Source: Reprinted from the table on page 49 in *The Future of American Politics*, 3rd Revised Edition by Samuel Lubell. © 1951, 1952, 1956, 1965 by Samuel Lubell. Reprinted by permission of Harper & Row, Publishers, Inc.

race, religion, culture, and social class so clearly that never again would the ethnics be unmindful of their stake in national politics. As Table 5–1 shows, the 1928 election brought a Democratic electoral plurality to the cities of the nation. Since then, those cities have normally voted heavily Democratic, and they were the mainstay of the Democratic party's electoral strength until the 1980s.

With Al Smith's candidacy, the ground was prepared for a recognition of the cities in American politics. What cemented the relationship between the cities and the Democratic party was the Great Depression and Franklin Delano Roosevelt.

The Depression and the Cities

The Great Depression came as a shock to Americans and to their public leaders. The 1920s had been a decade of prosperity and optimism, especially for the burgeoning middle class. Business leaders and politicians sold the idea that the potential for sustained economic growth was limitless. A strong undertow of poverty ran below the surface, in the immigrant slums, on farms, and in such depressed areas as the Appalachias, but on the surface the signs of prosperity prevailed. It was an age that extolled mass consumption and complacency. The discontents about the industrial order seemed long past.

The symbolic beginning of the Great Depression occurred on October 24, 1929. On that day, "Black Thursday," disorder, panic, and confusion reigned on the New York Stock Exchange. Stock prices virtually collapsed. For several months prices had sagged, then risen, then sagged again, with each trough lower than the previous and each peak less convincing. When the bottom fell out, "the Market . . . degenerated into a wild, mad scramble to sell, . . . the Market . . . surrendered to blind, relentless fear."[15] In one morning, eleven well-known speculators committed suicide. From Wall Street the economic catastrophe rippled outward, with consequences that would fundamentally alter American politics.

Over the next three years the nation sank deeper into economic stagnation. In 1929, the unemployment rate stood at only 3.2 percent. Within a few months, the number of unemployed exceeded 4 million, representing 8.7 percent of the labor force.[16] This number doubled to 8 million unemployed in 1931—15.9 percent of the labor force. In 1932, more than 12 million workers, 23.6 percent of all workers, could not find jobs. In the depths of the depression, during the spring of 1933, about 13 million workers were unemployed, more than a quarter of a labor force of 51.5 million.[17]

Until 1940, unemployment levels dropped below 15 percent only in 1937; they remained above 20 percent in both 1934 and 1935. Most of those who managed to find work made less than before. From 1929 to 1933, the average income of workers fell by 42.5 percent.[18] Weekly wages fell from $28 in 1929 to $17 by 1932, and workers always faced the ominous threat of unemployment. Many jobs were reduced from full-time to parttime status, and employers cut wages and hours to meet payrolls. For example, U.S. Steel's payroll was cut in half from 1929 to 1933, and in 1933 it had no full-time workers at all.[19]

The productive capacity of business seemed irreparably damaged. National income fell 44.5 percent in the three years following the stock market collapse. Steel mills operated at only 12 percent capacity by 1932.[20] By that summer, stocks had fallen 83 percent below their value in September 1929.[21] By the end of 1932, 5,096 commercial banks had failed. In rural areas the picture was equally bleak. Between 1929 and 1932, farm income declined from $7 billion to $2.5 billion.[22] For many farmers the depression was simply the final blow, for their incomes had been sharply dropping throughout the 1920s.

The statistics only hint at the extent of human suffering. Between 1 and 2 million men rode the rails and gathered in "hobo jungles," or camped in thickets and railroad cars. Others lived in "Hoovervilles," collections of shacks made of boxes, scrap wood, and corrugated steel located on empty lots and city parks. Those who had been chronically poor in the 1920s were now hungry and destitute. They stood in bread lines, ate from garbage cans, or went from door to door begging. Many of the home-owning middle class lost their homes and savings. One-quarter of all homeowners lost their homes in 1932, and more than 1,000 homes a day were foreclosed in the first half of 1933.[23] By March 1933, when Franklin D. Roosevelt was inaugurated, 9 million savings accounts had been lost.[24]

Never before had the nation faced such a catastrophic economic crisis, nor was there a tradition of federal government assistance for the unemployed and destitute.[25] In earlier depressions, including the panics of the 1870s and 1890s, production and employment declined much less severely and the recovery began within a year or two.[26] What made this depression unique was that it touched all classes, its effects felt by rich and poor alike. Not that unemployment and poverty were new; far from it. In the period from 1897 to 1926, unemployment levels in four major industries constantly fluctuated around the 10 percent level.[27] Poverty was a chronic condition of industrialization and immigration. The measure of the crisis of the 1930s was the wholesale breakdown of economic institutions, not just unemployment and poverty.

No one knew how to respond. President Herbert Hoover firmly resisted intervention by the federal government and instead launched two national drives to encourage private relief. Late in 1930, he appointed the President's Emergency Committee for Employment. Its main task was to encourage state and local committees to expedite public construction (to help create jobs) and to coordinate the public and private giving of relief. In August 1931, he formed the President's Organization on Unemployment Relief, whose job was to help organize private unemployment committees in states and communities.

Despite Hoover's undying opposition to federal intervention, two major programs were funded during his administration. The Federal Home Loan Bank Act supplied capital advances to a very small number of mortgage institutions so that they could forbear rather than foreclose on mortgages in default. A few banks were saved by this program. Second, the Emergency Relief and Construction Act made $300 million in relief loans to state and local governments that could not meet their relief needs.

Hoover was hardly alone in opposing an expanded federal role. Until 1932, most governors took a "do it ourselves" attitude toward solving unemployment and its associated problems.[28] Two governors refused to work with the President's Organization on Unemployment Relief, even though federal funds were not involved.[29] The officials of financially strapped local governments were also skeptical of federal aid. In July 1931, Milwaukee's mayor wrote to the mayors of the 100 largest cities to call for a mayors' conference to request a national relief program. He got no response at all from several of the big cities, and some mayors criticized the idea on the premise that federal aid would constitute "an invasion of community rights."[30]

In the 1932 campaign, the Democrats accused Hoover of doing too much, not too little. The Democratic nominee, Franklin Delano Roosevelt, promised to balance the budget while he accused Hoover of having presided over "the greatest spending administration in peace times in all our history."[31] It was apparent that the weight of the past lay heavily on both political parties. In the face of a cultural tradition that extolled individualism and free enterprise, there was great reluctance to expand the powers of government, especially the federal government, to meet the crisis.

Nevertheless, when Roosevelt was inaugurated on March 4, 1933, he set in motion a concentrated period of reform that vastly increased the powers of the federal government in areas of business regulation, farm policy, and social insurance. Why did Roosevelt break so thoroughly with the traditions of the past?

Roosevelt's activity was motivated by the pervading sense of crisis that ushered him into the White House. Between his election in November 1932 and his inauguration the following March, the nation passed through the worst months of the depression. The economy teetered on the brink of complete collapse. In February 1933, some of the nation's biggest banks failed. "People stood in long queues with satchels and paper bags to take gold and currency away from the banks to store in mattresses and old shoe boxes. It seemed safer to put your life's savings in the attic than to trust the financial institutions in the country."[32] Roosevelt wondered if there would be anything left to salvage by inauguration day. Indeed, by March 4, thirty-eight states had closed their banks and, on that day, the governors of New York and Illinois closed the nation's biggest banks.[33] The New York Stock Exchange had stopped trading. The Kansas City and Chicago Board of Trade had closed their doors. "In the once-busy grain pits of Chicago, in the canyons of Wall Street, all was silent."[34]

It was also one of the harshest winters on record. In desperation, people overran relief offices and rioted at bank closings. Relief marchers invaded state legislative chambers. Farmers tried to stop foreclosure proceedings and blockaded roads. Amid marches, riots, arrests, and jailings, politicians feared revolution and Communism.

The first 100 days of Roosevelt's administration were characterized by frenetic activity in the executive branch and by a compliant Congress.[35] On March 9, Roosevelt signed the Emergency Banking Act. The act extended financial assistance to bankers so they could reopen their doors, and also gave the government authority to reorganize banks and to control bank credit policies. It received a unanimous vote from a panicked Congress, sight unseen. There were other major pieces of legislation. The

Civilian Conservation Corps (CCC) was formed (signed, March 31); this was followed by the Agricultural Adjustment Act and the Federal Emergency Relief Act (May 12); the Tennessee Valley Authority (May 18); the Federal "Truth in Securities" Act (May 27); the Home Owners' Loan Act (June 13), establishing the Home Owners' Loan Corporation (HOLC); the National Industrial Recovery Act (June 16); and more than a score of other bills. Most of the legislative onslaught was designed to stimulate, regulate, and stabilize the most important institutions in the economy. But the benefits filtered down. After the Emergency Banking Act was passed, depositors gained confidence and redeposited their savings. Under the National Housing Act (adopted in 1934), home buyers could secure long-term mortgages from banks whose loans were guaranteed by the federal government. Foreclosures on farms and homes were sharply reduced when the government agreed, through the Farm Credit Administration and HOLC, to buy up defaulted mortgages. Thus, New Deal programs affected many people's lives by salvaging their houses, farms, and savings. Nevertheless, the New Deal's attempts to reform the economy were designed more to bring stability and growth to financial institutions than to fight poverty and destitution. Home and farm programs primarily helped the nation's important economic institutions and secondarily aided the heavily mortgaged middle class.

The other side of the New Deal included its public works and relief programs. These programs assisted millions of unemployed and penniless people. They vastly expanded the Democratic coalition by bringing into the fold the same elements that had identified with Al Smith. For millions of families, the New Deal meant the difference between hunger and having food; between ego-crippling unemployment and finding a job. Between 1933 and 1937, the federal government administered public works programs for several million people and supplied direct relief to several million more.

The earliest of the public works programs was the Civilian Conservation Corps, established on March 31, 1933. In all, more than 2.5 million boys and young men were employed by the CCC. In 1935 alone, 500,000 men were living in CCC camps. They planted trees, built dams, fought fires, stocked fish, built lookout towers, dug ditches and canals, strung telephone lines, and built and improved bridges, roads, and trails. Their contribution to conservation was enormous; the CCC was responsible for more than half of all the forest ever planted in the United States.[36]

The Civil Works Administration (CWA) was much larger and broader in scope. Established in November 1933, it employed 4.1 million people by the third week of January 1934.[37] In a few months it employed nearly a third of the unemployed labor force. Although the CWA lasted for less than a year—Roosevelt ended it in the spring of 1934 because he thought it was too costly—it enabled many families to survive the bitter winter of 1934. The CWA was "immensely popular—with merchants, with local officials, and with workers," and its demise was resisted in Congress.[38]

The Public Works Administration (PWA) enjoyed a longer run, and its impact was more lasting. In six years, from 1933 to 1939, the PWA built 70 percent of the new school buildings in the nation, and 35 percent of the hospitals and public health facilities.[39]

The Federal Emergency Relief Act (FERA), signed into law on May 12, 1935, was never as popular as the public works programs, for it undercut the cherished principles of work and independence. Roosevelt himself viewed the Federal Emergency Relief Administration with distaste, thinking that it would sap the moral strength of the poor. Although Roosevelt constantly sought ways to cut its budget, and though its benefit levels were extraordinarily low, the FERA was mandated by the want and the civil disorder that prevailed in Roosevelt's first term. In the winter of 1934, 20 million people received FERA funds.[40]

The FERA was treated as an embarrassing necessity. The government's response was understood to be an emergency measure; it was comparable to helping victims of such catastrophes as floods, earthquakes, and tornadoes. Despite its importance and scope, it was never given widespread publicity. Congressional debate on the FERA received no consequential coverage. When the act was passed on May 9, 1933, *The New York Times* mentioned it only on page 3, in a column listing legislation passed by Congress. When it was signed by President Roosevelt on May 12, it made page 21 of the *Times*, but only in reference to the appointment of the administrator. The FERA was a black sheep in a culture that extolled individualism, competition, and hard work.

Franklin Roosevelt often expressed doubts about relief and public works programs. He preferred economic recovery to government spending. But his response to the economic emergency broadened the base of the Democratic party. Public works and relief created a loyal following among minorities and ethnics in the cities and among the working class everywhere. The party became identified in many people's minds as the "little man's" party. Voting in small towns then (and now) often split between the Republicans on the "right" side of the tracks and the working class and poor on the other.

The most reliable Democratic following was located in the cities. Urban ethnics became solidly Democratic, and the loyalty of black voters to the Republican party was broken by New Deal programs. Before the 1936 election, a prominent black publisher counseled, "My friends, go turn Lincoln's picture to the wall. That debt has been paid in full."[41] In the 1936 election, blacks gave Roosevelt 75 percent of their votes.

The Great Depression revolutionized the group composition of the party system in the United States. Both parties became class-oriented, a fact that shifted the center of gravity for the Democrats to the northern cities, where large numbers of the working class and poor were concentrated. Additionally, so many people benefited through New Deal programs that the voting coalition supporting the party broadened sufficiently to ensure that the Democrats would become the ascendant national party. In 1936, a Gallup poll found that 59 percent of farmers favored Roosevelt (Agricultural Adjustment Act, Farm Credit Administration, Farm Mortgage Corporation, abolition of the gold standard), 61 percent of white-collar workers (bank regulation, FHA, savings deposit insurance), 80 percent of organized labor (government recognition of collective bargaining, unemployment insurance, work relief), and 68 percent of people under twenty-five (Civilian Conservation Corps, National Youth Administration). Among lower income groups, 76 percent favored Roosevelt, compared with 60 percent of the middle class.[42] In contrast, upper-income groups identified overwhelmingly with the Republican party.

The political parties became *both* class-based and organized on the basis of appeals to particular interest groups in the electorate. But no major bloc of votes became more solidly Democratic than in the cities, and this helps explain why city voters became the mainstay of the Democrats. Union members, ethnics, and blacks voted more heavily for Roosevelt in the 1936 election than any other groups in the country.

The Cities in the Intergovernmental System

The Depression years were a turning point for cities in the United States. The cities' electoral importance to the Democratic party was but one area in which they gained political clout. At least as important, especially over the long run, was that the Depression altered the structure of intergovernmental relations by bringing about a direct relationship between the cities and the federal government. The states emerged from the 1930s weakened in their ability to control the cities. Three elements stand out as key facilitators of these changes: (1) the crisis in the cities; (2) the intransigence of the states; and (3) the forging of an alliance among city officials for the purpose of securing a federal response to their problems.

The Depression initiated a financial crisis for city governments and a social crisis for the cities. In the 1920s, the cities had heavily borrowed to finance public improvements and capital construction. Already seriously in debt at the onset of the Depression, they now faced rising unemployment and poverty. Local officials could not avoid seeing at first hand the misery and want on their streets. Faced with a manifest emergency, they provided relief funds as rapidly as they could, but it was not enough.

Municipal governments simply lacked the financial resources to cope with the emergency.

During the 1920s, counties and municipalities financed a multitude of new public improvement programs. The renewed government activity represented a response to the automobile, to middle-class demands for improved public education, and to public demands for parks and recreational facilities. The auto imposed heavy new costs on local governments, as cities invested in traffic signals, police cars, garbage trucks, schoolbuses, snowplows, roads, and bus and airline terminals.

The cities also increased spending for education, constructing newer public school buildings, especially high schools, and public school libraries. Park and stadium construction also increased substantially.

Local governments made heavier investments in these areas than did either the state or federal governments. During the 1920s, counties and municipalities spent 55 to 60 percent of all public funds in the nation, and debts mounted to $9 billion.[43] From 1923 to 1927, while the states increased expenditures by 43 percent, the largest 145 cities added 79 percent in spending, and cities of 100,000 or more in population increased their budgets by 82 percent.[44] These latter cities expanded public welfare expenditures (work relief and welfare) by 391 percent from 1923 to 1932, while the states in this period added only 63 percent to their budgets. In the last year of the Hoover administration, thirteen big cities alone spent $53 million more than all the states for public welfare. In the decade of the 1920s, federal grants as a percentage of all public expenditures actually declined from 2 to 1.3 percent.[45] The thirteen biggest cities incurred 50 percent more debt during this period, and many of them were hard-pressed even at the beginning of the Depression to pay for government services and public improvements.[46]

The Depression placed unprecedented responsibilities on city officials. In an attempt to provide relief and, in some cities, public works jobs, the cities quickly exhausted their resources. Cities could not expand tax revenues to keep pace with increased responsibilities. State-imposed debt limitations did not allow the cities to borrow for general government expenditures. Additionally, by 1932 cities faced a full-scale demoralization of municipal credit when they found it impossible to sell long-term bond issues to investors. In 1932 and 1933, many states and municipalities could market no new bond issues at all, including Buffalo, Philadelphia, Cleveland, and Toledo, and the states of Mississippi and Montana.[47] Temporary loans with high interest rates replaced long-term notes.

Two-thirds of the revenue for city budgets derived from property taxes, and these declined precipitously between 1929 and 1933. As assessments on deteriorating property plummeted, property tax revenues were reduced by 20 percent during the four-year period.[48] The rate of tax delinquency increased at the same time, from 10 to 26 percent (1930–1933) in cities of over 50,000 in population.[49] Tax losses resulted in an actual reduction in the budgets of the largest thirteen cities between 1931 and 1933, from $1.8 to $1.6 billion.[50]

The cities' attempts to help the unemployed plunged them into financial crisis. Municipal governments lacked sufficient resources to treat the Depression's symptoms, yet many mayors saw this as their principal mission. Detroit's experience revealed the impossibility of the task. In the fall of 1930, Frank Murphy won a surprise victory in a special mayoralty election on a campaign promising unemployment relief.[51] His efforts to provide relief by expanding public jobs and welfare in Detroit attracted national attention. He appointed an unemployment committee, operated an employment bureau, sponsored public works, raised private donations, and consulted with private firms. Detroit did more than any other city for its unemployed, but its compassion was costly. With over 40,000 families receiving relief and one-third of the work force unemployed, it was spending $2 million a month for relief in 1931, far more than second-place Boston.[52] The burden soon brought financial disaster to the city.

By the spring of 1931, Detroit faced municipal bankruptcy. To avoid default, Murphy curtailed the city's health and recreational services and slashed the fire and police department budgets. Only an emergency bank loan allowed him to meet the June 1931 payroll. But these efforts were not sufficient. Under pressure from the New York banks that held Detroit's bonds, Murphy was forced to cut relief expenditures in half during 1932. Thousands of families were dropped from the relief rolls as it became obvious that Detroit could not solve its unemployment problems.

Other cities around the country were in the process of learning the same lesson. Finally, their problems galvanized them into concerted action. In the spring of 1932, Murphy invited the mayors of the major cities to a conference. On June 1, representatives from twenty-nine cities met in Detroit with a single purpose in mind: to get the federal government to help them with their problems. At the conference, Murphy stated the cities' case succinctly: "We have done everything humanly possible to do, and it has not been enough. The hour is at hand for the federal government to cooperate."[53] New York City's mayor likewise pleaded for assistance:

> The municipal government is the maternal, the intimate side of government; the side with heart. The Federal Government doesn't have to wander through darkened hallways of our hospitals, to witness the pain and suffering there. It doesn't have to stand in the bread lines, but the time has come when it must face the facts and its responsibility.
>
> We of the cities have diagnosed and thus far met the problem; but we have come to the end of our resources. It is now up to the Federal Government to assume its share. We can't cure conditions by ourselves.[54]

The mayors' demands for federal assistance marked a historic turning point for the cities. Historically, cities had been mere creatures of the states, with no direct ties to Washington. Only a few months before, most of the mayors had declined to attend a mayors' conference suggested by the mayor of Milwaukee.[55] Many local officials felt it was illegitimate to ask the federal government for help, and others feared any aid, lest it lead to a loss of local autonomy. But desperation finally overcame tradition.

The situation was made worse by the fact that state governments refused to respond to the cities' plight. While municipal governments' expenditures for jobs and relief skyrocketed, the states cut expenses: "As tax revenues dwindled and unemployment increased, economy in government became a magic word."[56] State governments were more concerned with balancing budgets than with alleviating human suffering. As state tax revenues declined, wholesale reductions were made in public works and construction programs. Whereas in 1928 the states had spent $1.35 billion for public works projects, this spending was reduced to $630 million by 1932 and to $290 million for the first eight months of 1933.[57] The states' budget cuts compounded the unemployment crisis.

Other government expenditures were likewise reduced. Per capita spending for highways and education declined only slightly from 1927 to 1932,[58] but in some states budgets were slashed. Tennessee, for example, failed to provide funds for its rural schools for much of 1931.[59] In 1932, many states cut deeply into their budgets: Arizona by 35 percent; Texas, Illinois, and Vermont by 25 percent; South Carolina by 33 percent. State educational institutions, especially universities, were hard hit. During 1933, education budgets were curtailed by 40 percent in Maryland, by 53 percent in Wyoming, and by more than 30 percent in several other states.[60]

Relief spending by the states went up in the early years of the Depression, from $1.00 per capita in 1927 to $3.50 four years later.[61] But the overall amount of relief spending was small and failed to come close to what was needed. The overall statistics, in any case, mask the tremendous variations among the states. From mid-1931 to the end of 1932, relief spending by the states increased from $500,000 to $100 million, but most of the money was provided by a few states, especially New York, New Jersey, and Pennsylvania.[62] When the New Deal began, only eight states were providing any money at all for relief.[63]

Local officials petitioned the states for help, and their pleas sounded more and more desperate as the Depression wore on.[64] Except in the very few states providing relief, however, no response was forthcoming. The mayors of Michigan's cities, led by Frank Murphy, became so discouraged about the possibility of receiving help from the state government that they were forced to appeal for federal assistance. Their fears that such aid would compromise local autonomy were overcome by the corruption and conservatism of their state's government.[65]

State governments were slow to respond to the needs of their cities because their legislatures were controlled by rural representatives. In state after state, legislative districts were drawn up to ensure that rural counties could outvote cities in the state legislative chambers. In Georgia, each county was represented equally in the legislature, regardless of its population.[66] Louisiana provided that each parish would have at least one representative in the state senate and house, no matter what its population, and Rhode Island applied this standard to each town.[67] Without exception, rural districts were ensured control over the legislatures of all the states. The rationale for these arrangements was sometimes stated in emotional terms, as at the Louisiana Constitution Convention of 1845, when a delegate referred to city people's tendencies to carry "those sudden passions which pervert and carry men's minds to fearful extremities."[68] Such emotionalism aside, the political stakes involved were important. If cities were allowed to gain majorities in legislatures because of their growing populations, political alignments and party structures would fundamentally change. Incumbent legislators would lose their positions, and a shift in legislative power would inevitably result in new governmental policies.

Underrepresentation of urban areas resulted in indifference to urban problems. Traffic congestion, slums, inadequate park space, and smoke pollution did not interest rural and small-town legislators. Governors, too, tended to be sensitive to rural and small-town interests. Governors' and legislators' national conferences persistently ignored the Depression. At a 1930 governors' conference in Salt Lake City, for example, the major topics of discussion included such weighty matters as "'the essentials of a model state constitution,' 'the need for constitutional revisions,' 'constitutional vs. legislative home rule for cities' and 'the extent of legislative control of city governments.'"[69] The 1931 conference also studiously ignored the economic crisis. The cities had nowhere to go but to the federal government.

The federal response to the Depression was designed to deal with a national, not an urban, crisis. Conditions in many rural areas were worse than in the cities. The Appalachian region, the Ozarks, and most of the South witnessed grinding poverty, where families lived in drafty one-room hovels, children walked about with bellies distended by malnutrition, and parents could not afford adequate clothing and shoes for their children. A drought from the Midwest to the Rockies turned much of the plains into a vast dust bowl. In the winter of 1934, New England's snow turned red from the dust of Texas, Kansas, and Oklahoma.

Not only was there compelling need in rural areas, but Roosevelt and his advisors distrusted city politics and culture. For example, Roosevelt's first public works program, the Civilian Conservation Corps, was based on his feeling that the moral character of unemployed youth in the cities would be improved by living in the countryside.[70] Roosevelt felt "small love for the city."[71] One of the president's closest advisers confessed that "since my graduate-school days, I have always been able to excite myself more about the wrongs of farmers than those of urban workers."[72] The New Deal accomplished a comprehensive farm policy of price supports, crop allotments, and federally guaranteed mortgages. In contrast, it produced its first program specifically for the cities, the Wagner-Steagall Housing Act, in 1937, and that program provided slum clearance and public housing only on a limited scale.

Despite the deep-seated antagonism to the cities, city officials were able to develop close relationships with politicians and administrators in Washington, D.C. The New Deal's first relief and recovery programs depended on the states for their administration. But federal programs were later enacted that put local officials in charge of administration. The three major public works programs for adults, Public Works Administration, Civilian Works Administration, and Works Progress Administration, were administered directly by federal officials in cooperation with state and local officials. The Federal Emergency Relief funds were channeled through the states, but local relief agencies actually administered the funds. Local officials found themselves testifying to congressional committees about programs that affected the cities. By 1934, a southern mayor observed: "Mayors are a familiar sight in Washington these days. Whether we like it or not, the destinies of our cities are clearly tied in with national politics."[73]

During the New Deal, a transformation in American politics occurred, in which local officials learned to petition the federal government for help. This learning process took two forms. First, it became "legitimate" to seek federal assistance. Second, local officials formed an urban lobby organized specifically to represent the cities in the federal system. It was the "coming of age" for cities in American national politics.

Through the United States Conference of Mayors, formed in 1932, the mayors met annually to discuss their mutual problems. They financed a permanent office in Washington to lobby for urban programs. Together with the International City Management Association, the National Municipal League, the American Municipal League, and other officials' organizations, an urban lobbying structure became elaborated, which in times of urban crisis, such as the 1960s, would constitute a powerful lobbying force in the halls of Congress and at the White House.

The Cities in National Politics

By the mid-1930s, the nation had completed one political cycle and entered another. During the century of city growth, the conflict between rural America and the cities steadily worsened. Overall, the cities seemed to be the losers. State governments kept jealous watch over their cities. Even though cities gained "home rule" charters in the Progressive Era, their powers remained limited. They could supply only those services specified in their charters, and their ability to borrow and raise money was severely restricted. It seemed unlikely that this situation would change. State legislatures were careful to apportion seats in their legislatures to guarantee rural control.

Cities were the losers in a cultural sense as well. Rural America reacted to the cities by imposing rural Protestant moral ethics, by law. Though ethnic community life and the party machines provided some buffer against the attacks, there was little prospect for political change. Except in a few big cities, governments represented anticity political interests.

The Great Depression changed the role of the federal government in the United States. The federal government asserted powers to regulate the economy and to assist its citizens during times of need. Urban working-class people were affected by government recognition of collective bargaining. Section 7a of the National Industrial Recovery Act and the Wagner Labor Act encouraged workers to organize. Unemployment compensation, job protection, and factory regulations were important political reforms that the party machines had never sought. Craft and industrial unions became important political forces especially in the national Democratic party.

Working-class whites and blacks became the mainstay of the Democratic party in the north. Though it was a long way from their collective vote to Congress and the White House, the potential for political influence was there.

Cities as governmental units gained attention. In the 1937 Housing Act, the federal government committed itself to slum clearance and public housing. This precedent was followed in urban renewal legislation after World War II. In the late 1930s, the national government took a positive interest in the cities. The National Resources Committee published a report in 1937 entitled *Our Cities: Their Role in the National Economy.*[74] In 1941, the National Resources Planning Board prepared a report entitled *Action for Cities: A Guide for Community Planning.* The report proposed formal local planning for treating city problems and stated that the federal government should assist in the planning process.[75] During the war, national legislation for urban highways was implemented, and the foundation for federally assisted urban redevelopment was laid.

The cities' new position in the federal system was only partially assured when they learned to vote Democratic. It was further enhanced when city officials became convinced that they could rightfully lobby for their shared interests in Washington. It is true that between 1953 and 1961, when a Republican president served in the White House, urban interests were not able to push through significant new programs. In fact, from 1959 to 1961, President Eisenhower eliminated public housing requests from the budget. But with the election of John F. Kennedy in 1960, the urban lobby groups found a receptive environment, and it did not take long for them to exploit it.

References

1. W. B. Munro, *The Government of American Cities* (New York: Macmillan, 1913), p. 27.
2. For a discussion of suburbanization before World War II, see chapter 6.
3. Francis E. Rourke, "Urbanism and the National Party Organizations," *Western Political Quarterly* 18 (March 1965):150.
4. Wilfred E. Binkley, *American Political Parties: Their Natural History* (New York: Alfred A. Knopf, 1943), p. 285.
5. Binkley, pp. 285–286.
6. Robert A. Caro, *The Power Broker: Robert Moses and the Fall of New York* (New York: Alfred A. Knopf, 1974), pp. 118–119.
7. William E. Leuchtenburg, *The Perils of Prosperity, 1914–32* (Chicago: University of Chicago Press, 1958), pp. 213–214.
8. Robert K. Murray, *The 103rd Ballot: Democrats and the Disaster in Madison Square Garden* (New York: Harper and Row, 1976), p. 9.
9. Kenneth T. Jackson, *The Ku Klux Klan in the City, 1915–1930* (New York: Oxford University Press, 1967).
10. Murray, *The 103rd Ballot*, p. 7.
11. Murray, p. 7.
12. Murray, p. 103.
13. For good accounts of the 1924 convention, see Murray, *The 103rd Ballot*; Edmund A. Moore, *A Catholic Runs for President: The Campaign of 1928* (New York: The Ronald Press, 1956); Arthur M. Schlesinger, *The Crisis of the Old Order, 1919–1933* (Boston: Houghton Mifflin, 1956).
14. John D. Hicks, *Republican Ascendancy, 1921–1933* (New York: Harper and Brothers, 1960), p. 212.
15. John Kenneth Galbraith, *The Great Crash, 1929*, rev. ed. (Boston: Houghton Mifflin, 1979 [first published 1961]), p. 99.
16. Lester V. Chandler, *America's Greatest Depression, 1929–1941* (New York: Harper and Row, 1970), p. 5.

17. Chandler, p. 5.

18. Chandler, p. 35.

19. William E. Leuchtenburg, *Franklin D. Roosevelt and the New Deal, 1932–1940* (New York: Harper and Row, 1963), p. 19.

20. Leuchtenburg, *FDR and the New Deal*, p. 1.

21. Chandler, *America's Greatest Depression*, p. 19.

22. Chandler, p. 57.

23. Arthur M. Schlesinger, *The Coming of the New Deal* (Boston: Houghton Mifflin, 1957), p. 3.

24. Leuchtenburg, *FDR and the New Deal*, p. 18.

25. Most relief was given by local public and private agencies. Although many states had programs for relief to designated categories of people—dependent children, the blind, and the disabled—few of these were actually funded.

26. Arthur E. Burns and Edward A. Williams, *Federal Work, Security, and Relief Programs* (New York: Da Capo Press, 1971), pp. 1–2. First published as Research Monograph 24, Works Progress Administration, Division of Social Research, 1941.

27. Burns and Williams, p. 15.

28. James T. Patterson, *The New Deal and the States: Federalism in Transition* (Princeton, N.J.: Princeton University Press, 1969), p. 30.

29. Patterson, p. 30.

30. Mark I. Gelfand, *A Nation of Cities: The Federal Government and Urban America, 1933–1965* (New York: Oxford University Press, 1975), p. 35.

31. Leuchtenburg, *FDR and the New Deal*, p. 11.

32. Leuchtenburg, *FDR and the New Deal*, p. 39.

33. Leuchtenburg, *FDR and the New Deal*, p. 39.

34. Leuchtenburg, *FDR and the New Deal*, p. 40.

35. For a thorough account of New Deal programs, see Burns and Williams, *Federal Work*.

36. Leuchtenburg, *FDR and the New Deal*, p. 174.

37. Burns and Williams, *Federal Work*, pp. 29–36.

38. Leuchtenburg, *FDR and the New Deal*, pp. 122–123.

39. Leuchtenburg, *FDR and the New Deal*, p. 133.

40. Josephine Chapin Brown, *Public Relief, 1929–1939* (New York: Holt, 1940), p. 249.

41. Binkley, *American Political Parties*, p. 284.

42. Binkley, pp. 380–381.

43. Patterson, *The New Deal and the States*, p. 26.

44. Calculated from James A. Maxwell, *Federal Grants and the Business Cycle* (New York: National Bureau of Economic Research, 1952), p. 23, table 7.

45. Maxwell, p. 23, table 7.

46. Gelfand, *A Nation of Cities*, p. 49.

47. Maxwell, *Federal Grants and the Business Cycle*, p. 29.

48. U.S. Bureau of the Census, *Historical Statistics on State and Local Government Revenues, 1902–1953* (Washington, D.C.: U.S. Government Printing Office, 1955), p. 12.

49. Maxwell, *Federal Grants and the Business Cycle*, p. 27, table 11.

50. Maxwell, p. 24, table 8.

51. Gelfand, *A Nation of Cities*, p. 31.

52. Gelfand, p. 32.

53. Gelfand, p. 36.

54. Gelfand, p. 36.

55. Gelfand, p. 34.

56. Patterson, *The New Deal and the States*, p. 39.

57. Patterson, p. 40.

58. Patterson, p. 40.

59. Patterson, p. 44.

60. Patterson, p. 47.

61. Patterson, p. 40.

62. Brown, *Public Relief*, pp. 72–96.

63. Brown, pp. 72–96.

64. George C. S. Benson, *The New Centralization: A Study in Intergovernmental Relationships in the United States* (New York: Farrar and Rinehart, 1941), pp. 104–105.

65. Gelfand, *A Nation of Cities*, p. 34.

66. Robert G. Dixon, Jr., *Democratic Representation: Reapportionment in Law and Politics* (New York: Oxford University Press, 1968), p. 174.

67. Dixon, pp. 71–75, 80, 86–87.

68. Dixon, p. 71.

69. Patterson, *The New Deal and the States*, p. 45.

70. Leuchtenburg, *FDR and the New Deal*, p. 52.

71. Leuchtenburg, *FDR and the New Deal*, p. 136.

72. Leuchtenburg, *FDR and the New Deal*, p. 35, quoting a statement by Guy Rexford Tugwell.

73. Quoted in Gelfand, *A Nation of Cities*, p. 66.

74. U.S. Department of the Interior, National Resources Committee, Urbanism Committee, *Our Cities: Their Role in the National Economy* (Washington, D.C.: U.S. Government Printing Office, 1937).

75. Philip J. Funigiello, "City Planning in World War II: The Experience of the National Resources Planning Board," *Social Science Quarterly 53* (June 1972):91–104.

Part II

THE DEVELOPMENT OF AN URBAN CRISIS

Chapter 6

THE SUBURBS AGAINST THE CITIES

Suburbs and the Urban Crisis

The cities' influence in the national Democratic party developed at a time when they faced a significant danger that they would become completely powerless in national politics. Two demographic movements threatened to doom the cities to permanent political impotence. A suburban noose was tightening around the industrial cities, limiting their spatial growth and drawing from them a disproportionate share of affluent people. Collectively, the suburbs became a bastion of indifference and hostility toward the cities, and their explosive growth in the 1920s and following World War II initiated a resurgence of anticity politics.

At the same time, minorities and poor people poured into the older industrial cities. This process, set in motion during World War I and accelerating during and following World War II, resulted in expanding racial ghettos in the older central cities. Historically, American cities had been viewed as dangerous outposts within American civilization, where foreign immigrants clustered together. In the twentieth century, this legacy was embellished when millions of blacks, Hispanics, and poor whites moved into the cities. As much as ever, the cities were pitted against the rest of the nation, but now the "rest of the nation" was not only rural; it was also suburban.

The 1970 Census represented a statistical milestone in the urbanization of the United States. For the first time in the nation's history, a majority of urban residents lived outside the central cities, a fact that had taken half a century to accomplish. In every decade from the 1920s to the present, population growth in the suburbs exceeded growth in the cities. Most of the new suburbanites had moved out of the cities. The exodus reached floodtide proportions after World War II, emptying the cities of middle-income and affluent whites, and leaving behind blacks, Hispanics, the aged, and poor whites recently arrived from depressed rural areas.

It was widely predicted that these movements would result in the strangling of the central cities by a suburban noose. The significance of this problem can be appreciated by considering the attention devoted to it. The National Commission on Urban Problems (1958), the National Commission on Civil Disorders (1967; called the Kerner Commission after its chairman, Illinois Governor Otto B. Kerner), the President's Task Force on Suburban Problems (1967), President Nixon's Commission on Population Growth and the American Future (1972), and a host of state and city task force reports decried the segregation of the poor, and aged, and the nonwhite in the cities. University professors and urban analysts documented and theorized about the emerging "urban crisis."

The old industrial cities were becoming more and more different from the suburbs. These differences seemed to herald a city-suburban conflict in which affluent suburban whites would erect barriers against the minorities living in the cities, protecting their homes and schools from invasion by "undesirable" elements.

Although analyses of the central city–suburban dichotomy forewarned of a national crisis ("two nations, one black, one white," stated the Kerner Commission), the urban political situation was more complex than a war between the cities and the suburbs. Within the cities, neighborhoods divided along social class and racial lines continued to exist. Most of the school busing controversies of the mid-1970s, for example, involved disputes between blacks and whites living within the cities, not between cities and suburbs. The suburbs also differed substantially from one another. In fact, the gap between the poorest and the richest suburbs in most metropolitan areas was wider than the gap between the suburbs (considered as a whole) and the central cities.

Books and articles about suburbia focused exclusively on white, middle-class, family-centered communities. Yet there were exceptions. White working-class suburbs, some of them quite old, sat cheek by jowl near manufacturing plants. A few older black communities were located in suburbia, too. For example, Kinloch, a suburb of St. Louis, originally was settled by blacks forced out of East St. Louis by the riots of 1917. Two other types of suburbs also existed. Heavy industries had located outside the central cities even before World War I. These "industrial" suburbs tended to be completely segregated from the residential suburbs of the middle and upper classes. Excluding themselves on large lots, living in large houses with landscaped yards, the "upper-class" suburbanites constituted the final, although least typical, suburban stereotype. The political conflicts *between suburbs* promised to be rooted as much in racial and class antagonisms as those between city and suburb.

Nevertheless, a fundamental rift appeared between the central cities and their suburbs. In the postwar suburban boom, the great majority of the people leaving the cities were white and relatively affluent. While millions of them were moving from the urban center to the periphery, poverty-stricken migrants were replacing them in the cities. This *dual migration* created the city-suburban statistical differences (affluent whites in the suburbs, poor minorities and whites in the cities) that came to be defined as "the urban crisis."

The Movement to the Cities

Three streams of migration in the twentieth century created vast ghettos in American central cities (see Table 6–1).[1] Millions of blacks, Mexicans, and Appalachian whites were forced off the land and into the cities by economic and political conditions. The first large movements occurred between 1910 and 1930, when 700,000 Mexicans moved into Texas, New Mexico, Arizona, and California; and 1 million blacks left the southern states for Chicago, Detroit, Cleveland, New York City, Pittsburgh, Philadelphia, and other cities of the industrial Midwest and Northeast. The second, much broader stream of migration began during World War II and continued into the late 1960s. These migrants, Appalachian whites, Hispanics, and southern blacks, faced considerable hardship in adjusting to city life.

The new citybound migrants were pushed by crisis and pulled by opportunity, as had been the Europeans who preceded them. Between 1910 and 1920, 1 million blacks moved into the industrial states of the North. Boll weevil infestations destroyed cotton crops all across the South, beginning in southern Texas in the 1890s and sweeping through Georgia by 1921, forcing black sharecroppers and renters off the land. The availability of jobs in World War I armament industries in northern cities induced unemployed blacks to leave the South. During the 1930s, falling cotton and

TABLE 6–1 Rural to Urban Migrant Streams in Twentieth-Century America

Migrant groups	Principal migration periods	Approximate number of migrants*	Origin	Destination
Appalachian whites	1940–1970	1,600,000	Southern Appalachian Mountains (Kentucky and West Virginia)	North Central United States
Mexicans	1910–1930	700,000	*Mesa Central* primarily, also *Mesa Del Norte*	Texas and southwestern United States
	1950–1970	700,000	*Mesa Central* primarily, also *Mesa Del Norte*	Texas and California
Blacks	1910–1930	1,000,000	Mississippi Delta, Black Belt, Atlantic Coastal Plain	Illinois, Ohio, Michigan, New York, Pennsylvania
	1940–1965	3,500,000	Mississippi Delta, Black Belt, Atlantic Coastal Plain	Cities everywhere

Source: Stanley B. Greenberg, *Politics and Poverty: Modernization and Response in Five Poor Neighborhoods* (New York: John Wiley, 1974), p. 19. Reprinted by permission.

*These figures are approximate. The data for the Mexican migration, for example, are obscured by contract labor, two-way migration, and illegal entrants.

tobacco prices brought further economic ruin to black sharecroppers. They were attracted to Northern cities by the employment opportunities opened up during World War II. After the war, the mechanization of southern agriculture threw hundreds of thousands of sharecroppers and farm laborers out of work. The push to migrate became compelling. A wave of movement during and after World War II concluded the black migration that placed 70 percent of the nation's blacks in cities in the West, the Northeast, and the Midwest by 1970.

Mexicans were driven into the American Southwest by the bloody and protracted violence of the Mexican Revolution of 1910 to 1926. Although the revolution allowed millions of peasants to leave feudal estates, it left them without the means to sustain an independent livelihood. Bloody confrontations between the Mexican government and landowners from the turn of the century until 1926 drove millions of the newly liberated peasants across the border in search of refuge. Five and one-half million Mexican-Americans lived in the American Southwest by 1970, the great majority in towns and cities.[2] Mexicans continued to stream into the southwestern states in the 1980s in search of jobs.

The southern Appalachian Mountains of West Virginia and Kentucky provided the setting for the migration of poor whites. Poverty and unemployment had forced hundreds of thousands of white families to leave their marginal farms and poverty-stricken towns. The theme of Harry M. Caudill's book *Night Comes to the Cumberlands* can be expressed partly in numbers: one-quarter of the population deserted the Cumberland Plateau in the 1950s, settling in the cities and towns of Kentucky, Tennessee, Maryland, Virginia and the cities of the northern industrial states.[3]

These three migrant streams created the islands of poverty within twentieth-century American cities. In search of a better life, the new city residents instead found segregated areas of dilapidated housing, high crime, and inadequate public services. Their migration helped create the city half of the statistics of the urban crisis.[4] The suburban half of those statistics resulted from another great population movement: the flight from the cities to the suburbs by those who could afford to pay the premium on the "good life" of the crabgrass frontier.

The Suburban Impulse: The Interwar Years

From the last quarter of the nineteenth century until about 1920, a nascent suburbanization was set in motion by the electric streetcar. Streetcars were used to reach neighborhoods, towns, villages, and subdivisions located at the urban periphery, often, but not always, beyond the boundaries of the city. Whether these communities located inside or outside the boundaries of the cities mattered little, for the cities were still experiencing economic development and population growth (as shown in Table 6–2). Suburban development did not seem to threaten the economic vitality of the industrial cities. Between 1900 and 1920, for example, New York City grew by 1.3 million (a 387 percent increase), compared to a population increase of 90,000 in its surrounding area (60.9 percent). In 1920, New York's population was 5.6 million; its suburban ring's, 379,000. In the first two decades of the twentieth century, even though suburban populations grew at a faster *rate* than that of the cities, the vast majority of people living in urban areas still lived in central cities. Between 1900 and 1910, when St. Louis's suburban population grew from 74,000 to 141,000 (more than 90 percent), St. Louis soared from 650,000 to 829,000 people, a 19.4 percent increase. It seemed unlikely that the cities would ever be eclipsed by the new suburban towns.

Industrial and manufacturing facilities remained near water and rail transportation links in the city centers. Between 1904 and 1914, St. Louis lost some of its manufacturing establishments to the suburbs (from 95 to 90 percent of the area's activity), as did Baltimore (96 to 93 percent), and Philadelphia (91 to 87 percent), but these cities were the exception rather than the rule.[5] The old industrial cities dominated the economies of their urban areas. Suburbs remained completely dependent on them.

In the 1920s the pace of suburbanization quickened, and although most central cities continued to grow significantly, for the first time the *population increase in the suburbs exceeded the population increase in the cities* in most large urban areas. New towns located just beyond the boundaries of the old cities were expanding at a *faster rate* than the cities, which was nothing new; but they were also, in many urban areas, attracting a larger number of people. Table 6–2 documents this development. In all the metropolitan districts of the nation, almost 5 million people were added to the suburbs in the 1920s and the central cities grew by nearly 6 million. However, if the New York and Chicago regions are subtracted from these totals, an interesting fact emerges: the suburbs of the other metropolitan areas added more people to their populations than did the old central cities. If this trend continued, cities soon would become smaller in population than the suburbs surrounding them.

During the Depression years, the fortunes of the older industrial cities declined precipitously and many of them lost population for the first time. Although the suburban movement slowed because of the economic crisis, the suburbs added 500,000 more people than the cities did during the 1930s. The consequences for the central cities, if such a trend continued, was described in apocalyptic tones in a 1936 report prepared by the St. Louis Plan Commission:

TABLE 6-2 Population Movements in Areas of the United States, 1900–1940 (Increases in population expressed as percent growth and number of people added)

Districts	1900–1910 Central city	1900–1910 Outside central city	1910–1920 Central city	1910–1920 Outside central city	1920–1930 Central city	1920–1930 Outside central city	1930–1940 Central city	1930–1940 Outside central city
New York City*	38.7 (1,329,681)	60.9 (91,636)	17.9 (853,165)	35.2 (98,692)	23.3 (1,310,398)	67.3 (424,785)	7.6 (524,549)	18.2 (193,291)
Chicago	28.7 (486,708)	87.7 (122,226)	23.4 (512,185)	79.1 (210,797)	24.9 (673,292)	73.9 (419,906)	0.6 (20,370)	10.4 (104,214)
Boston	19.6 (109,693)	23.4 (161,273)	9.0 (61,968)	21.2 (179,148)	4.4 (33,128)	21.2 (267,344)	–1.3 (–10,372)	3.1 (47,741)
St. Louis	19.4 (111,791)	90.6 (67,357)	12.5 (85,868)	26.4 (37,412)	6.7 (56,643)	71.3 (165,344)	–0.7 (–5,912)	15.7 (74,896)
Cleveland	46.0 (176,492)	46.5 (16,698)	40.1 (227,978)	140.0 (75,171)	11.8 (95,007)	125.8 (164,128)	–2.7 (–24,135)	13.0 (38,824)
Los Angeles	206.1 (214,932)	553.3 (100,232)	80.7 (257,475)	107.6 (156,692)	114.7 (661,375)	157.9 (661,548)	21.3 (263,918)	30.1 (324,138)
Mean for all Metro Districts	33.6	38.2	25.2 (5,385,116)	32.0 (2,236,795)	20.9 (5,851,909)	46.4 (4,819,770)	4.4 (1,498,186)	13.6 (2,086,607)
Non-Metro Pop. Increase	16.4		9.6		9.5		7.2	
Total U.S. Pop. Increase	21.0		14.9		16.1		7.2	

Source: U.S. Department of Commerce, Bureau of the Census, *The Growth of Metropolitan Districts in the United States 1900–1940*, by Warren S. Thompson (Washington, D.C.: Government Printing Office, 1947), especially table 2.
*Includes growth of population in New York City proper and in satellite areas of New York. New Jersey population is excluded.

The City of St. Louis consists of sixty-two and a half square miles of land, most of which has now been improved with buildings, streets, parks and other urban improvements. New growth now finds accommodation mostly outside the city limits. Population is moving out of the city. Land values have declined markedly in the central areas of the old city. Buildings are being demolished to save taxes, and little or no replacement occurs.

. . .To state the condition in its simplest terms—if adequate measures are not taken, the city is faced with gradual economic and social collapse. The older central areas of the city are being abandoned, and this insidious trend will continue until the entire city is engulfed.[6]

Though the situation may have been stated in overly stark terms by St. Louis's planners, it did seem apparent that the future belonged to the suburbs and not to the cities.

This enormous suburban growth was made possible by the prosperity of the 1920s. The expanding middle class invested much of its new-found affluence in suburban real estate. From 1915 to 1925, average hourly wages climbed from 32 to 70 cents.[7] Total national wealth doubled in the ten years from 1912 to 1922, and the value of residential land and improvements also doubled in the 1920s.[8] Economic prosperity was spread among those in middle-class occupations—junior executives, lawyers, physicians, real estate brokers, insurance salesmen, clerks, and store owners.

The key development underwriting suburban growth, however, was the mass production and consumption of the automobile. The automobile precipitated a revolution in mass transit. It was multipurpose, convenient, and fast, and it provided privacy and freedom for the consumer. During the 1920s, huge amounts of suburban land opened up for residential use by commuters who worked in the cities. The automobile provided the link between the two worlds.

Mass ownership of automobiles skyrocketed after World War I, facilitated by the Ford Model T (first produced in 1913) and falling used-car prices. Auto production increased from 63,000 cars in 1908 to 550,000 in 1914. Then production soared: 1.5 million automobiles were produced in 1916, 2.27 million in 1922, and 4.45 million in 1929.[9] With the auto came the bedroom suburb. Millions of Americans separated their community of work from their community of residence.

If the 1920s foreshadowed the post–World War II urban crisis, the 1930s made the nature of that crisis clear. Although the Great Depression sharply reduced movement to the suburbs, it even more drastically applied the brake to central city population growth. The Depression signaled the twilight of the city-building era in the older cities that had benefited from post–Civil War industrial expansion. As shown in Table 6–2, Boston, St. Louis, and Cleveland all lost population in the 1930s. So did Philadelphia, Kansas City, and the New Jersey cities—Elizabeth, Paterson, Jersey City, and Newark. San Francisco, which had grown by 27 percent in the 1920s, was no bigger in 1940 than it was in 1930. A great many small manufacturing cities of New England and the Midwest declined in population—Akron and Youngstown, Ohio; Albany, Schenectady, and Troy, New York; Joplin, Missouri; and New Bedford, Massachusetts.

The exigencies of the Great Depression affected the suburbs as well as the cities. Private industry provided neither the incentive nor the means for a suburban exodus at the 1920s rate. The growth rate of New York's suburbs declined to 18 percent for 1930–1940, compared with 67 percent for 1920–1930; Chicago's suburban expansion slowed from 74 to 10 percent; Cleveland's from 126 to 13 percent; and Los Angeles's from 158 to 30 percent.

To a perceptive observer it seemed likely that once constraints on suburbanization were lifted, residential development beyond the boundaries of the cities would accelerate. The older industrial cities would grow slowly, if at all. This scenario seemed inevitable, considering the experience of both the 1920s, the decade of prosperity, and the 1930s, the decade of want.

The Depression, however, was not followed by a lifting of constraints but by the imposition of new ones. During World War II, materials needed for housing were commandeered for the war effort. New housing construction stopped. The inevitable suburban boom was postponed until the late 1940s.

The Suburban Impulse: The Postwar Explosion

In the two decades following the war, a suburban population explosion fundamentally altered the urban landscape. Table 6–3 provides a glimpse of the magnitude of the population changes between 1940 and 1980.

During the war, central cities recovered somewhat from the Depression years, primarily because jobs in war industries lured millions of workers from rural areas. After the war ended, however, the pace of suburbanization quickened. While the cities added just over 6 million people to their populations during the 1940s, their suburbs gained over 9 million. These numbers were but a portent of things to come, for the 1950s and 1960s witnessed an unprecedented and still unparalleled suburban boom.

Between 1950 and 1960, central cities averaged an 11 percent increase in their populations. In comparison, the suburbs of these cities grew by 49 percent—19 million more people, compared with 6 million more in the cities. Growth in the suburbs was not new, but now, for the first time since the 1930s, most of the big cities in the Northeast and Midwest lost population. About the only cities still expanding were located in the South and

TABLE 6-3 Population Movements in Areas of the United States, 1940–1980 (Increases in population expressed as percent growth and number of people added)

Districts	1940–1950		1950–1960		1960–1970		1970–1980		1980
	Central city	Outside central city	Central city	Outside central city	Central city	Outside central city	Central city	Outside central city	% population in central city
Frostbelt									
New York City	5.9%	23.2%	-1.4%	75.0%	1.5%	26.0%	-10.4%	0.4%*	77.1%
Chicago	6.6	31.2	-2.0	71.5	-5.2	35.3	-10.8	13.6	42.1
Boston	4.0	11.5	-13.0	17.7	-8.1	11.3	-12.2	-2.6	20.3
St. Louis	5.0	33.8	-12.5	50.8	-17.0	28.5	-27.2	6.3	19.2
Cleveland	4.2	41.6	-4.2	67.3	-14.3	27.1	-23.6	0.4	30.3
Detroit	13.9	54.8	-9.7	79.3	-9.5	28.5	-20.5	7.8	27.6
Pittsburgh	0.8	8.9	-10.7	17.2	-13.9	4.4	-18.5	-2.2	18.7
Minneapolis	6.0	76.2	-7.5	115.7	-10.0	55.9	-14.6	20.6	17.5

Sunbelt

Atlanta	9.6	57.8	47.1	33.9	2.0	68.6	-14.1	45.8	78.9
Dallas	47.4	73.7	56.4	27.0	24.2	61.8	7.1	47.9	43.3
Denver	29.0	73.4	18.8	121.8	4.2	.63.7	-4.5	59.9	35.0
Phoenix	63.3	86.3	311.1	-0.3	32.4	72.0	30.9	92.1	50.7
Los Angeles	31.0	69.8	25.8	66.6	13.6	20.0	5.0	0.7	44.3
Miami	44.8	157.2	17.0	161.7	14.8	45.0	3.6	37.1	21.3
Mean for all SMSAs	14.0	35.9	10.7	48.6	6.4	26.8	0.1	18.2	
Number added	(6,021,074)	(9,199,931)	(6,251,181)	(19,081,702)	(3,849,814)	(15,974,243)	(80,054)	(15,631,197)	
Non-Metro Pop. Increase	6.1	7.1		6.8			15.1		
Total U.S. Pop. Increase	14.5	18.5		13.3			11.4		

Source: U.S. Department of Commerce, Bureau of the Census, 1950 Census of Population, vol. 1, Number of Inhabitants, pt. 1 (Washington, D.C.: U.S. Government Printing Office, 1952), p. 69, table 17; 1970 Census of Population, vol. 1, Characteristics of the Population, pt. A, p. 180, table 34; and 1980 Census of Population, Supplementary Reports, Standard Metropolitan Statistical Areas and Standard Consolidated Statistical Areas, p. 2, table B, p. 6, table 1, and p. 49, table 3.

*Nassau and Suffolk counties were deleted from the New York City SMSA in 1971. They have been included here for purposes of comparability. The actual "Outside Central City" figure for the revised New York City SMSA is -1.4.

West, and many of these were booming: Atlanta went from 331,314 in
1950 to 487,455 in 1960; Phoenix from 106,818 to 439,170 in the same
period. But the suburbs surrounding most of these cities were growing as
well. The exceptions were cities like Phoenix, which expanded its boundaries to encircle some of the new housing developments. Old cities in
industrial America were locked into their boundaries, because most were
already surrounded by incorporated suburban jurisdictions.

In the 1960s, central cities *on the average* grew by 6 percent, but this average is deceptive. Older Frostbelt cities suffered huge population losses. St.
Louis lost 17 percent; Cleveland, 14 percent; and Minneapolis, 20 percent.
Sunbelt cities continued to grow, though a slowdown was evident in two of
the older Sunbelt cities, Denver (4 percent) and Atlanta (2 percent). All
across the nation, affluent people continued to flee the cities, and even in
the Sunbelt, suburban expansion far exceeded city population growth. In
this decade the suburbs gained almost 16 million people.

The Rise of the Sunbelt

The long-term decline of the old industrial cities continued in the
1970s, despite a media focus on the "urban renaissance." Virtually all the
big cities in the North experienced huge population losses: St. Louis
declining by 27 percent, Pittsburgh by 18.5 percent, and Detroit by 20.5
percent. By 1980, only a small proportion of the metropolitan populations
of most Frostbelt urban areas lived within the central cities—less than 20
percent for St. Louis, Pittsburgh, and Minneapolis (see the right-hand column of Table 6–3).

And, in an important new development, the rate of suburban growth
outside these cities slowed to a crawl; the suburbs of Boston and Pittsburgh actually lost population. The *metropolitan areas as well as the central
cities* of the Frostbelt were stagnating. All the metropolitan areas located
in the eastern and central Frostbelt corridor expanded slowly in the
1960s, and fell into actual decline during the 1970s. In contrast, most
metropolitan areas in the Sunbelt were still growing. In the early 1950s, a
redistribution of national population to the South and West began, and it
is still occurring.

National economic growth and population movement favored suburbs, smaller towns, and cities outside the Northeast and Midwest.
Between 1970 and 1980, central cities in the Northeast lost 10.5
percent of their populations and cities in the Midwest declined by 9
percent. But central cities in the South grew by almost 9 percent and
Western cities by 15 percent.[10] Table 6–4 shows the on-going redistribution of the national population.

TABLE 6-4   Population Growth of Selected Metropolitan Areas of 1,000,000 or More, 1950 through 1980 (Ranked by Growth in 1970s)

Metropolitan area	% increase in population		
	1950–1960	1960–1970	1970–1980
Phoenix	100.0	45.8	55.3
Houston	51.6	40.0	45.3
San Diego	85.5	31.4	37.1
Anaheim	225.6	101.8	35.9
Denver–Boulder	51.8	32.1	30.7
Miami	88.9	35.6	28.3
Atlanta	39.9	36.7	27.2
Dallas–Fort Worth	43.4	39.0	25.1
Los Angeles–Long Beach	45.5	16.4	6.2
San Francisco–Oakland	24.0	17.4	4.6
Chicago	20.1	12.2	1.8
Detroit	27.7	11.6	−1.9
St. Louis	19.9	12.3	−2.3
New York City	11.9	8.2	−4.5
Boston	7.5	6.1	−4.7
Pittsburgh	8.7	−0.2	−5.7

Source: U.S. Department of Commerce, Bureau of the Census, *1970 Census of Population*, vol. 1, *Characteristics of the Population*, pt. A (Washington, D.C.: U.S. Government Printing Office, 1973), p. 171, table 32; and *1980 Census of Population*, Supplementary Reports, *Standard Metropolitan Statistical Areas and Standard Consolidated Areas*, p. 3, table 1.

In most of the Sunbelt metropolitan areas shown in Table 6–4, population increases have ranged from 20 to 50 percent and more in each of the decades since 1950. But for the six Frostbelt areas shown, population growth was modest in the 1950s and 1960s, and they fell into decline after 1970.

The concept of the Sunbelt was first advanced by Kevin Phillips in *The Emerging Republican Majority* (1969).[11] It came into popular usage in the 1970s to describe a broad region of the nation undergoing an economic and population boom. The Sunbelt encompasses (in most definitions) a region extending from North Carolina, reaching across the southern (but not border states), and extending to the West Coast, embracing on the way Oklahoma, Colorado, New Mexico, Arizona, and Southern California.

Within the Sunbelt, smaller metropolitan areas have been transformed since the 1970 Census. Table 6–5 shows the enormous growth taking place

TABLE 6-5 The Ten Fastest Growing Metropolitan Areas from 1970–1980 and 1980–1984

1970–1980		1980–1984	
Metropolitan Area	% increase in population	Metropolitan Area	% increase in population
Fort Meyers–Cape Coral, Fla.*	95	Midland, Tex.	38
Ocala, Fla.*	77	Anchorage, Alaska	30
Las Vegas, Nev.	69	Naples, Fla.	29
Sarasota, Fla.	68	Ocala, Fla.*	27
Fort Collins, Colo.	66	Fort Pierce, Fla.	26
West Palm Beach–Boca Raton, Fla.	64	Odessa, Tex.	25
Fort Lauderdale–Hollywood, Fla.	64	Fort Meyers–Cape Coral, Fla.*	23
Olympia, Wash.	62	Melbourne–Titusville–	
Bryan–College Station, Tex.*	61	Palm Bay, Fla.	21
Reno, Nev.	60	Austin, Tex.	20

Source: U.S. Bureau of the Census, 1980 Census of Population, Supplementary Reports, *Standard Metropolitan Statistical Areas and Standard Consolidated Statistical Areas* (Washington, D.C.: U.S. Government Printing Office, 1981), p. 2, table C; and U.S. Bureau of the Census, *State and Metropolitan Area Data Book*, 1986 (1986), p. 2, table 3.
*Contained in both lists.

in these areas. Five of the ten fastest growing metropolitan areas of the Sunbelt from 1970 to 1980 are located in Florida; nine of the ten that grew fastest from 1980 to 1984 are in Florida and Texas. (The crash in oil prices in the mid-1980s has slowed urban growth in Texas, however.)

The old industrial cities lost business and jobs to other regions of the country. Table 6-6 shows that in the 1970s, the Northeast gained only 8.4 percent of the nation's new jobs, and the Midwest region gained only 13.5 percent. From 1981 to 1985, the Midwest slowed down even more, but the Northeast's share of growth increased to 13.6 percent of the total. However, 77 percent of all job growth in the nation took place in the South and West, most of it in smaller metropolitan areas like those listed in Table 6-5. According to the *Wall Street Journal*, corporations in the early 1980s were relocating to or were interested in such places as Austin, Texas; Colorado Springs, Colorado; Tulsa, Oklahoma; and Las Vegas, Nevada.[12]

National economic growth was uneven; this was also the case within metropolitan areas. The central cities' share of employment in their metropolitan areas, shown for four cities in Table 6-7, declined from 1958 to 1972. The performance of these four cities was typical of all cities in the Frostbelt. The average loss of employment for fourteen relatively distressed cities in the Northeast and Midwest is also shown in Table 6-7. Between 1967 and 1972, employment losses for central cities ranged from almost 5 percent in manufacturing to more than 8 percent in retailing. These figures can be compared with the averages for fifteen better-off cities, of which eleven were located in the Sunbelt. These cities showed negligible declines in their share of retail jobs, and slight gains in their share of manufacturing and service jobs.

The movement of population, industry, and commerce away from the urban core does not indicate, by itself, an urban problem. This process has always characterized urban expansion. The problem of inner-city isolation and decline was created when city boundaries failed to embrace new population and economic expansion. If cities stayed within their historic boundaries—St. Louis's city limits, for example, were the same in 1980 as they had been 100 years before—then they would inevitably become surrounded by independent suburbs, and *they* would become the beneficiaries of growth.

Sunbelt cities have annexed huge amounts of new territory, while Frostbelt cities were long ago locked into their old boundaries. Oklahoma City contained about 51 square miles in 1950, but twenty years later it encompassed 636 square miles. Much of its territory is semirural land waiting for new housing tracts. Phoenix expanded from 17 square miles in 1950 to 277 square miles in 1978. Most Sunbelt cities added substantial territory in the 1950s and 1960s, and at least some additional territory in the 1970s. One exception was Atlanta, which reached the end of its territorial

TABLE 6-6   Comparison of Regional Shares of Employment and Shares of Job Growth, 1960–1985 (in Percentages)

Region	1960 share of U.S. employment	1960–1970 share of U.S. job growth	1970 share of U.S. employment	1970–1981 share of job growth	1981–1985 share of job growth	1985 share of U.S. employment
Northeast	29.1	18.3	26.4	8.4	13.6	21.0
Midwest[1]	29.3	25.5	28.3	13.5	9.7	25.2
South	26.5	35.1	28.7	47.8	48.3	33.7
West	15.1	21.2	16.6	30.4	28.5	20.2

Source: U.S. Department of Labor, Bureau of Labor Statistics, *Employment and Earnings,* Statistics for March 1960 (Vol. 6 No. 9), 1970 (Vol. 16 No. 9), 1981 (Vol. 28 No. 3, and *Profile of Employment and Unemployment,* 1985, Bulletin 2266 (Washington, D.C.: U.S. Government Printing Office, 1986), pp. 3–7.
*Regions defined according to Bureau of the Census definition.
[1]North Central changed to Midwest in 1985.

TABLE 6-7 Central City Employment as a Percentage of SMSA Employment, 1958–1972

	Retail			Manufacturing			Selected services		
	1958	1967	1972	1958	1967	1972	1958	1967	1972
New York City	76.8	69.1	76.6	84.3	82.0	80.3	88.4	84.2	86.0
Chicago	67.9	55.8	44.9	66.4	55.6	*	78.8	72.8	64.2
Boston	43.3	34.0	27.0	30.0	25.2	*	58.7	52.2	46.4
St. Louis	55.7	37.4	27.4	55.9	32.5	29.4	71.9	58.9	48.1
14 relatively distressed cities**	*	41.1	32.8	*	38.9	34.6	*	55.4	48.1
15 better-off cities**	*	61.3	59.1	*	53.1	53.5	*	67.4	66.7

Source: William G. Colman, *Cities, Cities, Suburbs and States: Governing and Financing Urban America* (New York: The Free Press, 1975), pp. 58–59, and the sources cited therein. Copyright © 1975 by the Free Press, a division of Macmillan Publishing Co., Inc. Also Harvey A. Garn and Larry Clinton Ledebur, "The Economic Performance and Prospects of Cities," in Arthur P. Solomon, ed., *The Prospective City: Economic, Population, Energy, and Environmental Developments* (Cambridge, Mass.: The M.I.T. Press, 1980), pp. 226–227, 234–235.

*Not available.

**In most cases, boundary changes caused by annexations between 1967 and 1972 have been adjusted to reflect 1972 boundaries.

expansion in 1970. It is interesting to note that Atlanta (as shown in Table 6–3) is one of the Sunbelt cities that lost population in the 1970s. Without annexing new territory, southern and western cities would soon fill in. These cities would have added fewer than half as many people as they did during the 1960s if they had stuck with their old boundaries.[13]

Older industrial cities found it impossible to keep up with new growth mostly because they already were surrounded by independent suburban municipalities decades ago. Very few of them have added significant territory through annexation since 1950. Suburban governments prevented annexation or merger moves. In 1979, there were 1,214 governmental units in the Chicago SMSA, 864 in the Philadelphia SMSA, and 615 in the St. Louis SMSA.[14]

Several of the older cities of the Sunbelt, like older cities elsewhere, have not been able to expand boundaries, and these cities contain a disproportionate share of the minority and poverty populations in their regions. Atlanta, for example, lost 14 percent of its population during the 1970s, while its suburbs grew by 46 percent (see Table 6–3). Denver lost population in the 1970s as well (−4.5 percent), and its suburbs went through a 60 percent population increase.

Racial and socioeconomic segregation between central cities and suburbs became well established in the 1950s. For the largest six metropolitan areas (shown in Table 6–8), the median income of central city residents (according to the 1950 census) was 95 percent of the income of the suburbanites in those areas. Ten years later, city residents earned only 88 percent as much as the people living in the suburbs. The gap widened even more in the 1960s and 1970s. By the time the 1980 census was taken, the average family in the six central cities made only 75 percent as much as families living outside the boundaries of those cities.

The six biggest SMSAs in the South and West show a similar pattern, except that the city-suburban disparities were created about a decade later than in the Frostbelt cities. There are two principal reasons for this lag. First, many of the Sunbelt cities annexed suburban populations in the 1950s and 1960s. Second, much of the growth in these areas occurred after 1960. But it is apparent that the racial and economic differences between central cities and suburbs, popularly associated with northern metropolitan areas, are also developing in the South and West. As late as the 1970 census, central city residents of Sunbelt cities made 92 percent as much money as their suburban counterparts. But their income ratio fell to 85 percent by 1980.

In the past, the "urban crisis" has been centered in the nation's industrial cities. The crisis was fixed in the 1950s. Old cities were the first to experience overcrowded housing, inadequate services, and generalized decay of

TABLE 6–8   Income of Central City Residents Compared with Rest of Metropolitan Area Residents in 12 Selected Areas

| | Central city family income as percentage of income outside central city | | | |
| | Census year | | | |
Six largest SMSAs	1950	1960	1970	1980
Northeast and Midwest				
New York City	95	93	89	87
Chicago	97	92	86	77
Philadelphia	96	90	85	77
Detroit	99	89	83	69
Washington, D.C.	89	79	74	69
Boston	92	86	80	70
Average of six SMSAs in Northeast and Midwest	95	88	83	75
South and West				
Los Angeles–Long Beach*	98	98	96	92
San Francisco–Oakland*	100	95	89	85
Dallas–Fort Worth*	103	101	97	90
Houston	102	98	96	90
Atlanta	91	87	79	64
Anaheim–Santa Ana–Garden Grove*	—	—	96	89
Average of six SMSAs in South and West	99	96	92	85

Source: Adapted from James Heilbrun, *Urban Economics and Public Policy,* 3rd ed. (New York: St. Martin's, 1981), p. 248, citing U.S. Bureau of the Census, *Census of Population,* 1950, 1960, 1970, 1980. Reprinted by permission.
*Ratio is for first-named central city only.

housing, business districts, and infrastructure—bridges, streets, parks, sewer and water mains. Most important, the old industrial cities were the first to be subjected to the conflicts that later plagued American urban society—the segregation of rich from poor, black from white, and old from young. But the elements that made up this crisis in the industrial cities may be developing in the newer cities of the Sunbelt as well. (This argument is developed fully in Chapter 8.)

The "Typical" Middle-Class Suburb

Stereotypical white middle-class suburbs proliferated during the 1950s. Most of the literature on suburbia examines these kinds of suburbs. It usually describes them almost as if they existed on another planet, populated with strange beings who share few qualities with other Americans. The outstanding features of this world, the elements that allegedly made it attractive to this special breed of people, were summed up by William H. Whyte in his study of Park Forest, Illinois:

> In most cases the dominant factors for the move to suburbia were the *space* for the money, the *amenities* not anywhere else available and most important, the fact that it was so well *set up for children*. Park Foresters went there for quite rational and eminently sensible reasons. Once there, however, they created something over and above the original bargain . . . a *social atmosphere* of striking vigor.[15]

In this quote we find all the main ingredients of what one author has called "the suburban mystique of the 1950s."[16] Suburbanites seemed to be in search of: (1) "open space"; (2)"amenities" (superior services and conveniences); (3) an atmosphere "set up for children" (a healthy environment for childrearing); and (4) a "social atmosphere." Are these, indeed, characteristics of the quintessential suburban development?

The physical environment of the "typical" middle- and upper-class suburb undeniably differs from the ambiance of the cities.[17] Suburbs are less crowded, and as a drive on a modern freeway reveals, both pollution and noise levels decrease with distance from the urban core. Crime rates are lower outside the central cities. In fact (except for coastal cities), suburbs are even cooler than cities in summer, sometimes by several degrees.[18]

Housing styles and costs lured people to the suburbs. Compelled to dissociate from the American city, which historically had attracted waves of immigrants who crowded together into tenement slums, a large number of Americans adopted single-family dwellings built on individual plots of ground as both a real and a symbolic rejection of the cities.[19] This preference neatly dovetailed with the fact that land at the urban rim was cheaper and uniquely appropriate for homes built on individual lots. Homes in the suburbs were usually larger and had more modern conveniences than houses in the cities. Suburban housing of the 1950s and 1960s generally contained more rooms in each dwelling, fewer structural problems, and high values than central city housing. Suburban lots normally were larger than in the cities. Suburbanites expected and got a living environment that felt and looked different from what was available in the cities. Possibly because their expectations were generally fulfilled, suburban residents were more satisfied than city residents with their communities.[20]

Besides preferring the physical features of the suburbs, suburbanites receive more services at less cost than do city dwellers. They usually pay lower taxes,[21] and they are far more satisfied with their public services and local amenities than their counterparts in the cities. Research on community satisfaction has found that a much greater proportion of suburbanites give highly favorable evaluations to such services as police protection, streets and roads, schools, garbage collection, and parks and play-grounds.[22] Thus, suburban expansion "should probably be attributed minimally to suburban ideals and maximally to suburban practicalities."[23]

To suburbanites, the public school is their most important community institution.[24] In a 1971 survey, 41 percent of suburban dwellers rated their public schools as "very good," compared with 21 percent of the respondents in all central cities over 100,000 in population.[25] These evaluations, of course, are subjective, but they translate into social reality when they become the basis for residential location decisions.

Because local communities carry the burden of public educational finance, suburbs with higher average incomes are able to spend more for each child's education than cities are. The suburban advantage results in higher-quality teachers, school facilities, and teaching resources. The typical suburban public school is highly homogeneous in race and social class characteristics and is typically a microcosm of the suburban community in which it is located.

The popular attacks aimed at suburbia in the 1950s and 1960s often focused on suburban lifestyles and social interactions. William H. Whyte, in his classic, *The Organization Man*,[26] asserted that concern for occupational status and corporate advancement dominated the social life of suburban families. The organization man, said Whyte, spent his time both on and off the job attempting to gain status and respect. Since social interactions were used to sort out the individuals that make up any suburban community, all were expected to participate. Conformity was demanded; individuality, suppressed.

Research conducted in the 1950s and 1960s found that suburbanites led a more active social life than city residents, mainly by participating in neighborhood activities.[27] Individuals who moved to suburbia often increased their social activities after the move.[28] Much of this activity seemed associated with the need to establish new ties with people of similar religious and occupational identifications, and to learn community norms. New friendships were easily made within suburban communities because of the social homogeneity and the similarity of status aspirations. This phenomenon was especially evident among suburban housewives. It was their primary method of adjusting to new social networks.[29] While suburbanites were highly conscious of occupational status and concerned about conformity, the other half of the "organization man" thesis pointed by implication to those who could not or did not assimilate into the new environment, as noted by Herbert Gans in his late 1950s study of a New Jersey suburb:

> The smallness and homogeneity of the population made it difficult for the culturally and socially deviant to find companions. Levittown benefitted the majority [with social interactions] but punished the minority with exclusion, . . . "the misery of the deviant."[30]

Because of income, occupational, or lifestyle differences, the suburban "misfit" was doomed to an isolated social position.

Nevertheless, middle-class suburbs were probably no more "exclusive" than middle-class neighborhoods anywhere. The history of American cities was always a history of ethnic, racial, and social class segregation. Thus, the segregated neighborhoods in the suburbs did not constitute a new phenomenon. America had never been a melting pot. In fact, the presence of so many nationalities and racial groups in the cities generally heightened a popular awareness of diversity. The idea of the melting pot was that America brought together its immigrant ethnic and racial groups into a common culture.[31] It was a myth born partly from fear; the "Americanization" ideal reached the zenith of its popularity during the decades of anti-immigrant feeling. "Despite the hope that a unified American culture might emerge from the seething cauldron, it didn't happen; instead, the formation of ethnically homogeneous communities-ghettos" occurred.[32] Suburban culture, with its tendency to segregate, conformed to the American tradition.

The notion that suburbanites created a unique culture of their own was of doubtful validity. People identified as "suburban" a stereotype produced by the fact that most researchers looked at middle-class communities as the "typical" suburban residence. But social class was being confused with place of residence. White middle-class suburbanites were little different from their white middle-class counterparts living in the cities. The alleged differences between city residents and suburbanites owed to the way groups were sorted out on the metropolitan landscape. As Herbert Gans concluded from his study of Levittown, New Jersey:

> the distinction between urban and suburban ways of living . . . is more imaginary than real . . . when one looks at similar populations in city and suburb, their ways of life are remarkably alike. For example, when suburbs are compared to the large urban residential areas beyond the downtown and inner districts, culture and social structure are virtually the same among people of similar age and class. Young lower middle-class families in these areas live much like their peers in the suburbs, but quite unlike older, upper middle-class ones, in either urban or suburban neighborhoods.[33]

Suburban communities that differ from one another in socioeconomic characteristics will also differ in lifestyles and political attitudes. Working-class families retained the same habits they cultivated before their move to the suburbs. People who moved to the suburbs took with them their values and outlooks. The suburbs, therefore, represented "new homes for old values" more than "new values."[34]

Despite its doubtful validity, the suburban myth exerted a powerful impact on the development of American suburbs because it was useful to developers and home builders. As the ensuing discussion shows, "the myth of suburbia conveniently suited the ideological purposes of several influential groups who market social and political opinion."[35] Realtors and home builders exploited "an image of a way of life that could be marketed to the nonsuburban public."[36] The suburbs were created in anticipation of the kinds of people who might be induced to move to them. In this sense, what the suburbs became was decided by the institutions that financed their development.

The Entrepreneurial Shaping of Suburbia

Although many suburbanites moved out of the cities to escape crime, crowding, noise, and the presence of minorities, the individuals who made the suburban move exercised less choice about it than is commonly supposed. Most home building after World War II occurred at the urban rim, but the tastes of home buyers were only one of several factors that determined this development. Availability of relatively inexpensive land in outlying areas encouraged real estate developers and builders to promote construction outside the cities. In their attempt to sell new subdivisions, developers virtually invented the "suburban dream." The suburbs were created not only by suburbanites but also by the actions of entrepreneurs. In this respect, the suburbs resembled the urban frontier of a hundred years earlier.

Developers influenced the character of the suburbs by selecting the clientele that could best supply profits, the middle to upper classes, and by anticipating the tastes and preferences of these consumers. The role of the entrepreneur could be recognized visually in the kind of housing structures that were constructed and symbolically in the advertising used to attract prospective buyers. This process was apparent in the first tract housing projects built after World War II.

During the long years of postwar suburbanization, from 1945 to the 1970s, the firm of Levitt and Sons became one of the largest home-building companies in the eastern United States. The company gained experience in building subdivisions during the Great Depression, constructing tract housing for upper-middle-class people leaving New York City for Long Island. After the war, the firm expanded its operations and began constructing two Levittowns, one in New York State and one in Pennsylvania. Designed to accommodate the flood of veterans returned from the war, the Levitt houses were small, wood frame look-alikes, sitting row after row on straight, parallel streets. Between 1947 and 1951, Levitt and Sons constructed 17,447 homes on Long Island.[37] In Bucks County, Pennsylvania, the firm built nearly 20,000 units in the mid-1950s.

Even without substantial advertising, the homes sold as fast as they were constructed. All metropolitan areas were beset by a serious housing shortage, a situation brought about by underconstruction during the Depression and war years, aggravated by the baby boom of the 1940s and 1950s, and worsened when President Truman imposed a housing moratorium during part of the Korean War. When Levitt opened his first homes on Long Island in 1947, prospective buyers waited for hours in lines blocks long for a chance to fill out a mortgage application.

Despite the demand for new housing, Levitt's homes failed to invite unanimous praise. Numerous social critics said that the Levitt projects were little more than mass-produced uniformity and boredom, and some writers even imagined the emergence of a suburban personality that conformed to the housing styles. "Levittown" entered the critics' slang as the epithet for all suburban developments characterized by uninteresting, mass-produced subdivisions. In the East, the word continues to be used in that fashion.

In the mid-1950s, one of the Levitt sons, William, decided to build a third Levittown in New Jersey, across the border from Philadelphia. This development became one of the desirable bedroom suburbs of the 1950s and 1960s. Opened in October 1958 and finished in 1965, Levittown, New Jersey, exhibited several new features. Fearing that the unfavorable image previously conveyed about the suburbs would damage sales, the Levitt Corporation varied its standard model by providing several house styles and floor plans. The idea of mixing styles was offered by William Levitt's wife, and was implemented by him over the objections of his executives.[38] Rather than being motivated by the concern to provide more esthetically pleasing suburban residential areas, Levitt had been confronted by a crucial economic reality—he needed to sell the houses and to ensure that they would continue to appeal to the aspiring middle class.

Levitt attracted purchasers by other means as well. His firm attempted to screen people who would not fit the middle-class attributes of, for example, nice clothing and appearance. All homes were expressly designed for families with young children. Advertisements stressed that it was a planned community with schools, churches, swimming pools, and parks. The company used the latest in mass-production preassembly techniques in order to keep the new homes within a $12,000 to $15,000 price range. Long-term financing with low monthly payments was made possible through the firm. In all these respects, the Levitt Corporation preselected its clientele.

Private entrepreneurs can manipulate the housing market only so far, since the social and political tendencies of consumers are independent of the developers' plans. People fleeing to suburbia are not *tabulae rasae*, to be written upon and created anew after the move. Lifestyles and world views are brought with them; the developer only provides a context, a situation. Types of housing advertising and credit policy work to encourage certain social groups and to exclude others. Because developers are constrained to specialize and limit their housing alternatives, segregation on the basis of incomes and lifestyles is a natural result of subdivision development. "[I]nhabitants of suburban developments are trapped in an environment which they have few means of changing. Levittown was privately developed and its areas were planned in advance of construction."[39] Some subdivisions are fated to become working-class suburbs, and others predictably attract high-income families. The intentions of developers, then, largely determine the type of community that will result from a development. Suburbanites "are very largely *prisoners* of that environment with but little opportunity of changing it."[40]

Private Enterprise in the Suburbs: Selling the American Dream

It has often been asserted that people moved to the suburbs in pursuit of a "dream" of the good life, replete with patios, barbecue grills, and curved streets. In fact, however, the suburban vision was created for prospective buyers. The mystique was invented by developers probably as much as by suburban residents. A reading of newspaper advertisements from the 1950s through the 1970s makes this fact evident. For example, an advertisement from *The New York Times* in 1953 reads:

> Babylon—An early American Waterside Village—Recreated! For the person who has reached that position in life where they desire complete comfort and relaxation. . . .[41]

Most advertisements in the 1950s promised exclusion, social class segregation, and residential status. The success theme appears repeatedly in the advertisements, as in this direct appeal for upward climbers to settle in Birchwood Park, a Long Island suburb:

> When you settle at East Hempstead you are "on the right side of the tracks" in more ways than one. It's the hub of Long Island's most desirable residential section.[42]

Another advertisement labeled one of its home models, "The Cadillac —Split Level Plus.... A most worthy addition to the 'Bluebloods of Distinctive Homes.'" For "living on a higher plane," said the builder, "you must get a 'Cadillac!'"[43] Still another builder pleaded to "Let us show you how to make your most elite dreams come true."[44]

Along with appeals to those desiring instant status and social class segregation, the developers specified the particular features of new developments that seemed attractive to family-oriented, upward-striving young executives. For example, one subdivision advertised that:

> The Cedar Hill Ranch Home, frankly, wasn't designed for the man in the street. There are many homes costing less that ably satisfy his needs. The size and appointments of Cedar Hill were fashioned for the family who considers anything less than the best inadequate. ... Yes, Cedar Hill was definitely designed *for the family accustomed to finer things.*[45]

The suburbs were not segregated only because of the preferences of the people moving there but also because of the *choices* offered. The suburbs were built and advertised as segregated environments, making it difficult or impossible for new residents *not* to live in a homogeneous community.

Developers often promised instant social status, and its attendant segregation, as one of many desirable features of their subdivisions. Most advertisements sold "healthy, happy living" in a "serene" environment, often encouraging people to "get out of the jungle" of the city.[46] Apparently not convinced that subtle messages would suffice, one builder promised:

> A Better Way of Life. ... For three years community planners, engineers, architects, yes, even sociologists, devoted themselves to the conception of Heartland Village, a new neighborhood of fine homes that would characterize the American Dream of wholesome living.[47]

It would certainly be difficult to improve on a community designed by "yes, even sociologists."

Starting in the late 1960s, some developers began to promote projects designed for clienteles other than young family-centered marrieds. Around many cities, and especially in Florida, Arizona, and southern California, developers began to construct condominiums and apartments targeted for the growing market of retired and older adults. Naturally, new advertisements were designed to sell these projects; the following one is typical:

> Jefferson Village: The first totally-electric condominium community for people 52 or over. Now that the children have moved out, is your house too large for you? Then consider the comfort of living in a full country apartment, provided for by a full staff of electric servants.[48]

Another advertisement in the same newspaper promoted The Gardens on the premise that "Retirement: *Where* you live it determines *how* you live it. The 'second lifetime' of retirement can be a delight or a delusion. It often depends on where you decide to live it."[49]

Young singles soon joined the elderly as a group targeted for special attention by suburban builders. Over the last two decades, the proportion of the population that is young and unmarried has increased dramatically (just as it has for those over sixty-five). It takes little imagination to discern how builders have attempted to tap this new market. The following advertisement from the *St. Louis Post-Dispatch* provides a clue:

> Your move—make it to Woodhollow—pick of the young professionals . . . great word association: Woodhollow and Young Professionals. Lawyers . . . nurses . . . teachers . . . engineers . . . anyone with success in mind.[50]

Another St. Louis project, Cypress Village, was "for smart young pace setters who like being together . . . for professionals who enjoy being adult and young at the same time. It's Cypress Village, where you share much more in common with your neighbors."[51]

Regardless of the group being courted by the developer, the theme behind suburban culture recurs: status and segregation from "undesirables." The promise to young singles, one that is made with greatly varied shades of explicitness, is sex and companionship. Thus, in this advertisement: "Today's young people are constantly seeking to fill their needs, whether working, playing or relaxing with a special kind of excitement. The Village gives you the opportunity to fill these needs."[52] The developers of Spanish Trace took no chances that young people in the St. Louis area might miss the point of their advertisement. Their development was, they said,

> a playpen for kids. Big Kids. It's our clubhouse. Top of the knoll. Sort of an adult playground. The kind of a place you go to with that certain someone. It's roomy and comfortable. A lounge for relaxing . . . cocktails and snapping logs in the fireplace. The games we play are rated M.[53]

In light of this evidence, which is thrust upon us every Sunday in the real estate supplement, it seems odd that most of the suburban literature focused on the suburbanite rather than the institutions that have financed, built, and advertised suburban communities. Home builders, realtors, developers, and financial institutions determined the choices available to consumers. Combined with the preferences of the individuals who made the suburban move, a system of racial and social class segregation evolved. Through their control of land use, housing styles, and sales and mortgage processes, developers encouraged segregation and social class hostility.

The messages carried in ads represent the orientation and self-interest of developers in exploiting these tendencies. Home sales, however, are only the last step in a complex chain that begins with the assembly and financing of land for future development. At every step, economic, social, and political institutions facilitate class and racial segregation.

Suburbs Against Cities: The Fight for Separation

Since the nineteenth century, when improvements in mass transit allowed the upper and upper-middle classes to escape the congestion of downtown districts, social and economic differences have been apparent in the spatial patterns of urban areas. Even before the suburbanization of the twentieth century, better-off native Americans separated themselves from recently arrived immigrants. The auto suburb accentuated this pattern. In the United States, the history of city building ensured that place of residence would be a primary indicator of social status. In fact, living in the "right" neighborhood was, for a long period, probably as important as occupation in indicating social status, for in the urban environment it was a sign that a family had risen above its origins. Immigrants moved out of the ethnic neighborhoods as a signal that they were becoming full-fledged Americans, while Anglo-Saxon middle-class families moved to show, in visible terms, their ascent in social standing. "Staying behind" was *prima facie* evidence of failure.

The habit of equating residence with social status bred fears that status would be compromised if "undesirable" racial and ethnic groups invaded the "better" neighborhoods. Spatial separation accentuated the perception of class and race differences and led to a territorial imperative. The interneighborhood squabbles of the nineteenth century translated into intrasuburban and city-suburban conflict in the twentieth century. The identification of status with residence compelled the privileged to isolate themselves in autonomous suburbs. Political separation, the creation of independent suburban municipalities, thus became the concomitant of spatial segregation.

The division of urban turf on the basis of ethnicity and social class was accomplished in the old urban centers before the movements of blacks and Hispanics in the twentieth century. When race became a dominant feature in the political and social life of cities, the suburbs became even more defensive of their separate status. By World War II, the modern metropolis, with its fragmented political makeup, was an accomplished fact.

Immigration bred an anticity bias that flourished during the age of reform. For native-born Americans, political separation promised an escape from the alleged corruption, anarchy, and immorality of the cities.

The motive for walling off Boston in the late nineteenth century, as described by Sam Bass Warner, rings familiar. It is a theme often repeated in the contemporary literature:

> Annexationists appealed to the idea of one great city where work and home, social and cultural activities, industry and commerce would be joined in a single political union. Boston, they said, would share the fate of Rome if the middle class, which heretofore had provided the governance of the city and the force of its reforms, abandoned the city for the suburbs.
>
> Opponents of annexation countered with the ideal of small town life: the simple informal community, the town meeting, the maintenance of the traditions of rural New England. They held out to their audience the idea of the suburban town as a refuge from the pressures of the new industrial metropolis. Nor were the opponents of annexation slow to point out that the high level of city services maintained by Boston meant higher taxes, and further, they frankly stated the independent suburban towns could maintain native American life free from Boston's waves of incoming poor immigrants.
>
> It was already apparent in the 1880's that to join Boston was to assume all the burdens and conflicts of a modern industrial metropolis. To remain apart was to escape, at least for a time, some of these problems. In the face of this choice the metropolitan middle class abandoned their central city.[54]

At the edges of all the big cities, incorporation of municipalities proceeded very rapidly from the 1890s to the Great Depression, and again in the postwar era. In 1890, Cook County, whose principal city is Chicago, had 55 governments. By 1920, it had 109. Similarly, the number of general-purpose governments in the New York area grew from 127 in 1900 to 204 in 1920. There were 91 incorporated municipalities in the Pittsburgh area in 1890 and 107 by 1920.[55] During the 1920s, new suburbs were created by the score. It seemed that people had developed a taste for living outside the city; indeed, the literature in the first three decades of the century exuded an intellectual and sentimental reaction against the city and waxed bucolic about the suburban sanctuary.

Cities had few defenders and a host of critics. Academic writers promoted the idea that "our great cities, as those who have studied them have learned, are full of junk, much of it human."[56] A Boston University professor called city life "a self-chosen enslavement" and indicated that "the psychological causes of urban drift are socially most sinister."[57] Cities were thought to promote every conceivable sort of evil, as evidenced by such titles of sociological research as: *The Social Evil in Chicago; Five Hundred Criminal Careers, The City Where Crime Is Play; Family Disorganization; Sex Freedom and Social Control*; and *The Ghetto*.[58]

The other side of the coin entailed worshiping of rural and semirural environments through the "back to nature" movement, which swept the country from 1900 through the 1920s. Boy Scouts, Campfire Girls,

Woodcraft Indians, and other organizations attempted to expose children to the healthy influence of nature study. Children's literature and school-books were filled with stories of adventure in "natural" settings. Adults, too, were thought to be corrupted and worn down by city life and rejuvenated by visiting the countryside. Tourism to national parks boomed, especially with the availability of the automobile. Bird watching and nature photography became major pastimes.

Inevitably, the yearning for nature became linked to the suburban ideal. While, in fact, few urban residents had any intention of giving up the amenities and advantages of urban life, they could nevertheless attempt a fusion of both worlds, the urban and the rural, in the suburbs. Journals and magazines of the day carried a multitude of articles on the advantages of suburban life as an amalgam of city conveniences and rural charm. They "offer the best of chances for individualism and social cooperation," said the *Independent* in 1902.[59] The next year *Cosmopolitan* carried an article hailing the "new era" of suburban living.

> The woeful inadequacy of facilities of communication and transportation which formerly rendered every suburbanite a martyr to his faith have, in great measure, been remedied; and, moreover, residents in the environs have now reached the happy point where they consider as necessities the innumerable modern conveniences of the city house which were little short of luxuries in the suburban residence of yesterday.[60]

These themes were exploited by real estate brokers and speculators who sold suburban housing developments. After World War II, real estate promoters emphasized social standing and prestige. While these themes were present in the earlier period, they tended to be downplayed in favor of images of rural quietude and peace. Advertisements for suburban property just after the turn of the century stressed the availability of springs, orchards, forests, and such items as "oysters, bathing, fishing, and shooting"; healthfulness; and such modern conveniences as "hot water, lighted by gas, modern rooms, long distance telephone in house."[61] "A Country Home with All City Comforts," promised one advertisement, alongside others that offered crops of oats and hay, orchards, trees and shrubbery, fruit trees, and other accoutrements of the rural-suburban environment.[62] One advertisement selling a hot-air pump promised "safety in the suburbs."[63] Most of the advertisements carried photographs of wide expanses of lawn, trees, and meticulously tended gardens.

An anticity ideology both motivated and resulted from the suburbanization process in the first decades of the twentieth century. We have already noted the most important consequence, the political isolation of the central cities. But this isolation was evident not only in the segregation of the cities from their suburbs; it could also be seen in the lack of concern for the problems of the cities. State legislatures, dominated by rural interests, routinely ignored the cities within their boundaries. To the national government cities were nearly invisible. Only for a brief period during World War I did the government construct federally assisted housing for war workers, but as soon as the war ended the government sold or donated these units to local governments or private entrepreneurs. The cultural worship of the agrarian-suburban ideal militated against federal government concern for the ills that affected city residents. Alcoholism, bad housing, abandoned children, and poverty were to be treated by private philanthropy, not by government. In his State of the Union Message of 1925, Calvin Coolidge echoed the prevailing philosophy when he said:

> Local self-government is one of our most precious possessions. It is the great contributing factor to the stability, strength, liberty, and progress of the nation. It does not follow that because abuses exist [in the city] it is the concern of the Federal Government to attempt their reform.[64]

Even in the face of economic calamity, in December 1931 President Hoover clung to the notion that the federal government should not become involved. In a message to Congress, he assured the legislators that:

> Committees of leading citizens [in local communities] are now active at practically every point of unemployment. In the large majority they have been assured the funds necessary which, together with local government aids, will meet the situation.
>
> I am opposed to any direct or indirect government dole. The breakdown and increased unemployment in Europe is due in part to such practices. Our people are providing against distress from unemployment in true American fashion.[65]

There was a profound resistance to national involvement in the cities. It was founded on an amalgam of nineteenth-century agrarian ideals, twentieth-century suburban romanticism, and heavy doses of anticity prejudices. The urban prospect seemed dim indeed, and it was hardly improved by the post–World War II suburban explosion.

Political antagonisms between the suburbs and the cities waited until the post–World War II period because the consequences of separation were not severely felt until then. The two most important consequences included (1) a higher degree of racial segregation between cities and suburbs, and (2) severe financial difficulties for the central cities.

Suburban residents, on the whole, benefited by pursuing policies of political separation because they could escape the burden of trying to solve national social problems. Poverty was concentrated in the cities, and political independence allowed suburbanites to avoid the financial costs of supporting welfare programs, public hospitals, special school programs, high police expenditures, and other services that could not be provided by poor residents.

Political separation was, in effect, a redistribution scheme in favor of the privileged. Apart from the monetary benefits of separation, suburbanites escaped the difficult problem of racial integration. Nearly all the school integration battles in the urban North have been fought in the central cities, with suburban residents acting the role of critical onlookers. The fact that the cities were the centers of racial conflict, high crime, poor schools, and deterioration of buildings led to a perception among suburbanites that minorities caused these problems. Suburbanites placed high value on racial segregation and were quick to credit their privileged status to their separation from minorities. The post–World War II period saw the proliferation and sophistication of political techniques to exclude blacks precisely because they had become, for so many suburbanites, the symbols for the evils of urban society.

This racism often carried with it the ragged edge of violence. Blacks who tried to move to white, working-class suburban communities were frequently subjected to harassment. When blacks moved into white St. Louis suburbs in the 1960s and early 1970s, they were often subjected to broken windows, swastikas painted on doors, and damaged cars. In the mid-1980s blacks moving to white neighborhoods in Chicago received similar treatment.

For the most part, violent expressions of racism have been replaced by more subtle strategies of exclusion. Middle- and upper-class suburbanites who would be appalled by violence and harassment tactics uniformly support incorporation and zoning as ways of preserving the racial and class homogeneity of their communities. These strategies have been both pervasive and effective in suburban America, and a brief elaboration of them is important to our understanding of how the suburbs evolved, not only through urban growth processes, but also through a conscious politics of exclusion.

The Importance of Suburban Autonomy

The most effective strategy for protecting the social and racial composition of a community is incorporation. By becoming a separate political jurisdiction, a community gains substantial control over its own destiny. Local policy can be shaped according to the desires of a group of people occupying specific territory; and local residents and their officials, rather than larger county or city governments, make the critical decisions affecting housing construction permits, school construction and location, zoning, taxes, and services. When a community feels threatened by change, control of government and public policy becomes crucial. The importance of local control is illustrated by a New York land developer's complaint that: "I've got 500 to 600 acres and can't do anything with it because of zoning . . . we just can't run with little home town rule. Every idiot can come down to the town hall and have his say and the guys up front tremble because they're afraid they won't be reelected."[66]

Suburban officials are responsive to local constituencies on racial and residential issues, especially when the suburb is small and the composition of the population homogeneous. Politics in small suburbs tends to be simple and noncontroversial, and this fact is the most important reason for the existence of suburbs: so that local populations can gain control over the government policies that affect their lives.

> People sought suburbanization for essentially private purposes, revolving around better living conditions. The same people sought suburbs with independent local governments of their own for essentially public ones, namely the ability to maintain those conditions by joining with like-minded neighbors to preserve those life styles which they sought in suburbanization. They soon discovered that control of three great functions was necessary to provide a solid foundation for meaningful local self-government: (a) control of zoning to maintain the physical and social character of their surroundings; (b) control of the police to protect their property as they wished it protected and to maintain the public aspects of their common value system; and (c) control of their schools to develop an educational program for their children that met their perceived needs and pocketbooks. It has become evident over and over again that suburbanites will fight as hard as necessary to retain control over these broad functions as long as they see them threatened by "outsiders" who would change them in such a way as to alter the life styles of their communities.[67]

Incorporation works to the financial benefit of most, though not all, suburbanites. Obviously, high-income groups that protect themselves behind political boundaries evade the high taxes necessary to support central city services. High-income residents' suburban governments require low taxes (because of a larger tax base) and are generally able to provide high-quality services for their residents. By the same logic, autonomy can become a liability for small jurisdictions that lack a sufficient tax base to finance adequate services. For example, Kinloch, a predominantly black suburb of St. Louis, incorporated in 1948 to gain control of its local schools and to escape harassment from white county police. Since then, the community has been plagued by inadequate sewers, schools, and law enforcement.[68] Whereas Kinloch's troubles are extreme, many of the small suburbs surrounding St. Louis are notorious for their poor services and bad public management. The *St. Louis Post Dispatch* has repeatedly carried stories of municipal corruption in these communities, ranging from police incompetence and brutality, speed traps, and kickback schemes in municipal insurance to mismanagement of public funds.

In the St. Louis area, suburbanization has not always brought with it the suburban dream. Within St. Louis County, there were ninety-four independent municipal governments in 1970, fifty-six of them with fewer than 5,000 residents. Twenty-five had fewer than 1,000 residents, with the smallest one having 19. Huge variations existed in community wealth, housing quality, tax rates, and services. University City, a middle-income community with somewhat older housing stock (most of it built before the 1950s), had a tax rate of $1.46 per $100 assessed valuation on homes, and the community also supplied high-quality services to its residents. Clayton, which borders on University City, taxed at $0.79 per $100, but supplied even better services. In 1976, Clayton's budgetary surplus allowed it to recurb and resurface a large number of its streets. Meanwhile, Kinloch, with a $0.70 per $100 rate, got along with rutted, potholed streets and notoriously bad services. The main differences in these cases were community incomes, housing values, and willingness to tax. The median family income in Clayton was $17,541 in 1970, compared with an average income of $5,916 for Kinloch families.

The same story is told by school district data (see Table 6–9). The Clayton school district managed to spend $7,005 per pupil in 1984–1985, compared with University City's $3,640 per pupil expenditure. Yet

TABLE 6–9   **Financial Disparity Among School Districts, Selected St. Louis County School Districts, 1984–1985**

	1985 tax rate*	Assessed valuation per pupil	Expenditures per pupil
Clayton	2.40	$193,076	$7,005
Ferguson	3.76	62,634	4,321
University City	3.02	46,253	3,640
Jennings	3.66	40,594	2,726
Wellston	4.13	19,306	2,635
County Average (all districts)	2.77	74,076	4,110

Source: St. Louis County, Department of Planning, *1986 St. Louis County Data Book* (1986), pp. 66–67, 110–115.

*Dollars per $100 of assessed valuation.

Clayton, because of the high value of assessed property per pupil ($193,076), had a much lower tax rate than University City. The Wellston school district, with a low assessed valuation per pupil ($19,306), managed to spend $2,635 per pupil only by taxing its residents at a very high rate.

Not all suburban jurisdictions are able to afford high-quality services. Like the central cities, they are the losers in the battle to keep and attract residents and businesses that pay high taxes. They are financially strapped for exactly the same reasons that the central cities are: lowered property values, aging housing structures, and a high percentage of lower-income residents. Nevertheless, even in these cases, suburban residents are rarely willing to relinquish their independent status. They are willing, if necessary, to accept higher taxes and poorer services in order to maintain the class and racial composition of their communities. The basic purpose of political autonomy is to maintain residential stability and to guard against rapid change: "similarity of occupation or of race, or some special bond unique in the area serves to set down the roots of a modern small town culture."[69] If not united by a cultural or community bond, suburban residents nevertheless feel they have something to protect. Their "Government is a 'Chinese Wall' protecting the character of the people in the neighborhoods, the character of school and school children their children will know, and the investment in property."[70]

Zoning for Exclusion

Over the past half century, zoning has become the central strategy for preserving the racial and social composition of suburban communities. The history of zoning shows that it was born as an exclusionary instrument, and it became popular because it was a subtle, though effective, method of exclusion. Through zoning, communities are able to regulate the uses of land within their jurisdictions, making it difficult or impossible for "undesirables" to cross community boundaries. The list of "undesirables" is often quite lengthy, though it differs from one suburban jurisdiction to another.

The nation's first zoning law was enacted in New York City on July 25, 1916. By the end of the 1920s, 768 municipalities with 60 percent of the nation's urban population had enacted zoning ordinances.[71] As pointed out by Seymour Toll, "That such a swift spread of law could occur despite the intricate processes of many state legislatures and hundreds of local governments is at least statistically extraordinary."[72]

Quick adoption was made possible by the unanimity of real estate interests in advancing the concept that zoning was a useful tool for protecting valuable land against the slums. New York's ordinance was explained by its promoters in this fashion to audiences around the nation: "The small homeowner and the little shopkeeper were now protected against destructive uses next door. Land in the lower Fifth Avenue section, which had been a drag on the market when zoning arrived, was now undergoing so successful a residential improvement that rents were on the rise. 'Blighted districts are no longer produced in New York City.'"[73] The main theme used to promote zoning was that it kept land values high by segregating "better" from "inferior" land uses. In state after state, real estate groups and politicians lobbied for state laws enabling the cities to zone their property.

New York City's zoning ordinance had been prompted by fears that fashionable sections of Fifth Avenue might be invaded by loft buildings from the Garment District on the West Side. Indeed, there was abundant evidence that such an invasion might occur. From 1850 to 1900, New York's population increased from 661,000 to 3,437,000. Such growth rewarded speculators and entrepreneurs who had been discerning enough to predict the path of the city's expansion. But it was bothersome, too, for upper-class residents had repeatedly established themselves at the city's periphery, only to be pushed out again by encroaching waves of immigrants and businesses. By the turn of the century, the upper class had established a mansion district and an exclusive shopping area on upper Fifth Avenue.

Wealthy residents became interested in stable land values when they felt threatened by the teeming masses only a few blocks away. The Garment District, characterized by the clusters of tall loft buildings that employed thousands of poorly paid immigrant seamstresses and carters, threatened to destroy the exclusive shopping district. This threat inspired New York's zoning law. A way had to be found to restrict, by law, the uses of land. Most important, Fifth Avenue had to be protected. Fifth Avenue came to be defined (by the rich) as the cultural fulcrum of New York, "a unique place" in "the traditions of this city and in the imagination of its citizens," "probably the most important thoroughfare in this city, perhaps any city in the New World," "its history and associations rich in memories," "the common pride, of all citizens, rich and poor alike, their chief promenading avenue, and their principal shopping thoroughfare."[74] The Fifth Avenue Association, which employed lawyers to invent this kind of rhetoric, pleaded in 1916 that Fifth Avenue was a special area that should be protected from encroachment. Fifty-four years later, the rationale behind zoning had changed little: "We moved out here . . . to escape the city. I don't want the city following me here," explained a Long Island resident.[75]

Between 1913 and 1916, the Fifth Avenue Association, composed of wealthy retail merchants and landowners, lobbied to exclude tall loft buildings from their district. At first they sought restrictions only on building height. In 1916, the Buildings Heights Commission, first appointed in 1913 to investigate the problems of tall buildings in New York City, proposed carving Manhattan into distinct zoned areas. The philosophy contained in the proposal was "A place for everything and everything in its place."[76] According to the commission, "the purpose of zoning was to stabilize and protect lawful investment and not to injure assessed valuations or existing uses."[77]

New York's law specified five zones, the distinctions based on the different uses and values of the land. In the zoning pecking order, residential uses assumed first place, followed by business districts, differentiated on the basis of building height (the higher the buildings, the less desirable they were deemed). Warehouses and industries were allotted last place.

New York City officials were keen to publicize their law, in part to ensure that it would be widely adopted before courts could challenge its constitutionality. The law contained a tailor-made appeal to real estate interests across the nation. "By the spring of 1918 New York had become a Mecca for pilgrimages of citizens and officials," who wanted to enact a similar ordinance. Within a year after passage of the legislation, more than twenty cities had initiated "one of the most remarkable legislative campaigns in American history."[78] Zoning was literally mass-produced, most cities virtually copying the New York ordinance. Zoning soon became the chief weapon used by real estate interests within the cities to protect land prices. By 1924, the federal government had given zoning its sanction. A committee of the Department of Commerce drafted the Standard State Zoning Enabling Act, which comprised a model zoning law for all the nation's cities.

In a landmark decision, the U.S. Supreme Court subsequently reviewed a case from Euclid, Ohio, and in 1926 declared that zoning was a proper use of the police power of the municipality.[79] One interesting facet of the case revealed how zoning would be used in the future. The Ambler Real Estate Company had purchased property in the village of Euclid in hopes that it would become valuable as residential property. In 1922, the village zoned Ambler's property as commercial, thus instantly lowering its value. In bringing suit against the village, Ambler argued that Euclid's zoning law lowered property values without due process of the law.

In its decision, the Court set forth a classic statement in defense of restrictive zoning, arguing that the presence of apartment, commercial, or industrial buildings threatened the value of single-family dwellings. There was an assumed hierarchy of uses, which the Court itself enunciated:

> With particular reference to apartment houses, it is pointed out that the development of detached house sections is greatly retarded by the coming of apartment houses, which has sometimes resulted in destroying the entire section for

private house purposes; that in such sections very often the apartment house is a mere parasite, constructed in order to take advantage of the open spaces and attractive surroundings created by the residential character of the district. Moreover, the coming of one apartment house is followed by others, interfering by their height and bulk with the free circulation of air and monopolizing the rays of the sun which otherwise would fall upon the smaller homes, and bringing, as their necessary accompaniments, the disturbing noises incident to increased traffic and business, and the occupation, by means of moving and parked automobiles, of larger portions of the streets, thus detracting from their safety and depriving children of the quiet and open spaces and play, enjoyed by those in more favored localities—until, finally the residential character of the neighborhood and its desirability as a place of detached residences is utterly destroyed. Under these circumstances, apartment houses, which in a different environment would not only be entirely unobjectionable but highly desirable, come very near to being nuisances.[80]

In its decision, the court ruled that to separate residential from other land uses was a legitimate use of the city's police power to promote the order, safety, and well-being of its citizens.

If the zoning laws that appeared up through the 1920s discriminated on the basis of social or economic class, the standard practices adopted in later years by developers and realtors added another basis upon which to isolate highly valued property in the city, as well as in the suburbs. In 1924, the National Association of Real Estate Boards adopted a code of ethics which included the statement:

A Realtor should never be instrumental in introducing into a neighborhood . . . members of any race or nationality, or any individuals whose presence will clearly be detrimental to property values in that neighborhood.[81]

In both the North and the South, restrictive covenants attached to deeds forbade white property owners from selling to blacks (and sometimes to Jews). Not until 1948 did the Supreme Court bar the enforcement of racial covenants in courts of law.[82] The courts previously had not consistently protected the civil rights of blacks in exercising residential choice. In fact, in the years from 1934 to 1949, the federal government encouraged racial and social class segregation. According to the Federal Housing Administration manual providing guidelines for federally insured mortgage loans: "If a neighborhood is to retain stability, it is necessary that properties should continue to be occupied by the same social and racial groups."[83]

In part, the Supreme Court held that zoning was a legitimate function of local government on the ground that it protected property owners' investments by preserving and enhancing property values. Using this logic, zoning *did* interfere with the normal functioning of the marketplace by creating an environment favorable to land investment, similar to the government's role in stabilizing business transactions by enforcing laws of contract.

Because zoning was the best available technique for controlling land use, it was adopted by entrepreneurs as a way to protect their investments, and (on the other hand) by reformers who wished to rationalize city growth. With the automobile and the street railway providing the technology for suburban expansion, urban sprawl seemed more threatening than it had in the past. Zoning laws provided an alternative to runaway growth. But planned land use was not necessarily more efficient or better adapted to public needs. Instead, it protected investments made by developers and wealthier people. Zoning became popular at the same time that well-to-do suburbs proliferated around the large cities—Beverly Hills, Glendale, and a host of wealthy communities around Los Angeles, Cleveland Heights, Shaker Heights, Garfield Heights outside Cleveland, and Oak Park, Elmwood Park, and Park Ridge on the borders of Chicago. The utility of zoning for these communities was apparent. If suburbanization was one of the important movements of the 1920s, so was zoning. From its inception to the present, zoning became the legal justification to ensure what informal social class barriers might not have prevented—the exclusion of the Great Unwashed.

The possibility of dispersing the poor throughout urban areas threatened people living in exclusive neighborhoods in cities and suburbs. At the heart of zoning lay the fear of what urban life might become if it were not controlled: a hodgepodge of mixed land uses, the owners of properties always threatened by, or forced to mingle with, the poor. The wealthy (and the middle class, too, when they could afford it) had escaped the chaos of the city's center when transportation improvements had made the suburban move possible. The problem in the twentieth century was that the poor might be able to move about freely, even to the suburbs, and thus upset the segregated living patterns that the upper and middle classes had struggled to establish. By artificially raising the cost of housing available within a community, zoning effectively excluded "undesirables." Normally, restrictive residential zoning attempted to exclude apartments, place a minimum size on lots, or stop new construction altogether.

Apartments in the suburbs represented the possibility of social class, lifestyle, or racial changes. The "residential character" of a tree-lined, curved-street development with individual homes set well back was threatened by apartment buildings, which symbolized the city environment. "We don't want this kind of trash in our neighborhood" was an attitude applied even to luxury apartments. Apartments were seen as potential slums that might attract lower-class white or minority residents. Thus apartments symbolized the coming to suburbia of city problems, with crime, welfare, crowding, and minorities:

The apartment in general, and the high-rise apartment in particular, are seen as harbingers of urbanization, and their visibly higher densities appear to undermine the rationale for the development of the suburbs, which includes a reaction against the city and everything for which it stands. This is particularly significant, since the association is strong in suburbia between the visual characteristics of the city and what are perceived to be its social characteristics.[84]

Many suburban communities became deeply concerned when apartment projects were proposed. For example, an executive living in Westport, an exclusive suburb in Fairfield, Connecticut, exclaimed:

> Thank God we still have a system that rewards accomplishment, and that we can live in places where we want to live, without having apartments and the scum of the city pushed in on us.[85]

Most suburbs excluded apartment building entirely: until the early 1980s, over 99 percent of undeveloped land zoned residential in the New York region excluded apartments.[86] Although this did not mean apartments could not be constructed, it did require apartment builders to secure zoning variances, which maximized the chances for opposition.[87]

Suburban governments also attempted to regulate the social class and incomes of people who occupied single-family homes. Subdivision regulations and building codes made developers go through a costly review process that artificially raised the cost of new houses and provided local residents an opportunity to oppose new developments. But the most common device for raising the minimum cost of new construction was (and is) large-lot zoning.

Large-lot zoning is a device to keep out people with lower incomes. In some upper-class communities, this means keeping out the middle class. In middle-class communities, it excludes the working class. As pointed out by a defender of four-acre lot minimums in Greenwich, Connecticut, large-lot zoning is

> "just economics. It's like going into Tiffany and demanding a ring for $12.50. Tiffany doesn't have rings for $12.50. Well, Greenwich is like Tiffany." Large-lot zoning is defended by a New Jersey legislator as a means of making sure "that you can't buy a Cadillac at Chevrolet prices." An official of St. Louis County, where 90,000 acres were zoned for three-acre lots in 1965, indicates that this suburban county welcomes anyone "who had the economic capacity [to enjoy] the quality of life that we think our county represents . . . be they black or white."[88]

Minimum building size regulations have also become a popular tool for raising the price of purchasing into a suburb. Wealthy suburbs frequently mandate a minimum floor space requirement that exceeds what could be afforded by middle-income home buyers.

In the 1980s, there has been a boom in townhouse and luxury condominium construction, in both central cities and suburbs. The single family home no longer is automatically equated with status. But zoning regulations still are used to preserve high property values, low tax rates, and social class segregation. Though housing styles have changed, the uses of zoning have not.

The National Challenge to Zoning

The importance of zoning is its ability to manipulate the value of land. Thus, it cannot be neutral, for it protects some people's investments and costs other people money and opportunity. One measure of its importance is that it is frequently the subject of litigation in the courts. From 1948 to 1963, for example, 52 percent of all litigation in the local courts of suburban New York City involved zoning and land-use cases.[89]

As a tool for creating and perpetuating exclusion and privilege, zoning went largely unchallenged in the state and federal courts for nearly half a century.[90] In the 1970s, however, it became an important legal issue, even though legal challenges proved to be generally ineffectual. Zoning continued to be a viable tool for social class and racial exclusion. However, zoning cannot be used in an overly blatant fashion, especially if it is designed to work primarily against blacks. The problem with zoning if it is used too blatantly is illustrated by the Black Jack, Missouri, case, in which that city's zoning ordinance was overturned by a federal appeals court[91] after years of litigation.

On June 5, 1970, the Federal Housing Administration (FHA) granted approval to a federally subsidized housing project to be built near the unincorporated Black Jack subdivision in St. Louis County, just north of the city of St. Louis. The project, to be sponsored by St. Mark's United Methodist Church of Florissant and the United Methodist Metro Ministry of St. Louis, was to contain 210 two- and three-story townhouses for middle-income residents. The application for federal funding stated that the project would fill a need in St. Louis County for integrated, moderately priced housing.

On hearing of the proposed project, the residents of the Black Jack area held a rash of neighborhood meetings, circulated petitions against the project, and contacted public officials. A delegation of local residents journeyed to Washington, D.C., to present petitions to federal officials. They complained that the apartment project would overload their schools, crowd their highways, and threaten the value of their homes. Although cautious about saying so in Washington, the delegates and their constituents shared a fear that low-income blacks would move into their community. Residents freely expressed racist sentiments in their first discussions of the housing project, though they soon learned to be wary of reporters. After attending a Black Jack meeting in 1971, a *St. Louis Post-Dispatch* reporter wrote, "The most common statement we heard during the meeting in Black Jack was, 'we don't want those people, we don't want another Pruitt-Igoe in North St. Louis County.'"[92] Pruitt-Igoe was a nationally infamous public housing project built in St. Louis during the 1950s, noted for its crime, broken windows, and urine-stained hallways. It took little insight to guess to whom "those people" referred.

Black Jack residents perceived that they could best protect their interests by creating their own political jurisdiction. The county zoning ordinance had made sixty-seven acres available for apartment construction within the Black Jack area. The fact that the county council represented a large, complex constituency that included suburbs and thousands of acres of unincorporated territory made it unlikely that Black Jack residents could prevail without separating themselves as an independent political unit. As an incorporated city they could, in contrast, adopt a zoning ordinance appropriate to their needs—and fears.

In late June 1970, the Black Jack Improvement Association presented petitions to the St. Louis County Council requesting the incorporation of the new city of Black Jack. The proposed boundaries were to include about 2,900 residents, most of them living in recently constructed middle-income housing tracts.

It appeared to be unfortunate timing for such a request. Black Jack would be the first new incorporation in St. Louis County since 1959. Ninety-three separate suburbs in the county already had created a governmental mess. Two attempts had been made previously, in 1957 and 1959, to consolidate government services in the St. Louis area. The county planning department strongly discouraged the new incorporation, arguing that the community would not be able to support viable public services. Nevertheless, on August 6, 1970, incorporation was approved by the county council, terminating the county's zoning authority and passing it to the new Black Jack City Council.

The county's decision to allow incorporation reveals much about the fears held not only by Black Jack residents but by suburbanites elsewhere as well. The Black Jack Improvement Association lobbied throughout the North County area, linking their fate with that of other areas. Allowing the project in Black Jack, said the association, "could open the door to similar projects being located almost anywhere in the North County area. By stopping this project, you would lessen the chance of one perhaps appearing in your neighborhood."[93] Against persistent pressure, the council decided it could best get out of the situation by approving incorporation, thus washing its hands of the housing issue.

The Black Jack incorporation set off a legal controversy of national import. On September 16, the Park View Heights Corporation, (the nonprofit housing corporation formed by the original sponsors) had completed the purchase of twelve acres of land, which were subsequently put within the city of Black Jack's boundaries. Park View Heights filed suit against Black Jack, alleging that both the incorporation and the proposed zoning ordinance were intended to block the townhouse project and that Black Jack was attempting to use its zoning power to circumvent the Civil Rights Acts of 1866 and 1964, the National Housing Act of 1937, and the Fair Housing Act of 1968. Judge Roy W. Harper, in a brief hearing, dismissed the suit on October 16, 1970. Judge Harper refused to hear any witnesses. On October 20, 1970, the Black Jack City Council rezoned the land so that the townhouse project could not be built.

The decision was appealed, and the suit was still in the courts on December 10, 1970, when the National Committee Against Discrimination in Housing accused the Nixon administration of supporting the suburbs in integration conflicts. The case subsequently embroiled the Nixon administration in an internal conflict over its policies regarding the suburbs. The *Black Jack* case played out in an atmosphere of national concern over suburban racial politics.

In the months following the Black Jack incorporation, it seemed unlikely that its zoning ordinance would be allowed to stand. Lawton, Oklahoma, southwest of Oklahoma City, had attempted to use its zoning ordinance to exclude apartments, but the federal appellate court for its circuit had ruled that municipalities could not use zoning to exclude minorities or the poor unless they could show a nondiscriminatory intent concerning land-use objectives.[94] In the case of Black Jack, this would be extremely difficult.

In April 1971, another case gave hope to proponents of suburban integration. The United States Court of Appeals for the Second Circuit rejected an attempt by the city officials of Lackawanna, New York, to block the building of a black housing subdivision in a white neighborhood.[95] Comments in the editorials of the *St. Louis Post-Dispatch* compared the *Lackawanna* suit favorably with the *Black Jack* suit. "The unanimous action indicates that local governments will have legal difficulties if they try to zone out Negroes from white areas. The Lackawanna decision clarifies the fact that misuse of political powers to keep out minority groups is unconstitutional."[96]

Against this background, civil rights organizations pressured the Nixon administration to take a strong stand for integration. It was unclear which way the administration would go. In August 1970, concerned by disorders over school integration in Warren, Michigan, George Romney, secretary of the Department of Housing and Urban Development (HUD), had stated that there would be no HUD policy forcing racial integration in the suburbs. Yet Romney and his department favored housing programs to open up the suburbs. Not only did HUD promote housing in suburbs through the "Fair Share" housing program, which tied federal grants for sewers and other facilities to the willingness to build subsidized low-income housing, but Romney urged the Justice Department to challenge discriminatory zoning laws such as Black Jack's.

President Nixon sided with Attorney General John Mitchell's view that the federal government should stay out of "local" controversies. But both HUD and the housing branch of the Justice Department urged the federal government to institute a suit against Black Jack for using zoning power to block lower middle-income housing. The president and his advisers stalled. In January, 1971, the American Civil Liberties Union (ACLU) filed suit on behalf of the Park View Heights Corporation and eight individuals.

The White House's response to these events was not encouraging to open-housing proponents. Nixon indicated in December 1970 that his administration would never use the power of the federal government "for forced integration in the suburbs." In January, Nixon said, "to force integration in the suburbs, I think, is unrealistic."[97] Later, in March, Nixon said that the cause of most suburban segregation was economic rather than racial.[98] He also said the government was not justified in breaking up communities over housing integration. At this point, it appeared unlikely that Nixon would assist the cause of suburban integration.

When pressed to provide a clearer statement of the administration's position, Nixon refused on the ground that two important cases were under review by the Supreme Court. In one of these, the *Lackawanna* case, the Justice Department had intervened against the municipality because there seemed to be such a clear case of racial discrimination. The other, a case from California, was decided on April 26, 1971. The Supreme Court ruled in favor of a California constitutional provision that required a local referendum for approval of low-income housing project construction, empowering electorates to stop any similar housing projects. The Court stated that the California provision was not intended to be used for racial discrimination and did not therefore automatically deny minority groups equal protection of the law.[99] Not only was the administration unclear on integration, but so were the courts.

On June 11, 1971, Nixon announced his policy on suburban housing. There was little that was new in his statement; Nixon said that he would encourage but not force suburbs to provide housing for minority groups. And he made a distinction between economic and racial segregation:

We will not seek to impose economic integration upon an existing jurisdiction; at the same time, we will not countenance any use of economic measures as a subterfuge for racial discrimination.[100]

How could the president know when economic measures were in effect a strategem to discriminate against minorities? It was obvious that the subterfuge would have to be exceptionally transparent:

> Quite apart from racial considerations, residents of outlying areas may and often do object to the building in their communities of subsidized housing which they fear may have the effect of lowering property values and bringing in large numbers of persons who will contribute less in taxes than they consume in services. Beyond this, and whether rightly or wrongly, as they view the social conditions of urban slum life, many residents of the outlying areas are fearful that moving large numbers of persons—of whatever races—from the slums to their communities would bring a contagion of crime, violence, drugs, and other conditions from which so many of those who are trapped in the slums themselves want to escape.[101]

Only three days later, the Justice Department entered the suit against the city of Black Jack. At the same time, Secretary Romney announced that suburbs that used zoning for racial discrimination would not receive federal construction, sewer, or water grants. For one day, it appeared that Nixon's statement did not mean what it appeared to mean. The next day, June 15, the apparent discrepancy was clarified when administration officials emphasized that federal intervention in suburban housing would be limited to cases of manifest, overt racial discrimination.[102] Additionally, the federal government would not interfere in local zoning laws generally, but only in specific instances. It seemed that while Black Jack might lose the battle, the suburbs would win the war. The federal suit against Black Jack came more than nine months after the Black Jack controversy had been called to the attention of the Nixon administration. The suit also came five months after the suit by the ACLU. During this time, it had become a national issue, a symbol of suburban segregation, and an example of administrative indecision. The national attention focused on this case would make it the most important precedent in housing to date.

In December 1971, United States District Judge Roy W. Harper threw out the *Black Jack* suit on the ground that the litigants had no standing to sue: "there is no indication that anyone has been injured by the ordinance. . . . This court will not entertain jurisdiction of questions that are abstract, hypothetical and contingent, such as the one before it."[103]

On appeal, the Eighth Circuit Court of Appeals reversed this decision in September 1974. Throwing out the contention that the Black Jack zoning ordinance was intentionally discriminatory, the court nevertheless found that it had a discriminatory effect—a decision with great potential for changing zoning laws in the United States. In June 1975, the Supreme Court refused to review the decision, thus affirming it.

The *Black Jack* case was a pyrrhic victory for the Park View Heights Corporation. By the time the litigation was concluded, the housing program that funded the project had lapsed. Worse, the inflated costs of housing materials made the project infeasible for moderate-income families. Black Jack eventually paid a $450,000 settlement to the corporation, but the townhouses were never built.

The *Black Jack* case turned out not to be a reliable precedent. A Supreme Court decision on January 11, 1977, made it clear that discriminatory zoning would be difficult to challenge successfully. In reviewing the zoning ordinance of Arlington Heights, Illinois, which barred a federally subsidized townhouse project from being built, the court declared that the impact of zoning laws could not be used as the only argument against them; rather, they had to be shown to have racially motivated intent: "Disproportionate impact is not irrelevant, but it is not the sole touchstone of an invidious racial discrimination."[104] In the case of Arlington Heights, the city's zoning ordinance had predated the plans for the townhouse construction, as do most suburban zoning laws. If intent rather than effect must be proved, then few communities would be challenged. "As far as the constitutional question is concerned, it appears the court has made it even more difficult to prove racial discrimination," one of the attorneys in the case observed.[105]

But civil rights advocates can point to two other significant court cases when they try to challenge exclusionary zoning. In 1975, the New Jersey Supreme Court struck down the zoning ordinances of Mount Laurel, a New Jersey municipality that sits close by cities with large black and Puerto Rican populations. Mount Laurel's zoning prohibited all but single-family houses, and specified large lot and building sizes, four bedrooms minimum, and substantial setback from the street. The court found that this was illegal because it arbitrarily limited market choices by builders and consumers. The court found that Mount Laurel's law constituted "a blatantly exclusionary ordinance. Papered over with paper studies rationalized by hired experts, the ordinance at its core is true to nothing but Mount Laurel's determination to exclude the poor."[106]

A second court decision involving Mount Laurel (called Mount Laurel II) was handed down in 1983. This time, the New Jersey Supreme Court went even further to invalidate various amendments that had been made to Mount Laurel's laws. The court stated that the municipality was obligated to provide zoning legislation to allow a "fair share" of low- and moderate-income people from the region to move into Mount Laurel, if they wished. The decision was considered a resounding victory by opponents of exclusionary zoning.

Standing alone, court decisions such as the Mount Laurel cases cannot change metropolitan patterns of racial and social class segregation. Municipalities can stall in the courts for years, and litigation is expensive. Zoning laws must be somewhat extreme to invite challenge—Mount Laurel's, for example, were unusually restrictive.

For several reasons, zoning will continue as a popular and viable tool for exclusion. First, new housing, when it is not subsidized by the federal government, is too expensive for the poor. In 1987, the average home in the United States cost about $100,000, which excluded most people in the under-$40,000-per-year-income category. The greatest danger to zoning, therefore, is through subsidized housing funded through the federal government, and in which rent supplement tenants live. Such housing, however, constitutes a minuscule proportion of the entire housing market in the United States. All subsidized housing programs have been cut drastically by the Reagan administration. In the absence of a new commitment to subsidized low-income housing in the United States, zoning will continue to be exclusionary, partly because it will rarely be effectively contested.

The Costs of Suburbanization

The principal effect of suburbanization has been to increase opportunities for racial and social class segregation. To a large extent, segregation was fated by the actions of private entrepreneurs who saw that it was in their interest to package social status and segregation as essential components of the suburban myth. The effect of entrepreneurial decisions is everywhere apparent: housing styles, design, and function preselect the clientele with the income, lifestyles, and values appropriate to the living space. This explains the persistence of old suburbs. One study of suburbs that existed continually from 1920 to 1960 found that most of them had changed little in socioeconomic composition over the forty-year period.[107] Their original physical features continually select new residents.

The suburbs were promoted as ways to enhance social class, to escape the problems of the cities, and to live in a segregated social environment. Thus, the suburbs became sharply differentiated from the cities, both symbolically and in reality: the symbol of exclusion became actualized by entrepreneurs' selection of clientele.

The plain fact is that now as before, the main force in our process of urban development is the private developer. The primacy of the bulldozer in transforming rural land to urban uses, the capacity of the private company to build thousands of homes on quiet rolling hills is a predominant fact of American urban life.[108]

Obviously, segregation occurs for many reasons. One is that entrepreneurs encouraged it. It is also the case, however, that many—perhaps most—suburbanites wished to segregate themselves; they felt that they had escaped the problems of the crowded central cities.

Suburbanites have imposed increased costs on central cities in at least two ways. First, because the suburbs can be selective about who they let in, "the central city becomes a receptacle for all the functions the suburb does not care to support."[109] Those functions, ranging from public hospitals serving primarily the poor to shelter for the homeless, are public services for which suburbanites can escape paying.

Central cities also experience escalating expenses as a result of suburban exploitation of their services. This phenomenon stems from the importance of highly paid white-collar professional, managerial, and office employees in the service-oriented city economy, and the spatial segregation of work place from home. Suburban residents take the best jobs in central city service economies, leaving the minimum-wage jobs for city residents. Yet the commuting suburbanites wear out city streets and increase the need for police, fire, water, and recreational services.

But suburbanites do not pay their share of the city services they use. One study of 168 metropolitan areas found that the cost of central city services was explained more by the suburban population level than by any other factor.[110] A study of the Detroit area found that suburbanites' willingness to support local public services was determined, in part, by their access to central city services: if services were available in Detroit, suburbanites were less willing to pay for them in their own communities.[111]

Even in the 1980s, the suburbs still owe their status as viable communities to the central city's labor supply and economic markets. They cannot exist independently. They share a symbiotic relationship with the cities, in which the cities too often are the hosts and the suburbs the parasites: "Suburbanites are suburbanites precisely because they desire to be near enough to the city to enjoy its benefits, but not near enough to have to shoulder its burdens."[112]

References

1. A brief but excellent account of these movements may be found in Stanley B. Greenberg, *Politics and Poverty: Modernization and Response in Five Poor Neighborhoods* (New York: John Wiley, 1974), pp. 15–27.

2. See Greenberg, pp. 15–27, and Leo Grebler, Joan W. Moore, and Ralph C.

Guzman, *The Mexican-American People* (New York: The Free Press, 1970), p. 113.

3. *Night Comes to the Cumberlands* is Harry M. Caudill's moving account of the political and social decay of the Cumberland plateau (Boston: Little, Brown, 1962).

4. The social crisis of the central cities is the subject of Chapter 8.

5. Gary A. Tobin, "Suburbanization and the Development of Motor Transportation: Transportation Technology and the Suburbanization Process," in *The Changing Face of the Suburbs*, ed. Barry Schwartz (Chicago: University of Chicago Press, 1976), p. 100; see also U.S. Bureau of the Census, *Industrial Districts: 1905, Manufactures and Population*, Bulletin 101 (Washington, D.C.: U.S. Government Printing Office, 1909), pp. 9–80, and the U.S. Bureau of the Census, *Census of Manufactures: 1914, vol. 1:* Reports by States with Statistics for Principal Cities and Metropolitan Districts (Washington, D.C.: U.S. Government Printing Office, 1918), pp. 564, 787, 1292.

6. See Institute for Urban and Regional Studies, "Urban Decay in St. Louis," Washington University, St. Louis, March 1972.

7. National Industrial Conference Board, *The Economic Almanac 1956: A Handbook of Useful Facts about Business, Labor and Government in the United States and Other Areas* (New York: Thomas Y. Crowell for The Conference Board, 1956).

8. NICB, *The Economic Almanac, 1956.*

9. These data are cited in Tobin, "Suburbanization and the Development of Motor Transportation," pp. 102, 104, and are also available in NICB, *The Economic Almanac 1956.*

10. U.S. Bureau of the Census, *1980 Census of Population*, Supplementary Reports, *Standard Metropolitan Statistical Areas and Standard Consolidated Statistical Areas* (Washington, D.C.: U.S. Government Printing Office, 1981), p. 49, table 3.

11. Published by Arlington House, New Rochelle, N.Y., 1969. For an excellent discussion of the origins and usage of the term, see Carl Abbott, *The New Urban America: Growth and Politics in Sunbelt Cities* (Chapel Hill: The University of North Carolina Press, 1981).

12. *Wall Street Journal*, March 14, 1980, p. 1.

13. Ira S. Lowry, "The Dismal Future of Cities," in *The Prospective City: Economic, Population, Energy, and Environmental Developments*, ed. Arthur P. Solomon (Cambridge, Mass.: MIT Press, 1980), p. 176.

14. U.S. Bureau of the Census, *Local Government Finances in Selected Metropolitan Areas and Large Counties: 1970–80* (Washington, D.C.: U.S. Government Printing Office, 1981), p. 2.

15. William H. Whyte, Jr., *The Organization Man* (New York: Simon and Schuster, 1956), p. 26.

16. This is the title of Chapter 5 of Dennis Sobin's book, *The Future of the American Suburbs: Survival or Extinction?* (Port Washington, N.Y.: Kennikat Press, 1971).

17. For an excellent discussion of the ecology of suburbs and cities, see Claude S. Fischer, *The Urban Experience* (New York: Harcourt Brace Jovanovich, 1976), and his "The Metropolitan Experience," in *Metropolitan America in Contemporary Perspective*, ed. Amos H. Hawley and Vincent P. Rock (New York: John Wiley, 1975), pp. 201–234.

18. See both of Fischer's works, and R. A. Bryson and J. E. Ross, "The Climate of the City," in *Urbanization and the Environment*, ed. T. R. Detwyler and M. G. Marcus (Belmont, Calif.: Duxbury Press, 1972), pp. 51–68.

19. See J. B. Lansing, *Residential Relocation and Urban Mobility* (Ann Arbor: Survey Research Center, University of Michigan, 1966).

20. Robert W. Marans and Willard Rodgers, "Toward an Understanding of Community Satisfaction," in *Metropolitan America*, ed. Hawley and Rock, pp. 299–352.

21. Robert B. Pettengill and Jogindar S. Uppal, *Can the Cities Survive? The Fiscal Plight of American Cities* (New York: St. Martin's Press, 1974).

22. Marans and Rodgers, "Toward an Understanding of Community Satisfaction," 320.

23. Fischer, *The Urban Experience*, p. 210.

24. Marans and Rodgers, "Toward an Understanding of Community Satisfaction," pp. 311–332; Robert C. Wood, *Suburbia, Its People and Their Politics* (Boston: Houghton Mifflin, 1958); and Gary A. Tobin, "Ethnic Mobility in a Suburban Community" (Ph.D. diss., Department of City and Regional Planning, University of California, 1975).

25. Marans and Rodgers, "Toward an Understanding of Community Satisfaction," p. 320.

26. See Whyte, *The Organization Man*.

27. I. Tallman and R. Morgser, "Life-Style Differences Among Urban and Suburban Blue Collar Families," *Social Forces* 48 (March 1970):334–348, and A. K. Torich, "Informal Group Participation and Residential Patterns," *American Journal of Sociology* 70 (July 1964): 28–35. See also Scott Greer, *The Urban View: Life and Politics in Metropolitan America* (New York: Oxford University Press, 1972), pp. 24–33.

28. See Herbert Gans, *The Levittowners: Ways of Life and Politics in a Suburban Community* (New York: Pantheon, 1967), and S. D. Clark, *The Suburban Society* (Toronto: University of Toronto Press, 1966).

29. See Gans, *The Levittowners*.

30. Gans, p. 239.

31. The classic statement of this idea is found in Israel Zangwill, *The Melting Pot* (New York: Macmillan, 1909).

32. Bennett M. Berger, "Suburbs, Subcultures, and the Urban Future," in *Planning for a Nation of Cities*, ed. Sam Bass Warner (Cambridge, Mass.: MIT Press, 1966), p. 148.

33. Gans, *The Levittowners*, pp. 288–289.

34. See Leonard Reissman and Thomas Ktsanes, "Suburbia—New Homes for Old Values," *Social Problems* 7 (Winter 1959–60):187–195; Berger, *Working-Class Suburb*; and Wood, *Suburbia*, p. 143.

35. Berger, "Suburbs, Subcultures, and the Urban Future," p. 147.

36. Berger, p. 147.

37. Harold Wattel, "Levittown: A Suburban Community," *The Suburban Community*, ed. William M. Dobriner (New York: G. P. Putnam's Sons, 1958), p. 287.
38. Gans, *The Levittowners*, pp. 8–9.
39. Robert Goldston, *Suburbia: Civic Denial* (New York: Macmillan, 1970), p. 67.
40. Goldston, p. 68.
41. *New York Times*, March 31, 1953.
42. *New York Times*, March 22, 1953.
43. *New York Times.*
44. *New York Times*, January 5, 1962.
45. *New York Times*, October 26, 1952. Emphasis in the original.
46. These quotations are from ads in the *New York Times.*
47. *New York Times*, May 26, 1968.
48. *New York Times.*
49. *New York Times.*
50. *St. Louis Post-Dispatch*, April 16, 1972.
51. *St. Louis Post-Dispatch*, August 18, 1974.
52. *St. Louis Post-Dispatch*, July 5, 1970.
53. *St. Louis Post-Dispatch.*
54. Sam Bass Warner, *Streetcar Suburbs: The Process of Growth in Boston, 1870–1900* (Cambridge, Mass.: Harvard University Press, 1962), pp. 164–165.
55. Data cited in Wood, *Suburbia*, p. 69, and in National Municipal League, Committee on Metropolitan Government, *The Government of Metropolitan Areas in the United States*, prepared by Paul Studenski with the assistance of the Committee on Metropolitan Government (New York: National Municipal League, 1930), p. 26.
56. Robert Park, Ernest W. Burgess, and Roderick D. McKenzie, *The City* (Chicago: University of Chicago Press, 1925), p. 109.
57. Quoted in Peter J. Schmitt, *Back to Nature: The Arcadian Myth in Urban America* (New York: Oxford University Press, 1969), p. 180; original quotation found in Ernest Groves, "The Urban Complex," *Sociological Review* 12 (Fall 1920) :74, 76.
58. A more complete list of titles can be found in Schmitt, *Back to Nature.*
59. Editorial ("Suburbanism"), the *Independent*, February 27, 1902, p. 52.
60. Weldon Fawcett, "Suburban Life in America," *Cosmopolitan*, July 1903, p. 309.
61. Advertisement in *Country Life in America*, November 1906, p. 3.
62. Advertisement in *Country Life*, March 1907, p. 474.
63. Advertisement in *Country Life*, June 1907, p. 240.
64. U.S. Congress, House, *Message of the President of the United States*, H. Doc. 2, 69th Cong., 1st sess. (1925), p. 1; also found in Fred L. Israel, ed., *State of the Union Messages of the Presidents, 1790–1966*, vol. 4 (New York: Chelsea House, 1966), pp. 2699–2670.
65. Quoted in Josephine Chapin Brown, *Public Relief, 1929–1939* (New York: Henry Holt, 1940), pp. 98–99.

66. Louis H. Masotti and Jeffrey K. Hadden, eds., *Suburbia in Transition* (New York: Franklin Watts, 1974), p. 305.

67. Daniel J. Elazer, "Suburbanization: Reviving the Town on the Metropolitan Frontier," *Publius, The Journal of Federalism* 5 (Winter 1975):59.

68. John Kramer, "The Other Mayor Lee," in *North American Suburbs: Politics, Diversity, and Change*, ed. John Kramer (Berkeley, Calif.: The Glendessary Press, 1972), pp. 192–198.

69. Wood, *Suburbia*, p. 105.

70. Scott Greer, *The Emerging City: Myth and Reality* (New York: The Free Press, 1962), p. 147.

71. Seymour I. Toll, *Zoned America* (New York: Grossman, 1969), p. 193.

72. Toll, p. 193.

73. Toll, p. 197.

74. Toll, p. 159.

75. Quoted in Michael N. Danielson, *The Politics of Exclusion* (New York: Columbia University Press, 1976), p. 54.

76. Toll, *Zoned America*, p. 183.

77. Toll, pp. 182–183.

78. Toll, p. 187.

79. The "police power" refers to the implied powers of government to adopt and enforce laws necessary for preserving and protecting the immediate health and welfare of citizens. The meaning of this is, of course, subject to a wide variety of interpretations.

80. *Village of Euclid v. Ambler Realty Co.*, 272 U.S. 365, 47 Sup. Ct. 114, 71 L. Ed. 303 (1926).

81. Quoted in James L. Hecht, *Because It Is Right: Integration in Housing* (Boston: Little, Brown, 1970), p. 19.

82. Refer to Hecht for a discussion of the landmark case, *Shelley v. Kraemer.*

83. Quoted in Hecht, p. 20.

84. Quoted in Danielson, *The Politics of Exclusion*, pp. 53–54.

85. "The End of the Exurban Dream," *New York Times*, December 13, 1976.

86. Danielson, *The Politics of Exclusion*, p. 53.

87. Because of the fears concerning apartment developments, the planning process involving their construction is complicated, requiring petitions for zoning variances, public hearings, and lengthy review proceedings. For an excellent account of these complexities, see Daniel R. Mandelker, *The Zoning Dilemma: A Legal Strategy for Urban Change* (Indianapolis: Bobbs-Merrill, 1971).

88. Quoted in Danielson, *The Politics of Exclusion*, p. 60.

89. Kenneth M. Dolbeare, "Who Uses the State Trial Courts?" in *The Politics of Local Justice*, ed. James R. Klonoski and Robert I. Mendelsohn (Boston: Little, Brown, 1970), p. 69.

90. A detailed discussion of the legal status of zoning is not included in this section. For further research, the following sources are especially useful: Michael N. Danielson, *The Politics of Exclusion* (New York: Columbia University Press, 1976); Richard F. Babcock, *The Zoning Game* (Madison: University of Wisconsin Press, 1969); Richard F. Babcock and Fred P. Bosselman, *Exclusionary Zoning: Land Use*

Regulation and Housing in the 1970s (New York: Praeger, 1973); Daniel R. Mandelker, *Managing Our Urban Environment* (Indianapolis: Bobbs-Merrill, 1971); Daniel R. Mandelker, *The Zoning Dilemma* (Indianapolis: Bobbs-Merrill, 1971); Randall W. Scott, ed., *Management and Control of Growth*, Vol. 1 (New York: The Urban Land Institute, 1975); David Listokin, ed., *Land Use Controls: Present Problems and Future Reform* (New Brunswick, N.J.: Center for Urban Policy Research, Rutgers University, 1975); and other books and articles cited in these works.

91. The following account draws upon many sources, including articles in the *St. Louis Globe-Democrat* and *St. Louis Post-Dispatch*; Ronald F. Kirby, Frank deLeeuw, and William Silverman, *Residential Zoning and Equal Housing Opportunities: A Case Study in Black Jack, Missouri* (Washington, D.C.: The Urban Institute, 1972); *Park View Heights Corp. v. City of Black Jack*, 467 F. 2d (1972), reversing: 335. F. Supp. 899 (1971); *U.S. v. City of Black Jack*, Civ. Action No. 71; "Confrontation in Black Jack," in *Land-Use Controls Annual* (Chicago: American Society of Planning Officials, 1972); and from discussions in several places in Danielson, *The Politics of Exclusion*.

92. Jack Quigley, *St. Louis Post-Dispatch*, June 15, 1971.

93. Quoted in William K. Reilly, ed., *The Use of Land: A Citizen's Guide for Urban Growth* (New York: Thomas Y. Crowell, 1973), p. 90.

94. *Dailey v. City of Lawton*, 425 F. 2d 1037 (1970).

95. *Kennedy Park Homes v. City of Lackawanna*, 436 F. 2d 108 (1971).

96. Editorial, *St. Louis Post-Dispatch*, April 5, 1971.

97. *St. Louis Post-Dispatch*, June 3, 1971.

98. *St. Louis Post-Dispatch*.

99. *James v. Valtierra*, 91 S. Ct. 1331 (1971).

100. "Federal Policies Relative to Equal Housing Opportunity: A Statement of the President," press release, the White House, Washington, D.C.: June 11, 1971.

101. White House press release, June 11, 1971.

102. *St. Louis Post-Dispatch*, June 15, 1971.

103. Quoted in *St. Louis Post-Dispatch*, December 22, 1971.

104. Quoted in *St. Louis Globe Democrat*, January 11, 1977.

105. *St. Louis Globe-Democrat*.

106. Quoted in Nicholas Henry, *Governing at the Grass Roots*, 3rd ed. (Englewood Cliffs, N.J.: Prentice Hall, 1987), p. 492.

107. Reynolds Farley, "Suburban Persistence," in *North American Suburbs*, ed. Kramer, pp. 82–96.

108. Robert Wood, "Suburban Politics and Policies: Retrospect and Prospect," *Publius, The Journal of Federalism* 5 (Winter 1975):51.

109. Wood, *Suburbia*, p. 106.

110. John D. Kasarda, "The Impact of Suburban Population Growth on Central City Service Functions," *American Journal of Sociology*, 77(6) (May 1972):1111–1124.

111. William B. Neenan, *The Political Economy of Urban Areas* (Chicago: Markham, 1972), pp. 137–138.

112. Goldston, *Suburbia: Civic Denial*, p. 22.

Chapter 7

THE FISCAL CRISIS

The Squeeze on Public Budgets

In an attempt to balance their fiscal year 1976 budget, officials in the city of Detroit announced that 25 percent of the city's employees would be laid off. This action, taken to trim $96 million from a budget otherwise faced with a deficit of between $65 and $85 million, followed on the heels of an earlier 10 percent reduction in the payrolls. Detroit officials were trying to avoid their twenty-first budget deficit in the past twenty-five years.[1]

At the other end of Lake Erie, the city of Buffalo was confronted with a $17 million deficit in its $229 million budget, even though its municipal payroll had been cut by 16 percent over the previous four years. Local revenues were not keeping pace with costs, and the city found it nearly impossible to borrow. The money market had closed tight on Buffalo in the wake of the fiscal difficulties of two other cities in the state, Yonkers and New York City, and the city was unable to find any buyers for a multimillion dollar bond issue.[2]

The St. Louis Board of Estimate and Apportionment proposed an increase in the property tax rate and a simultaneous payroll cutback of

4 percent in order to avoid a $20 million deficit for the fiscal year beginning May 1, 1975. By state law, the city was not allowed to have a deficit. The city's action followed previous cutbacks amounting to 7 percent of the municipal work force since 1971.[3]

City officials in Boston, already presiding over the highest tax rate among the nation's thirty largest cities, had to reduce the city's payroll by 10 percent in order to approach a balanced budget in fiscal 1976.[4]

In Cleveland, debt service payments—current interest charges and repayment of principal on maturing long-term debt—cost 18 percent of current operating expenditures. Cleveland led the nation in this category. Massive local layoffs in the auto industry and voter refusal to approve a municipal income tax increase left the city with a projected $16 million deficit in its 1976 budget. In response, Mayor Ralph Perk laid off 1,100 city workers, reduced service levels, and closed four firehouses.[5]

At the beginning of 1975, Newark faced a $36 million deficit. To balance the budget, Mayor Kenneth Gibson announced that 370 city employees would be removed from the payrolls. Four months later he announced that the city's public school staff would be reduced by 20 percent, 1,600 jobs.[6]

Scenes such as these were repeated across the nation as the recession of the mid-1970s caught up with city finances. The National League of Cities noted (from a far less than complete survey) that thirty-six cities intended to postpone needed capital improvements as a result of the recession. Twenty-one municipalities reported that they were laying off city workers or imposing a hiring freeze. While twenty-eight cities intended to raise tax rates, twenty-three planned to reduce service levels to balance their budgets. Forty-three cities reported to the League that they anticipated budget deficits in the upcoming fiscal year.[7]

By June 1975, the recession, at the time the nation's worse economic downturn in forty years, was estimated by one congressional committee to have cost state and local governments about $8 billion. More than 140,000 government employees had been forced off the payrolls and into the ranks of the unemployed. About 85 percent of these reductions came in eighteen states where unemployment rates already exceeded the national average.[8]

Similar stories of municipal hardship abounded during the recession that started in July 1980. Service levels were again slashed, capital improvements delayed, and city employees laid off, only this time, the cities had even fewer options than before. During the earlier recession, the federal government had come to the cities' rescue. Revenue-sharing funds began to flow in 1973. Under the Carter administration, an Economic Stimulus Package was put together to help the cities. Funds made available under the Concentrated Employment and Training Act were increased.

Total federal grants-in-aid grew from $43.4 billion in 1974 to $77.9 billion in 1978.[9] State governments also increased their urban aid, an effort made possible by the budgetary surpluses held by many states.

By the time the recession of the early 1980s hit, circumstances had changed considerably. Beginning with the adoption of Proposition 13 by California voters in 1978, a tax revolt swept the states; by the end of 1982 more than two-thirds had adopted property tax limitations, budget ceilings, or other spending or revenue restrictions. The timing for these measures was unfortunate for cities, for the recession also cut into the revenues of the states. As a result, Connecticut faced a $110 million revenue shortfall in fiscal 1982; the governor of Illinois recommended $220 million in budget cuts for fiscal 1982; Iowa reduced its 1981 budget by 4.6 percent; Michigan cut its fiscal 1981 budget by 6 percent and laid off 4,300 state employees; Minnesota was confronted with a $500 million shortfall in 1982; Oregon's governor sought $200 million in spending cuts and $240 million in tax increases (in 1978 the Oregon legislature had cut property taxes).[10] Even the state of Colorado, where unemployment lagged behind the national rate by 2 to 3 percent, found itself facing a $100 million deficit in 1983, forcing the legislature to seek a package of tax increases.[11] Only six years earlier, the same legislature had cut state income taxes.

All this occurred against a background of deep cuts in federal grants-in-aid to the cities. Thus, even when the economy recovered in 1984, city budgets could not easily rebound. In 1979, federal grants-in-aid supplied 26 percent of city revenues. This declined to 23 percent by 1984, and state grants to cities dropped even more. Just to stay even, which most cities managed to do because of new private investment, cities were forced to raise their property taxes or continue delaying capital improvements.

City Expenditures

Cities are especially sensitive to fluctuations in the economy. During economic downturns, revenue sources decline, but demands for local services increase. Even in prosperity, revenue sources go up more slowly than do expenditures. Thus, cities are caught in a constantly recurring fiscal squeeze.

Because cities are the front-line providers of critical governmental services, it is difficult for them to hold down expenditures. Poverty and unemployment, high crime rates, homelessness, heavy winter snows, demands for recreational and cultural facilities—these are only a few of many conditions that lead to high service costs.

Most categories of municipal expenditure are familiar to everyone. Cities provide everyday government services: police and fire protection, education, water distribution and sewage collection, parks, highways, museums, and libraries. The relative importance of the various functional areas of municipal expenditure for 1983–1984 are shown in Table 7–1. The six biggest cities spend a large proportion of their funds on public welfare and health and hospitals, which together account for 23 percent of their expenditures. Education also is a leading item, accounting for 15 percent of their budgets. This is followed by police protection, which takes 9 percent.

TABLE 7–1 **Distribution of Revenues and Expenditures for Selected Urban Governments, 1983–1984 (in Percentages)**

	All municipalities*	6 cities 1,000,000+	18 cities 500,000– 999,999
Intergovernmental revenue	32	37	36
State aid	20	27	18
Federal aid	10	11	16
Local revenue	69	63	64
Property taxes	21	30	19
Sales taxes	17	21	18
Income taxes	8	20	10
All other taxes and changes	44	30	42
Expenditures by function			
Education	11	15	12
Public welfare	5	15	11
Health and hospitals	6	8	8
Police protection	12	9	11
Highways	8	3	6
Sewerage	7	4	7
Parks and recreation	5	2	5
Fire protection	6	4	6
General control	3	2	3
Financial administration	3	1	2
Interest on debt	6	4	6
Other	27	31	27

Source: Calculated from U.S. Bureau of the Census, *City Government Finances in 1983–84*, Government Finances 16F84, No. 4 (Washington, D.C.: U.S. Government Printing Office, 1985), table 2.
*These data are estimates subject to sampling variation.

Smaller municipalities located within metropolitan areas less frequently run the schools, which are financed through independent school districts, and they spend much less of their budgets on public welfare and public health. Standard municipal services, such as police and roads, account for a larger share of their budgets. Most central cities are not responsible for education, which is provided through separate school districts. The exceptions are some old cities, such as New York, Boston, San Francisco, and Baltimore. Public welfare is a relatively small item in all city budgets except in the six biggest cities.

Collectively, cities spend substantial sums of money. In fiscal 1981, for example, they spent $70.4 billion, which was 31.5 percent of all local government expenditures in the United States. School districts and counties, with 36 percent and 23 percent respectively, accounted for most of the rest of local government expenditures.[12] In fiscal year 1983, the leading budget by far was New York City's, at $16.4 billion. Eight other cities spent more than $1 billion: Washington, D.C. ($2.3 billion), Chicago ($2.1 billion), Philadelphia ($1.8 billion), Los Angeles ($1.7 billion), Baltimore ($1.3 billion), Detroit ($1.2 billion), San Francisco ($1.1 billion), and Houston ($1.0 billion).[13]

Municipal expenditures rose sharply throughout the 1960s and until the recession of 1974–1975. Between 1962 and 1972, per capita spending in the twenty-eight largest cities rose 198 percent.[14] These cities added to their budgets at a much faster rate than other local governments, which increased spending by 142 percent. As indicated in Table 7–2, a steep rate of increase for all local governments was maintained until 1975. From 1970 to 1975, the six cities with populations exceeding 1 million increased their budgets *even after adjustments for inflation* by 26 percent, only lagging behind smaller cities very slightly.

But after 1975, the brakes were applied to municipal budgets. The six biggest cities upped their budgets by 30 percent from 1975 to 1980, but after adjustments for inflation this meant a 9.7 percent *drop* in real spending power. The twenty cities with populations exceeding 500,000 in the 1970 Census had no real increases after adjustments for inflation during the same five years. Other municipalities did no better.

In the 1980s, all cities, on the average, continued to hold the line on spending; between 1980 and 1984 there were no per capita increases, after adjustments for inflation are considered. The largest six cities increased expenditures 3.4 percent (after inflation), but cities of 500,000 to 1 million in population *reduced* expenditures.

Per capita expenditures of cities are closely related to city size. Big cities spend more for a variety of reasons: they support a wider array of services, often provide service of better quality (for example, well-trained police officers and firefighters), pay higher salaries to their public employees,

TABLE 7-2 Changes in Spending for Cities of Different Size, 1970–1984

	Growth rate, percentage					
	1970-1975		1975-1980		1980-1984	
	Unadjusted	(Adjusted for inflation)*	Unadjusted	(Adjusted for inflation)*	Unadjusted	(Adjusted for inflation)*
All municipalities	76	(21.6)‡	47	(.02)	31	(0)
Cities of 500,000 to 999,999†	76	(21.6)	45	(.01)	26	(–3.8)
Big six cities	72.5	(19.2)	30	(–9.7)	35	(3.4)

Sources: U.S. Bureau of the Census, *Local Government Finances in Selected Metropolitan Areas and Large Counties: 1969–70*, GF 70 no. 6 (Washington, D.C.: U.S. Government Printing Office, 1971), table 4; *Local Government Finances: 1974–75*, GF 75 no. 6 (1976); *City Government Finances in 1974–75*, GF 75 no. 5, table D; *Local Government Finances: 1979–80*, GF 80 no. 5, (1981), table D; U.S. Advisory Commission on Intergovernmental Relations, *Significant Features of Fiscal Federalism, 1980–81 Edition* (December 1981), p. 19; *City Government Finances in 1983–84*, GF 84 no. 4 (1985), table 3.
*Using GNP implicit price deflator for state and local government purchases, U.S. Bureau of the Census, *Statistical Abstract of the United States* (1986), p. 470.
†Population in 1982.

and experience the high service costs that high-density populations and poverty and unemployment make necessary. In 1983–1984, the six biggest cities spent $1,489 for each of their citizens; the average for all municipalities in the United States was $672.

Throughout the 1960s, the cities of the industrial North in effect tried to ignore the fiscal constraints imposed on them by their deteriorating tax bases. Faced with social unrest and urban decay, they attempted to improve business districts and neighborhoods by investing in municipal and social services.

In the 1970s, the most important reason for rising municipal expenditures was the cost of necessary goods and services. From 1964 to 1970, about two-thirds of total adjustments in expenditures were attributable to inflation. After 1970, inflation takes a bigger bite, until by 1974, there is scarcely any real (adjusted for inflation) rise in expenditures at all. A survey conducted by the Senate Subcommittee on Intergovernmental Relations in 1977 found that some local officials believed inflation to be a worse problem for their budgets than the recession of the mid-1970s. According to an official from Norwalk, Connecticut, "our community has found its fiscal problems far less influenced by the consequences of recession than from the substantially higher operating costs resulting from inflation."[15]

Inflation affects local governments much more than it affects the private sector. In the eight years between 1963 and 1971, while the costs of goods and services as a whole (the Gross National Product) rose 32 percent, the costs of goods and services purchased by state and local governments rose by 51 percent.[16] Between 1970 an 1977, prices paid by state and local governments rose faster than the Gross National Product (GNP) in every year but one. Often the difference was substantial: in 1974, for example, GNP inflation was 5.6 percent, but for city goods and services inflation was 10.3 percent.[17]

This rate of inflation can be explained, in part, by the fact that most municipal services are labor intensive. In the private sector of the economy, labor costs are susceptible to being offset by efficiencies brought about by the use of labor-saving technologies. Such technologies have limited application in the public sector. The labor costs of police protection cannot be reduced to any appreciable extent by the use of computers. Police service demands a human response; it is not possible to get around the fact that police protection requires police officers.

The labor costs of city government are heavily influenced by the economic and social forces that influence the price of labor throughout the economy. Wage adjustments in the private sector together with the salary scale of federal employees (especially after the federal government made wage parity with the private sector its official policy) raised both the expectations and the aspirations of city workers across the country. Between

1960 and 1975, wages paid to state and local government employees rose from 89 to 98 percent of the earnings of private sector workers.[18] During the second half of the 1970s, however, the ratio of public to private employee wages fell to 93 percent. After 1975, for the first time since 1955, wage gains in the public sector lagged behind earnings in the private sector.[19]

Until the mid-1970s, growth in the number of public employees had consistently outpaced employment in the private sector.[20] Local government expenditures had accounted for an ever-increasing proportion of the GNP, rising from 4.4 percent in 1959 to 5.2 percent in 1975.[21] Spending by municipalities grew at a faster rate up to 1975 than did federal budgets,[22] and public employees found that they could demand higher wages. But after 1975, when they were faced with tighter municipal budgets and layoffs, their bargaining positions eroded.

During the years of rising labor costs, public employee unions were adding more members. During the 1960s, the membership rolls of such labor organizations as the American Federation of State, County, and Municipal Employees (AFSCME) and the American Federation of Government Employees, both affiliated with the AFL-CIO, grew rapidly. Union membership rose from 1,070,000 in 1960 to 2,318,000 in 1970. At the same time, the unions became more militant. Worker-days lost through work stoppages by state and local employees escalated from 58,000 in 1960 to 1,375,000 a decade later, and to 2,299,000 by 1973.[23] Unionization of city workers, which is more widespread in the older northern cities, appears to account for 10 to 15 percent higher compensation for public employees, thus partially explaining the cost of municipal services in those cities.[24]

Competition among rival unions forced union negotiators to bargain very hard. Much of the improvement in the compensation of city workers took the form of hidden or delayed benefits. As one observer noted:

> Between 1940 and 1965 the number of policemen in New York City increased by 50% (from 16,000 to 24,000) but the total number of hours worked by the entire force in 1965 was actually less than in 1940. The increase in manpower was completely eaten up by a shorter work week, a longer lunch break, more vacation days, more holidays, and more sick leave.[25]

Many personnel costs are "hidden." Pension and early retirement obligations, for example, are delayed until they must actually be paid, out of future budgets. Pension contributions make up a significant proportion of general fund spending in big cities: in 1976, 18 percent in Detroit and Buffalo, 12 percent in Cleveland.[26] When cities have to cut budgets, they find that pension costs are "fixed," arranged and guaranteed through previous contractual agreements.

State and local governments raised their total personnel levels during the 1960s. In the ten years between 1960 and 1970, state and local government payrolls rose from 6.4 to 10.1 million persons, a leap of 59 percent, in sharp contrast to the 16 percent increase in the "growing federal bureaucracy" so decried by vote-seeking political candidates.[27] This expansion of public employment continued through the minor recession of 1970 and grew faster than any other employment in the economy during the temporary recovery of 1971–72. It abated only in the recession of 1974–75.[28]

During this recessionary period, public employment provided jobs in the economically depressed central cities. In the five major cities listed in Table 7–3, for instance, nearly 33,000 new public service jobs between 1967 and 1972 helped offset a decline of 73,000 jobs in the private sector. Without the rise in public employment, unemployment rates would have been far worse than they were in the nation's large cities.

Between 1977 and 1983, however, there was a loss of more than 15,000 public service jobs in these cities, and also a loss of private sector jobs (more than 20,000). Cutbacks in federal and state programs for cities aggravated rather than buffered the recession that began in 1980.

TABLE 7–3   Changes in Private and Public Sector Central City Employment, 1967–1972 and 1977–1983

| | Change in number of jobs | | | |
| | 1967–1972 | | 1977–1983 | |
Five Cities	Private sector*	Public sector†	Private sector*	Public sector†
Baltimore	− 7,000	+ 3,900	−13,342	− 4,617
New Orleans	+ 7,000	+ 2,500	+ 5,349	− 2,542
Philadelphia	−53,000	+18,400	−19,705	− 4,445
St. Louis	−23,000	+ 2,300	−29,508	− 3,854
San Francisco	+ 6,000	+ 5,700	+37,000	+ 7
Total: 5 cities	−73,000	+32,800	−20,206	−15,451

Sources: Adapted from George E. Peterson, "Finance," in *The Urban Predicament*, ed. William Gorham and Nathan Glazer (Washington, D.C.: The Urban Institute, 1976), p. 112, citing U.S. Bureau of the Census, *Compendium of Public Employment*, 1967 and 1972; and U.S. Bureau of the Census, *State and Metropolitan Data Book* (1982), table A; (1986), table A; U.S. Bureau of the Census, *County Business Patterns*, 1983 and 1977, table 2 (Washington, D.C.: U.S. Government Printing Office).

*Jobs covered by Social Security only.
†Includes city school district.

Up to 1975, state and local payrolls made up a constantly larger share of the nation's personal income.[29] After 1975, these payrolls went into a steep decline in relation to the average national personal income, and the steepest declines occurred in New England and the midwestern states.[30]

The ability of cities to maintain expenditure levels was closely related to local economic vitality. All but two of the cities shown in Table 7–4 as reducing city budgets between 1976 and 1983 are located in the Frostbelt. Certainly budgetary reductions increased local unemployment levels and made it more difficult for cities to provide adequate services. In these cities, funds for health services were usually reduced, at a time when infant mortality rates and other indicators of ill health were skyrocketing among minority residents of older cities. In contrast, six of the ten cities that increased expenditures by large amounts were Sunbelt cities. Four of the cities that increased their budgets, however, were older industrial cities, showing that special circumstances (such as ability to raise taxes or find new tax sources) can be important.

Meanwhile, there are strong pressures on cities to maintain or to assume new expenditures. Cities compete with one another and with their suburbs for economic growth. Any city that allows its services or facilities to deteriorate runs the significant risk that business will locate elsewhere and that the affluent families still living in central cities will move away in even larger numbers than they are now doing. Thus, the revitalization of business districts and neighborhoods could be aborted.

Social pressure is also important. As a consequence of cuts in federal programs, rates of crime, ill health, and other problems associated with poverty have shot up in central cities. Homelessness has become a mounting problem, and cities can ill afford to allow street people and the unemployed to become even more desperate.

How Cities Raise Money

The cost of supplying city government services constitutes one-half the fiscal crisis that faces the cities. The other half is the problem of raising enough money. For a long period, cities have found it difficult to increase revenues sufficiently to keep up with expenditures.

The principal source of local revenue historically has been the property tax. The most important and widely used form of property tax is the *ad valorem* real property tax, a levy on land and its improvements. From colonial times through the early years of the republic, there was a belief that real property was a valid indicator of both wealth and the ability to pay taxes. In fact, this was generally so. Most of the wealth of the era was tied to the land, and fortunes were made in land speculation. A person's

TABLE 7–4 General Government Expenditures for Selected Large Cities, Fiscal Year 1976 to Fiscal Year 1983 (in millions of 1983 dollars)

	FY 1976 Expenditures	FY 1983 Expenditures	% Change
Cities with declining expenditures:			
New York	$20,933	$16,412	−22
Baltimore	1,716	1,262	−26.5
Cleveland	466	335	−28
Boston	1,270	848	−33
Denver	560	509	−11
Jacksonville, Fla.	409	332	−19
Washington, D.C.	2,512	2,337	−7
St. Louis	409	406	−1
Cities with increasing expenditures:			
El Paso	97	145	50
Houston	616	1,065	73
Pittsburgh	226	271	20
New Orleans	403	463	15
Milwaukee	345	393	14
San Jose	229	262	14
Dallas	375	477	27
Detroit	1,068	1,283	20
Phoenix	346	510	47.5
Chicago	1,758	2,087	19

Source: Alexander Ganz, "Where Has the Urban Crisis Gone? How Boston and Other Large Cities Have Stemmed Economic Decline," *Urban Affairs Quarterly,* 20, No. 4 (June 1985), p. 460. Copyright © by Sage Publications. Reprinted by permission of Sage Publications, Inc.

wealth was roughly proportional to landholdings. The real property tax, therefore, was used to underwrite state and local governmental expenditures.[31]

This method of taxation had several advantages. Real property was impossible to conceal. And insofar as the tax was levied on the land and not on the taxpayer per se, the tax could not easily be evaded. Even if the owner were unknown, the tax could be levied and extracted, if need be, by confiscation of the property.

The spatial location of land and improvements determined the value of property. The closer a manufacturer or warehouse was to the waterfront, the more valuable the property. If one recalls that early urban services were developed by local entrepreneurs largely out of a concern for the safety of their investments, it becomes clear the *ad valorem* levy was a relatively reliable index of the value of public services received by property holders. The owner of a $1,000 property received twice as much benefit from fire protection service as did a neighbor who owned a $500 property; the former had twice as much to lose in a fire and twice as much to gain if the property was saved. It was considered equitable if the levy were proportional to the value of the property.

Taxation of personal property—that is, assets other than real property —developed as the cities became more complex. As trade and manufacturing grew in importance, more and more wealth was represented in bank accounts, merchandise, patent rights, machinery, capital stock, and corporate assets. Cities (and states) began to levy taxes on them in order to maintain some relationship between tax assessment and wealth.

Such assets were hard to find and assess, especially following the Civil War when the nation underwent unprecedented capital accumulation and industrialization. In this period, although personal and corporate wealth grew at a rapid rate, the proportion of the property tax attributable to nonreal property actually declined.[32]

In 1902, personal and real property taxes accounted for 73 percent of all municipal revenues. They continued to provide approximately three-fourths of all local receipts until the late 1930s and early 1940s, when the proportion began to decline in the face of new revenue sources, especially sales and income taxes.[33]

By 1962, property taxes accounted for barely 50 percent of municipal revenues in the seventy-two largest SMSAs (although for nearly all the revenue for school districts). In the 1960s, the expansion of federal and state assistance to localities decreased the proportion of all revenues derived from property taxes, because taxes did not generate the entire city budget. By fiscal 1975, property taxes accounted for little more than one-third (35 percent) of the revenues in the largest metropolitan areas, despite a 130 percent increase in the average per capita levy since the early 1960s.[34]

Reliance on the property tax dropped to 21 percent of local revenues for municipalities in metropolitan areas by 1983–1984; in 1970, this tax had generated 39.1 percent of all municipal revenues.[35]

In the big cities, the property tax provided an even smaller proportion of local revenues. In the six cities with more than 1 million residents, it accounted for 30 percent, but in the eighteen other cities with 500,000 or more in population, property taxes netted only 19 percent of locally generated revenues in 1983–1984 (refer to Table 7–1). For all cities, the property tax only raised 21 percent of general revenues. The figure was somewhat higher for all local governments, as opposed to municipalities, because school districts and counties relied heavily on the property tax (school districts, 97 percent in 1984; counties, 76 percent).

For example, in Philadelphia and St. Louis, property taxes accounted for only 16 and 9 percent of 1984 local revenues, respectively. Between 1965 and 1975, both cities barely increased property taxes (10 and 9 percent), but other taxes increased much more, and intergovernmental revenues went up by more than 600 percent in Philadelphia and more than 1,000 percent in St. Louis. Between 1974 and 1984, property tax increases of 119 percent in Philadelphia nearly kept up with the increase in total revenues, but in St. Louis property tax revenue *declined* by 7 percent. Between 1975 and 1980, while municipal revenues for all municipalities in the United States rose by 45 percent (not adjusted for inflation), the property tax increased by only 30 percent.[36]

Only in some cities of the Sunbelt has the property tax been an important source of revenue growth since the 1960s. In those cities, property values escalated as a result of new business and residential investment. For example, taxable property value went up 251 percent in Phoenix from 1965 to 1973. In contrast, it rose only 2 percent in Newark and 14 percent in Detroit during the same period.[37] But stagnant property values in the industrial cities were only part of the problem. Antiquated assessment procedures existed in many cities, systems that fail to keep the assessed valuations of property in line with their market values in periods of inflation.[38]

Another problem is the high proportion of tax-exempt property. In 1982, in just twenty-three states and the District of Columbia, there was $15 billion in exempt property for religious institutions, $22 billion for educational, $15 billion for charitable, and $128 billion for government property.[39] In addition, many cities and states provide lower property tax rates to businesses in an attempt to create a good climate for investment.

As of 1969, 54 percent of the real property in Boston was tax-exempt. Nearly 35 percent of the real estate in New York City was so designated in 1970, and 25 percent of the real estate in Baltimore. A comparable 1971 figure for Washington, D.C., was 50 percent.[40] The situation in New York so incensed one taxpayer that he sued the city tax commission over the "subsidy of religion" issue, going all the way to the U.S. Supreme Court before finally losing the case.[41]

In the 1980s, the proportion of tax-exempt property has increased; many cities have provided tax relief for the aged or people in poverty ("circuit breaker" laws), and cities try to keep businesses from moving to other jurisdictions by forgiving or reducing their taxes.

Thus, cities have attempted to raise money through more "modern" taxes, chiefly through sales or income taxes, and user fees (e.g., charges for entry to zoos, museums, and sporting events).

Although Charleston, South Carolina, is reported to have levied a tax on income prior to the Civil War, the modern municipal income tax movement began in Philadelphia in 1939. That levy, a flat-rate payroll tax on all earnings of persons who lived or worked in the city, was adopted to relieve financial pressures during the Great Depression. Since that time it has been used in thousands of communities, more than 3,500 by 1970, but most of them, all but forty-two, were located in Pennsylvania or Ohio. It "was not adopted because cities thought it was in some sense a 'fairer' tax than the property tax, but solely because it was a tax that could generate large amounts of revenue."[42]

The revenue source that saved the cities during the 1960s, allowing them to expand both the level and scope of services, was intergovernmental aid. Between 1965 and 1974, intergovernmental transfers to all cities rose 370 percent, more than twice the 153 percent increase in municipal expenditures.[43] For some of the big cities the increase in intergovernmental aid was even larger: St. Louis, for example, was on the receiving end of a 1,039 percent increase.

State and federal aid facilitated budgetary expansion in northern industrial cities during the period 1965 to about 1978. Such aid was the single largest new source of revenue for most cities. It accounted for an average of 56 percent of all new revenues for the older northern cities. In contrast, it accounted for an average of only 30 percent of new revenues for southern and western cities.[44]

Although federal assistance grew at a faster rate than state government aid, the bulk of all intergovernmental assistance comes from the states. The cities as a whole received nearly $2 in state revenue for each federal dollar in 1974, though this ratio declined to $1.47 of state aid for each federal dollar by 1980.[45] A few large cities, however, receive more federal aid than state aid; examples in 1980 were St. Louis ($2.35 in federal dollars for each state $1) and Chicago ($2.18 to $1).[46]

As local revenue sources lagged further and further behind expenditure levels, the cities, especially the big ones, became more dependent on external revenue, meaning state and federal grants. So long as federal aid to the cities continued to rise, the expanding services and rising expenses of the cities could be funded. When federal and state aid began to decline in the late 1970s, cities found it difficult to replace it with their own revenues. Perhaps as a result, local government debt climbed steeply in the early 1980s, by 21 percent from fiscal 1979 to fiscal 1981.[47]

Cities also have found it difficult to increase taxes, for they have not escaped the "taxpayer's revolt" initiated in the late 1970s. Since 1970, at least fourteen state legislatures have enacted laws that limit property tax rates or spending by local governments.[48] Even more important, however, have been the citizen initiatives. The first well-publicized of these was Proposition 13 in California, which was passed in June 1978. From March to November 1978, sixteen states held initiatives or referenda to limit taxes or spending, though not all were binding on public officials.[49] Thirteen of the citizen-initiated proposals passed. More such proposals were approved after 1978. Consequently, even though cities were faced with social problems arising from the recession of the early 1980s, their budgetary options were sharply reduced.

The Fiscal Crisis and the Private Sector

The private institutions of the economy have contributed to the financial problems of the cities. Over the years, private capital has gravitated to the suburban and exurban rings that encircle the cities. It has also moved from the old cities of the Frostbelt to the cities of the Sunbelt. This movement of capital has been accompanied by active disinvestment in the old central cities. Banks and other financial institutions have been reluctant to finance home mortgages and commercial ventures in the cities, whereas money is readily available for these activities in the suburbs. In 1975, for example, four St. Louis-based banks, with combined assets of over $766 million, invested in only two conventional home mortgages in the city, totaling $50,000. The city's Department of Community Development also found that only five home mortgages, totaling $79,000, were made on properties by three city savings and loan associations, which held assets of well over $1 billion.[50]

The Association of Community Organizations for Reform Now (ACORN), a St. Louis social action group, "found that only 5.6 percent of the mortgage money lent by St. Louis banks and savings and loan institutions in recent years had gone to finance property in the city," while about 78 percent, or fourteen times as much, "had been lent financing property in high income suburban areas."[51]

A similar situation existed in all the old industrial cities. In New York

City, according to a report published by the New York Public Interest Research Group (NYPIRG), three of the largest savings banks in Brooklyn (Dime Savings Bank, Greater New York Bank for Savings, and Williamsburgh Savings Bank) received between 73 and 93 percent of their deposits from city residents, but only 15 to 17 percent of their mortgages were invested in properties within the city limits. The vast majority of the mortgages they held were on homes outside the city of New York, and many were even on properties outside the state.[52]

Disinvestment in the central cities by financial institutions accelerated the long-term decline of the cities, and was a major reason for their fiscal plight.

> As the banks have facilitated their withdrawal from the city housing market, they have required faster repayments of financing at higher rates of interest, making it difficult for even the best landlord to upgrade profitably.
> ...The banks themselves have created the abandonment problem, which they then point to as the rationale for reducing investment in the city.[53]

The lack of available mortgage capital deterred potential home buyers and businesses from locating in the central city. They were forced, for lack of an alternative, to seek locations at the suburban fringe. By the normal workings of the private financial market, cities were denied capital and, in turn, new residents, businesses, jobs, and—most important for municipal finances—taxpayers. Such property as already existed within the city declined in relative value. Assessed valuation fell because of the lack of a capital market to finance maintenance and improvements. The city's tax base further decayed, thus fulfilling the prophecy of the banking industry that the cities were poor investment risks.

The Case of New York City

No American city compares in size or complexity with New York City. New York's financial status as a public corporation is important to the entire American economy. New York's budget of $12.5 billion in fiscal 1980 was 6.5 times as large as that of the city with the second biggest budget, Washington, D.C. Table 7–5 gives some indication of New York's comparative status. In fiscal 1974, New York generated 43 percent of the total revenue of all forty-eight largest cities, spent 40 percent of the funds, and held nearly 43 percent of the debt. When New York City's financial situation came to a crisis in 1975, investors everywhere were worried. Banks in California, Missouri, and even overseas held New York's bonds. A default would reverberate throughout the economy of the nation and even of the world.

TABLE 7-5   New York City Finances in Comparative Perspective,
Fiscal Year 1973-1974 (Dollar Amounts in Millions)

	48 largest cities	New York City	New York as a % of 48 largest cities
Population, 1973 (est.)	39,444,916	7,646,818	19.3
Revenue, total	27,342	11,877	43.3
Revenue, own sources	13,741	5,460	40.2
Gross debt outstanding	31,672	13,509	42.7
Long term debt outstanding:	26,301	9,808	37.2
for housing and urban renewal	3,061	2,424	79.0
for Transit	2,047	2,024	99.0

Source: Adapted from Robert Fitch, "Planning New York City," in *The Fiscal Crisis of American Cities: Essays on the Political Economy of Urban America with Special Reference to New York*, ed. Roger E. Alcaly and David Mermelstein (New York: Random House, Vintage Books, 1977), p. 250.

After registering a slight (1.4 percent) increase in population during the 1960s, New York City lost more than 4 percent (328,500) of its population between 1970 and 1974. At the same time, the dependent population of the city grew. In 1970, nearly half (49 percent) of the city's families had incomes below the poverty line.[54] By 1975, the welfare rolls contained 1.1 million persons.[55] During a twenty-year period ending in 1970, the proportion of New York's population over 65 years of age increased from 8 percent to more than 12 percent.[56]

New York City has felt the trauma of economic deterioration, as have other similarly situated cities. Between 1970 and 1975, for instance, the city suffered a net loss of 379,000 private sector jobs (11 percent of the 1970 total)[57] as the decentralization of industry and commerce continued.[58] The garment industry, long a key part of New York's manufacturing base, lost an average of 12,000 jobs a year between 1969 and 1974. Much of the industry moved to the southern states. The printing industry lost 5,600 jobs annually. Even the white-collar real estate, banking, and insurance industries lost an average of 7,500 positions per year in New York.[59] As a result of this long-term decline and the recession of 1974 to 1977, the unemployment rate in New York City climbed dramatically, from 4.8 percent in 1970 to 12 percent in mid-1975.[60]

These private sector economic phenomena had a direct impact on the balance of New York City's finances. In 1973-74, for example, consumer prices rose 9.3 percent. Taxable sales within the city, however, rose only 1.7 percent.[61]

The budgetary impact of these demographic and economic trends was aggravated by the political climate. One observer noted that:

> The Big Apple's budgets in the last decade—because the two men who had the most influence on them—John Lindsay and Nelson Rockefeller, both wanted, still want, to be president—grew fat with so-called social legislation because it was easy to say yes.[62]

The availability of federal social programs, all of which required some local spending to match the federal money, led to a great expansion in New York's budget. Between 1965 and 1970, the city's budget doubled, from $3.9 to $7.8 billion. The number of city residents on the welfare rolls likewise doubled, reaching 1 million by 1970.[63]

The retrenchment in federal spending under the Nixon administration played havoc with the city's budget. Between 1965 and 1973, New York had relied on external sources of funding to absorb new budgeted expenditures. During that period, intergovernmental aid raised 55 percent of the city's new revenues.

The impact of Nixon's New Federalism was felt in 1973. Between 1973 and 1975, federal and state aid accounted for only 8 percent (an average of $125 million per year) of the growth in revenues. Net annual borrowing, on the average of $1.13 billion per year, was relied upon to take up the slack (70 percent). As a result, New York's general-purpose debt rose from $9 to $12.4 billion between 1973 and 1975.[64]

Even worse was the projected situation at the time of the fiscal crisis of 1975. The preliminary 1976 budget showed a net decrease in intergovernmental assistance ($7 million) and an unfunded budget gap of $641 million, a gap that could not be filled by borrowing.[65]

The pressures of spiraling expenditures presented New York with an annual financial crisis. First, there was the crisis of the deficit. Projected revenues continually fell short of budgeted expenditures, with the 8 percent gap in the 1976 budget constituting but one example of this difficulty.[66] This problem was largely solved through an annual exercise in "creative accounting." The philosophy underlying this system had been developed in the 1960s, as articulated by one of the Lindsay administration's budget directors, David Grossman: "You get a million dollars here and a million dollars there and, before you know it, you've got some real money."[67]

The system included a method of accounting that projected revenue *earned*, rather than revenue received or anticipated during the fiscal year. The flaw lies in the fact that not all revenue was collectible. Between 1970 and 1976, between $2 and $3 billion in city taxes, fees, and fines went uncollected—$1 billion in 1976 alone. Between 1970 and 1975, the delinquency rate for real property taxes rose from 4 to 7 percent and totaled $571 million by June 30, 1975.[68]

Other creative techniques included advancing the last payday of the year into the next fiscal year. Some current operating expenses, such as planning and engineering operations and manpower programs, were tucked into the capital expenditures budget. In 1975–76, some $600 million was so counted.[69] Vendors and other creditors were held off. Contributions to the city's pension funds were delayed and underfinanced, while the interest on those accounts above the statutory minimum was "borrowed" for the city's general fund.[70]

Present expenses were shifted onto future taxpayers by calling borrowed funds "income" and issuing Revenue Anticipating Notes (RANs) and Tax Anticipation Notes (TANs). These were short-term bonds against which future intergovernmental receipts and taxes were pledged. Over the years the city's accumulated operating deficit continued to climb, reaching approximately $2.5 billion by 1975.[71]

Another problem involved cash flow. This particular aspect of New York's chronic financial problem was an immediate contributing factor to the 1975·crisis. Because operating expenses occur on a regular, day-to-day, week-to-week basis, they require a steady flow of funds. Revenues and receipts, on the other hand, are sporadic. Federal and state aid payments do not always coincide with expenditure dates. Assessed real property taxes are not immediately collectible. Money often had to be spent, therefore, before it was actually received. The cash-flow problem led to a reliance on short-term borrowing. Over a ten-year period ending in 1975, such borrowing increased from $1.5 to $8.4 billion.

Because of persisting operating deficits, New York's accumulated debt continued to mount. The deficits were "rolled over" from year to year by issuing new bonds to cover debt service on bonds coming due. Short-term debt, which represented the bulk of this accumulated, "rolled-over" debt, grew by over 400 percent in ten years. (On a personal basis, this practice is similar to someone who charges living expenses on one credit card, uses a second credit card to cover the first, a third to cover the second, *ad infinitum*, and never comes up with the cash to cover the expenses.)

Despite the obvious culpability of successive administrations in New York, they were not solely responsible for the imaginative budgetary techniques used. In their in-depth analysis of the political situation surrounding New York's financial plight, Jack Newfield and Paul DuBrul concluded that "the banks have been the central villain. . . . Frankly, this was not our original thesis. But the deeper we probed, the more interviews we conducted, the more we realized that behind almost every horror stood a banker."[72]

This major tie between the city's banking institutions and the government was accomplished through the bond market. An enormous amount of money could be made in underwriting and marketing city securities. Between 1965 and 1975, New York issued nearly *$58 billion* in bonds. Of this total, $48.5 billion was in short-term, high-interest notes used to "roll over" the accumulating deficit and rectify the cash-flow problems of the city. Bankers and brokers made commissions on every bond sale. Thus, New York City's problems were immediately beneficial to banks and brokerage houses.

The banks were represented in the financial processes of the city through the Bond Counsel and the Comptroller's Technical Debt Advisory Committee. The latter body, which "was to advise the city on its securities-selling practices," gave implicit approval to the city's practices as it passed on the continuous stream of bonds. One observer-participant of these meetings remarked that "all Simon and some of the other bankers wanted to do was sell bonds, make their profits, and look the other way."[73] This was the same William E. Simon—"We're going to sell New York to the Shah of Iran. It's a hell of an investment."[74]—who, as President Gerald Ford's Secretary of the Treasury, advocated a policy of "punitive" measures against New York City. Simon, who served two years (1971–72) on the Comptroller's Committee, and who earned $2 million one year as a senior partner in the firm of Salomon Brothers, "was personally in charge of Salomon's [substantial] municipal and governmental bond sales."[75]

The fiscal crisis of New York in the spring of 1975 was intimately tied to the fortunes of the nation's, indeed the world's, economy. As the nation's private economy sputtered, the United States fell into what was at the time its worst depression in forty years. Ten million workers joined the ranks of the unemployed, 11 percent of the work force in New York City by March.[76] At the same time, the country experienced the worst inflationary rates for "any period of similar length in all of American history."[77] The recession threatened to bring a $25 trillion mountain of debt tumbling down on the nation's financial institutions.[78]

Toward the end of the previous economic boom, the banks had been "skating on thin ice."[79] By the end of 1974, the large commercial banking institutions had lent out 82 percent of their deposits, a historic high level. The highest loans-to-deposits ratio in the seventy years prior to 1970 had been 79 percent (in 1921). Even in the black year of 1929, the proportion had been only 73 percent.[80]

The deteriorating economy and the troubles of many private business firms (such as the failure of the retail chain W. T. Grant, which left banks holding $640 million in debts[81]) led banks to reevaluate their holdings. New York's bonds were doubly threatening. Not only were they deemed marginal, but should the city default, the banks could not control the resolution of the problem or the attendant "write-down" in the value of the bonds. A rapid write-down would weaken the banks' ability to raise capital.[82] As a result, the banks sold New York City bonds as fast as they could, creating a near-panic atmosphere about the financial viability of the city. A legislative investigation summarized the situation as follows:

> They began to rapidly and quietly (and perhaps improperly and illegally) unload their New York City bonds *and thus saturated the market.* You recall, they claimed the market was saturated and hence they could not sell their bonds. This seems to be untrue. In fact it appears that Chase [Manhattan Bank] unloaded two billion dollars' worth of bonds in a very short time!
>
>   . . . .Here is where the problem gets sticky for the banks. They had knowledge of the problems ahead, but they kept this knowledge to themselves while unloading their portfolios on others. They created the panic by their heavy sales. . . .
>
> In short, Chase alone unloaded two billion dollars of paper they knew was going bad without telling their customers. They not only created the panic, but profited from it.
>
> When the banks saturated the market with their own paper [i.e., city bonds originally purchased for their own accounts] they turned to the State and City and shouted "Help." The market was flooded and they could not sell their bonds. This, in turn, led to us bailing them out, and to higher interest rates for every municipality in the country. It led to the EFCB [Emergency Financial Control Board for New York City] and a substantial portion of the enormous debt service we are now carrying.[83]

The culpability of the banks in precipitating the fiscal crisis was subsequently charged in a ten-pound, 800-page investigative report issued by the Securities and Exchange Commission.[84]

The rest of the fiscal crisis unfolded very unfavorably for New York City. The banks refused to underwrite the city's bonds, and New York's near-default thus became a self-fulfilling prophecy. First the State of New York and finally the federal government were brought in to save the situation. The state established the Municipal Assistance Corporation ("Big Mac") in June to help the city convert its pressing, "rolled-over" short-term debt into long-term obligations. In return, "Big Mac" was given some measure of control over the city's budget. In September, the crisis-ridden city was placed in virtual receivership as the state-appointed Emergency Financial Control Board (EFCB) was given control of New York's revenues. The Financial Control Board devised a method for refinancing some of the city's debt, but the plan floundered under adverse court decisions and continued public skepticism of city and state bonds. Some state issues were being traded at discounts that brought the effective yield to 20.956 percent.[85]

As the situation continued to deteriorate, the Ford administration was forced to intercede to save the city, the state, and the banks. The possibility of a $1.6 billion default was imminent. On December 9, 1975, Gerald Ford reluctantly signed a $2.3 billion loan program for New York City.

Municipal Bonds

New York City's flirtation with fiscal disaster underscores the importance of the municipal bond market. It is through the bond market that cities are tied directly to the private capital market.

Cities turn to the private capital market to finance expensive, permanent capital projects. Schools, highways, bridges, hospitals, and parks are commonly financed in this manner. Such municipal borrowings typically represent 20 to 25 percent of all state and local spending.[86] About 96 percent of all municipal bonds issued are for capital investment projects.[87]

Cities make use of the capital market for several reasons. Most cities cannot afford to finance major capital expenditures out of current revenues, and given the general public abhorrence for overtaxation that might create governmental surpluses, cities are unable to accumulate excess reserves.

Cities also borrow for other purposes. Big cities, especially Chicago and New York City, use short-term bonds to increase budgetary flexibility and to improve their cash flow. New York City, as noted previously, made extensive use of short-term debt, having issued $48.5 billion in this fashion between 1965 and 1975. In 1974, New York accounted for 69 percent of the outstanding short-term debt of the nation's forty-eight largest cities.[88]

The volume of municipal bonds is considerable. Approximately 8,000 separate bond issues totaling $58.2 billion were issued by state and local jurisdictions in 1975.[89] The municipal bond market is effectively limited to corporations and wealthy individuals. Two factors account for this situation. First, bonds are typically issued in large denominations, $25,000 or greater. Second, the federal tax exemption for income derived from municipal bonds has a greater appeal to persons in higher-income brackets.

Commercial banks, because they "alone, among the major institutions, are taxed at the full marginal income tax rate," have invested heavily in tax-exempt municipal debt. Because they control such a large portion of the outstanding bonds (32 percent in 1984), city finances are heavily dependent on their investment decisions.[90] The New York fiscal crisis is a case in point. New York's problem coincided with the commercial banking industry's disinvestment in municipal bonds.

Fluctuations in bondholding are closely tied to the tax advantages of insurance and loan losses of corporate investors. Such losses reduce their tax liabilities, thereby making tax-exempt bonds less attractive. This phenomenon can be seen in the declining proportion of new issues absorbed by commercial banks during periods of economic recession.[91]

The interest rates paid by cities on municipal bonds have characteristically been lower than those paid on corporate securities. This is primarily attributable to their tax-exempt status. The actual interest level, however, depends on several factors. One factor is the length of maturity of the particular issue. The longer the term of the bond, the higher the interest rate.[92]

A second factor is competition on the tax-exempt bond market. Private industry is now entitled to sell nontaxable securities to finance pollution control investments. This type of bond was estimated to have appropriated 25 percent of the tax-exempt market in 1975. The additional cost to cities because of higher interest rates was $500 million by 1980.[93] States and local governments also sell tax-exempt industrial development bonds for the purpose of subsidizing land, sports stadiums, shopping malls, access roads, and even industrial buildings.

The Municipal Bond Market

The cost of borrowing for cities is basically determined by bond ratings. Each of several studies that have analyzed determinants of interest rates have made this conclusion.[94] Bond ratings are purported to represent the relative credit quality of the issuing municipality.

Bond ratings are published by two national rating firms: Moody's Investors Service, Inc., and Standard and Poor's Corporation. Until the late 1960s, both firms routinely rated most bond issues. Since that time, however, these two firms have rated municipal bonds only for an annual fee, ranging from $500 to $2,500 or more.[95]

Ratings represent a combination of subjective and objective evaluations. The exact formulas and procedures for making the ratings, however, are unknown. Both "rating agencies are loath to divulge the particular factors taken into account."[96] One commentator on the rating system noted:

> Instead of using systematic and objective measurements, both municipal bond rating agencies emphasize the importance of careful study and [subjective] decisions made by experienced municipal bond analysts and committees.[97]

If the amount of time spent is in any way indicative of the quality of analysis, it is interesting to note that while initial ratings typically take a few days, "ratings on subsequent sales of outstanding bonds take only a couple of hours," or less.[98]

The rating of municipal bonds has "shown a lack of consistency over time." Accurate duplication of ratings, using objective data about cities' financial conditions, occurs in only 50 to 70 percent of the cases. "Hidden factors" must therefore account for the discrepancies in rating between otherwise similar communities.[99]

Nevertheless, distinct patterns in ratings can be identified. Cities that were downgraded in their ratings between 1975 and 1980 lost population in the 1970s, while cities whose bonds were upgraded were adding population. The downgraded cities also experienced slower growth in per capita income.[100] Fiscal factors correlate highly with bond ratings. The cities that became most dependent on intergovernmental resources were the most frequently downgraded.[101] All these factors are associated with older cities of the Northeast and Midwest. Table 7–6 makes this relationship obvious, as does a study of larger cities published in 1980.[102] Every one of the seven big cities downgraded between 1965 and 1978 was an older industrial city noted for its social and economic problems. Of eleven big cities downgraded from 1978 to 1986, nine were older industrial cities in the Northwest or Midwest. The one Sunbelt city, Houston, was hit hard by the drop in oil prices in the mid-1980s.

Despite the attempt to link ratings to risk, ratings have proved to be an inadequate measure of the possibility of default. From 1929 to 1933, when 77 percent of all defaults occurred, the highest-rated bonds recorded the

---

TABLE 7–6   Changes in Ratings on General Obligation Bonds (Moody's Ratings)

Rating downgraded, 1965–1978	Rating downgraded, 1978–1986
St. Louis	St. Louis
Newark	San Francisco
Buffalo	Chicago
New York	Houston
Cleveland	Cleveland
Philadelphia	Detroit
Pittsburgh	Cincinnati
	Columbus, Ohio
	Toledo
	Milwaukee
	Louisville

Source: Moody's Municipal and Government Manual. 2 vols. (New York: Moody's Investors Service, Inc., 1986).

highest incidence of default.[103] The discrepancy in the interest rates between the highest and lowest investment grade bonds seems to be inexplicable on the basis of relative risk.[104]

Major cities simply do not fail to pay their debts. True, from the first recorded default in 1838 (Mobile, Alabama) through 1969 there were more than 6,000 recorded bond defaults. Fewer than one-third of these, however, involved incorporated municipalities (cities). Seventy-five percent of all such failures occurred between 1930 and 1939. Less than 10 percent were post-Depression defaults.[105] During the worst period for municipal bonds, 1929 through 1937, only 8 percent of all cities and 19.9 percent of their bonded debt were ever in default.[106] In nearly all these cases, the debts were eventually paid.

From World War II through early 1970, a total of 431 state and local units defaulted on their obligations. The total principal involved was $450 million, approximately 0.4 percent of the outstanding state and local debt. Three noncity units, the West Virginia Turnpike Commission, the Calumet Skyway Toll Bridge, and the Chesapeake Bay Bridge and Tunnel Commission, accounted for over 74 percent of this amount. Only two of twenty-four major default situations ($1 million or more) involved general-obligation bonds.[107]

Of 114 defaults by cities during the 1960s, most were temporary or technical defaults. Only thirty-four involved general-obligation bonds, and in all these cases the cities involved had populations under 5,000 and the amount in default was less than $1 million.[108]

An analysis of cases filed in federal district courts between 1938 and 1971 reveals that nine cities took advantage of federal municipal bankruptcy legislation. With one exception (Saluda, North Carolina), all the cases involved small, rather obscure cities in Texas (Ranger, Talco, Benevides) or Florida (Manatee, Medley, Center Hill, Webster, Wanchula). Only in the case of Benevides (population 2,500) were general-obligation bonds of post–World War II origin involved. In all other cases, the defaulted debt was of prewar origin, related to revenue bonds, or unrelated to bonds altogether.[109]

When a city does default on its obligations, it is generally only a technical failure to pay on time. In the few instances where cities have failed to meet debt service payments, the failure has been temporary. Bondholders have always recovered their money, but sometimes it took longer than they had anticipated. On December 15, 1978, Cleveland became the first major city to default, even in a technical sense, since 1933. On that day the city failed to make payments on $20 million in bonds. Cleveland's default, however, was technical and short-term: the city had already worked out an arrangement with major banks that allowed it to withhold payments until February 27, 1979. It successfully met the new deadline.[110]

There would appear to be little justification for differential rating of city bonds, especially general-obligation bonds. "Where the full faith and credit has been pledged . . . there simply has been no record of meaningful risk for forty years."[111]

Cities as Private Institutions

Cities are, in a sense, bought and sold in the same manner as any other commodities in the private marketplace. They have only a limited ability to determine their own fiscal destiny. If the rating services decide that a city is a poor investment risk, the cost and difficulty of borrowing escalates, yet the actual basis for the rating is rarely known. If the economy gets into trouble, cities find it difficult to raise enough revenues to pay for normal services. Yet the cities are generally blamed by the popular press for their fiscal difficulties. Only rarely, if ever, are private institutions held responsible for decisions they make regarding city finances.

Nearly all big city mayors find themselves in an impossible situation regarding the city budget. They are constantly besieged by demands for more and better services—police to solve the problem of crime, summer jobs for unemployed youths, street repairs, park improvements. Yet mayors risk their political careers if they take the unpopular step of pressing for higher taxes, so they are tempted to borrow. When they do, they put their cities at the substantial mercy of the private sector institutions that buy municipal bonds. As private institutions, cities are constantly at risk and highly vulnerable.

References

1. Lester A. Sobel, ed., *New York and the Urban Dilemma*; Mary Elizabeth Clifford, Joseph Fickes, Chris Larson, and Stephen Orlofsky, contributing eds.; Grace M. Ferrara, indexer (New York: Facts on File, 1976), p. 165.
2. Sobel, p. 165.
3. Sobel, p. 165.
4. Sobel, p. 165.
5. Sobel, p. 165.
6. Sobel, p. 165.
7. The National League of Cities, as reported in *The New York Times*, March 28, 1975.
8. U.S. Congress, Joint Economic Committee, *The Current Fiscal Position of*

State and Local Governments: A Survey of 48 State Governments and 140 Local Governments, Subcommittee on Urban Affairs, Joint Economic Committee, House, 94th Cong., 1st sess., 1975, pp. 20–21.

9. U.S. Advisory Commission on Intergovernmental Relations, *Significant Features of Fiscal Federalism, 1980–81 Edition* (Washington, D.C.: U.S. Government Printing Office, December 1981), p. 58.

10. U.S. Advisory Commission on Intergovernmental Relations, *The States and Distressed Communities: The 1981 Report* (Washington, D.C.: U.S. Government Printing Office, May 1982), p. 9.

11. *Rocky Mountain News*, February 8, 1983, p. 1.

12. U.S. Advisory Commission, *Significant Features, 1980–81*, p. 19.

13. Alexander Ganz, "Where Has the Urban Crisis Gone? How Boston and Other Large Cities Have Stemmed Economic Decline," Vol. 20, No. 4, *Urban Affairs Quarterly* (June 1985), p. 460.

14. George E. Peterson, "Finance," in *The Urban Predicament*, ed. William Gorham and Nathan Glazer (Washington, D.C.: The Urban Institute, 1976), p. 41.

15. U.S. Congress, Senate, Committee on Governmental Affairs, Subcommittee on Intergovernmental Relations, *The Counter-Cyclical Assistance Program: An Analysis of Its Initial Impact*, 95th Cong., 1st Sess., February 28, 1977, p. 10; also quoted in U.S. Advisory Commission on Intergovernmental Relations, *State-Local Finances in Recession and Inflation: An Economic Analysis* (Washington, D.C.: U.S. Government Printing Office, May 1979), p. 32.

16. U.S. Advisory Commission, *State-Local Finances*, p. 14.

17. U.S. Advisory Commission, *State-Local Finances*, p. 14.

18. U.S. Advisory Commission, *Significant Features*, p. 71. These data exclude school district employees. If they were included, public employee earnings would be 104.7 percent of private wages in 1975.

19. U.S. Advisory Commission, *Significant Features, 1980–81*, p. 71.

20. U.S. Advisory Commission, *Significant Features, 1980–81*, p. 69.

21. U.S. Advisory Commission, *Significant Features, 1980–81*, p. 10.

22. U.S. Advisory Commission, *Significant Features, 1980–81*, p. 19.

23. U.S. Advisory Commission, *Significant Features, 1980–81*, p. 19.

24. See Roger W. Schmenner, "The Determination of Municipal Employee Wages," *Review of Economics and Statistics* 60 (February 1973):83–90; Orley Ashenfetter, "The Effect of Unions on Wages in the Public Sector: The Case of Fire Fighters," *Industrial and Labor Relations Review* 24 (January 1971):191–202; and Peterson, "Finance," pp. 108–109.

25. E. S. Savas, "Municipal Monopoly," *Harper's Magazine*, December 1971, cited in U.S. Advisory Commission on Intergovernmental Relations, *City Financial Emergencies: The Intergovernmental Dimension* (Washington, D.C.: U.S. Government Printing Office, 1973), p. 33n. See also David T. Stanley, *Cities in Trouble*, National Urban Policy Roundtable (Columbus, Ohio: Academy for Contemporary Problems, December 1976), p. 6.

26. George E. Peterson, "Transmitting the Municipal Fiscal Squeeze to a New Generation of Taxpayers: Pension Obligations and Capital Investment Needs," in

Cities Under Stress: The Fiscal Crisis of Urban America, ed. Robert W. Burchell and David Listokin (New Brunswick, N.J.: Rutgers, The State University of New Jersey, 1981), p. 252.

27. U.S. Advisory Commission, *City Financial Emergencies*, pp. 31–32.

28. U.S. Advisory Commission, *City Financial Emergencies*, p. 32.

29. U.S. Advisory Commission, *Significant Features, 1980–81*, p. 67.

30. U.S. Advisory Commission, *Significant Features, 1980–81*, p. 67.

31. Refer to Richard T. Ely, *Taxation in American States and Cities* (New York: Thomas Y. Crowell, 1888), pp. 109–113; and Sumner Benson, "A History of the General Property Tax," in *The American Property Tax: Its History, Administration, and Economic Impact*, ed. C. G. S. Benson, S. Benson, H. McClelland, and P. Thompson (Claremont, Calif.: College Press, 1965), p. 24.

32. E. R. A. Seligman, *Essays in Taxation*, 9th ed. (New York: Macmillan, 1923), p. 24.

33. U.S. Bureau of the Census, *Historical Statistics of the United States: Colonial Times to 1970*, p. 2, Bicentennial ed. (Washington, D.C.: U.S. Government Printing Office, 1975), p. 1133.

34. Calculated from data in U.S. Bureau of the Census, *Local Government Finances in Selected Metropolitan Areas and Large Counties, 1969–70*, Government Finances, GF70 no. 6 (Washington, D.C.: U.S. Government Printing Office, 1971), p. 7; and the same publication, 1974–75 (1976), p. 7.

35. U.S. Bureau of the Census, *Governmental Finances in 1978–79*, GF79 no. 5 (Washington, D.C.: U.S. Government Printing Office, 1980), p. 64.

36. U.S. Advisory Commission, *Significant Features 1980–81*, p. 42.

37. Peterson, "Finance," p. 52.

38. Peterson, p. 53.

39. J. Richard Aronson and John L. Hilley, *Financing State and Local Governments*, 4th ed. (Washington, D.C.: The Brookings Institution, 1986), p. 136.

40. John R. Meyer and John M. Quigley, *Local Public Finance and the Fiscal Squeeze: A Case Study*, with contributions by Christopher H. Gadsden, Malcom Getz, Peter Kemper, Robert A. Leone, and Roger W. Schmenner (Cambridge, Mass.: Ballinger, 1977), p. 14.

41. *Walz v. Tax Commission of the City of New York*, 397 U.S. 664. See also Boris I. Bittker, "Churches, Taxes and the Constitution," *Yale Law Review* 78 (July 1969):1285–1310.

42. Christopher H. Gadsden and Roger W. Schmenner, "Municipal Income Taxation," in *Local Public Finance and the Fiscal Squeeze*, ed. Meyer and Quigley, p. 70.

43. Eric A. Anderson, "Changing Municipal Finances," *Urban Data Service Reports* 7, no. 12 (Washington, D.C.: International City Management Association, December 1975), p. 2.

44. Peterson, "Finance," p. 60.

45. U.S. Advisory Commission, *Significant Features, 1980–81*, p. 59.

46. U.S. Bureau of the Census, *Finances of Selected Metropolitan Areas and Large Counties, 1980–81*, GF81 no. 6 (Washington, D.C.: U.S. Government Printing Office, 1981), table 4.

47. U.S. Advisory Commission, *Significant Features, 1980–81*, p. 74.

48. John L. Mikesell, "The Season of Tax Revolt," in *Fiscal Retrenchment and Urban Policy*, ed. John P. Blair and David Nachmias (Beverly Hills, Calif.: Sage Publications, 1979), p. 109.

49. Mikesell, p. 109.

50. *St. Louis Post-Dispatch*, June 29, 1977, pp. 1A, 6A.

51. *St. Louis Post-Dispatch*.

52. Jack Newfield and Paul DuBrul, *The Abuse of Power: The Permanent Government and the Fall of New York* (New York: Viking, 1977), pp. 101–102.

53. Newfield and DuBrul, p. 105.

54. U.S. Congress, Congressional Budget Office, "New York City's Fiscal Problem," a background paper prepared by Robert D. Reischauer, Peter K. Clark, and Peggy L. Cuciti, as edited and published in *The Fiscal Crisis of American Cities: Essays on the Political Economy of Urban America with Special Reference to New York*, ed. Roger A. Alcaly and David Mermelstein (New York: Random House, 1977), p. 290.

55. Jason Epstein, "The Last Days of New York," as reprinted from the *New York Review of Books*, February 16, 1976, in *The Fiscal Crisis of American Cities*, ed. Alcaly and Mermelstein, p. 62.

56. Congressional Budget Office, "New York City's Fiscal Problem," p. 289.

57. Congressional Budget Office, p. 290.

58. George Sternlieb and James W. Hughes, "Metropolitan Decline and Inter-Regional Job Shifts," as excerpted in *The Fiscal Crisis of American Cities*, ed. Alcaly and Mermelstein, p. 152.

59. Sternlieb and Hughes, p. 158.

60. Congressional Budget Office, "New York City's Fiscal Problem," p. 288.

61. Congressional Budget Office, pp. 287–289.

62. Fred Ferretti, *The Year The Big Apple Went Bust* (New York: G. P. Putnam's Sons, 1976), p. 26. See also Frances Fox Piven, "The Urban Crisis: Who Got What and Why," in *The Fiscal Crisis of American Cities*, ed. Alcaly and Mermelstein, pp. 131–144.

63. Ferretti, p. 44.

64. Peterson, "Finance," pp. 64–65.

65. Peterson, p. 54.

66. Seymour Melman, "The Federal Rip-off of New York's Money," in *The Fiscal Crisis of American Cities*, ed. Alcaly and Mermelstein, p. 181.

67. Quoted in Ferretti, *The Big Apple*, p. 28.

68. Newfield and DuBrul, *The Abuse of Power*, p. 31.

69. Ferretti, *The Big Apple*, p. 46.

70. Peterson, "Finance," p. 65.

71. Peterson, p. 65.

72. Newfield and DuBrul, *The Abuse of Power*, p. 328.

73. Ferretti, *The Big Apple*, p. 45.

74. Ferretti, p. 6.

75. Roger E. Alcaly and Helen Bodian, "New York's Fiscal Crisis and the Economy," in *The Fiscal Crisis of American Cities*, ed. Alcaly and Mermelstein, p. 288.

76. Newfield and DuBrul, *The Abuse of Power*, p. 12; and Congressional Budget Office, "New York City's Fiscal Problem," p. 288.

77. Robert Zevin, "New York City Crisis: First Act in a New Age of Reaction," in *The Fiscal Crisis of American Cities*, ed. Alcaly and Mermelstein, p. 12. The annual inflation rate reached 12 percent in 1974.

78. See *Business Week*, "Never Enough Money for the States," October 12, 1974, p. 106.

79. Harry Magdoff and Paul M. Sweezy, "Banks: Skating on Thin Ice," *Monthly Review* 26 (February 1975):1–21.

80. Magdoff and Sweezy.

81. Alcaly and Bodian, "New York's Fiscal Crisis and the Economy," p. 53.

82. Alcaly and Bodian, pp. 53–54, citing Edward J. Kane, "Why 'Bad Paper' Worries Economic Policies," *Bulletin of Business Research*, July 1975.

83. From a confidential memorandum from William Haddad, Director of the Office of Legislative Oversight and Analysis, to George Cincotta, Chairman of the New York Assembly Banking Committee, July 7, 1976, as quoted in Newfield and DuBrul, *The Abuse of Power*, p. 42.

84. CBS Evening News, August 26, 1977.

85. Sobel, *New York and the Urban Dilemma*, p. 130.

86. Twentieth Century Fund Task Force on Municipal Bond Credit Ratings, *The Rating Game*, with a background paper by John E. Peterson (New York: The Twentieth Century Fund, 1974), p. 25.

87. Twentieth Century Fund Task Force, p. 153; also see John E. Peterson and Harvey Galper, *Forecasting State and Local Capital Outlays and Their Financing* (Washington, D.C.: The Urban Institute, 1970), pp. 2–5.

88. Calculated from data presented in Table 7–5.

89. U.S. Advisory Commission on Intergovernmental Relations, *Understanding the Market for State and Local Debt* (Washington, D.C.: U.S. Government Printing Office, 1976), p. 1.

90. Aronson and Hilley, *Financing State and Local Governments*, p. 174.

91. U.S. Advisory Commission, *Understanding the Market*, p. 16; and Twentieth Century Fund Task Force, *The Rating Game*, pp. 32–33. See also John E. Peterson, "An Analysis of Subsidy Plans to Support State and Local Borrowing," *National Tax Journal* 24 (September 1971):208ff.

92. U.S. Advisory Commission, *Understanding the Market*, pp. 19, 21.

93. Cited by National League of Cities, *The Tax System: Consequences for Urban Policy*, National League of Cities Working Paper, 2d ed. (Washington, D.C.: National League of Cities, 1975), p. 4.

94. Twentieth Century Fund Task Force, *The Rating Game*, pp. 44, 49–50. See Jess B. Yawitz, "Risk Premiums on Municipal Bonds," unpublished working paper, Graduate School of Business, Washington University, St. Louis, for interesting insights on another factor—revenue sharing.

95. Twentieth Century Fund Task Force, p. 55.

96. Twentieth Century Fund Task Force, p. 78.

97. George H. Hempel, *Measures of Municipal Bond Quality,* Michigan Reports no. 53 (Ann Arbor: Bureau of Business Research, Graduate School of Business Administration, University of Michigan, 1967), p. 124.

98. Twentieth Century Fund Task Force, *The Rating Game,* p. 83.

99. Twentieth Century Fund Task Force, p. 107; and Allen J. Michel, "Municipal Bond Ratings: A Discriminant Analysis Approach," *Journal of Financial and Quantitative Analysis,* 12 (November 1977):587–598; W. T. Carleton and E. M. Lerner, "Statistical Credit Scoring and Municipal Bonds," *Journal of Money, Credit and Banking* (November 1969):750–764; and Larry K. Hastie, "Determinants of Municipal Bond Yields," *Journal of Financial and Quantitative Analysis,* 7 (June 1972):1729–1748.

100. Jesse F. Marguette, R. Penny Marguette, and Katherine A. Hinkley, "Bond Rating Changes and Urban Fiscal Stress: Linkage and Prediction," *Journal of Urban Affairs* 4 (Winter 1982):92.

101. Marguette, Marguette, and Hinkley, p. 93.

102. John E. Petersen, "Changing Fiscal Structure and Credit Quality: Large U.S. Cities, in *Fiscal Stress and Public Policy,* ed. Charles H. Levine and Irene Rubin (Beverly Hills, Calif.: Sage Publications, 1980), pp. 179–202.

103. Thomas Geis, "Municipal Credit and Bond Rating System," paper delivered at the Municipal Officers Association Meeting, Denver, Colorado, May 31, 1972.

104. Geis, pp. 5–6.

105. U.S. Advisory Commission, *City Financial Emergencies,* p. 10.

106. U.S. Advisory Commission, *City Financial Emergencies,* p. 12.

107. U.S. Advisory Commission, *City Financial Emergencies,* p. 16.

108. U.S. Advisory Commission, *City Financial Emergencies,* p. 17.

109. U.S. Advisory Commission, *City Financial Emergencies,* p. 81–82.

110. U.S. Advisory Council on Intergovernmental Relations, *Intergovernmental Perspective* 8 (Winter 1982):25.

111. Twentieth Century Fund Task Force, *The Rating Game,* p. 117. See also Geis, and Hempel, p. 74.

Chapter 8

THE SOCIAL CRISIS
OF THE CITIES

Blacks Move to the Cities

The political isolation of the cities from the suburbs was an accomplished fact by 1960. What made this isolation assume the proportions of a crisis was its intimate connection to the segregation of race and class. By the 1960s, old central cities held millions of low-income minorities in ghettos of dilapidated housing, riddled with crime, poverty, and other social ills. Surrounding the cities were nearly all-white, relatively affluent suburbs willing to use all the means at their disposal to preserve their racial and class composition.

Table 6–1 documented the population migrations of the twentieth century. Between 1910 and 1930, about 1 million blacks, one-tenth of the black population living in the South, moved to cities in the Northeast and Midwest.[1] In 1910, 89 percent of the nation's black population resided in the South. By 1930, this proportion had declined to 79 percent. From 1890 to 1910, the black population in the South increased by 29 percent; but during the next twenty years, it grew in the South by only 8 percent, compared with 134 percent in the North.[2]

Nearly all the blacks leaving the South left poverty-stricken rural areas, but they located in Northern cities. Only 10 percent of the nation's blacks lived in cities of 100,000 or more in 1910. This percentage increased to 16 in 1920 and to 24 by 1930.[3] Big cities lured most of the migrants. The proportion of blacks living in cities smaller than 100,000 actually declined from 1910 to 1930, but increased substantially in cities of over 100,000 in population.[4] Thus, the Great Migration, so labeled by historians, had two principal components: blacks were becoming northern *and* urban. In several of the largest cities, black populations doubled within twenty years, as shown in Table 8–1.

Few cities of the North had many black residents in 1910. By 1930, heavily industrial Gary, Indiana, was 18 percent black, and East St. Louis, Illinois, was 16 percent black. In big cities, the numbers ranged from 5 percent in New York City to more than 11 percent in St. Louis and Philadelphia. Blacks in northern cities were concentrated in well-defined ghettos. In North Harlem, New York City, about one-third (36 percent) of the population was black in 1920, but this proportion increased to 81 percent by the 1930 census.[5]

The Great Migration of 1910 to 1930 and the reaction by Northern whites presaged the racial crisis of the 1960s. Three factors stand out. First, the migration from Southern farms to Northern cities was so extensive that it created competition among blacks for jobs and housing, thus making their adjustment to urban life extraordinarily difficult.

TABLE 8–1   Growth of Black Population in Several Cities, 1910–1930

City	1910	1920	1930	% increase 1910–1930	% of total population 1910	1930
New York City	91,709	152,467	327,706	257.3	1.9	4.7
Chicago	44,103	109,458	233,903	429.3	2.0	6.9
Philadelphia	84,459	134,229	219,599	160.0	5.5	11.3
St. Louis	43,960	69,854	93,580	112.9	6.4	11.4
Cleveland	8,448	35,451	71,889	751.0	1.5	8.0

Source: U.S. Bureau of the Census, *Negroes in the United States, 1920–1932* (Washington, D.C.: U.S. Government Printing Office, 1935), p. 55.

Second, the movement intensified racism throughout the North. Northern whites evinced intense hostility to blacks. Third, a wide range of political actions was taken by whites in northern cities to keep blacks "in their place."

There were many reasons for the migration to Northern cities, but the basic factors were employment opportunities in the North, and dissatisfaction with southern life. The two were inextricably entwined: information about the North often promised freedom from "Jim Crow" treatment and ample opportunity; the vision of the North as a "promised land" in turn created discontent with southern conditions.

The black-run newspaper, the *Chicago Defender*, founded in 1905, circulated widely throughout the South, reaching a circulation of 100,000 in 1917. Its great popularity south of the Mason-Dixon line was a result of the message it carried. The *Defender's* editorials advised blacks to come north to the land of opportunity, where they could find employment and, if not equality, at least an escape from harassment and violence. Its columns of job advertisements added to the "promised land" vision. At the same time, the *Defender* attacked conditions in the South. Lynchings and incidents of discrimination were frequently highlighted in lurid detail. Moving out of the South was interpreted as a way to advance the cause of racial equality.[6]

The *Defender* was only one of many voices encouraging blacks to leave the South. Blacks who had already moved wrote letters to relatives and friends describing their new life in glowing terms. Despite pervasive job and housing discrimination, they found conditions preferable to what they had left behind. Added to these testimonies were the facts of Southern unemployment and labor shortages in Northern factories. Labor agents representing Northern factories combed the Southern states in search of cheap labor, often offering free train tickets in exchange for labor agreements.

In reaction, Southern white employers tried to prevent the exodus of cheap agricultural labor. Magazines, newspapers, and business organizations decried the movement, as in this October 5, 1916, editorial in the *Memphis Commercial Appeal*:

> The enormous demand for labor and the changing conditions brought about by the boll weevil in certain parts of the South have caused an exodus of negroes which may be serious. Great colonies of negroes have gone north to work in factories, in packing houses and on the railroads. . . .
>
> The South needs every able-bodied negro that is now south of the line, and every negro who remains south of the line will in the end do better than he will do in the North. . . .
>
> The negroes who are in the South should be encouraged to remain there, and those white people who are in the boll weevil territory should make every

sacrifice to keep their negro labor until there can be adjustments to the new and quickly prosperous conditions that will later exist.[7]

Some communities went to considerable length to discourage migration. Jacksonville, Florida, passed an ordinance in 1916 levying heavy fines on unlicensed labor agents from the North. Macon, Georgia, made it impossible for labor agents to get licenses and outlawed unlicensed agents. The mayor of Atlanta talked to blacks about how "dreadfully cold" the northern winters were.[8] In some communities, police were sent to railroad stations to keep blacks from boarding trains.

But the "promised land" beckoned, and the exodus continued throughout the 1920s. What the new arrivals found was not opportunity, at least not equal opportunity, but persistent discrimination, especially in housing and jobs. Whenever blacks attempted to move into white neighborhoods, they were harassed and often violently assaulted. They were the last hired and first fired from their jobs. Everywhere in the North, they were kept in the most menial occupations. Job opportunities were limited not only by employers, but even more so by labor unions, which generally prohibited blacks from membership. Because the North was more heavily unionized than the South, there were actually fewer opportunities in some occupations, especially for skilled laborers.[9] In both union and nonunion shops, white workers often refused to work alongside blacks. To maintain labor peace, employers in such situations voluntarily agreed to hire only white laborers or to limit black employment to the less desirable jobs.

The difficulty of adjusting to urban life added to the problems faced by blacks. Hardly any of them had previously lived in an urban environment. Many had never even participated directly in the economic system. For example, sharecroppers recently arriving in northern cities had usually worked under contracts that contained provisions that they deal only with the landowners' stores, and then with credit rather than cash. As was the case with previous immigrant groups, they were often cheated, overpaying for food, housing, and other necessities.

These conditions, amplified by segregation in dilapidated, overcrowded ghettos, led to astonishing levels of social disorders. The arrest rate for blacks in Detroit in 1926 was four times that for whites. Blacks constituted 31 percent of the nation's prison population in 1923, although they were only 9 percent of the total population. In Harlem, the death rate between 1923 and 1927 was 42 percent higher than for the city as a whole, despite the fact that its population was much younger. The infant mortality rate was 111 per 1,000 births, compared with the city's rate of 64 per 1,000. Tuberculosis, heart disease, and other illnesses also far exceeded the rates for the city's general population.[10]

Blacks moving into northern cities were often surprised to find intense racism and discrimination. They quickly learned that southern whites were not so peculiar in their racial attitudes. Many restaurants and stores in the North refused to serve blacks, though the policies of segregation were not so rigidly enforced as they were in the South. Banks typically refused them loans; cemeteries, parks, bathing beaches, and other facilities were put off limits or divided into "white" and "colored" sections. Many dentists, doctors, and hospitals refused treatment to blacks. Worse, the violence that had plagued blacks in the South followed them everywhere they went. On July 2, 1917, a riot that erupted in East St. Louis took forty-six lives, thirty-nine of them blacks.[11] In the "Red Summer" of 1919, more than twenty cities experienced race riots, all of them initiated by whites attacking blacks. The cause of Chicago's riot of that summer was a black youth swimming across the "no-man's land" separating a colored beach from a white beach. Whites stoned the boy to death, then for days terrorized blacks throughout the city. From July 1, 1917, to March 1, 1921, Chicago experienced fifty-eight racial bombings.[12] Other cities followed suit. Unemployed blacks were forced out of Buffalo by city police in 1920. In 1925, blacks who attempted to move into white neighborhoods in Detroit were terrorized by cross burnings, vandalism, and mob violence.

The attitudes that motivated actions like these found ample expression in newspapers and books. Blacks were sketched as less than human, not only by Ku Klux Klan pamphlets but by academicians masquerading as scientific investigators. Sociologists writing about race in the 1920s concluded from IQ tests administered during World War I that blacks were inherently less intelligent than whites. While flimsy at best, such evidence supported what most white people wanted to believe. Political actions to keep blacks "in their place" reached into every sector of society.

The federal government provided the example. In 1916, President Wilson ordered the segregation of such government public facilities as rest rooms and cafeterias, and during World War I he barred integrated fighting units. Army camps made no recreational facilities available to blacks, and the War Department refused to protect black soldiers from civilian harassment.[13]

In virtually all cities, restrictive covenants were attached to property deeds to keep blacks from buying into white neighborhoods. Deeds with these restrictions were filed in the office of the county clerk or the registrar of deeds and were enforced by the courts. Chicago, with more than 11 square miles covered by restricted deeds in 1944, was typical of northern cities.[14] Neighborhood Improvement Associations formed in new subdivisions and, by legal prosecution and social persuasion, forced homeowners to accept and abide by racial restrictive covenants.

Blacks responded to white racism in a variety of ways. Probably the most common reaction was to avoid contact with whites as much as possible.

All-black churches and fraternal organizations provided opportunities for social interaction safely beyond white people's surveillance. But there was an elite of black leaders who organized protest against unjust conditions. One of the most militant of these leaders, Marcus A. Garvey, formed the Universal Negro Improvement Association in 1917. Garvey preached that blacks should be proud of their color and that they should withdraw from white society by organizing their own economic enterprises. He also held out the hope of creating a new black nation by encouraging American blacks to emigrate to Africa. But Garvey's organization failed to galvanize the new northern migrants into unified action. The failure of his organization was assured in 1928 when he was deported by the United States government for mail fraud.

Like previous immigrant groups, blacks were split on organizational tactics and goals. Conservatives, led and dominated by Booker T. Washington and his followers, encouraged both self-help and accommodation to white society. Washington's message was simple: to achieve equality, he said, blacks should become skilled, useful, and talented workers and should practice virtues such as thrift and cleanliness. Other organizations ran the gamut from Garvey's utopianism to Washington's accommodation.

The most important group in this spectrum was the National Association for the Advancement of Colored People (NAACP), a distinctly middle-class and, until the late 1950s, white-dominated organization. The NAACP's main strategy for accomplishing change was to use the legal system. It fought court battles and won significant victories, as in a 1917 Supreme Court decision striking down racial zoning in several southern cities. But overall, blacks won few meaningful concessions.

> The rise of the NAACP, some favorable court decisions, and lobbying by Booker T. Washington and other Negro leaders gained some minor legal and political concessions, but the black man in America was in almost total political eclipse from the 1890's until well in the 1920's.[15]

The New Deal signaled a clearcut change in the racial attitudes of some white Americans. Prominent members of the New Deal administration evinced concern for the plight of blacks. Harold Hopkins, who administered the Federal Emergency Relief Program and the Works Progress Administration, attempted to administer relief and public works on a nondiscriminatory basis. Because black unemployment levels far exceeded those for whites, a higher percentage of blacks actually received government aid than did whites.[16] In addition, the Roosevelt administration put blacks in several visible positions, a complete turnabout from policies in previous decades. The administration appointed race relations advisers to some federal departments and responded positively to NAACP requests to place prominent blacks in these positions.

In the 1936 election, blacks overwhelmingly voted for the national Democratic ticket. As with other low-income groups, their votes reflected the fact that the New Deal had given them relief and jobs. In the late 1930s, about half of Harlem's blacks still were receiving relief.[17] Further, the Congress of Industrial Organizations (CIO), a labor federation that burgeoned during Roosevelt's presidency, pursued a generally nondiscriminatory policy (in the North) toward blacks, putting them into the garment industry and into janitor, waiter, porter, redcap, and other previously all-white service jobs. Some blacks were accepted into skilled occupations. Support for unionization efforts by the Roosevelt administration guaranteed that blacks benefiting from CIO activities would vote Democratic.

Eleanor Roosevelt enraged many whites by her open support for black equality. In 1939, when soprano Marian Anderson was denied the use of Washington, D.C.'s, Constitution Hall by the Daughters of the American Revolution, the president's wife resigned from the organization and helped arrange an open-air concert at the Lincoln Memorial.[18] Such an event would have been unthinkable ten years earlier.

The Racial Crisis in Urban America

In the thirty years between 1940 and 1970, more than 4 million Southern blacks moved to northern cities. From Texas and Louisiana, blacks streamed into cities of the West, especially California; from the middle South, hundreds of thousands moved to St. Louis, Chicago, Detroit, and the cities of the Midwest; and from Mississippi eastward in the Deep South, blacks moved to the cities of the eastern seaboard. In 1940, 77 percent of the nation's blacks still lived in the southern states (compared with 87 percent in 1910). By 1950, only 60 percent of the country's blacks lived in the South, and in the next two decades the South's share declined to 56 percent (1960) and to 53 percent (1970).[19] Almost all the northbound migrants ended up in the cities. According to the 1970 census, 90 percent of all the blacks who lived outside Standard Metropolitan Statistical Areas were located in the South.

A movement of this magnitude would have created a crisis in its own right, since most of the migrants were of rural origin and predictably found the adjustment to city life difficult. But the crisis was made worse by the same factors that had plagued earlier black migrants: housing and job discrimination, racism, and extreme segregation. All the problems faced by northern blacks in the 1920s still existed after World War II. Furthermore, whites were leaving the cities by the millions every year, seeking their own "promised land" in the suburbs. While the cities became increasingly black, the suburbs remained nearly all-white. Table 8–2 shows that racial segregation between cities and suburbs had become pronounced by 1950, and worsened over the next decades.

For most of the twelve cities shown in Table 8–2, the fastest surge in black population occurred between 1950 and 1970. Northern migration was prompted by the employment opportunities in northern industry during World War II, but many white families stayed in the cities until the suburban housing boom that picked up full steam following the Korean War. Thus, although the proportion of black residents climbed during the 1940s in all the cities except St. Louis, the increase understated the extent of the migration. With the white depopulation of the central cities that occurred later, black proportions of central cities' populations shot up dramatically by 1970, to over 72 percent in Washington, D.C., to 47 percent in Cleveland, and to more than 41 percent in St. Louis.

During the same period, the suburbs exploded in population, and remained mostly white. The number of blacks in the suburbs increased 1.5 million between 1950 and 1970, but the number of suburban whites increased by 33.5 million. Thus, the proportion of suburbanites who were black changed little, increasing for all metropolitan areas from 4.5 to 4.9 percent during the 1960s.[20]

In the 1970s, Los Angeles, San Francisco, and Pittsburgh lost black population, and several others added less than 5 percent to their total black population base. Of the cities listed in Table 8–2, only Detroit increased its proportion of blacks by a large margin. Significant increases in black population occurred in the suburban rings of Los Angeles, St. Louis, Washington, Cleveland, and Baltimore. It was obvious that blacks were moving outside the central cities in increasing numbers during the 1970s.

Statistics like these, however, understate the degree of racial segregation in metropolitan areas. Within the cities and the suburbs, as well, blacks remain highly segregated from whites. Most suburbs have very few blacks. Within suburban communities with black populations, the black areas are usually distinct enclaves. Such suburbs are not integrated in any meaningful sense.

In the United States, there is only a handful of integrated suburbs, defined as communities in which a high proportion of census tracts contain a significant proportion of both blacks and whites. These include University City, Missouri, on the border of St. Louis; Shaker Heights and Warrensville Heights, near Cleveland; Zion, near Chicago; Hillcrest Heights and Tacoma Park, outside Washington, D.C., and Bloomfield, near Hartford, Connecticut.[21] In all these communities, black residents have much higher incomes than their central city counterparts. Even more significant, the blacks in these communities either have about the same

TABLE 8–2 Percentage of Blacks in Central Cities and Suburban Rings in 12 Selected SMSAs, 1940–1980

	Central city					Suburban ring				
	1940	1950	1960	1970	1980	1940	1950	1960	1970	1980
All 12 SMSAs	9.0	13.7	21.4	30.8	32.6	3.9	4.4	4.4	6.0	7.4*
New York	6.4	9.8	14.7	23.4	25.2	4.6	4.5	4.8	6.4	6.8*
Los Angeles–Long Beach	6.0	9.8	15.3	21.2	16.4	2.3	2.7	4.1	7.4	9.6
Chicago	8.3	14.1	23.6	34.4	39.8	2.2	2.9	3.1	4.1	5.6
Philadelphia	13.1	18.3	26.7	34.4	37.8	6.6	6.6	0.3	7.1	8.1
Detroit	9.3	16.4	29.2	44.0	63.1	2.9	5.0	3.8	4.0	4.2
San Francisco–Oakland	4.9	11.8	21.1	32.7	24.1	3.6	6.8	6.8	9.4	6.5
Boston	3.3	12.3	9.8	18.2	22.4	0.9	0.8	1.0	1.6	1.6
Pittsburgh	9.3	18.0	16.8	27.0	24.0	3.6	3.5	3.4	3.6	4.0
St. Louis	13.4	5.3	28.8	41.3	45.6	6.7	7.3	6.3	7.7	10.6
Washington, D.C.	28.5	35.4	54.8	72.3	76.6	13.7	8.7	6.4	9.1	16.7
Cleveland	9.7	16.3	28.9	39.0	43.8	0.9	0.8	0.8	1.1	7.1
Baltimore	19.4	23.8	35.0	47.0	54.8	11.9	10.2	6.9	6.2	9.1

Source: Adapted from Leo F. Schnore, Carolyn D. André, and Harry Sharp, "Black Surburbanization, 1930–1970," in *The Changing Face of the Suburbs,* ed. Barry Schwartz (Chicago: University of Chicago Press, 1976), p. 80. Reprinted by permission. The figures here were transposed to yield data on black percentages. 1980 data from U.S. Bureau of the Census, *1980 Census of the Population,* Supplementary Reports, *Standard Metropolitan Statistical Areas and Standard Consolidated Statistical Areas* (Washington, D.C.: U.S. Government Printing Office, 1981), p. 3, table 1.

*This figure includes data from the Nassau-Suffolk SMSA, which was deleted from the New York City SMSA in 1971. They are included to maintain comparability across time periods. The suburban ring figure for the redefined New York SMSA is 7.6%; the figure for all twelve SMSAs is 7.5%.

social status as their white neighbors or are middle-class blacks settled in moderate numbers in upper-income white suburbs.[22] In the Detroit area in 1960, only 11 percent of poor black families lived in the suburbs, but 45 percent of poor white families were suburbanites. A similar pattern existed in all the ten largest metropolitan areas.[23] Essentially the same relationships still existed at the time of the 1980 Census, when more than 60 percent of all poor white families living in metropolitan areas lived outside the central cities, compared with only 12 percent of all poor black families in metropolitan areas.

These statistics seem to suggest that racial as opposed to social class discrimination is still important for explaining patterns of segregation. For the most part, white suburbs remain white. Black suburban growth is not (in the main) integration into the suburbs, but central city segregation spilling beyond city boundaries. A study using 1970 data found that in Orange County, California, 70 percent of the black population lived in one town, Santa Ana. Three towns in northern New Jersey held 89 percent of Essex County's suburban black residents. More than 80 percent of the Chicago area's black suburbanites lived in 15 of the 237 suburban municipalities.[24] In the Detroit area, blacks constituted more than 4 percent of the population in only 7 of 65 suburbs.[25]

Many of these communities border on the central cities. Their housing quality is older and less sound than that of newer, more distant suburbs, with only a few exceptions. Yet blacks who moved to the suburbs in the 1960s had higher incomes, better education, and higher-status jobs than inner-city blacks.[26] Income is only one barrier that keeps blacks out of suburban communities, and in fact, income is not nearly as important as racial prejudice. A much higher proportion of poor whites than poor blacks have been able to locate in the suburbs.[27] Within every income class, a much higher proportion of whites can be found in the suburbs.[28]

Civil Rights and the New Black Politics

It is clear that the move to northern cities did not bring an end to racism and discrimination. Nevertheless, the worst and most symbolically crude racism continued to exist in the South. Against a background of white resistance to demands for change, the Civil Rights movement departed from a politics of accommodation to a politics of confrontation. At first centered in the South, its political effects would soon be felt in northern cities.

The Great Depression was a crisis of such proportions that it alone was sufficient to propel governments into action. The 1960s was a crisis bringing about even greater government involvement, but the crisis was one of social disorder more than of heightened social problems. Widespread poverty, racial segregation, juvenile delinquency and crime, bad schools, and a host of other social problems were "discovered" only in the sense that they were no longer "out of sight, out of mind." They had existed for a long period and were no worse and little different by the advent of the Kennedy administration than they had been under Roosevelt, Truman, or Eisenhower. What made them seem worse was their greater visibility. Martin Luther King, Jr., understood the task of creating visibility during the Civil Rights demonstrations in 1963: "I saw no way," he later commented, "of dealing with things without bringing the indignation to the attention of the nation."[29] By creating a crisis of social order in the South, King and other civil rights leaders translated a nascent, invisible social fact into a calculated crisis.

The struggle for racial equality entered a new phase in the summer of 1955, when a coalition of black ministers launched a boycott against segregated buses in Montgomery, Alabama. The boycott, which ended the "back of the bus" policy in Montgomery, brought Martin Luther King, Jr., to the attention of the national press. Until the Civil Rights Act of 1964 and the Voting Rights Act of 1965, his philosophy of creative nonviolent protest dominated the Civil Rights movement. What made civil disobedience so logical was its challenge to laws of doubtful constitutionality, and its effectiveness in dramatizing the issue of racial prejudice. In particular, the 1954 Supreme Court decision, *Brown v. Topeka Board of Education*, held out the prospect of a broad assault against "Jim Crow" segregation laws. That decision, which struck down separate schools for blacks and whites, fundamentally altered the strategies for achieving equality. The NAACP had challenged segregationist laws in the courts for many years and had won some victories. By the mid-1950s, encouraged by the *Brown* decision, civil rights leaders turned to direct action.

Until the mid-1960s, civil rights protest focused on the South. Certainly the worst abuses existed there, a legacy of the racist legislation that preoccupied southern legislators from the 1880s through the first twenty years of the twentieth century. In 1881, Tennessee passed a law requiring railroad companies to segregate their cars. Following this, perhaps the first Jim Crow law after the Civil War,[30] the states evolved a system of legal segregation that touched every aspect of life. Most railroads were segregated during the next twenty-five years. South Carolina, in 1906, also required segregation in restaurants and eating houses, and later in all forms of transportation. In 1915, the state required that textile factories designate separate work rooms for whites and blacks, and provide separate drinking glasses, toilet facilities, stairways, doors, and tools.[31] Parks; zoos; fishing, bathing, and boating areas; phone booths; textbooks and schools; taxicabs; orphanages; churches; courtrooms; drinking fountains; lavatories; waiting rooms; even courtroom bibles—all were segregated by state law in the South.[32] Most of these laws still existed in the 1950s.

There was little that blacks could do to challenge the system. Poll taxes and literacy requirements administered by white registrars kept most blacks out of the electorate. Between 1916 and 1963, black registration in eight southern states increased only 3.3 percent, from 5 to 8.3 percent. Registration dropped in Mississippi.[33] The NAACP and other organizations were illegal in some states. In any case, black political activity brought forth white repression—arrests, intimidation, even murder—when it was tried.

With the election of John F. Kennedy in 1960, the civil rights movement picked up momentum. When it was located in and focused primarily upon the Southern states, the movement had limited exposure and effectiveness. Until civil rights became a national commitment, southern resistance would be hard to break.

Martin Luther King, Jr., turned the civil rights movement into a national crisis in Birmingham, Alabama, in the summer of 1963. Here, the combination of King's nonviolent demonstrations, police chief "Bull" Conner's fire hoses and dogs, and the American television network's sense of spectacle brought the civil rights movement before the nation. Birmingham, Alabama, did in one week what 100 years of social protest had failed to accomplish: it forced a popular realization that the modern black experience in America was ugly, brutal, and revolting.

What started in Birmingham spread across the South and border states. Demonstrations were not confined to the South; in such northern cities as Detroit, Chicago, and New York, blacks were actively demonstrating for their rights. In the ten weeks that followed Birmingham, the Justice Department counted 758 demonstrations across the nation. During the course of the summer, there were 13,786 arrests of demonstrators in seventy-five cities of the eleven major southern states alone.[34] These demonstrations, and the civil rights movement in general, became dramatic continuing news items in 1963. Newspapers, magazines, television, and every other form of news media smothered the American public with the tale of King and his movement. The Civil Rights and Voting Rights Acts of 1964 and 1965 represented, symbolically, the crowning achievements in the fight for equality.

It soon became apparent that equal rights alone would not magically alter the condition of blacks in the nation. The March on Washington in August 1963 revealed a developing schism within the civil rights movement. A. Philip Randolph, the black labor leader who first suggested the march, wanted it to focus on jobs. King argued that it should be broadened to a demand for equality on all fronts.[35] Even while protest leaders joined in a broad coalition for the march, there were deep differences among them. The Urban League and the NAACP temporarily dropped their refusal to participate in direct action, and militant groups softened their demands in order not to offend white liberals involved in the march. There was disagreement, however, between those who focused on civil rights and those who concentrated on poverty, housing and jobs. To black leaders representing ghetto residents in northern cities, poverty and its related issues were far more important than legal equality.

Previous migrations to northern cities had concentrated blacks in vast ghettos characterized by unemployment, poverty, and dilapidated housing. Blacks had moved north out of desperation and hope, seeking economic improvement and personal freedom. Instead, they found poverty, unemployment, and despair. As James Baldwin stated in his essay, "Fifth Avenue, Uptown," blacks "did not escape Jim Crow; they just encountered another, not less deadly variety. They did not move to Chicago, they moved to the South Side; they did not move to New York City, they moved to Harlem."[36]

Urban Violence

On July 16, 1964, there was an outbreak of violence in Harlem following the death of a fifteen-year-old boy who was shot by an off-duty police officer. In Rochester, New York, 400 state troopers, together with 1,300 National Guardsmen, were called out to put down disorders during the summer of 1964. It took three days to control the riot. Other cities that experienced riots or violence during 1964 included Philadelphia; Jersey City, Paterson, and Elizabeth, New Jersey; and Dixmore, Illinois, a black suburb of Chicago. These disorders did not arise from planned demonstrations or protests, but were instead expressions of pent-up anger. The turmoil in the ghettos of northern cities indicated the frustrations blacks felt about the white racism that was pervasive in the northern cities. Attention had been focused on the South for a long time, and had helped to obscure the extent of discrimination and racism in the North.

A riot involving thousands of residents broke out on August 11, 1965, in the Watts area of Los Angeles. Like so many riots in subsequent years, this one ignited when a crowd of blacks gathered and angrily protested police actions in arresting a black youth. About 329 major incidents occurred from 1965 through 1968, with 220 deaths.[37]

The failure to achieve equal opportunity fed the resentments of blacks who lived in the ghettos of northern cities. Blacks' incomes lagged far behind white incomes, and the gap did not seem to be closing. In 1959, the median income of black families was 52 percent of white family income. By 1969, this figure had risen to only 61 percent.[38] Then the gains stopped, and the relative position of blacks deteriorated in comparison with that of whites. In 1981, black families made only 58 percent as much as white families.

Unemployment rates reveal that blacks had fallen behind whites from the 1950s into the 1980s. In 1986, the unemployment rate for blacks was 2.3 times the rate for white workers. Table 8–3 shows that the gap has become slowly larger over time. In the 1950s it widened somewhat, to about a two to one ratio. In the 1980s, it is wider than since statistics have been kept.

The gap between middle-class blacks and low-income blacks also widened. Two forces were at work within the black community during the 1960s: "rising affluence in the expanding middle class, and persisting poverty in a shrinking lower class."[39] A study conducted in Cleveland, Ohio, showed that between 1960 and 1965, black families outside the poorest areas made substantial gains.[40] Incomes rose, the incidence of poverty dramatically dropped, and the number of broken families declined. In the poorest areas, conditions continued to deteriorate. A study in Los Angeles showed a similar result.[41] To blacks in the ghetto it appeared that those around them, black *and* white, were leaving them behind. As the gap grew, so did frustration and anger.

TABLE 8–3   **Average Annual Unemployment Rates for Whites Compared with Nonwhites***

Year	% white unemployment	% nonwhite* unemployment	Ratio
1948	3.5	5.9	1.7
1950	4.9	9.0	1.8
1960	4.9	10.2	2.1
1968	3.2	6.7	2.1
1972*	5.1	10.4	2.0
1975	7.8	14.8	1.9
1980	6.3	14.3	2.3
1986	6.1	14.3	2.3

Source: U.S. Bureau of the Census, *The Social and Economic Status of the Black Population in the United States: An Historical Overview 1790–1978,* Current Population Reports, Special Studies Series, P-23 n. 80 (Washington, D.C.: U.S. Government Printing Office n.d.), p. 69, citing the U.S. Bureau of Labor Statistics as the original source of the data; U.S. Department of Labor, Bureau of Labor Statistics, *Employment and Earnings;* and Statistical Abstract of the United States (1986), p. 422.

*From 1972 the statistic is for blacks only. No separate statistics exist for blacks (as opposed to all nonwhites) before 1972.

Even before the urban riots of the mid-1960s, disorder in urban ghettos was rising. During 1959, vandals broke 161,000 panes of glass in New York City school buildings.[42] Fires set by arsonists, break-ins, and rock-throwing became everyday occurrences. The high rate of juvenile crime prompted special studies by social workers at Columbia University. The Ford Foundation focused on urban schools by giving grants in the late 1950s, funding "community action" projects in "gray areas" (depressed by not fully declined communities) in an attempt to make the schools more responsive to the residents of local communities and to give community residents a stake in their schools.

In the third consecutive summer of urban rioting, in July, 1967, President Lyndon Johnson established the National Commission on Civil Disorders to investigate the causes of the riots and to recommend policy responses. Chaired by Governor Otto Kerner of Illinois and Mayor John V. Lindsay of New York, the commission undertook an ambitious investigation. A staff of more than thirty professional researchers compiled materials while the commission visited cities and conducted numerous hearings. In March 1968 the commission delivered the "Kerner Commission" report.

The commission's analysis of the causes of the riots was controversial: ". . .the most fundamental is the racial attitude and behavior of white Americans toward black Americans . . . white racism is essentially responsible for the explosive mixture which has been accumulating in our cities since the end of World War II."[43] The commission cited such factors as segregation and poverty, violence directed at blacks, and the widespread feeling of powerlessness among blacks as the main conditions leading to the riots.

The commission recommended the enactment of special housing, education, employment, and welfare programs to provide the conditions for greater equality. Failure to remedy the problems it identified would "make permanent the division of our country into two societies; one largely Negro and poor, located in central cities; the other, predominantly white and affluent, located in the suburbs and in outlying areas."[44]

In the years since the Kerner Commission report was issued, most blacks have made relatively few gains.[45] As we have seen, unemployment levels have worsened, both absolutely and in comparison with whites. The position of teenage blacks in the job market has deteriorated in comparison with the position of teenage whites: in 1982, unemployment among black teenagers stood at 43.8 percent, compared with 20.4 percent for their white counterparts.[46]

Inner-city blacks, who were of greatest concern to the Commission on Civil Disorders, have fallen further and further behind. Many wholesale, retail, and manufacturing jobs have moved outside the boundaries of the central cities since the 1950s. The only counterbalance to this trend is found in the service industries, especially those connected to a growing governmental role, in the location of office space for corporations, and in the hotels, restaurants, bars, and auxiliary facilities connected to the tourist trade. The lion's share of higher-paying professional jobs located in the central cities are taken by white suburbanites, while the lower-paying jobs in the service industries tend to go to blacks. "Recent research on unemployment in thirty of the nation's largest cities reveal that blacks do not experience employment barriers in low-paid, menial, and casual jobs but rather in the more desirable, higher-paying jobs in the large manufacturing, wholesale trade, construction, and finance industries representative of industries of the corporate sector."[47]

It is apparent, however, that the black middle class has enjoyed better opportunities, especially in the government sector. In 1960, 13 percent of the black labor force was located in the government sector. That proportion increased to 21 percent by 1970.[48] Nearly two-thirds of newly hired government employees between May 1973 and May 1974 were black.[49] Thus, there has been an increasing segmentation of the labor market, which starkly differentiates between black middle-class households and the large majority who remain in menial, low-skilled, and low-paying service jobs. The degree of this segmentation can be appreciated by considering that the median income of married black couples in 1980 was $18,953—86.5 percent as high as the median income for white families—but that female-headed black households made an average income of only $7,425, which is 34 percent of white family income.[50] Between 1970 and 1980, the incomes of married black couples rose by 16 percent, while female-headed black families increased their incomes by only 3 percent.[51] Other evidence is equally compelling: Between 1969 and 1979 the proportion of blacks living in the central cities who were classified as poor increased sharply, but the poverty rate among all other blacks declined.[52]

The Social Crisis Comes to the Sunbelt

It would be a serious oversight to fail to recognize the social and political significance of Hispanics in American cities.[53] In a large number of cities and metropolitan areas they now represent the largest minority group. Their numbers are increasing at a much faster rate than whites or blacks, and some researchers expect Hispanics to equal blacks in total national population by the year 2003. Their potential political power is enormous, especially because they are concentrated in the southwestern states and in urban areas. The high levels of poverty and segregation among Hispanics virtually guarantee that local governments and the national political system will be confronted with demands for effective policy to treat their concerns.

Mexican-Americans comprise 60 percent of all Hispanics in the United States (see Table 8–4). Mainland Puerto Ricans make up about 14 percent of the total, but more than half (61 percent) of mainland Puerto Ricans are concentrated in New York City and northern New Jersey. About 25 percent of Hispanics are recent immigrants from Cuba, the Caribbean, and Central and South America. This last group is concentrated overwhelmingly in the Miami area, where it makes up 58.5 percent of all Hispanics. As shown in Table 8–4, two states, California and Texas, have 51.5 percent of all people of Hispanic origin in the United States, and 73 percent of all Mexican-Americans live in these two states. Most Americans of Hispanic origin live in metropolitan areas, about 80 percent of Mexican-Americans, and more than 98 percent of Puerto Ricans, Cubans, and South and Central Americans.[54]

As shown in Table 8–5, people of Hispanic descent constitute about 25 percent of the population in eight key cities (and in many others not listed in the table). They are not as segregated in the central cities as are blacks, but they nevertheless live disproportionately in deteriorated neighborhoods within *and* outside the cities, neighborhoods characterized by bad housing, high crime rates, and other ailments associated with poverty.

Blacks make up more than 10 percent of the population in five cities listed in Table 8–5, and their average share of the population is 17.5 percent. The combined black and Hispanic populations of all these cities averages more than 42 percent, a fact that clearly demonstrates that these Sunbelt cities are not protected from the kinds of social tensions that characterize older cities in the North. And as the data in Tables 8–6 and 8–7 indicate, these cities have high levels of inequality and poverty.

Hispanics fall well below the general population on all indicators of economic well-being. Their median family income in 1985 was $19,027, only 65 percent of the median income for whites (see Tables 8–6 and 8–7). A wide disparity in educational attainment is obvious: more than 75 percent of all whites had completed high school in 1984, compared with 47 percent of Hispanics. A very small proportion of Hispanics, 8.2 percent, had earned a college degree. These figures were reflected in occupational status. While 39 percent of the white work force held relatively high status white-collar jobs in 1984, only 17 percent of Hispanics held these kinds of jobs. It is obvious that only a small minority of people of Hispanic descent have entered the middle class in income, education, and occupational status.

TABLE 8–4 Regional Settlement Patterns for Persons of Hispanic Origin

State or region	Number	% of region's total population	% of national Hispanic-origin population	National background
New York State	1,657,417	9.4	11.4	59.4% Puerto Rican origin;
New York City SMSA	1,492,559	16.4	10.2	only 2.3% Mexican origin
Five Southwestern States	8,776,660	19.6	60.2	82.2% Mexican origin
California	4,538,360	19.2	31.1	80% Mexican origin
Texas	2,983,111	21.0	20.4	92.2% Mexican origin
Arizona, New Mexico, Colorado	1,255,189	18.2	8.6	66.9% Mexican origin; most others identify selves as Latino, etc.
Florida	860,403	8.8	5.9	54.8% Cuban; 25% Latin American
Miami SMSA	580,927	35.7	4.0	
Remainder of United States	3,294,396		22.6	
Total United States	14,588,876	6.4	100.0	59.8% Mexican-American 13.8% Puerto Rican; 5.5% Cuban; 20.9% Other

Source: U.S. Bureau of Census, *1980 Census of Population,* Supplementary Reports, *Persons of Spanish Origin by State 1980* (Washington, D.C.: U.S. Government Printing Office, 1981).

TABLE 8–5 Black and Hispanic Population in Selected Cities and SMSAs, 1980

Metropolitan area	% black in central city	% Hispanic origin in central city	%black outside central city	% Hispanic origin outside central city	% minorities in central city
Los Angeles	17.0	27.5	9.6	28.9	44.5
San Diego	8.8	14.9	2.7	14.7	23.7
Phoenix	4.9	15.1	1.4	11.2	20.0
Denver	12.1	18.7	1.7	7.5	30.8
Dallas	29.4	12.3	3.9	5.3	41.7
Houston	27.6	17.6	6.7	11.0	45.2
San Antonio	7.3	53.7	5.3	20.8	61.0
Miami	25.1	53.3	15.1	30.3	78.4
Mean for eight cities	17.5	24.8	4.3	12.7	42.3

Source: U.S. Bureau of Census, *1980 Census of Population,* Supplementary Reports, *Standard Metropolitan Statistical Areas and Standard Consolidated Statistical Areas* (Washington, D.C.: U.S. Government Printing Office, 1981).

TABLE 8–6   Economic Status of White, Black and Hispanic-Origin Americans, 1984, 1985

Economic indicator	White	Black	Hispanic origin
Education			
Percentage who completed 4 years of high school (among those 25 years or older)	75.0	58.5	47.1
Percentage who completed 4 years of college (among those 25 years or older)	19.8	10.4	8.2
Income and Employment			
Median family income (1985)	$29,152	$16,786	$19,027
Percentage white collar	39.4	22.7	21.6
Unemployment rate* (1985)	6.2	15.1	10.5
Percentage below the poverty level	11.4	31.3	29.0

Sources: U.S. Bureau of the Census, *Money Income and Poverty Status of Families and Persons in the United States: 1985 (Advanced Report),* Current Population Reports, Series P. 60, No. 154 (Washington, D.C.: U.S. Government Printing Office: 1986); Current Population Reports, Series P 60, no. 151, *Money Income of Household, Families, and Persons in the U.S.: 1984,* April 1986, p. 154, table 38; *U.S. Statistical Abstract: 1986,* pp. 133–135, and *Employment and Earnings, 1985.

The data in Table 8–6 show that blacks lagged behind Hispanics on almost every measure of economic well-being. The fact of poverty and low wage status among both blacks and Hispanics makes the data on minority concentration in Sunbelt cities even more meaningful. Obviously, a potential social crisis is possible in those cities.

Since the early 1970s, neither blacks nor Hispanics have made significant gains in comparison with whites. Table 8–7 shows that in 1969, black median income was 61 percent of white median income (an increase from 52 percent in 1959). By 1985, blacks were making only 58 percent as much. The ratio of Hispanic income to white income has also worsened; from 1972 to 1985, it dropped from 71 to 65 percent.

Though the poverty levels among blacks and Hispanics are at or near the national average in most Sunbelt metropolitan areas, white residents in those areas usually make *above* the national median income, and fewer whites are poor than in the nation as a whole.[55] Such extremes of wealth and poverty are obvious to any casual observer who has spent time in the Sunbelt. Television series continue the popular misconception that the

TABLE 8-7   Ratios of Black and Hispanic Incomes to White Incomes

| | Median family income ratios | |
Year	Black to white	Hispanic-origin to white
1959	.52	—
1964	.54	—
1969	.61	—
1972	.59	.71
1975	.62	.67
1978	.59	.68
1981	.58	.67
1982	.55	.66
1985	.58	.65

Source: Adapted from James Heilbrun, *Urban Economics and Public Policy,* 3rd ed. (New York: St. Martin's Press, 1987), p. 244, copyright © 1987 by St. Martin's Press, Inc., reprinted by permission of the publisher; and U.S. Bureau of Census, *Current Population Reports,* "Population Profile of the United States" series P–23, No. 80, 1979, table 14, and series P–60, No. 154, August 1986, table 2 (Washington, D.C.: U.S. Government Printing Office, 1982), pp. 49–50.

Sunbelt is filled with wealthy, prosperous people. The truth is that the promise of prosperity is hollow for a large number of Sunbelt residents.

But the conditions Hispanics face have not been easily translated into effective political demands. Mexican-Americans have very low voter turn-out rates and do not often feel that they can influence the political system.[56] Districting designed to fragment their strength and the presence of Hispanics not yet naturalized also explains why they are vastly underrepresented in the states where they have an opportunity to exert political influence. In 1973, the number of Mexican-Americans in the state legislature of Texas was less than one-third the number that would be expected if they were represented proportionately. In Colorado, the number of Mexican-American representatives was one-fourth what it should have been by this standard, and in California, one-half. In New Mexico, representation was on target, almost certainly because a large proportion of New Mexico's Hispanic-origin residents are descended from people who lived there long before white settlers arrived.[57] They are natives in the true sense, not recent migrants, and in fact often refuse to identify themselves as Mexican-American to Census workers.

The Prospect for Unrest

A high potential for violence exists in America's urban centers. Economic and social deprivation continues. Cities still exhibit the high levels of poverty and segregation that were identified by the Kerner Commission as the basic causes of rioting in the 1960s. In the aftermath of those riots, one response of governments at all levels was to organize police and intelligence programs to suppress violence.[58] In 1967, FBI Director J. Edgar Hoover organized the Counter-Intelligence Program (COINTELPRO) to disrupt and neutralize militant black organizations, with special focus on Martin Luther King, Jr., and on the Black Panthers. Local police often cooperated with the FBI or organized their own special units. But such a response revealed a basic misunderstanding of the causes of the riots. The riots were spontaneous uprisings, not planned, organized rebellions. They originated from pent-up frustrations, and were invariably set off by a confrontation with white authority, usually symbolized by the police.

Social conditions in Sunbelt cities are worse than in the North. Economic development in the Sunbelt has not trickled down very much. In the early 1970s, for example, the rate of subemployment, a measure combining unemployment with low-wage labor, was higher in the Sunbelt than in the Northeast, and the extent of poverty throughout the Sunbelt states continued to exceed the national average.[59] Minorities account for most of this statistic.

One reason corporations have moved South and West is to escape higher labor costs in the North. There is a vast pool of low-wage, nonunionized labor in the Sunbelt, and most Sunbelt states have "right-to-work" laws and other official policies to discourage unionization and keep wages low. Right-to-work laws are prominent features of most Sunbelt states' promotional advertisements placed in business journals and trade association publications.

The states and cities of the Sunbelt also are less willing to provide social welfare benefits and public programs to help alleviate the effects of poverty. Sunbelt cities spend considerably less on public health and welfare than do northern cities.[60] They also spend less on basic municipal services. Southern and western states consistently spend the least on education and welfare programs. At the same time, southern and several Sunbelt states lead the nation in overall levels of poverty. In the early 1980s, high unemployment hit the Sunbelt as well as other parts of the nation, and cities began to collect thousands of unemployed workers turned transients who had gone south and west in search of employment. One response by Phoenix officials was a 1982 ordinance making it illegal to search through garbage cans for food.

References

1. The immigration of Hispanics is treated later in this chapter.

2. Robert B. Grant, ed., *The Black Man Comes to the City: A Documentary Account from the Great Migration to the Great Depression, 1915–1930* (Chicago: Nelson-Hall, 1972), p. 27. Pages 16 to 30 in this book contain a complete set of statistics on black migration from 1890 to 1930. These data are used throughout this section.

3. Grant, p. 22.

4. Grant, p. 23.

5. Winfred P. Nathan, *Health Conditions in North Harlem, 1923–1927*, Social Research Series no. 2 (New York: National Tuberculosis Association, 1932), pp. 44–45, as excerpted in Grant, pp. 59–61.

6. Article from the *Chicago Defender*, as excerpted in Grant, pp. 31–40.

7. From the *Memphis Commercial Appeal*, October 5, 1916, as reprinted in Grant, pp. 43–44.

8. From the *Chicago Defender*, August 12, 1916, as reprinted in Grant, p. 45.

9. Herbert Northrup, *Organized Labor and the Negro* (New York: Kraus Reprint Co., 1971).

10. These statistics are from several sources excerpted in Grant, *The Black Man Comes to the City*, pp. 58–61.

11. See Elliott M. Rudwick, *Race Riot at East St. Louis, July 2, 1917* (Carbondale: Southern Illinois University Press, 1964), for a discussion of this event.

12. Chicago Commission on Race Relations, *The Negro in Chicago: A Study of Race Relations and a Race Riot* (Chicago: University of Chicago Press, 1922), p. 122.

13. August Meier and Elliott M. Rudwick, *From Plantation to Ghetto: An Interpretive History of American Negroes* (New York: Hill and Wang, 1969), p. 193.

14. Grant, *The Black Man Comes to the City*, p. 71.

15. Thomas Sowell, *Race and Economics* (New York: McKay, 1975), p. 52.

16. Meier and Rudwick, *From Plantation to Ghetto*, p. 212.

17. Samuel Lubell, *The Future of American Politics*, 3rd ed. (New York: Harper and Row, Colophon Books, 1965), p. 65.

18. Meier and Rudwick, *From Plantation to Ghetto*, p. 211.

19. U.S. Bureau of the Census, *Census of Population 1970: General Social and Economic Characteristics* (Washington, D.C.: U.S. Government Printing Office, 1972), pp. 448–449, table 3.

20. U.S. Bureau of the Census, *Census, 1970*, pp. 448–449, table 3.

21. Harold K. Connolly, "Black Movement into the Suburbs," in *Suburbanization Dynamics and the Future of the City*, ed. James W. Hughes (New Brunswick, N.J.: Rutgers University, Center for Urban Policy Research, 1974), p. 203.

22. Connolly, pp. 205–211.

23. John F. Kain and Joseph J. Pesky, "Alternatives to the Gilded Ghetto," *The Public Interest* (Winter 1969), p. 76.

24. These data are reported in Michael N. Danielson, *The Politics of Exclusion* (New York: Columbia University Press, 1976), pp. 8–9.

25. Leo F. Schnore, Carolyn D. André and Harry Sharp, "Black Suburbanization 1930–1970," in *The Changing Face of the Suburbs*, ed. Barry Schwartz (Chicago: University of Chicago Press, 1976), pp. 88–90.

26. Connolly, pp. 205–208; and Frederick J. Wirt, Benjamin Walter, Francine F. Rabinovitz, and Deborah R. Hensler, *On the City's Rim: Politics and Policy in Suburbia* (Lexington, Mass.: D.C. Heath, 1972), p. 41.

27. Wirt et al., p. 43.

28. Danielson, *The Politics of Exclusion*, p. 10.

29. Quoted in Theodore H. White, *The Making of the President 1964* (New York: Atheneum, 1965), p. 165.

30. John Hope Franklin, "History of Racial Segregation in the United States," *Annals of the American Academy of Political and Social Science* 304 (March 1956):6.

31. Franklin, pp. 1–9.

32. Franklin, pp. 1–9; and John Hope Franklin, *From Slavery to Freedom: A History of American Negroes*, 2d ed. (New York: Alfred A. Knopf, 1956). See also C. Vann Woodward, *The Strange Career of Jim Crow*, rev. ed. (New York: Oxford University Press, 1965).

33. White, *The Making of the President, 1964*, p. 171.

34. White, p. 225.

35. Lucius J. Barker and Jesse J. McCorry, Jr., *Black Americans and the Political System* (Cambridge, Mass.: Winthrop, 1976), pp. 224–225.

36. James Baldwin, *Nobody Knows My Name: More Notes of a Native Son* (New York: Dial Press, 1961), p. 64.

37. Joe Feagin and Harlan Hahn, *Ghetto Revolts* (New York: Macmillan, 1937), p. 102.

38. See Table 8–7.

39. Frances Fox Piven and Richard A. Cloward, *Regulating the Poor: The Functions of Public Welfare* (New York: Pantheon, 1971), p. 233.

40. Herman P. Miller, *Rich Man, Poor Man* (New York: Crowell, 1964), p. 85.

41. Miller, pp. 85–86.

42. Piven and Cloward, *Regulating the Poor*, p. 235.

43. *Report of the Advisory Commission on Civil Disorders* (New York: Bantam Books, 1968), p. 9.

44. *Report of the Advisory Commission on Civil Disorders*, p. 22.

45. For a discussion of the consequences of this fact, see Philip Meranto and Lawrence Mosqueda, "Toward Revolution in Urban America: Problems and Prospects," paper delivered at the Annual Meeting of the American Political Science Association, Washington D.C., September 3, 1979.

46. U.S. Department of Labor, Bureau of Labor Statistics, *Employment and Earnings*, January 1977, p. 46, and January 1983, p. 31.

47. William Julius Wilson, *The Declining Significance of Race: Blacks and Changing American Institutions* (Chicago: University of Chicago Press, 1978), p. 97.

48. Wilson, p. 103.

49. Wilson, p. 103.

50. U.S. Department of Commerce, Bureau of the Census, *Current Population Reports, Population Profile of the United States: 1981*, Series P-20, no. 374 (Washington, D.C.: U.S. Government Printing Office, 1981), pp. 49–50.

51. U.S. Bureau of the Census, *Population Profile: 1981*, pp. 49–50.

52. James Heilbrun, *Urban Economics and Public Policy* (New York: St. Martin's Press, 1982), citing U.S. Department of Commerce, Bureau of the Census, *Current Population Reports*, series P-60, no. 124 (1980) and series P-23, no. 37 (1972) (Washington, D.C.: U.S. Government Printing Office).

53. The first edition to this book committed such a serious oversight.

54. U.S. Bureau of the Census, *Current Population Reports, Persons of Spanish Origin in the United States: March 1977*, series P-20, no. 329 (Washington, D.C.: U.S. Government Printing Office, September 1978), p. 2.

55. U.S. Bureau of the Census, Supplementary Reports, *General Social and Economic Characteristics by Race and Spanish Origin: 1980* (Washington, D.C.: U.S. Government Printing Office, September 1978), p. 2.

56. Clifton McCleskey and Bruce Merrill, "Mexican American Political Behavior in Texas," *Social Science Quarterly* 53 (March 1973):785–798; and Susan Welch, John Cower, and Michael Stenman, "Political Participation Among Mexican Americans: An Exploratory Examination," *Social Science Quarterly* 53 (March 1973):799–813.

57. F. Chris Garcia and Rudolpho de las Csarza, *The Chicano Political Experience* (North Scituate, Mass.: Duxbury Press, 1977), p. 107.

58. Meranto and Mosqueda, "Toward Revolution in Urban America," p. 15.

59. David C. Perry and Alfred S. Watkins, "People, Profit, and the Rise of the Sunbelt Cities," in *The Rise of the Sunbelt Cities*, ed. David C. Perry and Alfred S. Watkins, Urban Affairs Annual Reviews, vol. 14 (Beverly Hills, Calif.: Sage Publications, 1977), pp. 296–297.

60. Peter A. Lupsha and William J. Siembieda, "The Poverty of Public Services in the Land of Plenty: An Analysis and Interpretation," in Perry and Watkins, p. 173.

Part III

THE GOVERNMENTAL RESPONSE

Chapter 9

GOVERNMENT POLICIES AND PRIVATE INVESTMENT

Creating the
Segregated Metropolis

National Policy for the Cities

In the aftermath of the Great Depression and World War II, the cities faced an economic and social crisis. In the many years since the prosperity of the 1920s, the physical condition of the inner cities had deteriorated. Public improvements had lagged behind, while municipalities struggled to balance their budgets. World War II delayed further public investment.

The crisis was evidenced in the decay of inner city housing stock and the shortage of new housing. All the nation's cities contained at their centers block after block of dilapidated housing. For years, landlords and owners had invested little or no money in repairs and renovation. At the same time, depression and the exigencies of war kept the yearly construction of new housing at rates far below what was needed to keep pace with a growing population. The housing crisis was bad and growing worse on the eve of the war. After the war ended, it reached astonishing dimensions. Millions of veterans returned from the war and began new families, only to find waiting lists for decent apartments. Many of them moved in with friends and relatives. The nation faced two urban problems: a housing shortage, on the one hand, and urban slums, on the other.

The apparent solutions to the problems of housing and slums lay beyond the financial capacity of local public institutions. The slums that plagued the nation's cities were seen as a national problem, and local officials sought national solutions. They were joined by business elites in the cities who were concerned about deteriorating business and residential districts. The business community was motivated in no small part by a continuing quest to secure a greater measure of order and stability in the metropolitan economic environment, in this case, to redress the functional breakdown of the private real estate and housing market in the cities.

The Housing Act of 1949 emerged from this atmosphere. For the first time, Congress declared a national commitment to rebuild the cities, eliminate slums and blight, and provide decent housing for the nation's citizens. The "Declaration of National Housing Policy," which introduced the Act, stated that

> the general welfare and security of the Nation and the health and living standards of its people require housing production and related community development sufficient to remedy the serious housing shortage, eliminate substandard and other inadequate housing through the clearance of slums and blighted areas, and the realization as soon as feasible of the goal of a decent home and suitable living environment for every American family, thus contributing to the development and redevelopment of communities and the advancement of growth, wealth, and security of the nation.[1]

Never before had there been such a direct statement of national purpose to help the cities. As is the case with most policy initiatives, however, the Housing Act was more evolutionary than revolutionary. Pressures had been building in favor of a national commitment to the cities for a long time. The postwar shortage of housing and the conditions of inner city slums provided the final push.

The Search for Urban Policy

The first positive federal response to the problems of urban America came in 1892, when Congress appropriated $20,000 to investigate slum conditions in cities with populations over 200,000.[2] In his subsequent report to the Congress, the Commissioner of Labor noted, among other things, that the nation's slums had a higher incidence of arrests and saloons than the rest of the country. This conclusion fell obviously something short of a full commitment to the cities.

Federal activity in housing began one year after the entry of the United

States into World War I. Through the Emergency Fleet Corporation, Congress authorized direct federal loans to local realty companies. At a cost of $69.3 million, eight hotels, nineteen dormitories, 1,100 apartment units, and approximately 9,000 houses were constructed to house shipyard workers in twenty-seven cities and towns.[3] Later in that same year, Congress authorized the nation's first public housing program to accommodate additional defense plant workers.

The United States Housing Corporation was created and managed by the Department of Labor. In the 109 days of its operation, it spent $62.4 million, constructing about 6,000 single-family dwellings plus accommodations for 7,200 single men, on 140 project sites around the country.[4] At the conclusion of the war, all of these federally owned housing units were sold to private owners, and in deference to the prevailing philosophy of the time, the government removed itself from the housing business.

The direct precedents for the public housing and slum-clearance programs of the 1950s are found in the depths of the Great Depression. During the last year of the Hoover administration, Congress created the Reconstruction Finance Corporation (RFC) and authorized it to extend loans to private developers for the construction of "low-income" housing in slum areas.[5] Of a total of $8.2 million lent out for such projects (only two were ever authorized), over 98 percent of the money was spent in three slum blocks of Manhattan to construct "Knickerbocker Village," with its 1,573 apartments.[6] Because this project was part of a larger economic program designed to assist private enterprise, the necessity of sufficient profit incentives limited not only the extent of participation but also the success of its social (as opposed to the economic) intent—the provision of low-income housing. In the case of Knickerbocker Village, 82 percent of the slum families who lived on the site "were forced back into tenements in other slum areas" as a result of the higher rent.[7]

Franklin D. Roosevelt introduced a plethora of national programs designed to stimulate the economy and end the Depression. One of the first of these, the National Industrial Recovery Act, included a minor provision authorizing "construction, reconstruction, alteration, or repair, under public regulation or control, of low-rent housing and slum clearance projects."[8]

The Housing Division of the Public Works Administration (PWA) was charged with implementing this provision. At first, the PWA tried to entice private developers into constructing low-income housing through the "carrot" of low-interest federal loans. This strategy conformed with one of the major purposes of the program, which was "to deal with the unemployment situation by giving employment to workers, . . . [and] to demonstrate to private builders the practicability of large-scale community planning."[9] But the private housing industry showed little enthusiasm, and only seven projects ever met specifications and were approved. As a result, the PWA undertook the direct financing and construction of government-owned housing units. The United States Emergency Housing Corporation was created for this purpose in 1933.

Court decisions in Kentucky[10] and Michigan[11] removed the federal government's power to use eminent domain to take over slum land for clearance. In order to avoid the problems of direct federal action, the Emergency Housing Corporation decided to work through local public housing authorities. These were chartered by the states and unquestionably had the power to assemble slum land through condemnation of property. By funneling federal money through these agencies, the PWA constructed nearly 22,000 public, low-income housing units in thirty-seven cities.[12]

The PWA program, however, built fewer low-income units than it tore down. Its main accomplishment was to serve as a vehicle through which real estate agents unloaded undesirable properties on the government at excessive valuation.[13]

Despite its problems, the program set several important precedents. It established the legitimacy of federal involvement in public low-rent housing. The PWA experience also provided the administrative model for implementing future housing programs. Local housing agencies became the recipients of federal funds. Thus, there might be national purposes, but local communities would be responsible for carrying them out. By the end of the PWA public housing program in 1937, twenty-nine states had passed enabling legislation allowing local governments to create and operate local housing authorities. Forty-six local housing agencies had come into existence.[14]

The Public Housing Act of 1937 replaced the PWA program. Like its predecessor, its main objectives were to build low-income housing and to eradicate the slums. The Act adopted the principle that housing programs would be implemented through federal grants-in-aid to local housing authorities:

> An act to provide financial assistance to the states and political subdivisions thereof for the elimination of unsafe and unsanitary housing conditions, for the eradication of slums, for the provision of decent, safe, and sanitary dwellings for families of low income and for the reduction of unemployment and the stimulation of business activity, to create a United States Housing Authority, and for other purposes.[15]

Under the 1937 Act, public housing would be built and administered by local agencies, not by the federal government, and private enterprise would play a pivotal role.

The Wagner-Steagall Public Housing Act of 1937 illustrated the basic conflicts in the housing field. Unlike federally insured mortgage loans, which were designed to stimulate activity in the private sector, public housing was "designed to service the needs of those of low income who otherwise would not be able to afford decent, safe and sanitary dwellings."[16] The absence of substantial economic profits for realtors, builders, and banks meant that groups representing these interests would persistently oppose the channeling of public funds into public housing construction. As far as they were concerned, government-owned housing competed with the private housing market. Its only redeeming virtue was that public housing provided jobs in the construction industry. But this benefit failed to outweigh the unpopularity of providing housing subsidies to the bottom third of the population. Such subsidies were not nearly as popular as the massive FHA insurance programs, designed to make the American goal of home ownership more attainable for the growing middle class.[17] The private sector, led by realtors and home builders, much preferred the FHA programs, which provided low risk and maximum profit without the problems of race and geographical location that characterized low-income housing projects.

The federal government's venture into housing hit a raw nerve within the real estate and construction trade industries. The opponents of public housing were led by the National Association of Real Estate Boards (NAREB), which promoted the idea that housing was an entirely private industry, which government should leave alone. As Walter S. Schmidt, president of the National Association, explained:

> Housing should remain a matter of private enterprise and private ownership. It is contrary to the genius of the American people and the ideals they have established that government become landlord to its citizens. There is a sound logic in the continuance of the practice under which those who have the initiative and the will to save acquire better living facilities and yield their former quarters at modest rents to the group below.[18]

Public housing and slum clearance were bitterly opposed by real estate interests, but a broad coalition supported public housing, including the National Public Housing Conference, the AFL and CIO, the Labor Housing Conference, the National Association of Housing and Development Officials, the Urban League, the NAACP, and the National League of Cities. Senator Robert F. Wagner of New York, cosponsor of the 1937 bill and chief architect of much of the New Deal social legislation, explained the position of the "public housers" when he stated:

> The object of public housing, in a nutshell, is not to invade the field of home building for the middle class or the well-to-do which has been the only profitable area for private enterprise in the past. Nor is it even to exclude private

enterprise from major participation in a low-cost housing program. It is merely to supplement what private industry will do, by subsidies which will make up the difference between what the poor can afford to pay and what is necessary to assure decent living quarters.[19]

The United States Housing Administration (USHA) was authorized by the 1937 Act to extend up to $800 million in long-term (60 years), low-interest loans to local public housing agencies, covering up to 100 percent of the cost of financing the development of low-income housing units. It was also authorized to make capital grants or annual subsidies to local housing agencies for the construction and operation of the projects. In practice, however, most of the local projects were financed through a combination of federal (USHA) loans covering 90 percent of the development costs, and an annual subsidy for operations. Approximately 15 percent of the "economic rent" (the rent that would have to be extracted if the projects were to have been economically viable) was supplied by state and local governments through tax-exemption for bonds used to finance construction. Federal annual operating subsidies ranged from an average of 30 percent in the prewar years to 16 percent during World War II.[20]

Some of the requirements of the Act reveal the heritage of the PWA experience and the major approaches taken in subsequent legislation. These included a demonstrated community need for public housing, a local community contribution to the program, specific limitations on costs and quality of rental units, and a restriction that occupancy be limited to low-income families only.[21] In response to demands from the real estate industry, a requirement was added that the number of new housing units constructed could not exceed the number of slum dwellings torn down. The purpose of this requirement was to keep public housing from competing with the private housing market.

The United States Housing Administration and its successor agencies, the Federal Public Housing Authority (1942–46) and the Public Housing Administration (1946 to the present), completed a total of 169,451 low-income public housing units under the authority of the 1937 Housing Act.[22] Most of the units were placed under construction before the entry of the United States into World War II.

World War II was the third national emergency recognized by Congress as requiring the production of publicly built and financed housing. In addition to 50,000 units constructed under 1937 Housing Act authorizations, 2 million other housing units were provided through temporary and emergency programs. Of these, around 1 million were privately built with federal financial assistance.[23] Another 1 million were completed under programs that left ownership in the hands of the federal government. The opponents of public housing made sure that these war-spawned units were sold on the private market after the war had ended.

The Struggle over Housing Policy

Public housing legislation prompted several groups to take an interest in urban redevelopment. The coalition that supported the 1949 Housing Act was made up of a tenuous union of liberal and conservative interests. The legislation represented a basic compromise. Conservatives acquiesced to a continued public housing program *in exchange* for an affirmation of the principle that private enterprise would be the main vehicle for redevelopment.

The Housing Act of 1949 contained two distinct diagnoses of the urban crisis. Liberals emphasized the social crisis in the slums. Their cure for this crisis included slum clearance and construction of low-income housing. Conservatives, on the other hand, defined the crisis in economic terms— the "blight" of commercial and residential areas, which sapped the economic vitality of the central cities.

A blighted area was defined as one that had become unprofitable to both the private investor and the municipality. Because of the deterioration and obsolescence of its structures, it could no longer compete with other areas in the private marketplace. Falling rents and increasing vacancy rates led to less and less maintenance. All this had a spiraling effect, further lowering rental values and occupancy rates. Property owners would attempt to limit their losses by withholding property taxes. Blighted areas thus became a financial burden on the municipality. Much more money had to be expended for the provision of basic municipal services than could be recouped in tax receipts. The blighted areas of Atlanta during the 1930s, for example, absorbed 53 percent of the city's expenditures for public services while providing only 5.5 percent of its real property tax revenues.[24] Similarly, Chicago's 1933 tax assessment of $1.2 million in one blighted area was $2 million less than the cost of providing municipal services. Even then, less than half the taxes assessed had been collected by 1936.[25]

Slums carried a social as well as an economic connotation. They were characterized by a host of social problems, which were generally attributed to the structural inadequacies of the housing and physical environment. Slums allegedly bred disease, crime, and delinquency, and were perceived to be detrimental to the moral fiber and social fabric of the city. It was noted, for example, that although Cleveland's slum areas contained only 2.7 percent of the population, they accounted for 7.8 percent of the juvenile delinquency arrests and 21.3 percent of the city's murders in 1932.[26]

A large number of interest groups agreed that the economic health and social well-being of the cities were threatened by urban decay, and liberals and conservatives concurred on this general principle. For example, one of the most conservative groups, the United States Savings and Loan League, voiced support for the redevelopment of blighted areas: "Our people have studied the problem of slum clearance for some years and agree that it is an appropriate field for public action . . . we think it appropriate for . . . land assembly [to proceed] in the slum areas of our cities."[27]

Even the National Association of Real Estate Boards favored urban development, so long as it was implemented through private institutions, this despite a long-standing opposition to government involvement in the provision of housing.[28] Private business interests, primarily the real estate and organized housing trade associations, were deeply concerned over the adverse economic impact and attendant capital loss of blighted areas. As owners and investors in urban real estate, the business interests of the city "had a tremendous stake in the maintenance of residential and commercial property values."[29] Blight threatened this stake.

But conservative interests united in their opposition to public housing. The National Association of Real Estate Boards was by far the most vociferous of the groups. Although its headquarters was located in Chicago, the NAREB maintained an office in the nation's capital, the "Realtor's Washington Office," from which it exerted pressure on Congress and federal administrators. The executive vice-president of the association was Herbert U. Nelson, a self-proclaimed defender of free enterprise and critic of popular democracy. He was a well-known figure in the capital. The NAREB described itself as a "trade and professional association, [operating] to improve the real estate business, to exchange information and, incidentally, to seek to protect the commodity in which we deal, which is real property, and to make home ownership and the ownership of property both desirable and secure."[30]

The association pursued the "demon" of public low-rent housing throughout the country, on Capitol Hill, in the state houses, in city halls, and in communities and neighborhoods. Between 1939 and 1949, it was eminently successful in its efforts to thwart the expansion of low-rent housing. The blind hatred that the NAREB held for the public housing program led it to oppose the 1949 Housing Act.

The second powerful force in the private housing industry was the United States Savings and Loan League. In 1949, the League represented 3,700 member associations, including most of the savings and loan institutions across the country. These financial institutions issued long-term mortgage loans for the construction and purchase of homes. Although originally established to serve the working class as an alternative to conventional banking institutions, over the years savings and loan institutions acquired a middle- and upper-class bias in their policies.

The National Association of Home Builders (NAHB) was another important conservative group. This organization represented approximately 16,500 member companies in 1949. For the most part, these members were small, local construction companies.

These three groups were backed by an array of private industry, trade, and financial associations, including the United States Chamber of Commerce, the Mortgage Bankers Association of America, the Producers Council, the National Economic Council, and the National Association of Retail Lumber Dealers.[31]

The National Association of Real Estate Boards designed and promoted a bold scheme of urban redevelopment to be implemented in a manner consistent with the interests of private enterprise. The basic concept of the scheme was first developed in 1935, and a second proposal was publicly introduced in 1941. This proposal, in large part, provided the basis for Title I of the 1949 Housing Act.[32]

During the eight years between the introduction of the proposal and the enactment of the program, it received the support of the conservative coalition in the housing industry. The proposal included all the key aspects finally adopted in 1949: local authorities to supervise redevelopment, joint federal-local subsidies to "write-down" the costs of land below market rates, and reliance on private enterprise as the vehicle for redeveloping the cleared land.

Throughout the 1940s, though the NAREB and its allies promoted federally subsidized urban redevelopment, the issue remained subordinated to their venomous opposition to public housing programs. This unwavering opposition derived its force from Herbert Nelson's ideological stand against the evils of "socialism," defined as publically-subsidized housing, and was supported by the real estate industry's interest in preventing public competition to privately owned slum housing.[33]

The liberal coalition was composed of a wide range of groups. As might be expected, many religious-oriented welfare organizations (e.g., the National Conference of Catholic Charities and the National Council of Jewish Women), civic organizations (e.g., the League of Women Voters and the Citizen's Union of New York City), and social welfare groups (e.g., the American Council on Education and the American Association of Social Workers) constituted the coalition supporting slum elimination through public housing programs. Perhaps the key group on the liberal side was the National Public Housing Conference. Formed during the pre–New Deal days of the Depression, this group became a kind of "brain trust" for public housing policy. It was largely responsible for the research and staff work for the 1937 Housing Act. Unlike the real estate lobbies, it was not a federation of local groups, nor was it a mass-based organization. It was an elite group of individuals interested in housing policy and included some of the more influential academic authorities on housing problems and policies. The Public Housing Conference had close connections with the federal government's housing administrators, and thus was able to exercise considerable influence.

Organized labor was a critical component in the public low-rent housing lobby. Both the CIO and the AFL maintained housing committees and participated in the Washington-based Labor Housing Conference. Of all the liberal groups, only organized labor carried the substantial political clout attendant to broad, mass-based organizations. Labor's solution to urban housing shortages and to the social evils of slum living was the construction of low-rent public housing on vacant land, including some suburban land.

Organized labor led the way in criticizing the urban redevelopment proposals of the real estate industry. A booklet of the period published by the United Auto Workers succinctly stated labor's point of view:

> Climbing on the "slum clearance" band wagon, they [the real estate and building trade associations] are trying to hoodwink the public into buying city slum areas at a high price and turning such areas over to them at a fraction of such cost to the public. Not a word of "subsidy" here. Not a word of rehousing the families who now live in the slums. . . . With sanctimonious faces they piously prate the high standards of American living and of the fire that burns in American breasts for home ownership (supplied by themselves). . . . To the shields of "private enterprise," "home ownership," and "the high standard of American living," with which they have so successfully covered their operations, they have suddenly added that shiny new shield of "slum clearance." . . .without government assistance, they would not now be operating and there would be little or no private house building in the postwar period.[34]

A third key group was the National Association of Housing Officials (NAHO). This group was formed during the Depression years and was responsible for spreading information on public housing, and thus educating supporters of the low-rent programs, through its journal, *The Journal of Housing*. It, too, attacked the urban redevelopment program advocated by the real estate industry, although not as vociferously as its labor union allies. Reflecting the basic values that drew the liberal, prohousing coalition together, NAHO insisted that the provision of adequate housing was far more important than urban economic redevelopment.

Organizations representing local officials were important in supplying support for public housing in local communities. The United States Conference of Mayors, the National League of Cities, and the American Municipal Association all supported public housing.

The liberal coalition was sympathetic to the proposed urban redevelopment program. They appreciated the economic and social benefits to be derived from the elimination of blighted areas. They refused, however, to allow the real estate industry to substitute blight eradication for public low-rent housing.

Perhaps the best indicator of the unlikely nature of the political alliance that supported the 1949 Housing Act is to be found in its unofficial title, the Wagner-Ellender-Taft Act. These three senators spanned the spectrum of American political philosophy. The conservative Republican presidential aspirant from Ohio, Robert A. Taft, the New Deal big-city liberal Robert F. Wagner of New York, and the segregationist southern Democrat Allen J. Ellender of Louisiana united to see their bill through five rounds of hearings, four years of controversy, three redraftings, and two changes of leadership in Congress.

The housing bill was introduced in the Senate (S. 1592) in 1945, and approved in April, 1946, only to die in the hands of the House Banking and Currency Committee, killed by "very potent private lobby groups."[35]

The bill (now S. 866) again passed the Senate in April, 1948, having survived the change in congressional leadership that occurred as a result of the 1946 elections. Again it was killed in the House. This time, however, it succeeded in passing through the Banking and Currency Committee, with the aid of a heavy dose of public pressure and political arm twisting, only to die in the Rules Committee just before the opening of the Republican national convention in July, 1948.

The general elections of 1948 returned Democratic leadership to both houses of Congress. In the battle over the bill (S. 1070) in the Senate, the liberal Senate supporters of public housing were put to the test of fire. In the most devious of several obstructionist moves, Senator John W. Bricker (R-Ohio) introduced an amendment prohibiting racial segregation in the public housing program, thus hoping to place his liberal colleagues on the horns of a dilemma. Such northern liberal Democrats as Hubert H. Humphrey and Paul Douglas determined the ultimate fate of the bill in the Senate by voting against the open-housing amendments they had so recently advocated at the Democratic national convention in 1948. With a stipulation requiring integration, public housing would never have been approved by Congress, and the liberals knew it.

The political coalition that passed the bill in the Senate included both Republicans and Democrats, liberals and conservatives. On the key votes in the Senate the bill received a majority from both sides of the aisle, and from such disparate members as the maverick liberal Senator Wayne Morse of Oregon and the conservative Senator Joe McCarthy of Wisconsin.

In the House, a leadership threat to undermine the authority of the

Rules Committee succeeded in getting the bill (H. 4009) to the floor. Despite intensive lobbying efforts by the realtors and their allies, the public housing title was retained by a razor thin five-vote margin, and the entire bill was passed by a bipartisan majority. Thus, northern Democrats, urban Republicans, and a few prohousing conservatives from both parties enacted the nation's first comprehensive urban housing policy.[36]

Title I of the Act empowered the Housing and Home Finance Agency (HHFA) to assist local efforts at blight and slum removal. Through this agency, the federal government offered grants-in-aid to help local public agencies absorb the cost of the "write-down" on land that had been cleared of slum buildings. The "write-down" was the difference between the local agency's cost of assembling and clearing the site and the price paid for the land by subsequent private developers.

In addition to the $500 million authorized for the "write-down" subsidies, the HHFA was authorized to extend loans to local public agencies for land assembly and site clearance. The Act gave private developers preference in redeveloping the clearance sites. Tenants and slum dwellers displaced by renewal programs were to be supplied with "decent, safe and sanitary dwellings." The redevelopment effort was to be "predominantly residential" in character and was to conform to "general plans for the development of the locality as a whole."

Title III, "Low-Rent Public Housing," authorized the production of 810,000 government-subsidized housing units over the next six years. This amounted to 10 percent of the estimated national need for new dwellings. Congress authorized annual subsidies to local public housing agencies of up to $308 million. A temporary revolving loan fund of $1.5 billion was created to finance initial construction.

The 1949 housing statute established occupancy preferences for veterans and families displaced by Title I (renewal) activities. Per room and per unit cost limitations were imposed to prevent "extravagance and unnecessary" amenities. Rent levels and tenant eligibility requirements were regulated to prevent "unfair" competition with the private housing market and to ensure that public housing opportunities went only to the neediest families.

Urban Renewal and Its Problems

The stated objectives of the national legislation that funded urban renewal often conflicted with the political and economic interests of local communities. The 1949 Housing Act was designed specifically to clear slums and to construct low-income housing.

Amendments to the legislation adopted in 1954 allowed communities to use 10 percent of project funds for commercial revitalization. In 1960, this proportion was raised to 30 percent. In actual practice, half or more of all funds could be diverted away from low-income housing to commercial development. Any renewal project that allocated 51 percent or more of its funds to housing was designated by the federal administrators as a "100 percent housing" project. By manipulating this definition, local authorities could allocate as much as two-thirds of their funds for commercial development, but still remain within federal guidelines.

Thus urban renewal was turned into a political pawn for commercial and industrial development interests.[37] Though the national legislation emphasized the deleterious effects of a slum environment on its residents, local political and economic elites focused on the economic decline of Central Business Districts (CBDs). Business leaders and politicians were convinced that urban decay was caused by the loss of economic vitality at the urban core.

In the abstract, housing for low-income people might seem worthwhile, but few local politicians felt they could afford to tolerate it in their own neighborhoods. Site selection, for example, was of paramount concern to Chicago's politicians in the 1950s. None of them wanted the projects in their own wards.[38] The Chicago experience was duplicated in many cities across the country, demonstrating that the public housing issue had failed to develop strong grassroots support. In fact, with the prodding of local chapters of the National Association of Real Estate Boards (NAREB), organized opposition to public housing developed in city after city. The specter of racial integration was exploited to the fullest by opponents of subsidized housing. Between 1949 and the end of 1952, public housing programs were rejected by referenda (a tactic favored by the NAREB) in forty communities, including a few of the nation's larger cities, such as Akron, Houston, and Los Angeles. Social and political realities at the local level made public housing a volatile issue. Local officials were acutely aware that "there could hardly be many votes to be gained in championing the cause—and perhaps a great many lost."[39]

In contrast, economic redevelopment was "good politics." Seizing on redevelopment as a way to secure federal funds and an excellent source of political capital, an enterprising mayor could simultaneously advance his or her political fortunes and improve the public image of the city. To implement big renewal projects, an alliance had to be forged between the mayor and other local officials on the one hand, and the business community on the other.

One now classic example of such an urban renewal alliance occurred in New Haven, Connecticut, where the young Democrat Richard Lee hung his mayoral aspirations and his political future on the prospect of a successful urban redevelopment program. He won the 1952 election and several terms thereafter by putting together a broad alliance in favor of community renewal. Because

> the mayor was building his political career on the success of redevelopment, the Republicans could not damage him without attacking either redevelopment or his role in it, but because everything in the redevelopment plan was endorsed by Republican [business] notables to attack the mayor was to alienate established sources of Republican electoral and financial support.[40]

Lee's political capital derived from a coalition of government officials and local notables, particularly business leaders. It took shape in the formation of the Citizen's Action Committee (CAC), an advisory board required by law (under Title I), which included "businessmen concerned with traffic and retail sales, trade union leaders concerned with employment and local prosperity," and "political liberals concerned with slums, housing, and race relations." This group was characterized by Mayor Lee as

> the biggest set of muscles in New Haven. . . . They're muscular because they control wealth, they're muscular because they control industries, represent banks. They're muscular because they head up labor. They're muscular because they represent the intellectual portions of the community. They're muscular because they're articulate, because they're respectable, because of their financial power, and because of the accumulation of prestige they have built up over the years as individuals in all kinds of causes.[41]

The fact that this group was brought together by an entrepreneurial mayor does not mean, however, that they had been co-opted into a supporting role against their better judgments and own interests. One conservative banker, a CAC member, noted that the city's chamber of commerce had

> felt something had to be done here, it couldn't be done by private interests, it couldn't be done by the public entirely, it couldn't be political . . . if we are going to have a city, and it's going to be a shopping area . . . something had to be done. . . . Here's a dream that we've had for a long time and we're happy to see it culminated.[42]

A second banker, in an outburst of economic parochialism, said:

> If taxes are going to remain high and there is going to be a social program in the United States . . . why, there's only one thing to do and that is to devise ways and means so that we can share in it. That's pretty selfish. I'm not interested in building a highway through Montana . . . or a TVA down South, and I'd like to see some of those dollars come back to Connecticut so that we can enjoy some more benefits.[43]

Local labor leaders were also happy with urban redevelopment. One of them pointed out that

> everybody feels—that is, most everybody feels—that they benefit one way or another by a prosperous community, even if it just means a better economic atmosphere . . . the building trades benefit directly from the program, and so they are enthusiastic towards it and have even made contributions to the CAC committee itself. . . . On the other end of the scale from the conservative building trades, the more sophisticated trade union leaders . . . have been completely taken with the program because of the concern of the program leaders for the human relations aspect of it.[44]

New Haven's version of the new urban coalition sprang up in cities all over the country. In the early 1950s, for example, Mayor Joseph Darst of St. Louis received widespread publicity for his efforts to "turn St. Louis around" through a redevelopment program. There was apparently very broad support for inner city renewal. A former St. Louis mayor recalled these efforts early in 1952:

> About a year ago, a group of distinguished citizens of our community were called into the Mayor's office and there charged by Mayor Darst with the responsibility of giving leadership to a program to take advantage of the Housing Act of 1949, Title I, and the State Act of 1945. It was suggested that an urban redevelopment corporation be organized. There was much fine publicity on the part of the metropolitan press—they not only gave considerable space but they also subscribed to the extent of better than a quarter of a million dollars to the debentures and stock of that corporation. So, we salute the press on this occasion. I should add that many other fine business institutions, sixty-nine in number, subscribed a total in excess of $2,000,000 toward the capital structure of the corporation. It is a distinguished list. There's the May Department Stores, Stix, Baer and Fuller, Scruggs, Vandervoort and Barney, the Anheuser Busch Company, Ely Walker Company, the Falstaff Company, the First National Bank, . . .and others.[45]

In every older city, business and financial interests were similarly concerned about urban decay and its impact on their economic investment in downtown property.

The central theme in the politics of urban redevelopment is the public official–local business coalition. The programs of the 1949 Housing Act fit nicely into the general concern shared by the nation's mayors to secure their personal political futures and at the same time improve the economic fortunes of their cities. Mayors universally associated the latter with the health of the Central Business District (CBD), and downtown businesses identified their own economic fortunes with the future of the cities. The flight of the middle class following World War II had seriously undermined the economic viability of the city. Self-interest on the part of local business establishments led to a burst of civic activity unparalleled since the municipal reform movement earlier in the century.

> They believe in the free enterprise system and have gone into this work, not to lose their money; they certainly hope to get their money back. And they hope to earn a modest profit. I point out, however, that a good many of them have a selfish motive. They want to maintain downtown values where their businesses are centered.[46]

As a result of the nature of the alliance, most redevelopment projects were located in or near Central Business Districts. Those areas were generally the oldest in the cities and were therefore susceptible to blight. Chicago's Loop, for instance, was surrounded by a semicircle of slums and blight extending out, on the average, five miles.

Since the Central Business District was the center of activity, where the local business establishment held heavy real estate and business investments, it was only logical that businesses would seek to protect their investments through revitalization of their immediate environment. The need for political visibility by elected officials reinforced the selection of downtown sites for urban renewal projects. The political interests of local officials and business leaders coalesced.

The separate elements of the new urban coalition needed one another. Each alone was insufficient to accomplish the task at hand. Local officials needed the financial support and public prestige the business community possessed. This was obviously the case in New Haven. Mayor Lee's careful selection of notable figures for the Citizen's Action Committee attests to this fact of life: "If all the banks [and, by extrapolation, other business institutions and leaders] had opposed redevelopment, it could hardly have moved forward even under the skillful auspices of Lee" and his associates.[47]

The business community, in turn, was dependent on the resources of the public sector. The coercive power of the state was a necessary ingredient for a successful redevelopment effort. Public authority was, in the first instance, called upon to officially designate an area as "blighted" and thus make it eligible for federal redevelopment funds. The government's power of eminent domain was a critical factor in land-assembly operations, because property owners could not otherwise be compelled to sell. Also, the unique ability of local renewal agencies to receive the necessary "write-down" subsidies and loans from the federal government made local officials and agencies indispensable to business leaders who wanted urban redevelopment. "This strange coalition"[48] was thus a mutually reinforcing alliance. The object of the alliance—renewed vitality for the city—used publicly subsidized urban redevelopment as its tool.

To some degree, public housing benefitted from the character of this alliance. By simple deduction, the members of the urban renewal coalition understood that the families and individuals displaced by urban redevelopment would have to find new housing. The 1949 Housing Act had called attention to this obvious fact and provided, in Title III, that people displaced by renewal be given priority in public housing projects. The political feasibility of public housing was founded on the formation of the new redevelopment coalition, for "the necessity of public housing as a companion to these [urban redevelopment] efforts was accepted as a fact of life."[49] By the end of 1961, urban redevelopment and renewal had eliminated 126,000 housing units, 80 percent of which were substandard. The 28,000 new units that replaced them were in no way sufficient to house the 113,000 families and 36,000 individuals who were displaced.[50] Public housing helped make up some of the deficit in housing units lost as a result of urban renewal, but it fell short of making up the whole difference, particularly since public housing accounted for only 6 percent of the construction started and only 1 percent of additional construction planned in urban renewal areas as of April 1, 1961.[51]

Redevelopment and the Black Ghetto

Because of the dual stigma of class and race, recently arrived blacks were housed in the run-down areas of the central cities. The oldest and most dilapidated housing was generally located near the Central Business District, and therefore black populations were frequently displaced by renewal projects. The "black residents of the inner cities [and] black businesses were among the prime victims of federally sponsored urban renewal programs referred to as 'urban black removal.' "[52] The program was described by critics as "Negro clearance," recognizing the fact that over three-fourths of the people displaced by urban renewal in the first eight years of the program, and 66 percent of those displaced through 1961, were either Puerto Rican or (more likely) black.[53]

Redevelopment of the Central Business District and areas near it served the explicit purpose of removing unsightly economic blight, thus in principle making the city's downtown more attractive to prospective investors and suburban shoppers. Simultaneously, it served the implicit purpose of removing esthetically unpleasing black and lower-class neighborhoods from the immediate environs of the Central Business District. In its quest to protect these property values and to secure an attractive environment for the city's commercial activity, the urban renewal coalition extracted social costs that fell disproportionately on poor and black slum residents. Black tenants were forced into other parts of the city by clearance projects, usually to a slightly more distant slum. Economic and racial barriers left them no other choice: "Given the realities of the low-income housing market . . . it is likely that, for many families, relocation [meant] no more than keeping one step ahead of the bulldozer."[54] Thus a new game was added to the harsh realities of urban life, "musical slums."

Because public housing was tied closely to slum clearance, most tenants in the central cities were black. Their status as slum dwellers gave blacks "the dubious privilege of eligibility for public housing."[55] Nonwhites accounted for 38 percent of all the nation's public housing tenants in 1952, but by 1961 this proportion had risen to 46 percent. In individual projects, segregation was the norm. Whites who were eligible for public housing or who had been victims of slum clearance retained housing options in the private market that were unavailable to blacks. Blacks, therefore, tended to "take over" public low-rent housing in the cities by default and as a result of racial discrimination.

Public housing policy reinforced racial and class segregation. Urban renewal and slum clearance simultaneously reduced black housing options and increased the density of the black ghetto. In short, the policies promoted through the 1949 Housing Act were molded by the political and economic setting in the cities. Racism, class discrimination, residential segregation, land values, and the profit motive were all important factors that motivated the urban renewal coalition to keep the black minority isolated within American cities.

By the early 1960s, there was widespread disenchantment with federally-assisted urban renewal. Liberals and conservatives alike were appalled by the results of the program. At its inception and through its early years business leaders and politicians expected a miraculous reversal of central city decline. The optimism soon turned into frustration.

Redevelopment took too long. By the later 1960s, it took an estimated four years to plan a project, and then an additional six years for "completion," which often enough was defined as giving up the original goals.[56] Blighted neighborhoods and slums grew faster than the renewal projects could eliminate them.

Liberal critics viewed urban renewal as a "federally financed gimmick to provide relatively cheap land for a miscellany of profitable, prestigious [private] enterprises."[57] It failed to provide a solution to the social problems of slum living. Not only were the poor displaced, but they were forced to pay higher rents when the supply of low-rent housing units dwindled. With only 5 percent of the new housing units within the economic reach of low-income families, there had a been a 90 percent decrease in the supply of low-income housing within redevelopment areas during the first ten years of the program's operation.[58]

Slum dwellers, who were initially supposed to benefit from the urban renewal program, were often the biggest losers. In the first fourteen years of the program's operation, "urban renewal demolished the homes of 177,000 families and another 66,000 single individuals, most of them poor and most of them black."[59] Less than one-fourth of the housing units were replaced, and many of these were too expensive for those who were displaced.[60] Only $34.8 million of the urban renewal funds, less than 1 percent, were used for relocation assistance, placing a disproportionate share of the cost of the program on the slum residents who were forced to move.[61]

In 1965, rent supplement programs were enacted as an alternative to public housing for the poor. Through direct housing aid, the poor would presumably be able to choose their own housing on the private market. The Housing and Urban Development Act of 1968 required that a majority of housing units constructed on redevelopment sites be for low- and moderate-income families.[62]

Such tinkering with the urban renewal and public housing programs was designed to provide more benefits for the poor. The improvements, in the end, were modest. Low-income housing continued to be replaced on far less than a one-to-one basis. In fact, only 51 percent of the new units built in urban renewal areas after 1968 were for people of low or moderate income.[63]

Both public housing and urban renewal met their effective demise in the 1970s. The inability of either to significantly counter the decay of the nation's older urban areas weakened their bases of support. They had persisted in the face of bitter criticism because everyone felt that something should be done, but there was no agreement on alternatives. In 1974, urban redevelopment was merged into the Community Development Block Grant program. Public housing was allowed to decline under the Nixon administration, from 104,000 starts in 1970 to only 19,000 starts in 1974.[64]

Low-rent public housing and urban renewal, the nation's first major programs designed specifically for the cities, were unsuccessful in saving the cities from blight and slums. Nevertheless, massive numbers of the poor were relocated to areas less valued by investors. Many of these areas are now occupied by office buildings, sports stadiums, hotels, and cultural attractions. Urban renewal made the land available, but by itself it could not "save" the cities for business investment.

National Policies Promoting Suburban Expansion

The decline of the central cities made urban redevelopment a pressing issue. But powerful economic and social forces were working against redevelopment. Suburbanization of people and businesses accelerated after World War II. And the flight from the central cities was substantially underwritten by national policies.

In June, 1934, the Roosevelt administration embarked on a set of policies that would have a profound impact on the spatial development of metropolitan America. Through the National Housing Act, the administration attempted to revive the moribund construction industry. Second only to agriculture as an employer, the housing industry had experienced a devastating retrenchment. Before the stock market crash of October 1929, new housing units were being built at the rate of 900,000 a year. By 1934, only 90,000 units a year were being constructed. Throughout the decade, housing starts lagged far behind the demand for new housing.[65]

In Chicago, only 131 new housing units were constructed during 1933, compared with 18,837 in 1929 and 41,416 in 1926.[66] Across the nation, 63 percent of the workers in the housing industry were unemployed. The housing problem was further exacerbated by foreclosures on mortgages. Millions of families lost their homes through foreclosures, and millions more were faced with hardship in meeting their mortgage payments. They looked to the federal government for assistance. The New Deal responded with the National Housing Act of 1934.

The Act was intended to stimulate the housing market by shoring up the home mortgage credit industry. The act created the Federal Housing Administration (FHA) and the Federal Savings and Loan Insurance Corporation (FSLIC).

The intent of the National Housing Act was to ease credit in order to expand the capital market for the home-building industry, thereby reviving a major sector of the economy. The FSLIC insured individual accounts up to $5,000 (it has since risen through a series of steps to $100,000), hoping in this manner to instill confidence in the minds of potential savers and investors. In this way, people would be persuaded to put their savings into banks instead of under mattresses and in shoeboxes, and to encourage savings and loan institutions to invest more capital in the floundering housing market.

By far the most important and familiar part of the 1934 Housing Act is section 203, the basic home mortgage insurance program under which the bulk of FHA insurance has been written up to the present date. Fully 79 percent, about 9.5 million units, of all FHA-insured units from 1934 to 1975 was insured under this 203 program, representing a face value of more than $109 billion.[67] The purpose of the program was to finance the acquisition of proposed, under construction, or existing one- to four-family units. As enacted in 1934, the Act provided for FHA insurance of 80 percent of the value of the property. Through the Housing and Urban Development Act of 1974, this amount subsequently has been increased to 97 percent of the first $25,000 and 80 percent of the remaining value. The low risk involved for the lending institution permits the mortgagee to pay a low downpayment, with the remaining principal and interest spread out over a twenty-five or thirty-year period. Title I of the 1934 Act provided FHA insurance for loans used for "permanent repairs that add to the basic liveability and usefulness of the property."[68]

The way various groups viewed this legislation sheds light on the differing goals of urban political groups. A conflict was developing between those who wanted to revitalize the inner-city slums and those who wanted to promote new housing construction on the urban fringe. A struggle emerged between social welfare liberals on the one hand, and banks, savings and loan institutions, realtors, and contractors on the other. New construction under FHA came to mean new housing *outside the cities.*

Social welfare liberals saw Title I of the 1934 Housing Act as a means of eliminating substandard living conditions in the central cities by providing property owners with an opportunity to rehabilitate their property with a low-interest, low-risk loan. City officials hoped Title I would be a catalyst to entice affluent people to stay within the city limits and remodel their homes rather than move to new homes in the suburbs. Downtown business interests wanted Title I to bolster the value of the Central Business Districts. But most banks, savings and loans, realtors, and contractors saw section 203 as a way to finance new construction beyond the built-up city. In lobbying for the Housing Act, they had agreed to Title I only as a compromise to facilitate quick congressional action.

Very little money was ever appropriated to implement the inner-city Title I provisions of the 1934 Act. Section 203, in contrast, assisted millions of people in moving to the burgeoning suburbs after World War II. Several factors help account for this fact. First, a serious housing shortage confronted the nation following the war. Fifteen million veterans returned to civilian life, married, and started families. The "baby boom" exerted great pressures in favor of new housing construction.

Second, the postwar economy created unprecedented affluence for the expanding middle class. American families had more to spend on housing and automobiles. Thus both demographic and economic pressures pushed new housing construction. Operating in conjunction with the financial policies of the FHA and other government agencies, these social developments made the vision of home ownership feasible for thousands of young urban families.

Caught in the mainstream ethos of upward mobility, conspicuous consumption, and the "good life," a great number of families took advantage of the opportunities made possible by the FHA. Just before the end of World War II, Congress enacted the Servicemen's Readjustment Act of 1944—the so-called GI Bill of Rights. By insuring home mortgage loans to veterans, the Veterans Administration (VA) had much the same impact as the FHA. The two programs together loosened the credit market. The no-down-payment policy of the VA helped increase the federally insured share of the mortgage market from 15 percent in 1945 to 41 percent in 1954.[69]

Table 9–1 shows how much the FHA eased the task of buying a home. In the 1920s, downpayments of 40 to 50 percent were standard. Savings and loan institutions allowed a maximum of eleven years for loans to be repaid. Banks were not so generous: six years was the norm. In the 1960s, by way of contrast, conventional mortgage loans typically required 25 percent down, amortized over a twenty-year period. Under the FHA, a home buyer could finance a home for 5 percent down for thirty years and could obtain a much larger loan. The VA allowed financing with no downpayment at all.

TABLE 9–1   Relative Burden of Loan Terms, 1920s and 1960s*

Decade and Lender	Terms	% of annual income	
		Down payment	Annual payment
1920s			
Savings and Loan Association	60 percent of house value loaned for 11 years at 7 percent; fully amortized	100	20
Bank or Insurance Company	50 percent of house value loaned for 5 years at 6 percent; unamortized	125	7.5 plus 125 in 5th year
1960s			
Conventional Lender	75 percent of house value loaned for 20 years at 7 percent; fully amortized	62.5	18
FHA	95 percent of house value loaned for 30 years at 7.5 percent; fully amortized	12.5	20

Source: Henry J. Aaron, *Shelter and Subsidies: Who Benefits from Federal Housing Policies*, Studies in Social Economics (Washington, D.C.: The Brookings Institution, 1972), p. 77. Copyright © 1972 by the Brookings Institution. Reprinted by permission.
*For a house equal to approximately two-and-one-half times the purchaser's annual salary.

FHA-insured mortgages made their mark on the home credit market. Between 1935 and 1974, the FHA insured 11.4 million home mortgages totaling $109 billion. Nearly 9 million of these mortgages, 77 percent of the total, went for new housing.[70] Table 9–2 shows how much the FHA and VA programs influenced the housing market. About one-third of all homes purchased in the 1950s were financed through FHA or VA. The proportion of government-financed loans gradually declined until the late 1960s, increased for a brief period, and declined again in the 1970s. In 1984, the FHA-VA share fell below 10 percent for the first time since World War II.

Most of the new construction occurred in the suburbs. Throughout the 1940s and 1950s, the FHA exhibited a heavy bias in favor of the suburbs. In its first twelve years, for example, it did not insure a single dwelling on Manhattan island.

In part, the FHA's suburban bias reflected a preference for single-family, middle-class neighborhoods, as opposed to densely settled city neighborhoods. Thus, homes for purchase by individual buyers were insured more readily than were rental units. The exclusion of apartments in the suburbs also meant the exclusion of people who could not afford to buy homes.

TABLE 9–2   Use of FHA- and VA-insured Loans in the United States, 1950–1984

Year	% private housing financed through FHA or VA	Total number of housing starts (in thousands)
1950	34.7	1,952
1952	28.0	1,504
1955	40.7	1,646
1960	26.4	1,274
1965	16.3	1,510
1970	30.5	1,469
1973	12.0	2,057
1975	14.9	1,171
1980	20.7	1,313
1983	13.3	1,713
1984	9.1	1,756

Source: U.S. Department of Commerce, Bureau of the Census, *Statistical Abstract of the United States:* 1986 (Washington, D.C.: U.S. Government Printing Office, 1985), p. 725.

The proportion of rental units in the nation's housing stock dropped steeply in the first two postwar decades (see Figure 9–1). In 1890, more than half of all housing was for rent, and in 1940 this was still the case. By 1950, this proportion had declined to 45 percent. In 1953, only 8.3 percent of all new housing starts were rental.[71] The proportion of rental units declined to 35 percent by 1983. From 1970 to 1983, however, the proportion of rental units dropped very gradually. The housing market in the late 1970s was depressed, and the cost of new housing escalated in comparison to the incomes of potential buyers. Between 1967 and 1975, the annual average costs of home ownership (after tax deductions) increased from 29 percent of median household income to 36 percent, and it has remained at about this level in the 1980s.[72]

FIGURE 9–1   **Rental Units as a Percentage of Total Occupied Units, 1890–1983**

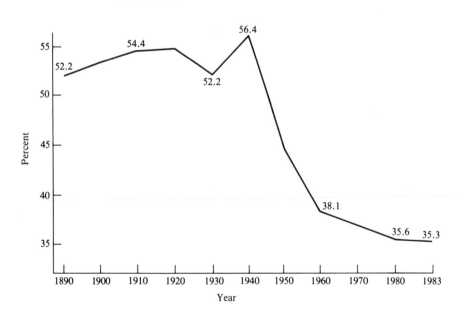

Source: Adapted from data in U.S. Department of Housing and Urban Development, *1974 Statistical Yearbook of the U.S. Department of Housing and Urban Development* (Washington, D.C.: U.S. Government Printing Office, 1976), p. 236, and U.S. Department of Commerce, Bureau of the Census, *1980 Census of Population,* Supplementary Reports, *Provisional Estimates of Social, Economic, and Housing Characteristics: States and Selected Standard Metropolitan Areas* (Washington, D.C.: U.S. Government Printing Office, 1984), p. 70, table H–1.

The Government's Role in Promoting Segregation

FHA mortgage insurance programs depend on the private sector for implementation. Even if the FHA had been willing to underwrite mortgages in the central cities, it would have found doing so difficult. It must be appreciated that FHA insurance was designed to protect the lending institution, not the home buyer. It was therefore available only on such loans as the lending institutions were willing to extend. Mortgage finance was typically available only in "economically sound" areas, where depreciation of capital investment was unlikely.

From the beginning, the FHA absorbed the "common values, policy orientations, and goals" of the real estate industry.[73] The personnel of the FHA were drawn from the ranks of the housing and banking industries. It was only logical that the FHA's philosophy would parallel the financial worlds; thus "FHA's interests went no farther than the safety of the mortgage it secured."[74]

FHA administrators shared the real estate industry's view that racial segregation was preferable to integration. In fact, when it issued its *Underwriting Manual* to banks in 1938, one of its guidelines for loan officers read:

> Areas surrounding a location are [to be] investigated to determine whether incompatible racial and social groups are present, for the purpose of making a prediction regarding the probability of the location being invaded by such groups. If a neighborhood is to retain stability, it is necessary that properties shall continue to be occupied by the same social and racial classes. A change in social or racial occupancy generally contributes to instability and a decline in values.[75]

The FHA's belief that the entry of a nonwhite family into a white neighborhood led to declining property values was based on reports by real estate analysts. But the most important reference for its policies was the work of a famous sociologist and demographer, Homer Hoyt. In a 1933 report, supplied later to the FHA, Hoyt had said:

> If the entrance of a colored family into a white neighborhood causes a general exodus of the white people it is reflected in property values. Except in the case of Negroes and Mexicans, however, these racial and national barriers disappear when the individuals of the foreign nationality groups rise in the economic scale or conform to the American standards of living. ... While the ranking may be scientifically wrong from the standpoint of inherent racial characteristics, it registers an opinion or prejudice that is reflected in land values; it is the ranking of races and nationalities with respect to their beneficial effect upon land values. Those having the most favorable effect come first in the list and those exerting the most detrimental effect appear last:

1. English, Germans, Scotch, Irish, Scandinavians
2. North Italians
3. Bohemians or Czechoslovakians
4. Poles
5. Lithuanians
6. Greeks
7. Russian Jews of lower class
8. South Italians
9. Negroes
10. Mexicans[76]

The real estate industry accepted as a fundamental law of economics the principle that the value of property was connected to the homogeneity of neighborhoods. From 1924 until 1950, article 34 of the realtors' National Code read: "A realtor should never be instrumental in introducing into a neighborhood a character of property or occupancy, members of any race or nationality, or any individual whose presence will clearly be detrimental to property values in the neighborhood."[77] In addition, most local real estate boards had codes of ethics prohibiting members from introducing "detrimental" minorities into white neighborhoods. Any realtor found breaking the code was subject to expulsion from the board. Even non-affiliated brokers felt compelled to accept these guidelines, because most of their business depended on referrals.

Many FHA administrators advised developers of residential projects to draw up restrictive covenants against nonwhites in order to obtain FHA-insured financing.[78] Between 1935 and 1950, "more than 11 million homes were built . . . and this federal policy did more to entrench housing bias in American neighborhoods than any court could undo by a ruling. It established federally sponsored mores for discrimination in suburban communities in which eighty percent of all new housing [was] being built and fixed the social and racial patterns in thousands of new neighborhoods."[79]

Less than 2 percent of all the housing financed with the assistance of federal mortgage insurance between 1946 and 1959 was purchased by blacks.[80] In the Miami area, only one black family received FHA backing for a home loan between 1934 and 1949, and there is "evidence that [the man who secured the loan] was not recognized as a black" at the time the transaction took place.[81]

In 1948, in the case of *Shelly v. Kraemer*, the United States Supreme Court ruled that racial covenants could not be enforced in the courts.[82] By 1950, the FHA had rewritten its underwriting manual so it no longer openly recommended racial segregation or restrictive covenants. Nevertheless, until at least the mid-1960s mortgages continued to be insured mainly in areas where minorities were excluded.

Provisions of the Civil Rights Act of 1968[83] proscribed discrimination by lenders through "either denying the loan or fixing the amount, interest rate, duration, or other terms of the loan." The statute also mandated that each of the federal regulatory agencies involved with the real estate industry take affirmative steps to enforce both the spirit and the letter of the law.[84]

Again, however, the bureaucracies were slow to change. Criticism escalated.[85] In response, the Federal Home Loan Bank Board (FHLB), which was responsible for regulating the nation's savings and loan institutions, issued new federal regulations on discrimination in lending. This was significant in that the nation's savings and loan associations, in 1973, held more than $186.8 billion in outstanding home mortgages, nearly three times the amount held by the second-largest source of home mortgage money, the commercial banks.[86] The new FHLB regulation recognized that

> refusal to lend in a particular area solely because of the age of the homes or the income level in the neighborhood may be discriminatory in effect since minority group persons are more likely to purchase used housing and to live in low income neighborhoods.[87]

In interpreting the dictate of the FHLB Board, the board's general counsel offered this opinion:

> There is substantial legal precedent for the board to assume that redlining that is discriminatory in effect (without any countervailing business purpose) is unlawful and to shift the burden of proof to the institution to demonstrate some reasonable genuine business purpose for redlining. . . . In any case, such a business necessity would not be established by the institution's unsubstantiated belief that no profitable loans could be made in a given area.[88]

Redlining is a tool used by financial institutions to increase the efficiency of their investment decisions. It derives its name from the "red line" drawn on maps to designate neighborhoods considered poor investment risks. By categorically excluding properties within certain areas from consideration, financial institutions can devote more time (and money) to loan applications from areas that promise a lower risk to their capital.

Part of the rationale for the practice of redlining lies in the fact that the neighborhood in which a property lies—its spatial location on the social, economic, and cultural map of an area—largely accounts for the value of the property. Thus, from the point of view of the lender, redlining is an entirely justifiable policy. From the perspective of a central city homeowner, redlining may have disastrous and far-reaching effects.

Redlining was practiced blatantly in the past, and although it is now illegal in many jurisdictions, it persists, though informally. Such behavior would be of little consequence were it limited to a few financial institutions or to specific periods of tight capital. But when aggregated, as it has been across institutions and over time, the individual decisions of the lenders make up a mutually reinforcing network of investment practices that end in the self-fulfilling prophecy of urban decay through disinvestment. The severe deterioration of housing stock in St. Louis, for example, has been related to redlining practices. Three savings and loan institutions, with more than $1 billion in assets, made less than $100,000 in loans on city residential property during 1975. Altogether, "only 5.6 percent of the mortgage money lent by St. Louis banks and savings and loan institutions in recent years had gone to finance property in the city."[89]

Similarly, in the District of Columbia, fewer than 12 percent of the real estate loans made by savings and loan institutions between 1972 and 1974 went for properties in the city. If condominiums and large (over $100,000) home loans are excluded, the figure drops to 7 percent. Most of the lending capital of financial institutions located in the city was used to finance housing in outlying areas.[90]

Racial bias in lending has resulted in serious underinvestment in the housing stock of black neighborhoods. In the nation's capital, for example, eleven areas (88 percent black, on the average) containing 69 percent of the district's population accounted for only 36 percent of the home loans made between 1972 and 1974. Half of those loans went to neighborhoods with rapidly increasing white populations. According to a study by several Washington-based public interest groups, economic class had little effect on the degree of racial bias. In four moderate to middle income areas dominated by owner-occupied and one- to four-unit housing structures, only 7.7 percent of the city's mortgage money was made available. Those areas contained 28 percent of the city's population and were 92 percent black.[91]

Such information as this has been collected under the provisions of the Equal Credit Opportunity Act of 1974[92] and the Home Mortgage Disclosure Act of 1975.[93] The rationale that exposing redlining activities would lead to public indignation and cause the practice to end underlies such federal reporting requirements. But segregation now exists on such a scale that it will be extraordinarily difficult to remedy.[94]

The Mechanisms of Segregation

Breaking down racial discrimination in housing has turned out to be a virtually insurmountable task. White attitudes have been very important. National Opinion Research Center surveys conducted intermittently between 1942 and 1968 indicate that a softening of white segregationist attitudes toward blacks of equal social status has occurred. Whites responded each year to the question, "If a Negro, with just as much income and education as you have moved into your block would it make a difference to you?" In 1942, 62 percent replied "yes"; in 1956, 46 percent; in 1963, 35 percent; in 1965, 32 percent; and by 1968, 21 percent.[95] But a researcher writing in the late 1970s concluded that such surveys were grossly misleading, and that the attitudes were different when people were presented with real as opposed to hypothetical situations. In his study of Chicago-area communities, he stated: "The general conclusion must be that, at each income level and regardless of socioeconomic characteristics, a concentration of black families is perceived negatively by whites."[96]

Evidence from several studies on the relationship between property values and race[97] indicates that although housing prices may fall temporarily during panic selling immediately after members of a minority group move into a neighborhood (thus leading to a self-fulfilling prophecy), "property values in neighborhoods entered by nonwhites do not generally fall and have sometimes risen because of the concentration of nonwhite demand."[98] Despite the general discrediting of the theory that property values decline with the arrival of nonwhite neighbors, the fear was widespread enough through the 1960s to contribute to the continued restrictions of housing opportunities for nonwhites by the private institutions that make up the housing market.

Strategies to maintain housing segregation are myriad, subtle, and complex. Among realtors, "blockbusting" was a common tactic. An unscrupulous real estate broker would forewarn a white neighborhood of the pending sale of a nearby home to nonwhites in order to cause a panic. Many white residents could then be convinced that the neighborhood was going to become undesirable because of this nonwhite entry and that their property values would fall quickly. The resulting panic selling of the homes to the broker would allow him or her to gain a huge profit on the resale of the houses to minorities for prices well above market value.[99]

Real estate brokers have been known to resort to a variety of tactics to bar the entry of nonwhites into white neighborhoods. They often refuse outright to show minorities houses in white sections of cities[100]; withhold listing information[101]; or use such devices as quoting excessive prices, saying a given house is already sold, demanding unfair down payments, removing "For Sale" signs, and not keeping appointments.[102]

Additionally, rental housing managers often serve as formidable gatekeepers to the rental housing market. Landlords exert a huge impact on the overall pattern of residential segregation, because most minority families rent their housing.[103]

The Open Housing Movement

Efforts to eliminate discrimination in the housing market originated during the civil rights crusades of the 1950s and early 1960s. Open housing did not become a priority, however, until after the Voting Rights Act of 1965. In a 1966 rally in Chicago, Martin Luther King, Jr., proclaimed: "For our primary target we have chosen housing. . . . We shall cease to be accomplices to a housing system of discrimination, segregation, and degradation. We shall begin to act as if Chicago were an open city."[104]

Although they stayed in the background, open housing advocates exercised some influence even before the 1960s. In 1950, a loose alliance of seventy-five national organizations came together to form the National Committee against Discrimination in Housing. The organization influenced the FHA and U.S. Public Housing Authority to abandon segregation policies. The committee was also involved in a historic eight-year battle with William Levitt, the developer of Levittown, Pennsylvania. Levitt's housing development was closed to blacks, but was located close to a U.S. Steel plant that had a large proportion of black employees. The Committee against Discrimination in Housing was able to persuade U.S. Steel that the company had a responsibility to assist its nonwhite employees in finding adequate housing. Levitt eventually conceded to the mounting pressure and opened a few of his units to blacks.[105]

By 1956, the national organization had grown to twenty-six affiliates, and it turned its attention to influencing federal policies against discrimination. Open-housing groups pressured both political parties to include planks opposing discrimination in housing in their presidential nominating convention platforms.[106]

The combined efforts of many local open-housing groups and the national committee exerted significant influence on the open-housing legislation passed in the 1960s. In 1962, President Kennedy signed an Executive Order declaring that all federal aid for housing and community development was to be granted on the condition that no discrimination be practiced. This action had limited consequences, because most housing was financed conventionally and thus was exempt from the order. Two years later, the 1964 Civil Rights Act prohibited discrimination in any program that used federal funds. Thus coverage was extended to all urban renewal and public housing projects.[107]

In 1968, Congress passed Title VIII of the Civil Rights Act, known as the Fair Housing Bill. This bill prohibited racial discrimination in about 80 percent of the nation's housing. It became unlawful "for an owner, manager, or any other person to refuse to rent an apartment to anyone because of race, color, religion, or national origin, or to discriminate by limiting rentals or length of a lease under which an apartment can be rented. Single family houses were covered as of January 1, 1970, unless sold directly by the owner without the use of a real-estate broker."[108] The Supreme Court decision in *Jones v. Mayer* in 1968 finally extended antidiscrimination coverage to all housing, including single-family homes sold directly by the owner without a real estate agent.

Developments at the national level were accompanied by corresponding efforts in states and communities. In 1957, only 14 cities had laws prohibiting discrimination in housing. By the end of 1964, 60 cities had passed laws against discrimination, and by 1970, 229 state and local fair housing laws were in place. Such a proliferation in legislation probably would not have been possible without extensive grassroots action. The National Committee against Discrimination in Housing's publication, *Trends in Housing*, enthusiastically described the nature of some of the local involvement in the open-housing movement in 1962:

> housing is the latest area in civil rights to be tackled by nonviolent direct action. Sit-ins, sleep-ins, equality vigils, picketing, protest marches, sympathy demonstrations, and "operation windowshop" are being used increasingly to further open occupancy in many sections of the country.[109]

A typical local action during the 1960s was for an informal committee composed of church and civic group members to organize in an attempt to open the housing market. The Committee on Special Housing, located in Indianapolis, was one such group. This committee sought to bring an end to segregation by working cooperatively with FHA, VA, and large development corporations. They began to offer on a nondiscriminatory basis 900 or more homes a year that became available because of repossessions or corporate executive transfers.[110] Other local organizations attempted to bring together willing white sellers and black buyers by developing their own listing service. Most of the communities reported very limited success and large-scale opposition by the real estate industry.[111]

Nonetheless, the real estate industry officially ceased its longstanding opposition to open-housing legislation after the passage of the Fair Housing Act and the *Jones v. Mayer* decision. The National Association of Real Estate Boards (NAREB), the most powerful and effective organization opposing fair housing legislation, called on its 85,000 members to comply with the new laws: "those who have opposed open-housing laws should now understand that their position is forever negated."[112]

Many of the barriers to open housing were still intact, despite legislative changes and political action. The enforcement of fair housing laws was especially complicated because of the complex institutional web involved:

> After decades of openly advocating housing discrimination and segregation, the federal government is now under a clear mandate to promote affirmative

action for open housing. But the mandate requires reciprocal action by housing consumers, private investors, builders and developers, as well as by the real estate industry, if open housing is to take a more than token reality.[113]

Another major difficulty in enforcing open-housing laws was that each case had to be brought before the courts individually. Class action suits have been rare. Thus, even though the 1968 *Jones v. Mayer* ruling enabled people who had been discriminated against to obtain injunctions prohibiting the sale or rental of the property in question until the case was settled, the effect on the real estate industry has been minimal. Compiling evidence of discriminatory behavior involves a complex set of legal tactics. Most minority families seeking housing "may decide that the cost and delay of going to court are not worth the effort."[114]

There have been varying assessments of the successes of local fair housing groups in bringing about positive action. Some of the alternative house listing services, legal tests of discriminatory practices, and lobbying efforts for stronger enforcement may have been somewhat effective.[115] By the early 1970s, however, most successes were limited to information campaigns and the placement of token minorities in white neighborhoods.[116] Of 537 applicants to the Chicago Equal Opportunity Housing Service in 1972, for example, only 46 were relocated by the program. Of those that were relocated, only 3 percent went to white neighborhoods; most found other housing in transitional or all-black areas.

The complex nature of the institutionalized forces that perpetuate housing segregation are beyond the scope of legislative remedies alone: "Neither federal, state nor local action can create integration by fiat."[117] Racial discrimination since 1968 has become more subtle. Gone are the days of racial covenants and FHA requirements of neighborhood homogeneity, along with most other overt mechanisms of segregation. Subtle but effective mechanisms persist, however, for "Every routine act, every bit of ritual in the sale or rental of a dwelling unit can be performed in a way calculated to make it impossible to consummate a deal."[118]

Highways and Urban Sprawl

Since the 1956 National Defense Highway Act, the federal government has spent billions of dollars to help construct a network of interstate highways across the country. In urban areas, these highways facilitated the movement of people and business to the suburbs.

The first commitment to federal highway building in urban areas came through the Highway Act of 1944. The act allocated 25 percent of all federal highway grants-in-aid for the construction of urban roads. Before this time, no such provision had existed. Federal highway programs had been designed by the Department of Agriculture to "get the farmer out of the mud." In fact, under the provisions of the 1916 Highway Act, the states were prohibited from spending any federal highway aid money in urban areas. At the time, this reflected not only the realities of rural-dominated legislatures but also the fact that urban streets were better developed than rural roads.

During the Great Depression, highway construction became a means of providing public works for the cities. Road construction, which consumed huge quantities of unskilled labor, could be used to provide relief for the unemployed of the cities and to supply necessary public improvements. Congress temporarily lifted the ban on the use of highway funds in urban areas to provide public works in the cities. Once put to work on urban roads and freed from the oversight of the Department of Agriculture (in 1939), the Bureau of Public Roads (BPR) was quick to make the cause of urban highways its own. By 1939, the BPR was calling the congestion of downtown streets the nation's most serious traffic problem. Too many automobiles were trying to get into the Central Business Districts on too few and inadequate roads. In both 1939 and 1944, the agency recommended that a national system of interregional and intraurban expressways be financed. These recommendations dovetailed with the President's concern that national defense required an improved interregional highway system for moving troops and supplies. Thus, the National System of Interstate Highways, later to become the National Interstate and Defense Highway System, was born.

The highway system was the key to urban transportation in the automobile age. As Americans grew more affluent and bought more automobiles, they required more and better roads. And as roads were subsidized with increased state and federal subsidies, the automobile became a dominant factor in influencing urban expansion.

The federal highway act of 1956 profoundly altered urban development and suburbanization. In that year, in order to expedite the construction of the then twelve-year-old interstate system, Congress changed the grant-in-aid formula from a federal contribution of 50 to 90 percent. By speeding the construction of the modern 41,000-mile expressway system, Congress inadvertently accelerated decline of the central cities. The new highways, designed to carry commerce and commuters into the heart of the cities efficiently and quickly, just as easily carried businesses and residents out toward the expanding urban fringe.[119]

Highway subsidies were pushed through by a powerful coalition led by the nation's largest auto, oil, and tire companies. The beginning of this coalition dates to June 28, 1932, when Alfred P. Sloan, Jr., president of General Motors, called together representatives from several companies to form the National Highway Users Conference. The purpose of the conference, which was chaired by Sloan until 1948, was to unite the petroleum-related industries against the railroads and the urban transit companies.

While the conference lobbied for highway legislation, GM, Standard Oil of California, the Firestone Tire Company, and other member companies began buying up electric streetcar lines in order to replace them with buses. GM took the lead in this effort when it formed the United Cities Motor Transit Company as a subsidiary in 1932. United Cities was used to buy up electric streetcar companies, replace the trolleys with buses, and then sell the bus companies to firms that agreed to use only GM products. The first cities successfully converted to buses were Kalamazoo and Saginaw, Michigan, and Springfield, Ohio. Many other cities were similarly converted: "In each case, General Motors successfully motorized the city, turned the management over to other interests and liquidated its investment."[120]

GM established two semi-independent holding companies that could be used to pool funds contributed by the petroleum-related corporations. The GM-created Omnibus Corporation and the National City Lines, Inc., systematically dismantled the streetcar companies of the nation's largest cities. Through National City Lines, buses had replaced electric streetcars in forty-five cities by 1949, including such big cities as New York City, Philadelphia, Baltimore, Salt Lake City, and Los Angeles. The capitalization required for all this was large, with GM, Standard Oil of California, Firestone Tire, and some suppliers raising $9 million to purchase streetcars. In most cases the new bus systems operated under contractual agreements stipulating that only gasoline or diesel fuel could be used in any of their vehicles. This ensured that the systems could not revert to electric trolleys in the future.[121]

The petroleum-related corporations continued their campaign to convert cities to buses, usually exclusively GM buses, until the mid-1950s, at which time Roger M. Keyes, GM's executive in charge of bus sales, pronounced the effort a success: "The motor coach has supplanted the interurban systems and has for all practical purposes eliminated the trolley."[122] By 1955, only 5,000 streetcars were still in service, compared to 40,000 in 1936, when National City Lines began its assault on the trolleys.

Meanwhile, the members of the National Highway Users Conference, which included the Motor Vehicle Manufacturers Association, the American Petroleum Institute, the American Trucking Association, the Rubber Manufacturers Association, and the American Automobile Association, launched a nationwide campaign to promote highway building. By the late 1950s, forty-four of the fifty states had adopted trust funds or similar devices to reserve state and local gasoline taxes for highway construction.

Between 1945 and 1970, the federal government spent $70 billion for highways, while states and localities spent $156 billion.[123] Federal mass transit legislation was not passed until 1962, and total federal expenditures on mass transit never exceeded 20 percent of highway spending, even in the 1970s, when mass transit expenditures were increased.[124]

The result of these covert policies in the private sector to eliminate streetcars and the overt lobbying to secure public funds for highway construction was the conversion of cities and metropolitan areas to nearly complete reliance on automobiles, trucks, and buses.

Only New York City, with its well-developed subway system, remained relatively dependent on a rail-based mass transit system. As shown in Table 9–3, 28 percent of New York's workers used public transit in 1980. In six other cities listed in Table 9–3, between 11 and 16 percent of commuters used mass transit. In all other cities in the United States, less than 10 percent of commuters rely on mass transit. Few cities, perhaps including Washington, D.C., and San Francisco (which have subway systems), can hope to reverse this pattern. Twenty metropolitan areas studied by the

TABLE 9–3 Percentage of Workers Using Public Transportation in Selected Metropolitan Areas,* 1980

Metropolitan area	% workers using public transportation
New York	28
Chicago	16
Washington, D.C.	15
Boston	13
Philadelphia	12
San Francisco	11
Pittsburgh	11
Minneapolis–St. Paul	9
St. Louis	6
Denver	6
Los Angeles	5
Salt Lake City	5
Dallas	4
Phoenix	2

Source: Adapted from U.S. Bureau of the Census, *State and Metropolitan Area Data Book, 1986* (U.S. Government Printing Office, 1986).

*CMSAs (Consolidated Metropolitan Statistical Areas) or SMSAs (Standard Metropolitan Statistical Areas).

Bureau of the Census in 1977 experienced an average decline of 3 percent in the proportion of people using public transportation between 1970 and 1977.[125] Most metropolitan areas are so spread out that an efficient public transportation system would cost astronomical sums to construct.

Working in conjunction with the FHA's preference for single-family dwellings, the highway system did much to influence the shape and direction of urban growth in the postwar world. The new urban highway system facilitated commuting into and out of the Central Business Districts. As the highways radiated outward, so too did urban growth. Already by the late 1940s, the suburban fringe of Chicago extended thirty miles from the Loop. Like every transportation innovation preceding it, the new highway system drew the affluent farther away from the city. And with the expansion of credit fostered by the FHA and the VA, the middle and working classes trailed along. The urban highway system made the land beyond the boundaries of the cities accessible, and the FHA and the VA made it affordable to urban residents.

The Impact of Subsidized Growth

The federal urban policies developed during the 1930s and 1940s, policies intended to address the problems that plagued the cities—blight, slums, and congestion—were replete with contradictions. Federal aid to urban areas disproportionately favored programs that were of benefit to the urban fringe. Urban renewal, for example, was a distinctly urban program; new suburban areas, which had no blighted areas comparable to those in the city, received little of the money. But the suburbs were benefitted through FHA policies and highway construction. Highways received huge direct subsidies from the federal government. As Table 9–4 demonstrates, until 1962 more than five times as many federal dollars were poured into the construction of concrete pathways to the suburbs than were spent in reconstructing the central cities.

Similarly, the two housing programs favored the suburbs because of the biased manner in which they were implemented. The FHA's policies were biased in favor of new suburban housing, while most of the FHA's low-rent public housing projects were located in the central cities. The federal subsidies for low-income housing were eclipsed by the subsidies extended for middle- and upper-income housing. For the year 1971, FHA subsidies and the associated homeowners' income tax deductions of mortgage interest amounted to more than eight times the total subsidy for public housing. Despite the intense ideological and political battles over subsidized public

TABLE 9–4   Federal Aid to Urban Areas: A Comparison of Grants for Highway Construction and Urban Renewal, 1950–1962 (in Millions of Dollars)

Year	Highway construction*	Urban renewal
1950	108.3	—
1951	108.3	—
1952	121.3	—
1953	120.3	8.7
1954	144.3	12.6
1955	145.1	37.6
1956	249.3	16.3
1957	731.2	30.6
1958	977.5	50.1
1959	1,203.2	78.9
1960	1,344.3	135.5
1961	1,030.8	180.0
1962	1,209.0	192.0

Source: George M. Smerk, *Urban Transportation: The Federal Role* (Bloomington, Indiana University Press, 1965), pp. 134, 135, reprinted by permission; and U.S. Housing and Home Finance Agency, *16th Annual Report* (Washington, D.C.: U.S. Government Printing Office, 1962), p. 295.

*Includes grants-in-aid for "urban highways" and "interstate highways in urban areas," but does not include those portions of the highway grants for "primary" and "secondary" highways that went through urban areas; thus the total should be larger.

housing, it is clear that the subsidies to the middle class were far more costly than were housing subsidies for the poor (see Table 9–5). Federal housing policies overwhelmingly favored upper- and middle-income groups.

The credit policies of the FHA, the transportation policies of the Bureau of Public Roads, and the economic interests of real estate developers all worked in harmony to open the urban fringe for development. The tracts of cheap, open land that appealed to the developers could not have been rapidly exploited without the development of the urban highway system, which connected the Central Business Districts to the urban fringe. The credit policies of the FHA meant that the new home buyers would be forced to go to these suburban developments in order to satisfy their desire for quality housing. Any incentives to renovate housing in the central cities were correspondingly undercut.

The development of the suburban fringe was heavily subsidized. Urban renewal and public housing increased racial segregation. "Negro removal" and public housing reinforced racial segregation in a vain attempt to save

TABLE 9-5   Federal Housing Assistance by Income Class—1971
(in Millions of Dollars)

Program	Under 3,500	3,500–10,000	10,000 and over
	Income class		
Public Housing	413	233	—
FHA sections 235 and 236	34	108	1
Farmer's Home Administration	2	18	16
FHA sections 312 and 115 (rehabilitation loan and grants)	25	18	—
Federal Income Tax deductions (mortgage interest, property taxes and depreciation)	58	2,552	3,190
Total	532	2,929	3,207

Source: From Chester W. Hartman, *Housing and Social Policy,* © 1975, p. 160. Reprinted by permission of Prentice-Hall, Inc., Englewood Cliffs, New Jersey.

the business community and the poor from the evils of slums and blight. Changes in federal housing and transportation policies in the 1960s, which placed greater emphasis on the needs of people with lower incomes, came too late to reverse the effects of previous programs.

References

1. Housing Act of 1949, Public Law 81-171, Preamble, sec. 2, 81st Cong. (1949).

2. Joint Resolution 52-22, 52d Cong. (1892); refer also to U.S. Congress, House, *Your Congress and American Housing—The Actions of Congress on Housing,* H. Doc. 82-532, 82d Cong., 2d sess., 1952 (Washington, D.C.: U.S. Government Printing Office, 1952), p. 1.

3. Public Law 65-102, 65th Cong. (1918); refer also to Congressional Quarterly Service, *Housing a Nation* (Washington, D.C.: Congressional Quarterly Service, 1966), p. 18; and Edith Elmer Wood, *Recent Trends in American Housing* (New York: Macmillan, 1931), p. 79.

4. Public Laws 65-149 and 65-164, 65th Cong. (1918); refer also to Twentieth Century Fund, *Housing for Defense* (New York: The Twentieth Century Fund, 1940), pp. 156–157; and Congressional Quarterly Service, *Housing a Nation,* p. 18.

5. Refer to the Emergency Relief and Reconstruction Act, Public Law 72-302, 72d Cong. (1932).

6. The only other loan extended under this authorization was in the amount of $155,000 for rural housing in Ford County, Kansas.

7. Edwin L. Scanton, "Public Housing Trends in New York City" (thesis, Graduate School of Banking, Rutgers University, 1952), p. 5.

8. Public Law 73-67, 72d Cong. (1933).

9. From a statement by Harold L. Ickes, Secretary of the Interior and Public Works Administrator, quoted in Bert Swanson, "The Public Policy of Urban Renewal: Its Goals, Trends, and Conditions in New York City," paper delivered at the American Political Science Association Meeting, New York, September 1963, p. 10.

10. *U.S. v. Certain Lands in City of Louisville, Jefferson County, Ky., et al.*, 78 F. 2d 64 (1935).

11. *U.S. v. Certain Lands in City of Detroit, et al.*, 12 F. Suppl. 345 (1935).

12. Refer to Glen H. Boyer, *Housing: A Factual Analysis* (New York: Macmillan, 1958), p. 247.

13. Richard D. Bingham, *Public Housing and Urban Renewal: An Analysis of Federal-Local Relations*, Praeger Special Studies in U.S. Economic, Social, and Political Issues (New York: Praeger, 1975), p. 30.

14. Nathaniel S. Keith, *Politics and the Housing Crisis Since 1930* (New York: Universe Books, 1973), p. 29.

15. Public Law 75-412, 75th Cong. (1937). Also found in U.S. Congress, House, Committee on Banking and Currency, *Basic Laws and Authorizations on Urban Housing*, 91st Cong., 1st sess., 1969 (Washington, D.C.: U.S. Government Printing Office, 1969), p. 225.

16. Roscoe Martin, "The Expanded Partnership," in *The New Urban Politics: Cities and the Federal Government*, ed. Douglas Fox (Pacific Palisades, Calif.: Goodyear Publishing Co., 1972), p. 51.

17. Mark Gelfand, *A Nation of Cities: The Federal Government and Urban America, 1933–1965*, Urban Life in America Series (New York: Oxford University Press, 1975), p. 199.

18. Keith, *Politics and the Housing Crisis*, p. 33.

19. Keith, pp. 32–33; citing a speech delivered before the fourth annual meeting of the National Public Housing Conference, New York, December 1935.

20. Charles Abrams, *The Future of Housing* (New York and London: Harper and Brothers, 1946), p. 260, p. 260n.

21. This last-mentioned feature, limiting participation to low-income families, seen from a comparative perspective is a root cause of the failure of public housing in America; see Arnold J. Heidenheimer, Hugh Heclo, and Carolyn Teich Adams, *Comparative Public Policy: The Politics of Social Choice in Europe and America* (New York: St. Martin's Press, 1975), pp. 69–96.

22. Public Law 76-671, 76th Cong. (1940), relating to defense housing needs; and Public Law 80-301, 80th Cong. (1946), suspending cost limitations for some low-income housing projects.

23. U.S. Housing and Home Finance Agency, *Fourteenth Annual Report* (Washington, D.C.: U.S. Government Printing Office, 1961), p. 380.

24. U.S. Congress, Senate, Special Committee on Post-War Economic Policy and Planning, *Housing and Urban Development, Hearings* pursuant to S. Res. 102 before a subcommittee of the Special Committee on Post-War Economic Policy and Planning, Senate, 79th Cong., 1st sess., 1945, pp. 1228–1237.

25. U.S. Senate, Special Committee on Post-War Economic Policy and Planning, pp. 1228–1237; also see John H. Haefner, *Housing in America: A Source Unit for the Social Studies*, Bulletin no. 14 (Washington, D.C.: National Council for the Social Studies, 1934), p. 6.

26. Refer to Robert B. Navin, *An Analysis of a Slum Area in Cleveland* (Cleveland: Cleveland Metropolitan Housing Authority, 1934), p. 6.

27. U.S. Congress, Senate, Committee on Banking and Currency, *General Housing Act of 1945, Hearings* before the Committee on Banking and Currency, Senate, 79th Cong., 1st sess., 1945, pp. 837–838.

28. U.S. Senate, Committee on Banking and Currency, p. 754.

29. Gelfand, *A Nation of Cities*, p. 112; refer also to pp. 112–118 for discussion of aspects of the NAREB plan.

30. U.S. Congress, House, Select Committee on Lobbying Activities, *Housing Lobby, Hearings* pursuant to H. Res. 288 before the Select Committee on Lobbying Activities, House, 81st Cong., 2d sess., 1950, Exhibit 349, p. 11.

31. U.S. House, Select Committee on Lobbying Activities, p. 11; also see Leonard Freedman, *Public Housing: The Politics of Poverty*, Public Policy Studies in American Government (New York: Holt, Rinehart and Winston, 1969), pp. 58–75; and Keith, *Politics and the Housing Crisis*, pp. 35–39.

32. For one explication of this policy see Guy Greer and Alvin Hansen, *Urban Redevelopment and Housing: A Program for Post-War*, Planning Pamphlets Series no. 10 (Washington, D.C.: National Planning Association, 1941).

33. Refer to Gelfand, *A Nation of Cities*, p. 14.

34. International Union, United Automobile, Aircraft, and Agricultural Implement Workers of America, *Memorandum on Post War Urban Housing* (Detroit: International Union, United Automobile, Aircraft, and Agricultural Implement Workers of America, 1944), p. 94 (original text italicized throughout).

35. Wilson W. Wyatt as quoted in Congressional Quarterly Service, *Housing a Nation*, p. 6.

36. See Keith, *Politics and the Housing Crisis*, pp. 41–100.

37. Chester Hartman et al., *Yerba Buena: Land Grab and Community Resistance in San Francisco* (San Francisco: Glide Publications, 1974); and John H. Mollenkopf, "The Post-War Politics of Urban Development," in *Marxism and the Metropolis: New Perspectives in Urban Political Economy*, ed. William Tabb and Larry Sawers (New York: Oxford University Press, 1978), pp. 117–152.

38. Martin Meyerson and Edward C. Banfield, *Politics, Planning, and the Public Interest* (Glencoe, Ill.: The Free Press, 1955).

39. Freedman, *Public Housing*, p. 55.

40. Robert A. Dahl, *Who Governs: Democracy and Power in an American City* (New Haven, Conn.: Yale University Press, 1961), p. 134. Also see Jewel Bellush and Murray Hausknecht, "Urban Renewal and the Reformer," in *Urban Renewal: People, Politics and Planning*, ed. Jewel Bellush and Murray Hausknecht (Garden

City, N.Y.: Doubleday, Anchor Books, 1967), pp. 189–197, for another insightful example of the use of urban renewal by a political entrepreneur.

41. Dahl, p. 136.

42. Dahl, p. 135.

43. Dahl, pp. 135–136.

44. Dahl, p. 136.

45. Institute of Housing, "Proceedings," University College, Washington University, St. Louis, March 21–22, 1952 (mimeo), p. 18. For studies of the coalition in other cities, see Harold Kaplan, *Urban Renewal Politics: Slum Clearance in Newark* (New York: Columbia University Press, 1963); Meyerson and Banfield, *Politics, Planning and the Public Interest*; and Peter H. Rossi and Robert A. Dentler, *The Politics of Urban Renewal—the Chicago Findings* (New York: The Free Press, 1961). Refer also to Jewel Bellush and Murray Hausknecht, "Entrepreneurs and Urban Renewal: The New Men of Power," *Journal, of the American Planning Institute* 32 (September 1961); George S. Duggar, "The Relation of Local Government Structure to Urban Renewal," in *Urban Renewal*, ed. Bellush and Hausknecht, pp. 179–187, 200–208, as reprinted from *Law and Contemporary Problems* 26 (Winter 1961); and Herbert Kay, "The Third Force in Urban Renewal," *Fortune*, October 1964.

46. Institute of Housing, "Proceedings," p. 18.

47. Dahl, *Who Governs*, p. 138.

48. Gelfand, *A Nation of Cities*, p. 161.

49. Keith, *Politics and the Housing Crisis*, p. 120.

50. Refer to Martin Anderson, *The Federal Bulldozer: A Critical Analysis of Urban Renewal, 1949–1962* (Cambridge, Mass.: MIT Press, 1964), pp. 65–66. Also see Bellush and Hausknecht, p. 13.

51. Anderson, p. 105.

52. Arthur I. Blaustein and Geoffrey Faux, *The Star-Spangled Hustle*, foreword by Ronald V. Dellums (Garden City, N.Y.: Doubleday, 1973), p. 71.

53. See Anderson, *The Federal Bulldozer*, p. 65; compare also Rossi and Dentler, *The Politics of Urban Renewal*, p. 224.

54. Chester Hartman, "The Housing of Relocated Families," in *Urban Renewal: The Record and the Controversy*, ed. James Q. Wilson (Cambridge, Mass.: MIT Press, 1966), p. 322, as reprinted from *Journal of the American Institute of Planners* 30 (November 1964):266–286.

55. Freedman, *Public Housing*, p. 140.

56. National Commission on Urban Problems, *Building the American City* (New York: Praeger, 1969), pp. 164–165.

57. National Commission on Urban Problems, p. 153. This presidentially appointed commission was established in January 1967 and headed by former Illinois senator and long-time urban policy advocate Paul H. Douglas.

58. Anderson, *The Federal Bulldozer*.

59. Bernard Frieden and Marshall Kaplan, *The Politics of Neglect: Aid from Model Cities to Revenue Sharing* (Cambridge, Mass.: MIT Press, 1975).

60. Anderson, *The Federal Bulldozer*, pp. 65–66.

61. Mollenkopf, "The Post-War Politics of Urban Development," p. 140.

62. Housing and Urban Development Act of 1968, Public Law 90-448, 90th Cong. (1968).

63. John C. Weicher, *Urban Renewal: National Program for Local Problems, Evaluative Studies Series* (Washington, D.C.: American Enterprise Institute for Public Policy Research, 1972), p. 6, citing unpublished HUD statistics: 101,461 of 200,687 new units were public low- or moderate-income housing—538,044 housing units had been demolished as a result of urban renewal activities through 1971.

64. U.S. Department of Housing and Urban Development, *1974 Statistical Yearbook of the U.S. Department of Housing and Urban Development* (Washington, D.C.: U.S. Government Printing Office, 1976), p. 104.

65. Stephen David and Paul Peterson, ed., *Urban Politics and Public Policy: The City in Crisis* (New York: Praeger, 1973), p. 94.

66. Abrams, *The Future of Housing*, p. 213.

67. *The Housing and Development Reporter* (Washington, D.C.: Bureau of National Affairs, 1976).

68. *The Housing and Development Reporter.*

69. Calculated from data in Congressional Quarterly Service, *Housing a Nation*, p. 6.

70. U.S. Department of Housing and Urban Development, *1974 Statistical Yearbook of the Department of Housing and Urban Development* (Washington, D.C.: U.S. Government Printing Office, 1976), pp. 116–117.

71. Abrams, *The Future of Housing*, p. 237.

72. Franklin J. James, "The Revitalization of Older Urban Housing and Neighborhoods," in *The Prospective City: Economic Population, Energy, and Environmental Developments*, ed. Arthur P. Solomon (Cambridge, Mass.: The MIT Press, 1980), p. 143.

73. For a discussion of this phenomenon, see Murray Edelman, *The Symbolic Uses of Politics*, 7th ed. (Champaign: University of Illinois Press, 1976), pp. 44–76. I am in debt to Jeffrey Gilbert for several of the ideas contained in this section.

74. Chester W. Hartman, *Housing and Social Policy*, Prentice-Hall Series in Social Policy (Englewood Cliffs, N.J.: Prentice-Hall, 1975), p. 30, citing Michael Stone, "Reconstructing American Housing" (unpublished).

75. Quoted in Brian J.L. Berry, *The Open Housing Question: Race and Housing in Chicago, 1966–1976* (Cambridge, Mass.: Ballinger, 1979), p. 9.

76. Quoted in Berry, pp. 9, 11.

77. National Association of Real Estate Boards, *Code of Ethics*, art. 34 (1924).

78. Luigi M. Laurenti, "Theories of Race and Property Value," in *Urban Analysis: Readings in Housing and Urban Development*, ed. Alfred N. Page and Warren R. Seyfried (Glenview, Ill.: Scott, Foresman, 1970), p. 274.

79. Quotation of Charles Abrams, in Norman N. Bradburn, Seymour Sudman, and Galen L. Gockel, *Side by Side: Integrated Neighborhoods in America* (Chicago: Quadrangle Books, 1971), p. 104.

80. Gelfand, *A Nation of Cities*, p. 221.

81. Nathan Glazer and David McEntire, eds., *Housing and Minority Groups* (Berkeley: University of California Press, 1960), p. 140.

82. *Shelly v. Kraemer*, 334 U.S. 1 (1948). The Court had struck down racial zoning some thirty years earlier, in *Buchanan v. Warley*, 245 U.S. 60 (1917).

83. Public Law 90-284, 90th Cong. (1968), Title VIII ("Fair Housing"), sec. 805.

84. D.C. Public Interest Research Group, Institute for Local Self-Reliance, and Institute for Policy Studies, *Redlining: Mortgage Disinvestment in the District of Columbia* (Washington, D.C.: DCPIRG, Institute for Local Self-Reliance, and Institute for Policy Studies, 1975), p. 3.

85. See Daniel Seering, "Discrimination in Home Finance," *Notre Dame Lawyer* 68 (June 1973):5ff; U.S. Commission on Civil Rights, *The Federal Civil Rights Enforcement Effort: Summary*, Clearinghouse Publication 31 (Washington, D.C.: U.S. Government Printing Office, 1971); and U.S. Commission on Civil Rights, *The Federal Civil Rights Enforcement Effort: One Year Later*, Clearinghouse Publication 34 (Washington, D.C.: U.S. Government Printing Office, 1972).

86. D.C. Public Interest Research Group et al., *Redlining*, p. 2.

87. D.C. Public Interest Research Group et al., p. 3.; see also "Nondiscrimination Requirements in Real Estate Loan Activities," *Federal Register*, February 8, 1973, pp. 3586–3587.

88. March 1974 opinion, cited in D.C. Public Interest Research Group et al., p. 3.

89. *St. Louis Post-Dispatch*, April 29, 1977.

90. D.C. Public Interest Research Group et al., p. 4.

91. D.C. Public Interest Research Group et al., p. 5; see also U.S. Commission on Civil Rights, *Mortgage Money: Who Gets It? A Case Study in Mortgage Lending Discrimination in Hartford, Connecticut*, Clearinghouse Publication 48 (Washington, D.C.: U.S. Government Printing Office, 1974).

92. Public Law 93-495, 93rd Cong. (1974), Title V, and amendments.

93. Public Law 94-200, 94th Cong. (1975), Title III.

94. See Rochelle L. Stanfield, "Housing Report: Home Loan Disclosure Plays the Numbers Game," *National Journal: The Weekly on Politics and Government*, December 11, 1976, pp. 1780–1781.

95. Frank de Leeuw, Anne B. Schnare, and Raymond J. Struyk, "Housing," in *The Urban Predicament*, ed. William Gorham and Nathan Glazer (Washington, D.C.: The Urban Institute, 1976), pp. 120–121.

96. Berry, *The Open Housing Question*, p. 375.

97. See Laurenti, "Theories of Race and Property Value."

98. HUD Advisory Commission, Social Sciences Panel, *Freedom of Choice in Housing: Opportunities and Constraints* (Washington, D.C.: National Academy of Sciences, 1972), p. 23.

99. Jon Pynoos, Robert Schafer, and Chester W. Hartman, *Housing Urban America* (Chicago: Aldine, 1973), pp. 208–209.

100. Rose Helper, *Racial Policies and Practices of Real Estate Brokers* (Minneapolis: University of Minnesota Press, 1969), p. 291.

101. HUD Advisory Commission, *Freedom of Choice in Housing*, p. 24.

102. R.L. Morrill, "The Negro Ghetto: Problems and Alternatives," in *Urban Social Segregation*, ed. Ceri Peach (London: Longman Group, 1975), p. 156.

103. Donald L. Foley, "Institutional and Contextual Factors Affecting the Housing Choices of Minority Residents," in *Segregation in Residential Areas: Papers on Racial and Socioeconomic Factors in Choice of Housing*, ed. Amos H. Hawley and Vincent P. Rock (Washington, D.C.: National Academy of Sciences, 1973), pp. 97–101.

104. Berry, *The Open Housing Question*, p. xix.

105. Juliet Saltman, *Open Housing: Dynamics of a Social Movement* (New York: Praeger, 1978), pp. 46–47.

106. Saltman, pp. 51–52.

107. Carter M. McFarland, *Federal Government and Urban Problems. HUD: Successes, Failures, and the Fate of Our Cities* (Boulder, Co.: Westview Press, 1978), pp. 187–188.

108. Morris Milgram, *Good Neighborhood: The Challenge of Open Housing* (New York: W.W. Norton, 1977).

109. Saltman, *Open Housing*, p. 59.

110. David Jay Baum, *Toward a Free Housing Market* (Coral Gables, Fla.: University of Miami Press, 1971).

111. Berry, *The Open Housing Question*, pp. 20–26.

112. Helper, *Racial Policies*, p. 70.

113. Milgram, *Good Neighborhood*, p. 200.

114. Foley, "Institutional and Contextual Factors," p. 127.

115. Foley, p. 128.

116. Berry, *The Open Housing Question*, pp. 46–47.

117. Nathan Glazer, "Bias of American Housing Policy," in *Housing Urban America*, ed. Pynoos, Schafer, Hartman, p. 417.

118. John F. Kain, "Effect of Housing Market Segregation on Urban Development," in *Housing Urban America*, ed. Pynoos, Schafer, and Hartman, p. 255.

119. Refer to A.Q. Mowbry, *Road to Ruin* (Philadelphia: J.B. Lippincott, 1968, 1969), pp. 59–73.

120. Bradford C. Snell, "American Ground Transport" in *The Urban Scene*, ed. Joe R. Feagin, 2nd ed. (New York: Random House, 1979), p. 247.

121. Snell, p. 248.

122. Quoted in Snell, p. 249.

123. Snell, p. 259.

124. U.S. Office of Management and Budget, *Special Analyses, Budget of the United States Government: Fiscal Year 1980* (Washington, D.C.: U.S. Government Printing Office, 1979); and *Fiscal Year 1976* (Washington, D.C.: U.S. Government Printing Office, 1975).

125. U.S. Department of Commerce, Bureau of the Census, *Special Studies, Selected Characteristics of Travel to Work in Twenty Metropolitan Areas: 1977*, Series P-23, No. 105 (Washington, D.C.: U.S. Government Printing Office, 1978), p. 4.

Chapter 10

THE RESPONSE TO THE URBAN CRISIS: 1960 to 1968

The Changing Federal Role

Before the Kennedy administration, the only major federal aid programs to be targeted specifically to cities were urban renewal and public housing. The partisan change in the White House in 1961 signalled the beginning of a new era. The national Democratic party's concern for urban problems developed into a full-fledged commitment to and even a preference toward metropolitan areas. Federal aid available to local governments increased dramatically. Federal assistance in urban areas rose from $3.9 billion in 1961, the last Republican fiscal year, to $14 billion in President Johnson's last budget, eight years later. Most of the new money and programs went to people and problems in the cities—a far cry from the pre–New Deal days when federal highway assistance funds to cities were forbidden by law.

The federal role in the cities expanded vastly in the 1960s behind the leadership of two Democratic presidents. This federal activism represented a new departure. Previous legislation had treated physical blight and housing decay in central cities. Public housing legislation was intended to build low-cost housing, but not to treat social problems. Urban renewal was designed exclusively to remove unsightly slums and to subsidize new investment in inner city property. Under Presidents Kennedy and Johnson, a new concern emerged about the *social problems* of the cities— juvenile delinquency, crime, poverty, bad education, racial conflict, and joblessness. In many respects the social programs of the 1960s, especially the Civil Rights Act of 1964, the antipoverty program, and the Model Cities legislation, were designed to enhance the Democratic party's electoral strength among inner-city blacks.

Beginning with the congressional elections of 1966, however, a backlash against social programs began building. It found expression in the 1968 presidential campaigns of George Wallace and Richard Nixon. Politicians built careers on the premise that the federal establishment had become overreaching and dangerous. When Nixon defeated George McGovern by a landslide in the presidential election of 1972, it seemed that old-time liberalism, of either the New Deal or Great Society variety, was dead.

The Social Welfare Explosion

When President John F. Kennedy was sworn in on January 20, 1961, his administration was already committed to an enhanced role for the cities. Even before his campaign, Kennedy had concluded that the problem of the cities was "the great unspoken issue in the 1960 election."[1] Not only did Kennedy feel that the election would be decided by the votes delivered in key cities in a few industrial states; he also felt that the problems of urban residents were worthy of special attention on their own merits. During the 1960 campaign, the Democrats played the city issue with scarcely a whisper from the opposition. The Republicans, in fact, tried to avoid such issues. "If you ever let them campaign only on domestic issues," confided presidential nominee Richard M. Nixon to his aides, "they'll beat us."[2] President Kennedy

emerged as an eloquent spokesman for a new political generation. In presidential message after message Kennedy spelled out in more detail than the Congress or the country could easily digest the most complete programs of domestic reforms in a quarter century.[3]

In August, 1965, the Watts riot in Los Angeles dramatically demonstrated the condition of life in the black ghettos of American cities. Under President Lyndon Johnson, the War on Poverty and many other major pieces of social legislation had been steered through Congress. The federal commitment began to pick up steam, and the trouble in the cities made this commitment seem imperative.

The growth of a grants economy tying the cities to the federal system is illustrated by the number and size of federal grants committed to cities and states during the 1960s. In 1960, forty-four separate grant-in-aid programs were available to state and local governments.[4] Four years later, a Senate subcommittee report compiled by the Library of Congress identified 115 grant programs and a total of 216 separate authorizations under these programs.[5] The next two years brought another large increase. An analysis done by the Legislative Reference Service in 1966 counted a total of 399 authorizations.[6] By 1969, the count was approaching 500; it reached about 530 a year later, before leveling off (Figure 10–1).[7] The number of programs declined in the 1970s, because many of them were folded into block-grant consolidations. There were fewer than 400 programs by 1985.[8]

FIGURE 10–1   Growth of Grants-in-Aid Authorizations, 1962–1986*

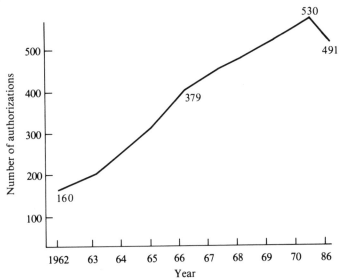

Source: Adapted from U.S. Congress, Senate, Committee on Governmental Operations, *Intergovernmental Revenue Act of 1971 and Related Legislation*, hearings before the Subcommittee on Intergovernmental Relations, Senate, 92nd Cong., 1st sess., 1971, p. 379; and Michael D. Reagan, *The New Federalism* (New York: Oxford University Press, 1972), p. 55; and Office of Management and Budget, *Catalog of Federal Domestic Assistance, 1986* (Washington, D.C.: U.S. Government Printing Office, 1986).

*For 1986, number of grant-in-aid programs to state and local governments. This may vary slightly from number of authorizations.

The amount of money spent through federal grants increased exponentially. In 1950, only $2.25 billion in grants was allocated to states and local governments, as shown in Table 10–1. By 1960, this amount had gone up to $7 billion. In 1969, the first year of the Nixon administration, the national government was spending $20.3 billion for grants-in-aid. When Nixon left office in 1974, the amount had more than doubled, to $43.3 billion. Spending rose rapidly until the late 1970s. Federal grants-in-aid totalled nearly $90 billion by 1980. Since 1980, real spending (controlled for inflation) has declined.

State and local governments became more and more dependent on federal dollars in the 1960s and 1970s. In 1950, about $1 of $10 spent by state and local governments originated in Washington. This proportion increased to 14.7 percent by 1960 and it rose to 19.4 percent by 1970. In 1978, more than 26 percent of state and local government dollars came from the federal treasury.

The importance of the stepped-up federal effort is illustrated by New York City's budget. In 1952, before any significant federal urban programs, New York relied on the federal government for only 3.8 percent of its expenditures. Even in 1963, after the implementation of the massive

TABLE 10–1   **Federal Aid Outlays in Relation to State and Local Expenditures, 1950–1984**

Fiscal year	Amount (billions of dollars)	Percent of state and local expenditures
1950	2.25	10.4
1955	3.21	10.1
1960	7.02	14.7
1965	10.90	15.3
1970	24.01	19.4
1972	34.37	22.0
1974	43.31	22.7
1976	59.09	24.4
1978	77.89	26.4
1980 (est.)	88.95	25.3
1981 (est.)	96.31	25.3
1982 (est.)	105.30	*
1983 (est.)	112.35	*
1984 (est.)	112.35	*

Source: U.S. Office of Management and Budget, *Special Analyses, Budget of the United States Government: Fiscal Year 1981* (Washington, D.C.: U.S. Government Printing Office, 1982), p. 254.
*Not available.

National Defense and Interstate Highway System, federal assistance amounted to only $142 million, or 5.5 percent. With the explosion of social welfare programs in the mid-1960s, however, the federal share of the city's budget rose rapidly. By 1965, the federal proportion of the budget reached 11 percent, and by 1969 it accounted for 16 percent. Finally, in the four years following, the total rose from $508 million to just over $2 billion—19 percent of the city's budget.⁹

Municipalities became heavily dependent on intergovernmental revenues flowing from both the federal government and the states. Table 10–2 shows that municipalities generated less than half of the revenues in their budgets by 1975; 19 percent came from the federal government and 42 percent from the states. The proportion of local revenues coming from the federal and state capitals declined in the late 1970s, however, from 61 percent in 1975, and 56 percent in 1980, to 43 percent in 1984.

Between 1962 and 1970, the federal government made 370 new programs available to states and localities. In the ten years between 1960 and 1970, Congress quintupled the number of programs that had accumulated over the preceding 175 years.¹⁰ Although the number of federal programs increased during the New Deal, the amount of money going to state and local governments remained small. In 1960, only 7.6 percent of the federal budget went to grant-in-aid programs, which, through specific grants, aided states and localities in giving relief and in building sewers, water mains, and highways.¹¹ By 1973, 16.9 percent of the federal budget took

TABLE 10–2   **Proportion of Municipal Revenues that Originates from Federal and State Transfers**

	Proportion of each municipal dollar received from		
Year	Federal government	State government	Federal and state government
1962	.05	.21	.26
1975	.19	.42	.61
1978	.26	.37	.63
1980	.23	.33	.56
1982	.17	.32	.49
1984	.14	.29	.43

Source: U.S. Advisory Commission on Intergovernmental Relations, *Significant Features of Fiscal Federalism,* 1985–86 edition (Washington, D.C.: U.S. Government Printing Office, February 1986), p. 64.

the form of grants-in-aid. The proportion of federal outlays for grants-in-aid plunged sharply in the 1980s, however, from 16.8 percent in 1979 to 12.7 percent in 1982.[12]

The explosion in federal spending for programs designed for specific localities during the 1960s was accompanied by an attempt to achieve *national purposes*. Not since the closing of the frontier in the 1870s had the national government attempted so clearly to define a domestic purpose. In giving away land to states and railroads, in establishing a post office and financing internal improvements, and in following a militant policy towards the Indians, the federal government in that period had declared its intention to open up the West and secure its territory.[13] Now, in the 1960s, the president and Congress again tried to formulate an overall national policy and to assert the right of the federal government to extend its authority. This assertion of purpose was, for example, particularly direct in the case of the Civil Rights Act of 1964, in which the government served notice that its new civil rights statutes would override state and local racial practices. In the case of grant programs, the preambles to legislation of the New Frontier and the Great Society articulated many new purposes. For example, from the Manpower Development and Training Act of 1962:

> *It is in the national interest that* current and prospective manpower shortages be identified and that persons who can be qualified for these positions through education and training be sought out and trained, *in order that the nation may meet the staffing requirements of the struggle for freedom.*[14]

Or the Economic Opportunity Act of 1964:

> *The United States can achieve its full economic and social potential as a nation* only if every individual has the opportunity to contribute the full extent of his capabilities and to participate in the workings of our society. *It is, therefore, the policy of the United States* to eliminate the paradox of poverty in the midst of plenty in this nation.[15]

Or the Demonstration Cities and Metropolitan Development Act of 1966:

> The Congress hereby finds and declares *that improving the quality of urban life is the most critical domestic problem facing the United States.*[16]

Imagine these kinds of statements of intention introducing hundreds of pieces of legislation, ranging from rent supplements and teacher training to federal school aid to crime control, and the complexity of the new system of grants becomes readily apparent. Hardly an economic or a social problem escaped attention, and each program carried with it complicated methods of implementation. Recipient institutions were subjected to close scrutiny and control, for it made no sense to announce a "national purpose" unless the money was going to be used carefully, according to prescribed guidelines and standards.[17]

This era of activist policymaking by the federal government was facilitated by a new conception of the legitimate role of the national government in relation to the individual and society. At the prodding of two Democratic administrations, the Congress

> enacted several programs which aimed primarily at broadening the scope of individual opportunity and development. The cumulative effect of these programs [was] to place the principal emphasis of federal aid . . . on health, labor, and welfare activities—as well as to give added impetus to education and housing and community development efforts.[18]

The shift to a social welfare orientation was accomplished between 1963 and 1967, when Congress enacted 136 new grant authorizations. Among the many programs added were the major social reforms of the 1960s, including, for example, food stamps, regional and community health facilities, the War on Poverty, Medicare, Medicaid, Appalachian regional development, aid for elementary and secondary education, and Model Cities.[19]

Most of the new programs fit within the general rubric of "human resources." Fiscal year 1965 marked the beginning of a dramatic upswing in outlays for social programs, particularly in the areas of health, education, and employment training. Grants-in-aid to state and local governments within these fields rose from 14 percent of federal domestic aid in 1960 to one-third of such aid in 1970. Similarly, the proportion of assistance outlays for housing and community development nearly quadrupled during the decade, rising from 3 to 11 percent of the domestic budget.[20] Obviously, urban issues were becoming more important. In fact, the 1960s were unique, for never before had the cities received so much direct attention. The extent of the new urban commitment is shown in Table 10–3.

While aid to urban areas shot upward 590 percent from 1961 to 1972, total federal aid spending increased by 405 percent. Aid to nonurban areas rose by only 182 percent. By far the largest increment in spending was in the new programs associated with community development and housing, which were distinctly urban in orientation.

The Dissatisfaction with Federal Activism

It is important to note that a significant portion of the new federal money did not go directly to city governments but to nongovernmental nonprofit organizations. Application procedures and funding arrange-

TABLE 10–3 Federal Aid Outlays to Urban Areas, by Functional Area, for Selected Years

Functional area	Fiscal year (millions of dollars)				% increase 1961–1972
	1961	1964	1969	1972 (est.)	
Agriculture and Rural Development	155	271	417	375	142
Natural Resources and Environment	54	18	180	943	1,646
Commerce and Transportation	1,434	2,142	2,539	3,205	124
other than highways	37	199	314	559	1,411
Community Development and Housing	214	338	1,612	3,328	1,501
Other than public housing and urban renewal	3	43	569	1,783	5,933
Education and Manpower	561	722	2,963	4,362	677
Health	99	300	2,296	3,262	2,194
Income Security	1,341	1,695	3,899	8,181	510
General Government and Defense	35	77	159	803	2,194
General Revenue Sharing	—	—	—	2,813	—
TOTAL for urban areas	3,893	5,588	14,045	26,848	590
TOTAL for federal aid outlays	7,112	10,141	20,255	35,490	405
Percentage of total federal aid outlays to urban areas	54.7	55.3	69.1	75.0	—

Sources: Adapted and calculated from U.S. Office of Management and Budget, *Special Analyses, Budget of the United States Government: Fiscal Year 1972* (Washington, D.C.: U.S. Government Printing Office, 1971), p. 241.

ments varied considerably. Grants-in-aid went directly to local governments, to state agencies performing urban functions, and to private and nonprofit institutions and groups. Many programs bypassed general-purpose municipal governments by requiring the creation of "special districts" or new agencies to receive funds. The rapid growth in the number of programs, their varying purposes, and their complex application procedures soon led to serious problems of coordination, impediments to congressional oversight, and conflicts among agencies and groups in local communities.

Governors, mayors, and other state and local officials expressed frequent consternation about the lack of coordination among programs, the complexities of application and administration, and the lack of available information on programs. The chief culprit in each case was institutional fragmentation.

There were numerous sources of information on grant programs. For example, in January 1967, the Advisory Commission on Intergovernmental Relations issued a bibliography entitled *Catalog and Other Information Sources on Federal and State Aid Programs* that was nine pages long.[21] It listed publications by federal agencies, organizations of public officials, and local governments. A study contracted by the Department of Housing and Urban Development reported in September, 1967, that federal agencies had no standardized procedures for conveying information on their grant programs and that there were few standard practices concerning the frequency of updating information.[22] During 1966, four agencies issued four different catalogues with information on programs of both their own agencies and those of others.[23]

This fragmentation was reflected at the local level. In July, 1967, administrators reported that they turned to an average of 8.2 sources to obtain information about grant programs.[24] The most frequently used sources were federal agency publications and federal agency personnel at local and regional offices. Newspapers were the next most widely used source.

In attempting to simplify the system, officials in the Johnson administration sometimes inadvertently made matters worse. HUD official Robert Wood testified before the Senate Subcommittee on Intergovernmental Relations in 1966 that HUD was participating in thirty-one interagency committees, task forces, and other coordinating groups.[25] At the same hearings, officials from the Office of Economic Opportunity testified that they cooperated in twenty-nine "committees and similar groups" with other federal agencies, and in twenty agreements with six other departments.[26] Secretary of Labor Willard Wirtz listed five interagency agreements in which the Department of Labor was participating.[27] But the Secretary of Health, Education, and Welfare enumerated the largest number of efforts. He served as the chairman of six committees, as a member of twenty-three others, and designated a person to represent him on six more. The Office of Education participated in seventeen "formal" committees, eleven informal ones, and five interagency agreements.[28]

Several formal mechanisms were developed to replace these voluntary attempts at administrative cooperation. The Economic Opportunity Council was established by the Economic Opportunity Act to help coordinate the federal government's antipoverty efforts. In August, 1966, an executive order authorized the Secretary of HUD to convene agency representatives for exchange of information.[29] The President also urged simplified grant procedures and authorized the Bureau of the Budget to study and report on intergovernmental relations problems.[30] The bureau subsequently reported some success in eliminating redundant data requirements among programs, reducing technical reviews, and implementing preapplication consultation among local, state, and federal officials.[31]

Federal agencies also encouraged local grant applicants to demonstrate strong efforts at comprehensive planning; in fact, in Model Cities and other programs, planning and coordination were the passwords for satisfactory applications. Between 1964 and 1966, forty-seven separate aid programs requiring some measure of planning were enacted. "Many of these were intended to improve areawide planning for metropolitan regions."[32] As with attempts at coordination, however, planning requirements often exacerbated rather than improved the grant process. In testimony before the House Subcommittee on Intergovernmental Relations in 1967, Secretary of the Treasury Fowler noted:

> Certain planning requirements necessarily demanded as a condition of grants may be overlapping. This duplication can defeat the very purpose for which planning is sought. Such requirements may themselves become a significant generator of confusion, and have an adverse effect on program policy and execution.[33]

Too many programs had been passed too fast for anyone to keep up. From the point of view of local public officials, the worst of it was not that there were so many programs but that so many of them went to agencies and groups outside city hall. The governmental apparatus of the cities was being bypassed in favor of new institutions, particularly those created through the antipoverty and Model Cities programs. In Oakland, California, for example, elected officials were disturbed that "substantial federal funding was going to a local organization which was openly hostile to the city government." The mayor's local nemesis, the local community action agency—the Oakland Economic Development Council, Inc.—received more than five times the $1 million in federal aid received by the city government in 1968.[34] Political officials and the local administrative agencies responsible for the delivery of municipal services felt that the federal government was fomenting "revolution" through its social programs.

The Attack on Inequality

Indeed, some programs initiated in the 1960s seemed to be explicitly designed to undermine political and economic elites in local communities. Attempts to address problems of economic inequality, combined with attacks on racial segregation and discrimination, inevitably would challenge politics-as-usual.

Until the 1960s the problems of economic inequality and poverty went largely unnoticed by political leaders. Social security, unemployment insurance, and the categorical aid programs were the "poverty" programs that existed, and all dated from the Social Security Act of 1935. These programs were not designed to address the problems of poverty or inequality *per se*, but to provide a bare subsistence to particular groups of individuals—mothers of dependent children, the blind, the aged—who were unable to participate in the economic system. The Social Security Act failed to achieve a redress of inequality and poverty, and the lack of further legislation in the ensuing decades illustrated the degree to which no further solutions were thought necessary.

In March, 1962, Michael Harrington published *The Other America*, a study of the "invisible land" of the poor existing in the midst of unprecedented prosperity. Harrington pointed out that there were few statistics on the poor in America; there were no congressional investigations, and the mass media sold the message of abundance, not want. Against this background of indifference, Harrington maintained, most of the poor lacked the means to change their condition. He attacked the general assumption that the "poor are that way because they are afraid of work."[35] Rather, he said, "the real explanation of why the poor are where they are is that they made the mistake of being born to the wrong parents, in the wrong section of the country, in the wrong industry, or in the wrong racial or ethnic group. Once that mistake has been made, they could have been paragons of will and morality, but most of them would never even have had a chance to get out of the other America."[36] Harrington discussed the factors of race, slum environments in the inner cities, the lack of job opportunities in depressed rural areas, and the jobs in the Arkansas belt and southeast Missouri that paid less than subsistence wages. His review of the few poverty studies that had been completed by 1961 revealed an estimate of 50 million poor people in the United States, a number that included almost one third of all Americans.

In the year following its publication, Harrington's book barely moved from the shelves. Finally, in March, 1963, Dwight MacDonald of *The New Yorker* wrote a lengthy review. Almost overnight Harrington's book became a best seller, and it was reprinted ten times by 1968. Poverty had arrived as an issue of general social concern.

The emergence of the poverty issue brought new political pressures to bear on the Kennedy Administration. The civil rights movement accelerated the pressures for a new domestic legislative agenda. Accompanying this was increasing statistical evidence of high unemployment and poverty among blacks as well as among whites in depressed areas of the nation. The issue of political discrimination was soon linked to economic discrimination. The time had come when it would be politically advantageous for the government to undertake a special program for the American poor. And the connection between poverty and race insured that the War on Poverty, as well as much subsequent legislation, would focus on inner-city black ghettos.

The electoral base of the national Democratic Party also led in this direction. As John C. Donovan observed in his book, *The Politics of Poverty*, "The greatest strength of the Negro communities lies in its voting power, in its numbers, and in their strategic location."[37] In the south, the black population was geographically diffused and systematically denied the power of the vote. In their migration to the North, blacks gained the franchise and concentrated their voting power in key urban areas, thus forcing a change in the strategy of presidential elections. The cities of all the large key states holding the majority of electoral college votes—Illinois, California, Massachusetts, Ohio, Michigan, New Jersey, New York, Texas, and Pennsylvania—contained substantial black populations by 1960.

With the beginning of the New Deal, the Democratic party established a new coalition based on the urban ethnic constituencies of northern cities and the old-line Democrats of the South. Blacks, who in 1936 had shifted from the Republican to the Democratic party, made up an important voting bloc in the new coalition, but exerted little influence on party platforms until the 1948 Democratic convention. In the 1950s, some members of the Democratic party began to respond to the growing black voting population in the North and the rise in civil rights activity in the South. At this point, painful decisions had to be made about where to seek votes, for southern Democrats would not abide forceful action on behalf of blacks. This can be discerned in the presidential election results of 1960: while Kennedy won the South, he did it with one of the poorest showings ever for a Democrat. In northern cities he carried enough of the vote to tip key industrial states into his column.

While the changing electoral calculus exerted its own subtle influence, overt pressures were brought to bear on the Kennedy administration. One important pressure was applied by the civil rights movement, culminating in the March on Washington in August 1963. Another was the discovery of poverty as a social issue.

The War on Poverty

The first steps toward a federal antipoverty effort were undertaken in early 1963 by Robert J. Lampman, a young staff member of the president's Council of Economic Advisors. In a series of memoranda to Walter

Heller, the chairman of the council, he stressed the failure of the Kennedy administration to fulfill its 1960 campaign promises to implement programs aimed at poverty and unemployment. Lampman's research generally supported the ideas set forth by Harrington in *The Other America*. When President Kennedy asked for a copy of Harrington's book, Heller supplied it with an enthusiastic endorsement. In June, 1963, Kennedy asked Heller to assemble a task force of economists to consider the possibility of a poverty program. In August, the president indicated that he was definitely interested in a legislative program to combat poverty.

When Kennedy was killed in Dallas in November, 1963, it was clear that a poverty program would be component in the 1964 presidential campaign. The program was to be rather small, however, funding no more than ten projects in ten cities. This was all changed when Lyndon Johnson succeeded to the presidency.

As the new president, Johnson was looking for a program that would both establish the unique identity of his administration and fulfill his desire to be remembered as a great reformer. It was logical that Johnson, a political product of the New Deal (he was first elected to Congress in 1938) who had publicly emulated Roosevelt, would choose poverty to set the theme for his domestic programs. When Walter Heller approached him two days after Kennedy's death and presented him with the idea of a poverty program, he enthusiastically embraced it and made it a cornerstone of his Great Society. "That's my kind of program," Johnson said. "It will help people. I want you to move full speed ahead."[38] Johnson envisioned the Great Society as his New Deal, and himself as the spokesman for the poor. "They had no voice and no champion," said Johnson, and "whatever the cost, I was determined to represent them. Through me they would have an advocate, and, I believe, new hope."[39]

It was the combination of Johnson's political astuteness and the demands of his own ego, the two most prominent characteristics of his personality, that led him to assert such a firm initiative with the antipoverty program. On January 8, 1964, while his poverty program was still being worked out, President Johnson announced in his State of the Union address a "total effort" to end poverty in the United States. As was his custom, the president spoke in heavy prose: "Let this session of Congress be known as the session . . . which declared all-out war on human poverty and unemployment in these United States. . . . This Administration here and now declares unconditional war on poverty in America, and I urge this Congress and all Americans to join with me in that effort."[40]

On January 31, in an effort to give the program his personal touch and to remove it from the competing interests of other government agencies, he established a presidential task force headed by Sargent Shriver, the former director of the Peace Corps. Johnson threw the full power and prestige of his office behind the Economic Opportunity Act of 1964, and his superb legislative skill eased the law through Congress in record time and with little debate. In July and August, 1964, the Senate and the House comfortably enacted the Economic Opportunity Act (EOA), in time for a Johnson signature during the presidential campaign.

Organizing the Poor As a Political Force

The rediscovery of poverty in the early 1960s entailed a great deal more than a quantitative analysis of the number of poor people in the United States. More important, it challenged old assumptions about the nature and causes of poverty, assumptions rooted in Social Darwinism, and probably dating even further back to Puritan notions that the elect can be discerned by their material progress on earth.

Traditional attitudes about poverty had fit into two categories, identified by sociologist Kenneth Clark as the "Puritan–Horatio Alger Tradition" and the "Good Samaritan–Lady Bountiful Tradition."[41] Under the former, the moral fiber and personal characteristics of the poor were identified as the chief causes of poverty. This tradition assumed that help from the prosperous individuals in the social community would have the effect of breaking down the moral strength and motivation of poor people. Left alone, the "deserving" poor would pull themselves up by their bootstraps. Only if society interfered in the natural social order would the profligate poor survive to breed future generations of poverty.

The "Good Samaritan–Lady Bountiful" tradition had its roots in the Progressive era, with its settlement houses, charities, and community chests, and emphasized such factors as "bad luck" and unfortunate circumstances: death of a breadwinner, unhealthy surroundings, or bad family environment. Giving aid to such victims meant having compassion and doing good deeds, and it was a sign of good policy besides, for it was assumed that the individuals thus helped (as distinct from the poor deserving of their fate) would use the aid to give themselves a new start in life.

An important new theory surfaced in the early 1960s, which, when adopted in the War on Poverty, provoked considerable anxiety among established political interests. The "structural opportunity" thesis emphasized the political relationships between the poor and the structures of the social and political system.

The assumption of this tradition is that unjust conditions of society have victimized the poor and that the prosperous are often exploitative in their relationship to the poor. The duty of the poor is to break the shackles that bind them and assert their independence and their rights as free men, and the duty of the wealthy is to compensate the victims, to lead the fight against injustice, and to transform the nature of society itself.[42]

According to this theory, social and political institutions systematically deny the poor access to better education, jobs, and social advancement. Educational requirements for jobs, for example, constitute opportunities to those with education but are barriers to lower-class individuals without access to adequate schooling. Likewise, unions that secure higher pay and better work conditions for their members systematically exclude minorities from the best jobs. Thus, according to the theory, poverty is as much a condition of powerlessness as of economic deprivation. The way out of poverty is not individual self-help but group action to challenge unequal opportunities and institutional barriers.

A variation on this theme stressed the effects of poverty on the motivations and attitudes of poor individuals. Poverty (suggested the theorists) was reinforced by feelings of powerlessness, alienation, frustration, and despair. Unable to affect the institutions around them, the poor had given up the struggle, thus losing whatever motivation they might have had to break out of their condition. The result was the "poverty cycle," wherein poverty bred feelings of inadequacy and frustration, which led to lack of motivation to look for better jobs or to seek better education, which led to low-paying, low-status jobs or to unemployment, which resulted in poverty, and on around the cycle again. The cycle was also thought to be generational; parents who lived in poverty passed on their defeatist attitudes to their children.

If this theory explained poverty, then the key to breaking the cycle seemed to be changing the motivations and attitudes of the poor. One effective way of doing this would be to involve them in their own salvation. Through participation in programs affecting their lives, they would learn specific skills of leadership and participation; generally, their attitudes about their own competence and worth would change.

The idea of increasing participation of the poor in the political system appealed to those who accepted the structural opportunity thesis as well as to those who believed in the cycle of poverty. To the structuralists, participation would lead to political pressures applied against institutions and elites; for the cycle-of-poverty enthusiasts, it would lead to change in the attitudes and aspirations of poor people. Individuals accepting both theories were numerous in the Kennedy and Johnson administrations. "Community action" programs, funded under section 2 of the Economic Opportunity Act, became highly controversial because they were interpreted by many federal administrators and by some of the poor as a means to attack the institutions in local communities—city hall, school boards, welfare agencies, housing offices, and even private employers. The reason the antipoverty program became a source of such criticism can be discerned in this interpretation of its purposes, offered by one of the important observers of the program:

> The anti-poverty program . . . can help to bring about the political preconditions for major economic changes. But this can happen only if the forms of involvement lead to new bases of organized power for low-income people. Economic deprivation is fundamentally a political problem, and power will be required to solve it.
>
> Community groups are beginning to realize that their stake . . . is the right to mount autonomous self-directed antipoverty programs in their own slums and ghettoes.[43]

Most political leaders would certainly have been alarmed to find community action interpreted as a way for the urban poor to fight political and economic elites. But the radical possibilities of community action did not become apparent to members of Congress and local government officials until after the antipoverty legislation was passed.

The antipoverty program was established to create a direct link between the federal government and inner-city black ghettos. New agencies were established in these communities to spend federal funds. Existing state and local governments were bypassed. In this regard, the poverty program shared a feature common to many of the Great Society programs. New governmental and quasigovernmental agencies that did not have to answer to city hall or other local authorities were established. Of all the community action funds spent by the Office of Economic Opportunity (OEO) by 1968, only 25 percent were given to public agencies at all, the remainder going to private organizations, including universities, churches, civil rights groups, settlement houses, family services agencies, United Way funds, or newly established nonprofit groups.[44] Likewise, only 10 percent of HEW project grants operating at the beginning of 1967 were limited to governmental units.[45] Of course, such arrangements upset local authorities, who saw federal monies flowing into their jurisdictions to groups and organizations over which they had little or no influence.

Community Action and Citizen Participation

In congressional hearings on the original legislation, the community action concept did not seem particularly unsettling, in part because few members of Congress had any notion of its meaning or potential for controversy. It was viewed mainly as a device for coordinating programs and improving government services. This impression is bolstered by a reading of section 202(a) of the legislation:

The term "community action program" means a program . . . (1) which mobilizes and utilizes resources, public and private, of any urban and rural . . . geographical area . . . in an attack on poverty; (2) which provides services, assistance, and other activities of sufficient scope and size to give promise of progress toward eliminating poverty or [the] causes of poverty through developing employment opportunities, improving human performance, motivation, and productivity, or bettering the condition under which people live and work; (3) which is developed, conducted, and administered with the maximum feasible participation of residents of the areas and members of the groups served; (4) which is conducted, administered, or coordinated by a public or private nonprofit agency. . . .

Significantly, 202 (1) (3), the clause calling for maximum feasible participation, was mentioned in testimony only once, by Robert F. Kennedy, in the hearings before Congress.

The ease with which the legislation passed through Congress illustrated the mundane interpretation given to it by members of Congress and also by those mayors and public officials who testified in its behalf. Community action programs were viewed as compatible with the political priorities of local officials. Even the conservative voices heard in opposition to this program earmarked specifically for the poor did not object strenuously to the basic structures being established to fight the antipoverty war.

The initial interpretation of maximum feasible participation chosen by OEO administrators quickly became a contentious political issue. Some political leaders saw it as a strategy to foment social and political revolution, as well it might have been if pursued vigorously and consistently. The first federal manual distributed to local community action administrators said that a "promising method" of implementing maximum feasible participation was "to assist the poor in developing autonomous and self-managed organizations which are competent to exert political influence on behalf of their own self-interest."[46] Likewise, in an early program guide, the OEO stated that local programs should involve the poor from the very first "in planning, policy-making, and operation . . . ".[47]

Representatives of the poor were to sit on governing or policy advisory boards and were to be selected by democratic means (preferably through elections). They were also to be involved in actual program operations. All of this held out the possibility that poor people would be able to organize pressure groups with active financial backing by the federal government.

Local officials soon reacted to this threat. In June, 1965, the United States Conference of Mayors adopted a resolution reflecting their own stakes in "properly" interpreting maximum feasible participation:

Whereas, no responsible mayor can accept the implications in the Office of Opportunity Workbook that the goals of this program can only be achieved by creating tensions between the poor and existing agencies and by fostering class struggle: . . . Now THEREFORE BE IT RESOLVED that the Administration be urged to assure that any policy . . . assure the continuing control of local expenditures relative to this program be fiscally responsible to local officials.[48]

Robert Wagner, mayor of New York City, echoed the mayors' concern before a House subcommittee when he argued that "the local governing bodies, through their chief executives or otherwise, should have the ultimate authority . . . for the conduct and operation of the antipoverty program."[49] Through 1965 and 1966, the mayors continued to vent their displeasure.

In August, 1965, two months after the Conference of Mayors resolution, Office of Economic Opportunity director Sargent Shriver denied that he had set arbitrary quotas for representation of poor people on poverty boards. Significantly, the subject of "autonomous organizations" of the poor was never again broached. Yet only a few months before, Shriver had told a congressional committee that the OEO was trying to

encourage at the local level the basic democratic processes which have made this country great . . . and that includes arguments, disputes, dissension, and what I like to call "community action" . . . When we see disputes at the local level, then we think we are getting exactly what Congress asked us to encourage.[50]

Both OEO administrators and the Johnson administration were subjected to pressures applied by the mayors and by members of Congress. President Johnson moved to placate the program's opponents. On October 21, 1965, he appointed Bernard L. Boutin, a former mayor of Laconia, New Hampshire, as the deputy director of the OEO. Boutin's first action was to refuse refunding for a controversial project in Syracuse, New York, in which community activists had led sit-ins and other protests. In November, 1965, the OEO's guidelines specified that one-third of the membership of poverty boards should be made up of representatives of the poor. Only three months later this requirement was revised to one-fourth. At other times, in fact, as early as August, Sargent Shriver had denied there was any quota at all. Shriver's increasing caution emerged in full bloom at a January 12, 1966, news conference, when he stated: "There is no requirement in this statute that a person be too poor to fulfill the statute and we are not trying to get poor people as such."[51]

The Reaction Against the "Radical" Poor

The most important point to be made about the coalition supporting the antipoverty program is that the poor were never a relevant part of it. The legislation was drafted entirely by bureaucrats within the executive branch. Representatives of poverty communities were absent from the hearings in Congress, and during implementation of the program they were excluded from contributing an important voice in the national antipoverty effort.

For its continued funding the antipoverty program required support from powerful political groups, and representatives of the poor were not important in this coalition. Members of Congress held the key to antipoverty appropriations. OEO director Sargent Shriver and his staff were keenly aware of the importance of their congressional image, and for the sake of this image OEO backed away from controversial projects, such as those in Syracuse, San Francisco, and the state of Mississippi. In each of these programs, local administrators of antipoverty funds led protests against mayors, welfare departments, or school boards, and demanded programs designed specifically in response to complaints from the black community. Governors, mayors and members of Congress responded by requesting meetings with the President and with federal officials. The OEO was forced to threaten a cutoff of funds unless "radical" activities in local programs were stopped.

An indicator of the OEO's sensitivity to political pressure was its attempt to build broad support for the antipoverty program by funding far more projects than had originally been envisioned. Members of Congress would be far more reluctant to vote against appropriations for the OEO if poverty funds were flowing into their districts. Thus, the administration quickly abandoned its initial plan to restrict the antipoverty effort to a few "demonstration" projects. Within the first year, the OEO funded 650 community action programs, and by 1967, the number of programs reached 1,100. The hope of concentrating the available money in order to exert maximum impact in a few areas gave way to the OEO's need to consolidate congressional support.

City mayors also could put the antipoverty program at risk. The mayors insisted on a "nonpolitical" definition of maximum feasible participation. The OEO's original definition of that phrase, that the poor should be encouraged to organize in their own self-interest, constituted a significant threat to the political position of the mayors:

> It cannot be ignored that stimulating new flow channels for the demands of the poor and minority groups is fraught with danger for any mayor. . . . An antiquated tax structure, for one thing, has created severe financial burdens for

city administrations, which would only be exacerbated by demands of newly formed groups for still additional services.[52]

Political demand also could escalate as a result of complaints of police brutality, calls for civilian review boards, the formation of tenant- and welfare-rights groups, and demands for community control of education. Only in unusual circumstances would a mayor be inclined to encourage the creation of new organizations to represent minority communities and poor people.

Similarly, groups representing established political interests had a stake in perpetuating existing political arrangements. Municipal reform coalitions, usually composed of business leaders, newspapers, civic groups, and middle-class voters, had little to gain by championing the cause of the poor. Public and private bureaucracies were chiefly interested in maintaining control of funds and programs, not in getting hassled for doing a bad job. Finally, even existing community organizations, including civil rights and neighborhood groups, usually opposed activity that threatened to alter the existing locus of neighborhood power. In short, vested interests at both the national and the local levels resisted mobilization of the poor except on their own terms.[53]

In most local communities, community action programs failed to involve any significant number of poor people. Two factors worked against independent political action by the poor. For one thing, individual poor people tended to be unorganized and apathetic, and it was difficult to persuade them that participation in public meetings or demonstrations would do any good. A second reason was that efforts to initiate change invited resistance from members of Congress, governors, mayors, and a variety of local officials. Programs involving protest marches, sit-ins, or other "radical" activities were either terminated by federal officials or forced to change as a condition of receiving federal funds.

Powerful members of the coalition described here succeeded in controlling almost every community action program agency created under the antipoverty legislation. For example, in a study of thirty-five community action agencies conducted for the Senate Subcommittee on Employment, Manpower, and Poverty, nearly all of the Community Action Agencies administered service programs, such as job referrals, special education classes, and the like, with very little participation by poor people. In fact, most of the money for services was filtered through the Community Action Agencies to school boards (e.g., for Head Start), to police departments, and to other established agencies. The strategy of enhancing the power of poor people by inciting political activity was *attempted* in only three communities studied by the subcommittee, San Francisco, Syracuse, and Newark (all the projects in the nation that had stirred controversy were included in the sample).[54] Significantly, these three programs soon became the subject of intense controversy and were either changed to eliminate radical activities, or their funds were cut off.

Most community action programs never were controversial, except perhaps in their rhetoric. Many of the early applications for poverty funds stressed social action by the poor because the OEO guidelines seemed to require this emphasis.[55] In practice, most programs were primarily concerned with delivery of social services, despite the language in the applications. To a large extent, the contradiction between rhetoric and actual operation was demanded by federal and local bureaucrats who dictated acceptable uses of poverty funds.[56]

Most local antipoverty programs defined citizen participation as either representation on community action boards or employment of the poor in service programs. That the OEO and local Community Action Agencies should choose these forms of participation is not surprising, because these were the most easily controlled and symbolically satisfying methods of "participation" available. After the first few months, the OEO consistently discouraged the one form of participation that would have stimulated new political demands in local communities—activities designed to mobilize poor people.

The Model Cities Program: The Second Experiment in Citizen Participation

The antipoverty program became controversial in the 1960s because it was targeted toward inner-city blacks and because for a time, it seemed to encourage participation by the poor in community action programs. A second program, Model Cities, shared these two features and offered another as well: while the War on Poverty's rhetoric unrealistically promised to end poverty, the Model Cities program was promoted as an all-out, coordinated, comprehensive attack on virtually all the social and physical problems confronting cities. Its strategies included citizen participation as well as the coordination of federal and local public and private resources available in local communities.

In a March 2, 1965, message to Congress, President Lyndon Johnson identified the quality of urban life as occupying the "front rank of national concern and interest" (the message was entitled "The Problems and Future of the Central City and Its Suburbs"). The president recommended a sweeping housing program to attack some of the problems of the cities. The new program would principally include rent supplements for poor families, grants for the planning and building of new towns and community facilities, an enlarged and revised urban renewal program, and increased public housing construction. In addition, the president urged the creation of a cabinet-level housing agency, to be named the Department of Housing and Urban Development (HUD), to coordinate all federal housing programs.

The idea of organizing a cabinet department responsible for housing programs soon expanded into proposals to create a department to administer all urban-related programs. Thus, by the time Congress approved legislation creating the Department of Housing and Urban Development, it was invested with a broad mandate to improve urban life. President Johnson signed the legislation on September 9, 1965. Less than two years later, HUD was given responsibility for administering the Model Cities program.

In a message sent to Congress to January 26, 1966, President Johnson spelled out his Demonstration Cities (Model Cities) proposal. The bill was promoted as "more comprehensive, more concentrated, than any that has gone before."[57]

The objectives of the proposed Demonstration Cities Act were exceedingly broad:

> The purposes of this title are to provide additional financial and technical assistance to enable cities of all sizes [to implement] new and imaginative proposals and rebuild and revitalize large slums and blighted areas; to expand housing, job, and income opportunities; to reduce dependence on welfare payments; to improve educational facilities and programs; to combat disease and ill health; to reduce the incidence of crime and delinquency; to enhance recreational and cultural opportunities; to establish better access between homes and jobs; and generally to improve living in such areas.[58]

These goals were to be accomplished through a "concentration and coordination of Federal, State, and local public and private efforts."[59]

The program was to be implemented on the local level through City Demonstration agencies, which would be established and operated under the authority of city governments. The agencies' primary role was to coordinate new programs that would be passed through local Model Cities Agencies, but administered by existing governmental, nonprofit, or private agencies and institutions. The city Demonstration Agencies would act as "umbrella" organizations, setting guidelines and project standards.

Another feature of the Model Cities Act called for "widespread citizen participation in the program" and "maximum opportunities for employing residents" in the program's phases.[60] Model Cities program administrators said that one of the most important features of the Demonstration Cities (later named Model Cities) program was its strategy of mobilizing community residents. Citizen participation was supposed to make the program "work" (i.e., to deliver services efficiently) and avoid the problems of local resistance that had been encountered in the urban renewal programs.

Unlike the Economic Opportunity Act, the Demonstration Cities Act did not sail through Congress easily. In fact, the politics of the program's enactment reveals a great deal about how difficult it was to secure approval, even in the mid-1960s, for social legislation targeted for the central cities. Though Lyndon Johnson's 1964 landslide victory had given him a 289 to 146 Democratic party majority in the House and a 67 to 33 Democratic majority in the Senate, not all of his Great Society Legislation had been treated kindly. An unprecedented volume of social welfare legislation had been proposed by the executive branch since 1964, and most of the major items had passed. But signs that congressional support might wane were evident even before the 1966 elections, when Republicans won several seats in the House and Senate. The HUD legislation in 1965 passed the House by thirty-three votes; rent supplements passed by six. In the same year, an amendment to kill the Economic Opportunity Act lost by forty-nine votes and the Teacher Corps passed by a seventy-two-vote margin. By the second session of the Eighty-ninth Congress (January 1965 to December 1966), many members were worried that a voter blacklash against federal spending might be imminent. The costs of the Vietnam War, a rising federal budget, riots in the cities, and reaction to the feverish pace in the previous session of Congress combined to spell trouble. The antipoverty program was the target of bitter popular criticism. The Demonstration Cities bill did not escape this atmosphere unscathed, and it barely escaped at all.

Many groups opposed the Model Cities legislation, ranging from the United States Chamber of Commerce, which traditionally opposes federal spending for social programs, to some mayors who feared that federal administrators would come into their communities and tell them what to do, to southern congressmen who thought that racial integration would be forced on them through the program. The administration had to promise to increase the flow of urban renewal funds to key cities to secure the support of influential mayors. Many members of Congress were promised federal projects in their districts if they voted for the legislation: "It isn't the kind of thing you talk about, but you wouldn't be wrong if you guessed that a lot of post offices, sewers, highways and other construction projects which had been hanging fire were promised."[61]

Model Cities in Local Communities

Like the antipoverty program before it, the Model Cities program held the potential for shaking up the political status quo of local communities, but it failed to deliver. The story paralleled the antipoverty program experience: Controversial programs were threatened with termination and federal officials, reacting to pressure from members of Congress, governors and mayors, and various interest groups, minimized the most controversial aspect of the program, citizen participation.

In city after city, professional planners and government officials fought residents for control of the programs. There were frequent mass meetings where local Model Cities administrators tried to secure ratification of their decisions from citizen committees. These meetings were frequently tumultuous, with community residents shouting that they were being ignored or pushed aside. However, it was inevitable that the residents would lose out, for the planning documents were judged as acceptable or insufficient by HUD administrators on the basis of their problem analysis and program description, all written in the jargon of planning and administration, and not on the basis of citizen participation. Citizen participation is a slow process, often involving protracted political struggles among the various participants. It gets in the way of technical planning analysis, and if such analysis is emphasized, professional administrators and planners will sooner or later view citizen participation as a nuisance.

In subsequent years, residents who participated in Model Cities activities were excluded even more thoroughly. Implementation of programs through the Model Cities agencies allowed even less room than planning had, for the programs were invariably run through institutions that had never been responsive to the poor. School boards got special education money, police departments received money for crime control programs, and city departments received funds to destroy old buildings and to improve streets or sewers. These monies were channeled through the Model Cities Agencies allegedly according to spending priorities and monitoring requirements arrived at through citizen participation, but the money was then allocated to school boards, police departments, and other agencies that always had been far removed from influence by minorities or the poor.

Did Inner-City Programs Increase the Power of the Poor?

No doubt, if participation by the poor were the standard for judging the War on Poverty and Model Cities programs, they would be considered political failures. But political pressure was sometimes applied by people claiming the poor as a constituency, for even if federal programs did not increase participation at the grassroots level in the cities over the long run, they might have created conditions favoring the emergence of an assertive middle-class leadership in segregated black communities in central cities.

Working through the new community action and Model Cities agencies, black leaders in inner-city ghettos exerted pressures on government institutions to become more sensitive to their communities.

According to an analysis by Frances Fox Piven and Richard A. Cloward in their book, *Regulating the Poor*, the Great Society programs were formulated to solve the political problems of the Democratic presidency; that is, their main purpose was to preserve and strengthen the Democratic party's advantage in the industrialized states holding the largest blocs of electoral college votes. Rather than work through local politicians who had repeatedly shown an unwillingness to mobilize the votes of inner-city blacks, the federal strategy bypassed local Democratic (and Republican) leaders and established direct links between the national government and the potential inner-city electoral constituency. "The hallmark of the Great Society programs was the direct relationship between the national government and the ghettoes, a relationship in which both state and local governments were undercut."[62] Great Society programs accomplished this result by providing services, funds, and patronage directly to black organizations and leaders.

New urban programs coopted the black leadership into mainstream politics by offering inducements similar to those offered by the old-style party machines at the turn of the century. Perhaps in the short run such programs as the War on Poverty and Model Cities created discontent, and encouraged blacks to demand more from local politicians. This presented a political problem to the Johnson administration. However, the main purpose of these programs was fulfilled: Black civil rights activists and leaders of organizations were brought into local political systems, with three important outcomes—political discontent was lowered, the political strength and effectiveness of black leaders were enhanced, and these same leaders were coopted into national Democratic politics. Piven and Cloward judge the Great Society to have been a "startling success" in accomplishing its goal of "absorbing and directing many of the agitational elements in the black population."[63]

> If civil rights workers often turned federal dollars to their purposes in the short run, in the longer run they became model-cities directors, community action executives—that is, they became federal employees and contractors, subject to the constraints of federal funding and federal guidelines. In many cities the Great Society agencies became the base for new black political organizations whose rhetoric may have been thunderous but whose activities came to consist mainly of vying for position and patronage within the urban political system.[64]

In sum, the black middle-class political leadership was invigorated by federal intervention.

It must be reemphasized that the poor as such did not increase their influence through federally funded programs. Elites living within ghetto communities—educated, professional people such as lawyers, social workers, and teachers—were elected to the boards of community action agencies or Model Cities programs, and they qualified for administrative positions in these programs. Their influence in segregated black communities depended on the volume of federal money passing through their hands. When Richard Nixon assumed the presidency, federal funds were slowly withdrawn from community action and Model Cities programs. By 1974 these programs were eliminated.

The Backlash

By the 1968 presidential campaign, a full-scale counterattack was launched against "national purpose" legislation. Many of the same people who had fought against the social programs began to argue against the use of federal power to dictate national goals. One of the vocal advocates for federal activism in the 1960s had been Senator, later Vice-President, Hubert Humphrey. However, by 1972, he testified before a Senate committee that

> I have listened to and talked to many thousands of people and hundreds of elected officials and if there is one unmistakable message, it is this—never before in the history of this nation has the diversity of our people, our cities, our countries, our communities, and our states placed such an importance on how government programs are constructed, how policies are implemented, and how revenue transfers are made.
>
> We can no longer pass legislation that through bureaucratic red tape and underfunding stifles the ability of local officials to deal with indigenous problems.
>
> We can no longer assume that solutions developed in Washington will automatically work in Louisiana, Montana, Utah, Connecticut, Iowa, and California.
>
> We can no longer make minute, detailed choices as to how funds will be spent in every city and community of this nation.
>
> We simply must recognize that cities, states, and local governments are different because people are different.
>
> These differences call for new departures—if the needs of the people are ever to be met.
>
> Revenue sharing is a new departure.[65]

Decrying the proliferation of federally sponsored programs and the long delays and uncertainties inherent in the federal bureaucracy, liberals began to shift their ground.

The political support for the Great Society social programs eroded rapidly. The congressional elections of 1966 and the presidential election of 1968 seemed to signal a political backlash against social legislation. In 1966, the Republicans gained four seats in the Senate, and in the House they raised their proportion of the membership from less than one third to 43 percent. In the 1970s and 1980s, a struggle over urban policy would ensue, one that Democratic liberals were destined to lose.

References

1. Reported in *The New York Times*, December 1, 1959, p. 27, and quoted in Mark I. Gelfand, *A Nation of Cities: The Federal Government and Urban America*, Urban Life in America Series (New York: Oxford University Press, 1975), p. 295. Also see John F. Kennedy, "The Great Unspoken Issue," *Proceedings, American Municipal Congress 1959* (Washington, D.C.: American Municipal League, n.d.), pp. 23–28; and John F. Kennedy, "The Shame of the States," *The New York Times Magazine*, May 18, 1958.

2. Quoted in Theodore H. White, *The Making of the President, 1960* (New York: Atheneum, 1962), p. 206. Nixon's strategy, which White contends was no strategy at all, was a "national" one, in which he committed himself to visit all fifty states; Kennedy, on the other hand, used an "urban" strategy centered around the industrial states (see pp. 267,352).

3. John C. Donovan, *The Politics of Poverty*, 2nd ed. (New York: Bobbs-Merrill, 1973), p. 19.

4. U.S. Advisory Commission on Intergovernmental Relations, *Eleventh Annual Report* (Washington, D.C.: U.S. Government Printing Office, 1970), p. 2.

5. U.S. Congress, Senate, Committee on Government Operations, *Catalogue of Federal Aids to State and Local Governments*, Senate, 88th Cong., 2d sess., April 15, 1964.

6. U.S. Congress, Library of Congress, Legislative Reference Service, *Number of Authorizations for Federal Assistance to State and Local Governments*, by I.M. Labovitz (Washington, D.C.: Legislative Reference Service, July 5, 1966).

7. Michael Reagan, *The New Federalism* (New York: Oxford University Press, 1972), p. 55. In 1971 and 1972 there was virtually no growth in the number of grant programs, largely because of presidential vetoes. Nixon vetoed sixteen bills in 1972. (See U.S. Advisory Commission on Intergovernmental Relations, *Fourteenth Annual Report: Striking a Better Balance* (Washington, D.C.: U.S. Government Printing Office, 1973), p. 12.

8. Office of Management and Budget, *1979 Catalog of Federal Domestic Assistance* (Washington, D.C.: U.S. Government Printing Office, 1980).

9. "Citizens Budget Commission Summaries, 1952–1973," and *Mayor's Annual Report and Expense Budget Message*, May, 1973, as cited in Donald H. Haider, *When Governments Come to Washington: Governors, Mayors, and Intergovernmental Lobbying* (New York: The Free Press, 1974), p. 94.

10. Reagan, *The New Federalism*, p. 55.

11. U.S. Office of Management and Budget, *Special Analyses, Budget of the United States Government: Fiscal Year 1975* (Washington, D.C.: U.S. Government Printing Office, 1974), p. 210.

12. U.S. Advisory Commission on Intergovernmental Relations, *Significant Features of Fiscal Federalism, 1980–81 Edition* (Washington, D.C.: U.S. Government Printing Office, December 1981), p. 58.

13. Refer to Daniel J. Elazar, *The American Partnership: Intergovernmental Cooperation in the Nineteenth Century United States* (Chicago: University of Chicago Press, 1962).

14. Manpower Development and Training Act of 1962, Public Law 87-415, 87th Cong. (1962); emphasis added.

15. Economic Opportunity Act of 1964, Public Law 88-452, 88th Cong. (1964); emphasis added.

16. Demonstration Cities and Metropolitan Development Act of 1966, Public Law 89-754, 89th Cong. (1966); emphasis added.

17. See James L. Sundquist and David W. Davis, *Making Federalism Work: A Study of Program Coordination at the Community Level* (Washington, D.C.: The Brookings Institution, 1969), pp. 3–5.

18. U.S. Bureau of the Budget, *Special Analyses, Budget of the United States Government: Fiscal Year 1969* (Washington, D.C.: U.S. Government Printing Office, 1968), p. 158.

19. Refer to U.S. Advisory Commission on Intergovernmental Relations, *Eleventh Annual Report*, p. 2; and U.S. Advisory Commission on Intergovernmental Relations, *Fiscal Balance in the American Federal System*, vol. 1 (Washington, D.C.: U.S. Government Printing Office, 1967), p. 151.

20. U.S. Office of Management and Budget, *Special Analyses: Fiscal Year 1975*, p. 207.

21. See U.S. Congress, Senate Committee on Government Operations, *Creative Federalism, Hearings* before the Subcommittee on Intergovernmental Relations, pt. 2a, *The State-Local-Regional Level*, Senate, 90th Cong., 1st sess., January 31, February 1, 2, and 6, 1967, pp. 576–585.

22. Midwest Research Institute, "Federal Aid Program Information—A Survey of Local Government Needs," September 1967, p. 15.

23. U.S. Bureau of the Budget, "Summary of Recent Activities to Promote Improved Intergovernmental Relations" (memorandum), March 14, 1967.

24. Midwest Research Institute, "Federal Aid Program Information," p. 64.

25. U.S. Congress, Senate, Committee on Government Operations, *Creative Federalism*, pt. 1, pp. 138–139. HUD was also participating in forty-one different "interagency agreements, understandings, Executive Orders, and Directives."

26. U.S. Senate, Committee on Government Operations, *Creative Federalism*, pt. 1, pp. 232–233.

27. U.S. Senate, Committee on Government Operations, *Creative Federalism*, pt. 1, pp. 264.

28. U.S. Senate, Committee on Government Operations, *Creative Federalism*, p. 1, pp. 287–289. He also listed interagency committees and agreements with the

Vocational Rehabilitation Administration and committees in which the Welfare Administration was participating.

29. U.S. Executive Office of the President, Executive Order 11297, August 11, 1966.

30. See "The Quality of American Government," *Weekly Compilation of Presidential Documents*, March 17, 1967, pp. 482–494.

31. U.S. Bureau of the Budget "Summary of Recent Activities to Promote Improved Intergovernmental Relations" (memorandum), June 21, 1968.

32. U.S. Advisory Commission on Intergovernmental Relations, *Fiscal Balance*, vol. 1, pp. 175–181. Also see H. Ralph Taylor, "Greatest Opportunity— Making Model Cities Work," *Public Management* 50 (February 1968):46; and Bernard J. Frieden and Marshall Kaplan, *The Politics of Neglect: Urban Aid from Model Cities to Revenue Sharing* (Cambridge, Mass.: The M.I.T. Press, 1975) for a discussion of the "efficiency and economy" values underlying the push for planning.

33. U.S. Congress, Senate, Committee on Government Operations, *Creative Federalism*, pt. 1, p. 391.

34. Jeffrey L. Pressman, *Federal Programs and City Politics: The Dynamics of the Aid Process in Oakland*, The Oakland Project (Berkeley: University of California Press, 1975), pp. 60–61.

35. Michael Harrington, *The Other America: Poverty in the United States* (New York: Macmillan, 1962), p. 14.

36. Harrington, p. 15.

37. John C. Donovan, *The Politics of Poverty*, p. 104.

38. Quoted in Richard Blumenthal, "The Bureaucracy: Antipoverty and the Community Action Program," in *American Political Institutions and Public Policy*, ed. Allen P. Sindler (Boston: Little, Brown, 1969), p. 149.

39. Lyndon Baines Johnson, *The Vantage Point: Perspectives on the Presidency, 1963–1969* (New York: Holt, Rinehart Winston, 1971), p. 71.

40. Message from the President to the Congress (reprinted in *Congressional Quarterly Weekly Report*, January 10, 1964).

41. Kenneth B. Clark, *A Relevant War against Poverty* (New York: Metropolitan Applied Research Center, 1969), p. 19.

42. Clark, p. 20.

43. Richard A. Cloward, "The War on Poverty—Are the Poor Left Out?" *Nation*, August 2, 1965, pp. 55–56.

44. Frances Fox Piven and Richard A. Cloward, *Regulating the Poor: The Functions of Public Welfare* (New York: Pantheon, 1971), p. 295.

45. U.S. Advisory Commission on Intergovernmental Relations, *Fiscal Balance in the American Federal System*, vol. 1 (Washington, D.C.: U.S. Government Printing Office, 1967), p. 169.

46. U.S. Office of Economic Opportunity, *Community Action Workbook*, pt. 1 (Washington, D.C.: U.S. Government Printing Office, 1965), p. 18.

47. U.S. Office of Economic Opportunity, *Community Action Program Guide* (Washington, D.C.: U.S. Government Printing Office, 1965).

48. Cited in J. David Greenstone and Paul E. Peterson, "Reformers, Machines, and the War on Poverty," in *City Politics and Public Policy*, ed. James Q. Wilson (New York: John Wiley, 1968), p. 275.

49. U.S. Congress, House, Committee on Education and Labor, *Examination of The War on Poverty Program, Hearings* before the Committee on Education and Labor, House, 89th Cong., 1st sess., 1965, p. 483.

50. Quoted in William C. Selaner, "View from Capitol Hill: Harassment and Survival," in *On Fighting Poverty*, ed. James L. Sundquist (New York: Basic Books, 1968), p. 166.

51. Cited in Barbara Carter, "Sargent Shriver and the Role of the Poor," in *Poverty: Power and Politics*, ed. Chaim Waxman (New York: Grossett Dunlap, 1968), p. 212.

52. Paul E. Peterson, "City Politics and Community Action: The Implementation of the Community Action Program in Three American Cities" (Ph.D. diss., University of Chicago, 1967), p. 116.

53. The best description of this process is contained in Peter Marris and Martin Rein, *The Dilemmas of Social Reform* (New York: Atherton Press, 1967).

54. Howard W. Hallman, "The Community Action Program: An Interpretive Analysis," in *Power, Poverty and Urban Policy*, ed. Warner Bloomberg, Jr., and Henry J. Schmandt, Urban Affairs Annual Reviews, vol. 2 (Beverly Hills, Calif.: Sage Publications, 1968), pp. 285–312.

55. See Clark, *A Relevant War against Poverty*.

56. Clark, p. 118.

57. Message from the President to Congress, transmitting recommendations for City Demonstration programs (January 26, 1966); see "A Program for American Cities," *Weekly Compilation of Presidential Documents*, January 31, 1966, pp. 107–117.

58. Demonstration Cities and Metropolitan Development Act of 1966, Public Law 89-754, 89th Cong. (1966), Title I.

59. Public Law 89-754, Title.

60. Public Law 89-754, Title I.

61. *Newsweek*, October 24, 1966, pp. 42, 44.

62. Piven and Cloward, *Regulating the Poor*, p. 261.

63. Piven and Cloward, p. 274.

64. Piven and Cloward, p. 275–276.

65. U.S. Congress, Senate, Committee on Governmental Operation, *Intergovernmental Revenue Act of 1971 and Related Legislation, Hearings* before the Subcommittee on Intergovernmental Relations, Senate, 92d Cong., 1st sess., 1971, pp. 102–103.

Chapter 11

THE STRUGGLE OVER URBAN POLICY: 1968 to 1988

Political Support for Urban Programs

During the Nixon and Ford administrations, there was a concerted effort to consolidate the categorical grant programs that funded social welfare and urban policies. These reforms were justified by a heavy dose of rhetoric about balancing the federal budget by paring the number and size of such programs. Despite the public posturing, federal social welfare and urban spending continued to rise. Outlays for grants-in-aid to state and local governments, including revenue sharing, increased from $20.3 billion in fiscal 1969 to $59 billion in fiscal 1976. The proportion disbursed through block grants increased from just 2.8 to 34.5 percent.[1] It is important to note that the block grant approach represented a tinkering with the manner in which money was disbursed, but certainly not a reduction in the overall amount of spending.

But by the late 1970s, political support for urban programs had weakened. Funds for social and urban problems began to decline, and when Ronald Reagan won the 1980 presidential contest, the handwriting was on the wall. In the 1980s, the urban agenda has all but disappeared from national budgets.

The Republican Agenda: Revenue Sharing and the New Federalism

As a result of the 1968 election, the Republicans held 62 percent of the governorships and installed a president pledged to clean up the federal assistance mess and to return "power to the people" through the decentralization of domestic policy and a New Federalism.[2]

"The Sixties are ending," observed the Advisory Commission on Intergovernmental Relations,

> with substantial support of a "New Federalism" championed by the Nixon Administration by which increased reliance is placed upon State and local governments to make the multitude of public decisions required in the pursuit of domestic goals.[3]

Immediately following his 1968 election victory, President Nixon emphasized his desire to decentralize domestic government programs, and he became more outspoken on the subject during 1971 and 1972. In his 1969 revenue-sharing message, he spoke of the grant programs as producing a "gathering of the reins of power in Washington," which he saw as "a radical departure from the vision of federal-state relations the nation's founders had in mind." He referred to his proposal as "a turning point in federal-state relations, the beginning of decentralized relations of governmental power, the restoration of a rightful balance between the state capital and the national capital."[4] Nixon returned to this theme often. In a radio address titled "The Philosophy of Government", he asked,

> Do we want to turn more power over to bureaucrats in Washington in the hope that they will do what is best for all the people? Or do we want to return more power to the people and to their state and local governments so that people can decide what is best for themselves? It is time that good, decent people stopped letting themselves be bulldozed by anybody who presumes to be the self-righteous moral judge of our society. In the next four years, as in the past four, I will continue to direct the flow of power away from Washington and back to the people.[5]

The president devised a two-fold strategy to achieve his objectives. First, he ordered reviews of the major programs left over from the Johnson administration. Throughout his first term, he repeatedly attempted to reduce spending on social programs. In a more positive vein, he proposed a new revenue-sharing program through which the federal government would give money to state and localities with few restrictions on how it could be spent. This would, he said,

> reverse the flow of power and resources from the States and communities to Washington, and start power and resources flowing back from Washington to the States and communities, and more important, to the people all across America.
> The time has come for a new partnership between the Federal government and the States and localities.[6]

His revenue-sharing proposal, submitted to Congress in 1971, promised to give state and local officials substantial freedom to spend federal money according to their own priorities. This was fundamentally different from the objectives that had been stated in the national purpose legislation under Democratic administrations. The preamble to the revenue-sharing legislation promised:

> to restore balance in the Federal system of government in the United States; to provide both the flexibility and resources for State and local government officials to exercise leadership in solving their own problems; to achieve a better allocation of total public resources and to provide for the sharing with State and local governments a portion of the tax revenues received by the United States.[7]

The revenue-sharing plan was intended to be the centerpiece of domestic policy for the Nixon administration. The administration contended that implementation of the plan would go a long way toward addressing the complaints that local officials had expressed about the complexity of the grants-in-aid system. Of the $16.1 billion proposed for distribution under revenue sharing for the first year, $5 billion was to be in the form of general revenue sharing and $11.1 billion was to be allocated to state and local governments through "special" or categorical revenue sharing in six functional areas.[8]

The presidential proposal stole the initiative from the Democrats. The idea of revenue sharing had been around for years. Initially it was developed by Walter Heller, a former University of Minnesota professor and chairman of the Council of Economic Advisors in the Democratic administrations of the early 1960s. Like so many others, he had noticed that "prosperity gives the national government the affluence and the local governments the effluents."[9] The federal income tax structure was such that tax revenues from this source grew at a rate 1.5 times that of the economy— for every 10 percent increase in economic growth, the government registered a 15 percent rise in tax revenues. The result, by 1963, was the prospect of excess revenues in the federal treasury.[10]

Concerned that the projected budgetary surpluses might slow economic growth, Heller proposed that the national government share its surplus with the nation's states and cities. Especially for the big cities, which were caught in a constant revenue crunch, federal revenue sharing would be a blessing.

Revenue sharing was never seriously considered by the Democratic presidents. Instead, the national purpose programs captured their attention. Additionally, much-publicized tax cuts were enacted in 1962 and 1964. Spending on social and economic programs and reductions in the tax rates were politically visible. The Democratic policymakers surmised that the public would take notice of such actions long before they appreciated intergovernmental transfers of revenue for general purposes.[11]

The adoption of revenue sharing was secured through the cooperation of two rather different political groups. One was composed of state and local public officials, including mayors, governors, city managers, county executives, and others. Their main incentive for pursuing the matter through the halls of Congress was to gain access to additional (i.e., federal) resources in order to ameliorate their fiscal problems.

The second major group was drawn together by ideological and political concerns over the expansion of the federal government's role in domestic policy. Conservatives were appalled by the centralization of domestic policy that had occurred during the Great Society years.

Political conservatives fully understood the dynamics of the political system with which they were tinkering. At the federal level, the power of political interest groups is balanced differently than in local politics. "The plain fact is that large population groups are better represented in the constituencies of the President and the Congress than they are in the constituencies of the governors and legislatures."[12] The values of equity, equality, and social justice receive a fuller hearing in national politics than they do at other levels of government.[13] In a congressional debate, for example, a civil rights law is somewhat abstract. In local politics, it translates into access to jobs, housing, and schools.

In the 1960s, this fact led to broad support for federal activism. Liberals had succeeded in elevating conflict about policy to the national arena because the electoral strength of the Democratic party was located in the cities. City officials wanted to move policy issues out of the state legislatures and into national politics because they knew national political leaders would be more sympathetic to their fiscal plight. "City leaders sought to promote direct federal aid as a defensive weapon against state intransigence."[14]

One consequence of removing social policy to the national arena, however, was that local political leaders lost some of their autonomy. Their control over politics slipped; for example, antipoverty workers protested city hall decisions, and nonprofit housing organizations proposed federally funded housing projects in white areas. Sometimes the political cost of accepting federal money was high, so of course local officials sought escape.

Support for revenue sharing was centered in a group of public interest organizations known as the Big Seven. The institutional members of this powerful coalition included the National League of Cities (NLC), the United States Conference of Mayors (USCM), the National Governors' Conference, the National Legislative Conference, the Council of State Governments, the National Association of Counties, and the International City Management Association (ICMA). These groups covered the spectrum of all important state and local policymaking institutions. The ICMA was a newcomer to the intergovernmental lobbying structure. It represented "professionals" who had long viewed political activities as beyond their purview; they now broke with a fifty-year tradition of "neutrality" vis à vis legislative issues to vigorously support revenue sharing.[15]

With these groups backing the concept of shared revenues, the ensuing political battle pitted the fiscal interests of local elected officials against the ideological and philosophical concerns of social welfare liberals.

Many of the social reform groups that had been an important part of the liberal-urban coalition that supported the expansion of the federal role now opposed the retrenchment implicit in the New Federalism's revenue sharing. Organized labor, except for the American Federation of State, County, and Municipal Employees (AFSCME), which correctly perceived that its members would be beneficiaries of the plan, decried the concept. The AFL-CIO, long a friend of urban interests and an important component of the Democratic electoral coalition, opposed the lack of national purpose and federal oversight in the proposed "giveaway" sharing plan.[16] The union group's executive council articulated its position in February 1971:

> The AFL-CIO urges complete rejection of this revenue sharing proposal. We are firmly convinced that such no-strings money will not add one Federal penny to the money available to the states and localities. It will merely be a substitute for the full funding of existing programs . . . critical needs could be by-passed in the expenditure of these federal monies. There is no reason to believe that each of the fifty states and 81,000 cities, boroughs, townships and school districts is in a better position to weigh and balance national priority needs, and use Federal Funds to meet them more effectively and efficiently. Moreover, without specified and enforceable federal performance standards, there is no assurance that federal civil rights guarantees and fair labor practices will be applied to projects supported by no-strings federal grants.[17]

Civil rights groups also opposed revenue sharing, fearing that social programs benefitting minorities would be abandoned.

Many liberals opposed revenue sharing because they thought it placed too much trust in the competence and intent of local governments. They argued that local governments lacked the vision and financial capacity to attempt social programs, and could not be depended on to respond to social needs:

> Fiscal poverty and poverty of ideas often go together in state government, especially when the programs are designed to help the least affluent and influential of citizens . . . states are loath to spend additional dollars unless compelled to.[18]

> . . .revenue sharing is a cop-out as regards the almost universally admitted inadequacies of state and local governmental structure and financial systems.[19]

Conservatives and liberals were not uniform in their positions regarding revenue sharing. Some conservative organizations, for example, did not see revenue sharing as an alternative to social programs: they didn't want either. One of the more active groups of this type was the United States Chamber of Commerce (USCC). Its opposition stemmed from its general ideological position opposing any expansion of the public sector at any level. It is significant to note, however, that the USCC Committee on Urban Problems advocated support of the revenue-sharing proposal within the organization. The organization's commitment to the philosophy of private enterprise and the unfettered market won out in the end, however, and the USCC became an active opponent of the Big Seven, going to the extreme of issuing an "action call" to all its affiliated local chambers to pressure their respective senators and representatives to vote against the revenue-sharing proposal.[20]

Another always conservative, antiurban group, the American Farm Bureau Federation, referred to the proposal as "deficit-sharing" during its testimony in opposition to the plan.[21]

The Democratic party and the liberal-urban coalition was deeply split over revenue sharing. The mayors, a key element in both the policy and electoral coalitions, strongly supported the proposal by this time. The fiscal crisis of the cities had deepened with no bottom in sight, and even the liberal mayors were forced to support practically any new source of revenues.

In a report commissioned by the National League of Cities in 1967, the nation's cities were estimated to be facing a gap between revenues and expenditures totaling $262 billion over the decade ending in 1975. Less than half of this staggering figure could be expected to be raised through federal grant programs. Even assuming increased municipal revenue tax rates and more state funding, total city debts could be expected to rise by $63 billion to meet the gap (see Table 11–1).[22] The National Urban

TABLE 11-1   Estimated Annual Revenue Gaps and Recommended
Funding Sources, 1966–1975 (Billions of Dollars)

		Funding sources			
				Increases	Increases
	Estimated	Federal		in city	in net
Year	gap	government	States	charges	city debt
1966	4.5	1.0	—	0.5	3.0
1967	8.0	3.0	1.0	1.0	3.0
1968	12.0	6.0	2.0	1.0	3.0
1969	16.5	8.0	3.0	1.5	4.0
1970	22.0	10.0	4.0	2.0	6.0
1971	28.5	13.0	5.0	2.5	8.0
1972	34.5	16.0	6.0	3.5	9.0
1973	40.0	19.0	8.0	4.0	9.0
1974	45.5	23.0	9.0	4.5	9.0
1975	50.0	26.0	11.0	4.5	9.0
TOTAL	262.0	125.0	49.0	25.0	63.0

Source: National League of Cities, U.S. Conference of Mayors, and International City Management Association, *The Fiscal Plight of American Cities*, table X, as presented in Richard E. Thompson, *Revenue Sharing: A New Era in Federalism* (Washington, D.C.: Revenue Sharing Advisory Service, 1973), p. 146. Reprinted by permission of the author.

Coalition predicted in 1971 that the difference between the revenues and expenditures of the nation's cities would reach $94 billion annually by 1976, even assuming passage of the revenue-sharing bill. The needs of the nation's cities were indeed critical.[23]

The seriousness of the fiscal gap was evidenced by major cutbacks in municipal services. The 1971 National Municipal Survey reported, for example, that:

Pittsburgh recently closed fourteen fire stations; *Philadelphia* would soon have to reduce various police support units; *Cincinnati* was cutting back on school libraries, kindergartens, and teaching staffs; *Hamtramck* was so very near bankruptcy that its mayor requested that HEW stop the flow of federal funds—the city could no longer supply the necessary matching funds; *Detroit* was forced to lay off 600 municipal employees and keep 2,200 authorized positions vacant due to the lack of sufficient funds, and, given the plight of the city's treasury, would need an additional 26 million new dollars to keep from backsliding any further—just to stay even; *New York* had 1 million persons on its welfare rolls— requiring annual welfare outlays of 600 million dollars in that category alone.[24]

In St. Louis, the budgetary crisis reached such proportions that Mayor A.J. Cervantes appeared before the board of aldermen with this speech:

> Having delivered several budget speeches over the years, I know that you will say that every year is another crisis. Today, however, the situation is even more desperate than in the past, and we must face up to the fact that we are scraping the bottom of the revenue barrel.
>
> This is the last year the City can make a budget which will come anywhere near adequately meeting the needs of our citizens. Working under the limitations of state constitution and state law, there are no other viable means of local revenue, in my opinion.[25]

As a result, the Metropolitan Youth Commission, the Regional Development Corporation, the Challenge of the 70s Committee, and the Meramec Hills Home for Delinquent Girls were eliminated from the budget. And in order to try to make ends meet, the St. Louis Board of Estimate and Apportionment also curtailed the following: the Child Guidance Program, Street Department, Human Development Corporation, Fire Department, Traffic Division, Forestry Division, Recreation Department, City Hospital, and maintenance for municipal buildings.[26]

The congressional leaders of the Democratic party, although sympathetic to the cities' plight, resisted the pressure to approve revenue sharing. With a national election only a year away, the Democratic legislative leadership and presidential aspirants were loath to give the Republican incumbent any type of domestic victory. Such Democratic mayors as Pittsburgh's Peter Flaherty and Cleveland's Carl Stokes considered this attitude an "ill-advised . . . partisan reflex"[27] to what they considered a nonpartisan issue.

The tension between the Democratic leadership's partisan needs and the fiscal needs of the big city mayors came to a head in a March, 1971, private meeting between the House leadership and the United States Conference of Mayors' Legislative Action Committee.

> As one of those in attendance recalls it, New York's Mayor John V. Lindsay had just gotten up to speak, when Majority Leader Hale Boggs (D-La.) suddenly slammed his fist on the desk and shouted: "You don't need to make any points. Revenue sharing is dead. I'll see that it never passes. So let's get on to something else." Flabbergasted, Lindsay slid back into his seat. There was a moment of embarrassed silence—and then a rolling southern drawl rang out from the back of the room. "Hale," said New Orleans Mayor Moon Landrieu, "that's the rudest treatment I have ever witnessed, and I think you better talk about revenue sharing and you better listen. Because, Hale, if you don't start thinking about helping the cities, I want you to know that you'll never be welcome in the city of New Orleans again." Now it was Boggs' turn to be flabbergasted.[28]

After this heated exchange, the Democratic leadership began to seriously reassess the soundness of its position. Party Chairman Lawrence O'Brien worked to mend the deteriorating urban pillar of the party's electoral coalition, straining to bind the party together. Finally, Representative Wilbur Mills, the powerful chair of the House Ways and Means Committee, dropped his opposition to the concept of revenue sharing. Being a back-burner presidential aspirant, he proposed a plan of his own—a $3.5 billion emergency aid plan for the cities—and opened the way for Democratic approval of the revenue-sharing concept. The internal wounds of the party began to heal.[29]

Even within the Big Seven lobby, there was dissention over the policy implications of the revenue-sharing proposals. The principal points of contention among the several groups centered around the appropriate formulas for dividing the federal monies. Both mayors and governors, logically enough, desired to maximize their own "equitable" share of the revenue pie. Ideas ranged from all the money going to the states with pass-through provisions to be worked out at that level, to all funding being allocated to the cities and the states being left out completely (the Mills plan). After several months of haggling, a compromise was reached. Two-thirds of the amount given to the states would be directly allocated to the cities (and other local governments), and one-third to the state governments.

Having emerged moderately victorious in that battle, urban interests turned toward the apportionment formula. In this vital matter, there was a direct conflict between the urbanized and the nonurbanized states. Reflecting the composition of the Ways and Means Committee membership that drafted the legislation, the House adopted a five-factor formula that closely approximated a "fair" per capita share, balancing allocation between urban and rural interests. The Senate, on the other hand, disagreed with the House allocation procedure. Again reflecting the makeup of the appropriate substantive committee (the Finance Committee, chaired by Russell Long of Louisiana) and the overall small-state bias of representation in the Senate as a body, the Senate adopted a three-factor allocation formula that reduced the proportion that would go to urban areas. By substituting a factor for poverty and total tax effort, the Senate version allocated a higher proportion of the total funds to the smaller, poorer, rural states of the South and Southwest.[30]

Urban interests watched intently as the two bills were sent to the House and Senate Conference Committees. Adoption of the House formula, as opposed to the Senate version of an allocation plan, would benefit the big cities. A classic compromise was worked out. Both formulas were to be used, with the choice left to the individual states.[31]

The passage of the State and Local Fiscal Assistance Act of 1972[32] marked the culmination of four years of intense efforts by big city mayors and other government officials to gain largely unrestricted access to the federal treasury. Revenue sharing was passed as a result of four basic political facts: (a) all the groups concerned, primarily the Big Seven, agreed on it as a high-priority measure; (2) a shaky but essential consensus was hammered out with respect to the division of money between the states and their local governments; (3) it received the highest priority from the president; and (4) the Democratic congressional leadership reluctantly agreed to allow the president a domestic policy victory on this issue.[33]

The signing of the revenue-sharing bill might have been interpreted as a bad omen by social welfare liberals who thought it presaged neglect of the nation's social problems. Officials representing every level of the American political system were present in Philadelphia for the outdoor ceremony. But after the signing, the new law was left behind as officials scurried off. The State and Local Fiscal Assistance Act of 1972 almost suffered the windy fate of a candy wrapper as the document was left unattended:

> . . . After the great ceremony of signing under the shadow of Independence Hall, nobody picked up the bill. And after everybody else had left, it was still sitting there. One of the policemen picked it up and asked: "Does anybody want this?"[34]

The Impact of the New Federalism

The revenue-sharing legislation granted local officials considerable autonomy in spending federal money. Unlike the grant-in-aid programs, few strings and little red tape were attached to the funds. Such guidelines as had to be followed were minimal and virtually meaningless in the face of the reality of government accounting procedures. Because of the lack of detailed federal oversight, revenue-sharing dollars were indistinguishable from other money in the over 39,000 state, county, township, and municipal treasuries across the nation. As such, they could not be traced beyond the actual use reports filed by local officials with the Treasury Department. They were, as they were intended to be by the Big Seven and the Nixon administration, a largely unrestricted supplement to the general revenues of state and local governments.

The actual amount of revenue-sharing money has constituted only a small component of the budgets of local governments. In 1974, the $4.5 billion apportioned among 35,077 local governments accounted for 3.1 percent of their revenues for that year. The relatively small size of the general revenue-sharing contribution to the total resources of the cities prevented it from having a significant impact on the municipal balance sheet.[35]

Local governments, and cities in particular, reported that they channeled the largest proportion of their revenue-sharing funds into governmental functions outside the general rubric of social services. Most cities during fiscal year 1973 put the money into transportation, environment and conservation, and public safety (see Table 11–2).

A substantial portion of these funds was allocated to public safety, meaning police and fire protection services. Townships and counties reported that they spent 33 percent of their revenue-sharing funds on such services in 1973. Cities spent even more—44 percent of their revenue-sharing funds—on public safety. Big cities, which were in the worst financial shape, put even more into fire and police: the nation's fifty-five largest cities spent 59 percent of their revenue-sharing funds this way.[36]

These figures stand in striking contrast to reported expenditure patterns by the states. Because of the tradition that police and fire services are principally local matters, the states spent very little (2 percent of the total in 1973) on public safety. The largest expenditure by the states, completely reversing the priorities of the cities, was education.

One of the significant aspects of the reported actual use of revenue sharing was the distinction between capital expenditures for such things as highways, parks, and new equipment, and operating and maintenance expenses. Only 33 percent of the revenue-sharing funds spent in 1973 went for capital improvements. Financially strapped big cities spent most of their funds just to "keep things going." While cities in general spent 56 percent on operations and maintenance, cities with populations over 250,000 reported spending 79 percent in this category. The five largest cities—New York, Chicago, Los Angeles, Philadelphia, and Detroit—reflecting their intractable day-to-day fiscal problems, reported spending 97 percent of their revenue-sharing funds for operations and maintenance.[37]

It appears that the enactment of general revenue sharing resulted in a drop of 10 percentage points for the human resources portion of federal assistance to states and localities. Human resources accounted for 69 percent of all grant-in-aid outlays in 1972, the last pre–revenue sharing fiscal year. Because 11 percent of domestic outlays went to the revenue-sharing program, human resources suffered a net loss of 14 percentage points in its share of the budget.[38] States and localities reported spending 35 percent of their revenue-sharing monies, or approximately 4 percent of the total federal outlays for grants-in-aid, on human resources. By adding this amount to the fiscal 1973 budget, we find that 59 percent of all federal assistance to state and local governments in 1973 went into human resources, a drop of 10 percentage points in a single year.[39] The big "winners," understandably, were general government services, which registered a gain in their proportion of the federal grant-in-aid budget, from 2 to 8 percent.[40]

TABLE 11–2 Reported Use of General Revenue Sharing Funds, January 1972–June 1973 (Amounts in Millions of Dollars)

Function	States (50 states and Puerto Rico)		All cities (15,785 cities)		Cities of 250,000 and over (55 cities)	
	Amount	%	Amount	%	Amount	%
Public Safety	20.0	2	434.0	44	208.9	59
Environment/Conservation	7.4	1	126.0	13	40.0	12
Transportation	55.6	5	148.7	15	35.2	10
Health	30.7	3	50.3	5	10.5	3
Recreation/Culture	3.7	*	76.6	8	27.8	8
Libraries**	—		10.4	1	3.8	1
Social Services	61.2	6	11.7	1	7.8	2
Financial Administration	18.5	2	16.0	2	3.8	1
Education	664.3	65	4.7	*	0.2	*
General Government	5.9	1	68.7	7	9.3	3
Housing/Community Development	1.1	*	14.4	2	1.2	*
Economic Development	2.2	*	7.3	1	3.3	1
Other***	151.9	15	11.7	1	0.4	*
Operations and Maintenance	959.1	94	546.3	56	277.9	79
Capital Expenditures	63.4	6	431.2	44	75.2	21

Source: Adapted from U.S. Department of the Treasury, Office of Revenue Sharing, *Revenue Sharing: The First Actual Use Reports*, by David A. Caputo and Richard L. Cole (Washington, D.C.: U.S. Government Printing Office, 1974), pp. 4, 10–11, 29.
*Less than 0.5 percent.
**State expenditures for libraries are included under "other"—"libraries" not being a separate reporting category for states.
***Includes "social development."

Most mayors were satisfied with the general revenue-sharing program. The program had given the city halls more autonomy from federal oversight. The only substantial criticisms of the program were offered by liberal and civil rights groups who objected to the political implications of policy decentralization. The Reverend Jesse Jackson, a Chicago civil rights activist and director of Operation PUSH, typified this sentiment when he decried the antipoor bias of general revenue sharing:

> Most statehouses, county courthouses, and city halls are dominated by the more advantaged sectors of the body politic.
> Revenue sharing funds, in contrast to certain categorical aids targeted on the poor as a group, do not flow in sufficient quantities to help those local governments, particularly the major central cities, with extraordinary concentrations of poor people.[41]

The Democratic leadership in Congress continued to be uneasy with general revenue sharing. Political self-interest alone would have led the Democrats to be unhappy with the decentralization of decision-making that accompanied distribution of the federal largesse. The orientation of the congressional party liberals led them to support federal authority in the formation and implementation of national goals. Many congressional liberals felt that the social needs that had been the object of so many policy initiatives during the 1960s were being undermined by the revenue-sharing program.[42]

Only months after the first checks were sent out by the Revenue Sharing Office, congressional Democrats began to complain about the manner in which the money was being spent. Representative Shirley Chisholm of New York voiced concern "that the program failed to aid the disadvantaged and minority groups."[43] Other members of Congress were concerned that revenue-sharing funds were not going to those who needed them the most but were being used to aid the "haves" instead.[44]

Liberal acquiescence to the program had been bought with the promise that general revenue sharing would exist in addition to, not instead of, the multitude of federal assistance programs. The outcry was immediate and loud when it became clear that in the Nixon administration's fiscal 1974 budget "the birth of general revenue sharing is being used to justify the homicide of selected social programs."[45]

Despite the offended ideological and political interests of congressional liberals and the Democratic leadership, general revenue sharing was extended in 1976. Again it was the unrelenting political pressure applied by representatives of the Big Seven, especially the big-city mayors, that prodded the Democratic Congress to act. The United States Conference of Mayors, a central organization in this coalition, adopted a resolution "supporting reenactment of the general revenue sharing program and promising to make renewal a key local issue in the Congressional campaigns."[46]

The extension of general revenue sharing reflected only a partial success for the interests of the Big Seven and the political conservatives. As adopted, the extension did not provide annual increments in the level of funding. Under the impact of inflation, the level of funding, measured in 1972 dollars, dropped 17 percent between 1972 and 1979.[47] Also, instead of extending the program for five and three-quarters years as proposed by the Ford administration, Congress extended revenue sharing for only three and three-quarters years. Both of these decisions reflected the wariness of Democratic members of Congress about revenue sharing. The ideological conflict over revenue sharing was far from settled.

In 1980, Congress amended the revenue sharing legislation, eliminating the states as recipients. Through the first half of the 1980s, revenue sharing constituted about 1.5 percent of municipal budgets, and was eliminated entirely at the end of Fiscal Year 1986.

Other Republican Initiatives

Although revenue sharing was surely the cornerstone of President Nixon's New Federalism, he pursued other policy initiatives that affected the interests of urban America. His domestic policy "centered around the New Federalism objectives of simplifying government operations and transferring planning and management functions to State and local governments."[48]

Early in his first term, the Office of Management and Budget issued a series of administrative orders that were intended to rationalize the grant-in-aid programs. Metropolitan and regional planning and coordination was encouraged through the most influential of these circulars, A-95. Other such memoranda strengthened the power of elected officials to control federal programs within their jurisdictions and required uniform federal practices in grant relationships.[49]

Another Nixon administration program included the "planned variations" component within the Model Cities program. Twenty cities were invited to participate. The first "variation" allowed cities to expand the Model Cities projects beyond the target neighborhoods to include the entire city, with additional funds being provided for that purpose. A second variation simplified Model Cities regulations. The third, and the most popular, variation required evaluation and recommendations by the city's chief executive on all federal grant applications arising from a city.[50] Mayors now had a coveted veto over all Model Cities operations.

The principal thrust of the Nixon administration's urban policy was an attempt to consolidate grant programs, to reduce the plethora of national purpose programs into a manageable handful of block grants. As in the case of general revenue sharing, the main objective of such consolidations was to minimize the relative power of the national government in domestic affairs and to maximize the authority of state and local government officials. The main administration initiatives along these lines were the special revenue-sharing proposals of 1971. Under these programs, $11.1 billion, twice the amount proposed for the subsequently enacted general revenue plan, was to be apportioned among the eligible jurisdictions. The monies were to be applied by state and local governments to programs within six broad areas: urban community development ($2 billion), rural community development ($1 billion), education ($3 billion), manpower training ($2 billion), law enforcement ($0.5 billion), and transportation ($2.6 billion).[51]

These proposals were not well received by the Democratic-controlled Congress, and were not enacted *en masse* as proposed by the Nixon administration. Portions of the plan, however, did find their way into the statute books.

Under the Comprehensive Education and Manpower Act of 1973, some 10,000 federal employment training contracts funded by the national purpose legislation of the 1960s were replaced with 50 state and 350 big city block grants. Consistent with the underlying philosophy of the New Federalism, the powers of the big city mayors to veto programs and allocate funds were enhanced under the provisions of the Act. Federal grant money for employment training programs in cities of 100,000 or larger was sent directly to the offices of the mayors. Implementation of the statute proceeded at the direction of the local chief executive.

The Housing and Community Development Act

The Housing and Community Development Act of 1974 constituted the most important attempt since the Model Cities program to formulate a comprehensive national policy for the cities. Like the Model Cities legislation, it recognized that urban communities had problems that required "systematic and sustained federal aid," and also like Model Cities, which hoped to coordinate private and public resources and promote planning, the Community Development Act promised "increased private investment and streamlining of all levels of government programming."[52]

President Nixon had initially proposed a consolidation of housing and urban programs in 1970. His proposal had invited an onslaught of counterproposals from Democrats in Congress. Finally, however, in August 1974, the Housing and Community Development Act was signed into law and took effect on January 1, 1975. The Act evolved as an amalgam of New Federalist efforts to decentralize domestic policymaking and Democratic efforts to increase funding levels for urban programs. The Act "secured a continuation of the traditional public housing and subsidized housing programs" as well as new, consolidated "community development and housing assistance programs that rely, heavily, on local government and private market activities."[53]

The Housing and Community Development Act of 1974 replaced seven categorical grant programs with a single block-grant authorization. Among the superceded programs were several of special importance to the nation's cities, grants for water and sewerage systems, neighborhood facilities and land acquisition programs, code enforcement and neighborhood development, urban renewal, and Model Cities. Of the $8.4 billion authorized by Congress for the first three years, Standard Metropolitan Statistical Areas were to receive 80 percent. Most, but not all, of the money was distributed according to a formula based on population, the extent of poverty, and housing overcrowding.

This program was significant to the urban areas of the nation, for it facilitated redistribution of grant funds administered by the Department of Housing and Urban Development away from the smaller cities and towns toward the larger cities (Table 11–3). The average city of more than 100,000 registered a 1 to 4 percent net increase in federal funding. The annual amounts of grants-in-aid under HUD-administered programs to cities of smaller size decreased, with cities of less than 10,000 persons experiencing an average 38 percent loss. Ironically, the implementation of the Nixon administration's philosophy of decentralization penalized the Republican party's natural base of support in "middle America," in the smaller cities and towns where conservative, pro-Republican sentiments were ascendant.

Unlike general revenue sharing, the new program required governments to apply for community development block-grant funds, with a portion of the monies awarded on a competitive basis and in accordance with performance standards and review procedures.[54] In fact, Congress specified unusually detailed administrative procedures, no doubt reflecting a lack of confidence in HUD's ability to formulate adequate standards. The legislation called for yearly application and evaluation, and required a three-year development plan from the applying community. Communities also were required, among other things, to project "long-range community objectives," to include a housing assistance plan for the poor and elderly, to respect equal opportunity and environmental protection guidelines, and to give "maximum feasible priority" to low- and moderate-income areas.[55] The last item probably was the most clearly stated "national purpose" in the legislation.

TABLE 11-3 Comparison of Community Development Block Grants and HUD Categorical Grants: Average Annual Monetary Grants, by City Size*

City size (1970 census)	Number of cities	Average annual grants (thousands of dollars)		% change
		Categorical grants (FY 1968–1972)	Community development block grants** (FY 1974)	
500,000+	26	23,459	23,776	+ 1
250,000–499,999	30	9,841	9,981	+ 4
100,000–249,999	97	3,381	3,722	+ 4
50,000– 99,999	232	1,191	1,149	– 4
25,000– 49,999	455	954	922	– 3
10,000– 24,999	1,127	600	554	– 8
Under 9,999	16,699	332	207	–38

Source: Adapted from U.S. Department of Housing and Urban Development, Office of Community Planning and Development, Office of Evaluation, *Housing and Community Development Act of 1974, Community Development Block Grant Program: First Annual Report* (Washington, D.C.: U.S. Government Printing Office, 1975), p. 142.

*Data exclude Puerto Rico, the Virgin Islands, and Guam, as well as places not considered incorporated by the Bureau of the Census.

**SMSA discretionary funds not included.

The first few months of implementation were characterized by delays and confusion. HUD was in the midst of a bureaucratic shake-up, which made policymaking extremely difficult. Carla Hills became Secretary of HUD in March 1975. But the real confusion was found in the middle ranks, where bureaucrats had to devise new regulations and procedures. For the first several months, the HUD bureaucracy repeatedly changed the rules on nearly everything: eligibility, review requirements, forms, and deadlines.[56]

Through all the chaos, HUD claimed big improvements over past practices. By the end of the first year, Secretary Hills said that HUD had reduced the average review period from two years for the programs that the Community Development Act replaced to forty-nine days, and that applications averaged 50 pages, compared with 1,400 pages for the old urban renewal applications.[57]

The most important features were not to be found in the procedures, however, but in the results. How was the money spent? In its first annual report, HUD reported that 71 percent of all community development funds were allocated to priority areas.[58] A year later, in its second annual report, HUD had revised its calculation to represent the actual proportion of lower-income residents in such areas, rather than counting the number of areas defined by municipalities as "low and moderate income." In the cities, the percentage of funds being spent for low- and moderate-income individuals averaged 44.1 percent.[59]

Evidence indicated that southern cities had allocated more money to affluent areas than the national studies suggested. According to the Southern Regional Council, "the very mixed achievements of southern cities had shown that local diversions from national purpose are not just occasional abuses, but rather form a pattern inherent in the implementation of the Act."[60] The national purpose the Council referred to was the congressional intent that most funds should be allocated to low- and moderate-income areas.

That community development funds would be spent in affluent areas was hardly a surprising turn of events. Since local discretion governed expenditures, local political elites held a controlling influence in the allocation process. Poorer areas, of course, lacked influence in these communities. In Little Rock, Arkansas, for example, $150,000 from the city's Community Development Block Grant (CDBG) was used to construct a tennis court in a wealthy section of town. When questioned about this use of funds, the director of the local Department of Human Resources noted that "ninety-nine percent of this money is going to low- and moderate-income areas." But he revealingly continued: "You cannot divorce politics from that much money. We remember the needs of the people who vote because they hold us accountable. Poor people don't vote."[61]

One strategy that local communities employed to make it appear that funds were flowing to priority (low- and moderate-income) areas was to draw their funding district boundaries in such a way as to include affluent and less affluent people within the same areas, a process much like gerrymandering congressional seats. In Gulfport, Mississippi, for example, the city council declared the entire city to be an urban renewal area in order to facilitate the use of CDBG funds on citywide projects, notably a new central fire station. "When you expand fire protection, everybody in every census tract benefits from lower insurance rates," including, ostensibly, the primary target population of the legislation, low- and moderate-income residents.[62] Whether census tracts or special planning districts were used, the result was often the same. Analyses of a number of individual cities demonstrated higher-than-expected Community Development Block Grant allocations in more affluent areas; a study by the Brookings Institution examined the distribution of CDBG funds in sixty-two cities and found that only 29 percent of the monies were spent in neighborhoods with lower than median family incomes.[63]

The Carter administration began to crack down on communities that flagrantly ignored the congressional intent that funds be targeted toward low- and moderate-income areas. "HUD Secretary Patricia R. Harris and Assistant Secretary Robert C. Embry . . . told mayors bluntly that they will have to concentrate their CD [Community Development] programs in poorer areas, instead of scattering projects all over town."[64] The administration examined the applications of the grant recipients more carefully than the Ford administration had. The impact of the new commitment was soon felt:

> An application by Hempstead, New York, was turned down . . . because of the community's poor record on low-income housing. . . . the city of Boca Raton, Florida, hurriedly approved a subsidized housing project in order to save a $400,000 grant.[65]

In May, 1979, HUD enforced new regulations that required communities to target 75 percent of their CDBG funds to benefit priority areas. But the way such areas were to be defined was left vague. One study of Denver, Colorado, found that a redistribution of funds to middle-income areas had taken place, with poor areas the biggest losers and better-off areas only modest losers.[66] Almost certainly this was because HUD's desire to put the money into relatively marginal areas conflicted with its desire to use federal money to "leverage" private investment, and investors were more likely to build projects in basically sound areas than in marginal areas of the city.

During the debates over the Housing and Community Development Act, and before its passage, Anthony Downs, then president of the Real Estate Research Corporation in Chicago and a consultant for HUD, recommended that urban programs be targeted to maximize their potential for securing private investment that would turn deteriorated neighborhoods around.[67] His "triage" model borrowed on the system of treating wounded French soldiers during World War I. Medical personnel classified the wounded into three groups: those who were so badly wounded that they could not be saved, and who were given painkillers (the equivalent, here, of fully deteriorated neighborhoods); those who would die without treatment, but would probably live with it, and to whom maximum treatment was given (partially deteriorated neighborhoods); and those who would survive even without medical care or with minimal care (healthy neighborhoods). Based on the triage concept, Downs recommended that areas within cities be divided up into three categories: healthy, transitional, and deteriorated. Transitional neighborhoods, he thought, should receive highly visible projects to stimulate private investment.[68] Under the terms of the Community Development Act, these transitional areas would normally qualify as "priority" areas. Thus poor neighborhoods might receive little or nothing.

Roger Starr took the triage analogy to what may have been its logical conclusion.[69] Starr advocated the idea that the most blighted urban areas should receive reduced public services and expenditures so that resources (both federal and local) could be concentrated in areas that were likely to attract private investment and, as a consequence, recover. Local governments generally denied that they used the triage strategy; to admit to such a policy would incite opposition from the residents of poorer neighborhoods.

But it is clear that the triage approach was used by many cities. Four years before Starr's drastic recommendation that city services be effectively withdrawn from deteriorated neighborhoods, a plan using the triage model was advocated in St. Louis. In a 1974 report to the city planning commission, a St. Louis consulting firm recommended that the city reduce services and discourage investment in severely blighted areas and allocate most of its resources to declined but salvagable neighborhoods.[70] Commenting in 1978 on the policy recommendations in the 1974 report, one of its authors wrote:

> The Land Reutilization Authority is increasing its holdings and its land banking property [in severely blighted areas] either by chance or design . . . other parts of the strategy memo are now in the process of being implemented.[71]

Another researcher showed that a similar triage approach underpinned the "Chicago 21" plan for redevelopment of the Loop in Chicago.[72] Similarly, community development funds in Denver were distributed in conformity with a triage strategy partly by policy design. According to two Denver researchers, it would be surprising indeed if this were not the case in other cities, considering the guidelines established by the federal government.[73]

During the Carter administration, HUD's policies emphasized strategies to stimulate private investment. According to Patricia R. Harris, the Secretary of HUD, "The specific intent of action programs will be to stimulate new and increased private investment while establishing private sector confidence that will protect current investment."[74] This philosophy dictated the federal government's implementation of the Housing and Community Development Act. The Act called for special attention to areas that were suitable for the strategy of using public funds to stimulate private investment. On March 27, 1978, the White House issued a document entitled "New Partnership to Conserve America's Communities."[75] The first section of this document emphasized the loss of private sector investment in the central cities, and the fiscal strain placed on local governments as a result of this loss. Thus "the loss of private sector activity, and of middle-income households, has eroded the tax base of many urban areas."[76] The logic behind the new partnership, and Carter's policy, was that urban programs should be directed toward leveraging private sector investment.

As a consequence, cities were encouraged to use the bulk of their funds as seed money to attract investment, whether the strategy involved downtown revitalization or neighborhoods. It was inevitable that the most completely declined areas would be neglected.

Amendments to the Community Development Act

By the end of 1975, there was concern, particularly in the urbanized areas of the Northeast, that the major urban centers would receive a progressively smaller share of community development funds. From a level of nearly 83 percent of the monies allocated in fiscal 1975, the Illinois Bureau of the Budget projected that only 60 percent would go to older cities of the North in 1980.[77] Under the 1974 formula, cities in critical need of community development funds were destined to suffer dramatic declines in assistance levels. By 1980, Newark would lose more than 52 percent of its block-grant allocation; Philadelphia, nearly 45 percent; Detroit, 22 percent; and Rochester, New York, almost 70 percent. The "lost" money would be largely allocated to the growing cities of the Sunbelt. Because of the biases of the allocation formula, Dallas would receive a 549 percent boost in its CBDG block grant amount by 1980, Fort Lauderdale would receive a 436 percent increase, and Phoenix would gain by 727 percent.[78]

The formula for distributing Community Development Block Grant (CDBG) money was deficient from the perspective of those who wanted to assist fiscally distressed cities. It was based on criteria that assigned equal weights for population and overcrowded housing and a double weight for the extent of poverty. Cities losing population, such as those in the Frostbelt, were disadvantaged by the formula, but Sunbelt cities experiencing rapid population growth stood to qualify for more money every year. Another component of the formula, poverty rate, also benefitted southern cities, since most of them had poverty rates above the national average for blacks and Hispanics.

These facts provoked several groups to initiate efforts to find a new formula. In response to requests from governors of fourteen northern industrial states who attended the Conference on Federal Economic Policies in October, 1976, an Illinois agency developed an alternative formula designed to benefit the older urbanized areas.[79] Similarly, the Brookings

Institution and HUD's Office of Policy Development and Research proposed changes in the allocation criteria to aid the declining Frostbelt cities.[80]

Urban interests representing northern cities pressured Congress to change the indicators used to distribute community development funds. The Northeast-Midwest Congressional Coalition in the House lined up behind a new formula that would give 20 percent weight to the degree of population *loss*, 30 percent to the poverty rate, and 50 percent to the age of the housing stock. These criteria gave maximum advantage to the Frostbelt cities, and it was chosen by Brookings and by HUD for precisely that reason.[81]

A bitter war broke out over the proposed change in the block grant formula. Two California representatives introduced amendments to retain the old criteria, which provided more money to cities in their districts.[82] The Southern Growth Policies Board lobbied vigorously against the new formula.

The House passed legislation in May, 1977, which had the effect of dramatically increasing the community development entitlement funds flowing to the distressed cities of the North. Using the HUD-sponsored amendments, New York City stood to receive a 50 percent boost in its 1978 entitlement and a $100 million increase (about 42 percent) in 1980.[83] Other older cities also expected large increases in their entitlements.

Several compromises were struck in order to get the amendments through Congress. To make the increases to Northern cities politically palatable, entitlements to these cities were allocated from a $1 billion per year addition to appropriations, so that the cities of the Sunbelt would not be total losers. The biggest compromise, however, involved the acceptance of a "dual formula," whereby a city could select between the original 1974 formula or the new one, depending on which of the two brought in the most money.

In an effort to aid distressed cities even more, Congress passed the Urban Development Action Grants (UDAG) program. These grants were to be distributed to cities that contained marginal areas needing particular attention, and were (in most cases) designed to supplement Community Development Act funds in distressed cities. In July, 1977, the Community Development Amendments and the UDAG grants were approved by Congress, and sent to the White House for President Carter's signature.

As a result of this legislation, cities in the Northeast received a 77 percent increase in fiscal year 1980 over the amount of block grant funds they would have received under the 1974 formula. Cities in the Midwest received a 66 percent boost in funding. But cities of the South were held to an 8 percent increase. Cities in western States were allocated an average of 14 percent more.[84]

The Contradictions in Carter's Urban Policy

As a Democratic president, Jimmy Carter normally would have responded favorably to the political interests representing the cities of the northern industrial states. These cities traditionally voted heavily for the Democratic Party in presidential elections, and thus the Carter administration tried to develop policies responsive to urban constituencies. Revenue-sharing funds were reallocated to benefit northern cities by an amendment that gave more money to cities with unemployment rates higher than the national average.[85] Jobs financed by large increases in the Comprehensive Employment Training Act (CETA) programs expanded the payrolls of local governments. In 1977, the Urban Development Action Grants (UDAG) were pushed through Congress. These grants were intended to provide federal dollars to stimulate private investment in selected cities; funds were provided to help construct convention centers, shopping malls, and private projects to stimulate business and shopping activities in central city areas. The 1977 amendments to the Community Development Act also were legislated in response to northern urban interests.

Democrats were successful in passing the Anti-Recession Fiscal Assistance Program over Ford's veto in July, 1976. Designed as an emergency measure to help distressed cities avert layoffs, maintain services, and avoid tax increases, this program was intended to end on September 30, 1977. By then, it was hoped, the recession's impact on these cities would have run its course. But in 1977, the Carter administration recommended that the Act be extended and funds increased. In the Intergovernmental Anti-Recession Act of 1977, $2.25 billion was added and antirecession assistance was extended to September 30, 1978.[86]

These programs were weighted heavily in favor of distressed cities. Five cities—New York, Philadelphia, Detroit, Chicago, and Los Angeles—received about 13 percent of the Anti-Recession Fiscal Assistance funds (together these cities made up 8 percent of the U.S. population).[87] By far the lowest allocations went to Sunbelt cities. Dallas, for example, received 4 cents per capita in funds through the program; Houston received $1.56; but Newark received $39.34 per capita.[88]

The various antirecession and public employment programs reversed a trend that had developed in the early 1970s, whereby federal programs disproportionately benefited Sunbelt cities. This pattern is shown in Table 11–4. Between fiscal 1972 and fiscal 1975, federal grants to the eight Frostbelt cities shown in the table increased by an average 62 percent, while grants to nine Sunbelt cities rose by 238 percent. Over the next three years, however, from 1975 to 1978, grants went up faster in the Frostbelt cities (133 percent) than in the Sunbelt cities (83 percent). The federal grants to distressed cities were extremely important to the financial

TABLE 11–4   Comparative Growth of Total Federal Grants to Selected
Northern and Sunbelt Cities, 1972–1978

City	% increase 1972–1975	% increase 1975–1978	% increase 1972–1978
Baltimore	146	68	314
Boston	9	81	97
Buffalo	107	154	427
Chicago	75	145	329
Cleveland	184	131	558
Detroit	26	87	136
Philadelphia	59	151	297
St. Louis	123	248	674
Mean for 8 Frostbelt cities	62	133	354
Atlanta	269	53	465
Birmingham	346	119	877
Dallas	405	74	777
Houston	267	88	591
Jacksonville	390	34	554
Louisville	68	86	214
New Orleans	209	90	488
Oklahoma City	237	107	599
Phoenix	423	94	689
Mean for 9 Sunbelt Cities	238	83	584

Source: Adapted from Paul R. Dommel, "Block Grants for Community Development: Decentralized Decision-Making," in *Fiscal Crisis in American Cities: The Federal Response*, ed. L. Kenneth Hubbell (Cambridge, Mass.: Ballinger, 1979), p. 254. Reprinted by permission of L. Kenneth Hubbell.

well-being of their municipal governments. In 1977, because of new federal funds, revenues in twenty-seven of the largest cities exceeded expenditures by 3.2 percent; in 1975 and 1976 these cities had (on an average) debts of $28.3 million and $150.7 million respectively.[89]

Beginning in 1978, a change in President Carter's urban policy began to deemphasize programs targeted to the distressed cities of the North. Two considerations led to the turnabout. First, the administration began to feel pressures to curb federal spending. The passage of Proposition 13 in California and the gathering strength of the tax revolt nationwide led to fiscal caution by Congress and the White House.[90] The National Development

Bank was the most important new proposal placed before Congress in 1978 by the White House. The bank would have promoted economic development by allocating loans and grants to depressed urban and rural areas. But the proposal failed to make it out of a conference committee after passing the House and Senate in a much-amended form.[91]

In the last year of the Carter administration, attention turned away from urban policy toward reindustrialization of the national economy. Such structural economic problems as the decline in manufacturing and the acceleration of foreign investment and imports became leading themes in Carter's 1980 campaign speeches. Urban policy was functionally abandoned by the administration by 1980. In its report issued in 1980, Carter's Presidential Commission on a National Agenda for the Eighties urged that people should move to the places where jobs were available. The commission emphasized that policies to promote national economic growth should be neutral about where that growth occurred:

> It may be in the best interest of the nation to commit itself to the promotion of locationally neutral economic and social policies rather than spatially sensitive urban policies that either explicitly or inadvertently seek to preserve cities in their historical roles.[92]

After Carter's 1976 election victory, Mayor Kenneth A. Gibson of Newark spoke for many Democratic mayors when he remarked that "We have every reason to believe that this is the beginning of a new relationship between the White House and the nation's mayors."[93] But by 1980, the stage was set for a fundamental shift in urban policy.

Urban Policy under Reagan

In a press conference held in October, 1981, President Reagan suggested that the residents of cities where unemployment was high should "vote with their feet" and move to more prosperous areas of the country.[94] His remark provoked controversy, but it could well have been lifted (although it probably was not) from the recommendations of the Presidential Commission on a National Agenda for the 1980s, whose members had been appointed by Carter:

> . . . the economy of the United States, like that of many of the older industrial societies, has for years now been undergoing a critical transition from being geographically-based to being deconcentrated, decentralized, and service-based. In the process, many cities of the old industrial heartland . . . are losing their status as thriving industrial capitals. . . .[95]
>
> The historical dominance of more central cities will be diminished as certain

production, residential, commercial, and cultural functions disperse to places beyond them.[96]

The commission's euphemism to describe this process was "transformation"; nowhere in their report did the world "decline" appear: "These cities are not dying, rather, they are transforming. . . ."[97]

The commission felt strongly that the federal government should not attempt to intervene in economic processes that were emptying out older cities. "Cities are not permanent," noted the commission; they adapt and change in response to economic and social forces. Their adaptation should be facilitated, not altered:

> To attempt to restrict or reverse the processes of change—for whatever noble intentions—is to deny the benefits that the future may hold for us as a nation.[98]
>
> Ultimately, the federal government's concern for national economic vitality should take precedence over the competition for advantage among communities and regions.[99]

The commission noted that some people might be left behind in this economic transformation, "consigned to become a nearly permanent urban underclass."[100] In its report the commission asserted that attempts to compensate the victims of economic change were misguided:

> Where the federal government steps in to try to alter these dynamics, it generates a flood of demands that may sap the initiative of urban governments because of the expectation of continuing support. There must be a better way.[101]

According to the commission, one of the "better ways" to help unemployed people was to provide retraining and relocation assistance so that people could move when necessary: "The principal purpose of such programs would be to increase people's mobility by helping them acquire the necessary skills to ensure their continuing relevance to a changing economy."[102]

The unique aspect of urban policy under the Reagan Administration (and the new element in the reports issued by Carter's commission), involves the judgment that individual cities are not valuable cultural, social, or economic spatial units except to the degree to which they contribute to a healthy national economy. Three University of Delaware researchers have characterized the new policy as "a form of Social Darwinism applied to cities as it has been previously applied, with pernicious consequences, to individuals and social classes."[103]

The Reagan Administration has sharply reduced federal urban aid, proclaiming that ". . .the private market is more efficient than federal program administrators in allocating dollars."[104] In line with its ideology and its political base, the Reagan administration has sought to withdraw the national government from urban policy and to restore state control over the urban programs that remain. In the administration's view, federal urban programs improperly finance

> . . . activities that logically and traditionally have been the responsibilities of State and local governments. . . . Individuals, firms, and State and local governments, properly unfettered, will make better decisions than the Federal government acting for them . . . it is State governments that are in the best position to encourage metropolitan-wide solutions to problems that spill over political boundaries . . . and to tackle the economic, financial, and social problems that affect the well-being of the State as it competes with others to attract and retain residents and businesses.[105]

The administration intended to devolve the "maximum feasible responsibility for urban matters to the states and through them to their local governments." Cities are instructed to improve their ability to compete with one another by ". . .increasing their attractiveness to potential investors, residents, and visitors."[106] Thus, national urban policy is to be built not on grant programs, but on advice guided by the assumption that free enterprise will provide a bounty of jobs, incomes, and neighborhood renewal.

The corollary to this approach is that social goals and national standards must be sacrificed to insure that business has maximum latitude to invest and profit. Any policies designed to redistribute resources to less viable areas or to less fortunate individuals violate the fundamental premise of supply-side theory, which holds that excessive taxation of the wealthy undercuts productivity and reduces investment capital. As dedicated budget-cutter Senator Phil Gramm (R-Texas) put the case in 1985 hearings on urban policy,

> . . . if our objective is to control spending what we've got to do is change the scope of the Federal Government. We have got to reduce functions that were set in place in another time, under other economic circumstances. While [Secretary of House and Urban Development Samuel Pierce] referred very fondly to programs he administers, the choice is between sustaining a recovery, which in terms of housing and urban development through low interest rates and jobs, is going to have more impact, favorably, on those things than the very programs we've got to control to sustain the recovery.[107]

Spending for social welfare and urban programs has been interpreted as dangerous to the priority of national economic growth. The logical next step is *not to have a national urban policy at all*. Soon after assuming office, Reagan moved in this direction. The Community Development Block Grants (CDBG) and Urban Development Action Grants (UDAG) programs won a reprieve from being sharply reduced until the 1985 budget year, and so did revenue sharing. Budget Director David Stockman wanted to kill these programs altogether, however, and attempted to write them out of the budget altogether as early as 1981. The administration, bending to the drastically weakened but still viable urban lobby, represented principally by governors and mayors, decided to save the program. The urban lobby came away relieved, even though some budget cuts were in store.

Table 11–5 shows the reductions for the major urban programs through 1988. Overall spending dropped from $6.1 billion in fiscal 1981 to $4.9 billion in fiscal 1983. The $5.2 billion spent for each fiscal year 1984 through 1986 constituted a decline in spending of almost 12 percent, when inflation is taken into account. By the 1988 budget year, money for urban programs is scheduled to be cut to $3.6 billion, a further reduction of about 40 percent from 1986 levels, when the effects of inflation are considered. By then, the only meaningful urban funding left will be through Community Development Block Grants. In addition, most subsidies for

---

TABLE 11–5 **Federal Outlays for Urban and Regional Programs to State and Local Governments in Fiscal Years 1981–1988 (in Billions of Dollars)**

	FY 1981	FY 1984	FY 1987 (est.)	FY 1988 (est.)
Community Development Block Grants	4.0	3.8	3.1	2.6
Urban Development Action Grants	.4	.5	.4	.3
Economic Development Administration and Appalachian Regional Commission	.7	.5	.3	.2
Other Community and Regional Development	1.0	.4	.7	.4
Total	6.1	5.2	4.5	3.6

Source: Executive Office of the President, Office of Management and Budget, *Historical Tables, Budget of the United States Government, Fiscal Year 1987* (Washington, D.C.: U.S. Government Printing Office, 1986), Table 12.3.

the construction of public housing have been ended. Only 10,000 new units a year were authorized after 1983, compared to the 111,600 new or rehabilitated units authorized in 1981 alone.[108]

Other budget cuts also were implemented. Urban mass transit aid was reduced 28 percent from 1981 to 1983, and cut another 20 percent by 1986 (in constant dollars).[109] The programs of the Comprehensive Employment and Training Act (CETA) were eliminated entirely after the 1983 budget. And all countercyclical aid programs ended early in the Reagan administration.

Urban Enterprise Zones

Until March 23, 1982, when President Reagan publicly proposed "enterprise zones" for depressed areas within cities, there had been no urban initiatives from his administration. In June, 1980, two New York representatives, Jack Kemp, the conservative Republican who was a principal architect of the 1981 Tax Reform Act, and Robert Garcia, a liberal Democrat from New York City, introduced the Urban Jobs and Enterprise Zone Act into Congress. A year later they introduced modified legislation.

The 1980 bill proposed to cut property taxes in designated zones by 20 percent over a four-year period, to allow depreciation of business property over a three-year period (compared with five years elsewhere), to eliminate federal capital gains taxes, to lower corporate taxes, and to reduce employer social security tax contributions. All of this was designed to encourage businesses to locate in depressed urban areas. In 1981, the legislation was altered to require a state and local commitment to reduce tax burdens on businesses located in enterprise zones. The new proposal also removed the accelerated depreciation allowance and the social security tax reduction. As a substitute, businesses in the zones were to be allowed up to $1,500 in tax credits for each of their employees.

Deregulation provisions were included in both bills. In the 1981 bill, participating cities would have been required to waive and relax various building codes, zoning requirements, and other regulations, the specific package to be proposed by each city. The administration pushed for a waiver of federal minimum wage laws, but Garcia adamantly opposed this recommendation.

Beginning in the fall of 1981, Secretary of Commerce Malcolm Baldridge chaired a study group composed mostly of HUD and Treasury staff members, with the purpose of modifying the Kemp-Garcia bill. The administration's proposal, announced in March, 1982, proposed the creation of twenty-five zones a year for three years. Businesses in these zones would have 75 percent or more of their corporate income tax forgiven, would pay no capital gains tax, and would pay no tariffs or duties in areas also designated by the federal government as "free trade zones." Employees in the zones would be given tax credits. No relief from minimum wage laws would be granted. The proposal also required that states and localities reduce regulations and support privatization of some neighborhood services.

The urban enterprise zones concept was inspired by supply-side economic theory. As described by President Reagan, "The program will identify and remove government barriers to entrepreneurs who can create jobs and economic growth. It will spark the latent talents and abilities already in existence in our nation's most depressed areas."[110] Both public subsidies and the easing of environmental and zoning restrictions were important components of the enterprise zones proposal.

Enterprise zones did not constitute a comprehensive new urban policy. First, relatively few zones were proposed—after three years, seventy-five in all. The total cost to the treasury was estimated to be $310 million in the first year and to peak at $930 million after four years.

Perhaps even more significant, the incentives offered to businesses in the zones would have been relatively unimportant. According to Rochelle Stansfield of the *National Journal*, "...federal taxes are far down the list of factors involved about where to locate." The tax relief promised in the zones proposal was expected to help "at the margins." Further, the enterprise zones would not have generated additional business volume for the nation; they would only have redistributed businesses from one location to another.

President Reagan promised to push for passage of urban enterprise zone legislation during the special session of Congress in November and December of 1982. But in the press of other business, the legislation was not considered. Finally, on March 7, 1983, the president sent his Urban Enterprise Zone Act to Congress, claiming that the legislation was a sharp departure from past policy:

> ... Enterprise zones are a fresh approach for promoting economic growth in the inner cities. The old approach relied on heavy government subsidies and central planning. A prime example was the model cities program in the 1960s, which concentrated government programs, subsidies and regulations in distressed urban areas. The enterprise zone approach is to remove government barriers, bringing individuals to create, produce and earn their own wages and profits.[111]

But, in fact, the legislation was not a "fresh approach," but a logical unfolding of past policies, Democratic as well as Republican. As of November,

1983, Congress had not acted on enterprise zones legislation, and the president had allowed the idea to drop from sight.

Dissolving National Urban Policy

In his State of the Union address of January 27, 1982, President Reagan unveiled a revolutionary "New Federalism" that would, he said, return power to the people in their states and communities. The president outlined a ten-year program for turning over to the states $47 billion in federal program, all to be accomplished by 1991. After his speech, he asserted that "those who still advocate far-removed federal solutions are dinosaurs mindlessly carrying on as they always have, unaware that times have changed."[112]

If this program had been implemented, Aid to Families with Dependent Children and Food Stamps, at a combined federal and state cost of $16.5 billion, would have been turned over to the states in fiscal year 1984. As a "bribe" to secure support for the proposal from state government officials, the federal government proposed to assume all costs of the Medicaid program, saving the states $19.1 billion. From fiscal 1984 through fiscal 1988, the states were to go through a voluntary transition period, assuming responsibility for up to forty-three separate grant programs then funded in part by the federal government. To help the states pay for these programs, a trust fund would have been established, composed of federal excise taxes on gasoline, tobacco, alcohol, and telephones, plus part of the federal "excess profits" tax on oil. After fiscal 1988, the trust fund would be phased out over four years, leaving the states with full responsibility to fund and administer the programs.

The CDBG and UDAG programs were scheduled for continued (though reduced) funding, but they were included in President Reagan's New Federalism proposals announced in 1982. If those proposals were implemented, states would inherit all responsibility for these urban programs, and the federal role would be dissolved entirely by fiscal year 1988.

Many states and localities would not have been able to finance the grant programs included in the New Federalist proposal. Even where financial capacity existed, political will might have been absent. David Cohen, the former president of Common Cause, noted that about half of the state legislatures did not possess the staff and expertise that were needed for the types of programs they were being asked to assume. Based on all prior experiences, the states would not choose to fund many urban programs. A 1982 Conference of Mayors report stated: "The history of city-state relations has too often been one of neglect of city needs by the state."[113] A former Atlanta mayor pointed out that "at best, there are only four states—Massachusetts, Michigan, Minnesota, and California—that have shown responsibility on urban issues. The other forty-six have shown either neglect or downright hostility."[114]

The New Federalism would have spelled the end to urban programs with a national intent or focus. It also would have doomed most urban programs in most states. David Stockman, in a briefing for reporters on January 28, 1982, warned, "This is not a solution to the fiscal disparities problem, which is inherent in a country as diverse as ours. If that dimension of the governmental issue gets interpreted into this process again, I think that we reach a prohibitive condition where no programs are made."[115] But it was not likely that Stockman would succeed in turning attention away from the fiscal capacities of the states. That, after all, was at the heart of the debate, along with concern about the willingness of the states—their *political* capacity—to continue funding programs turned over to them by the federal government.

Urban interests, civil rights groups, and social welfare organizations mounted a formidable campaign against the New Federalism. Negotiations between the Reagan administration and the U.S. Conference of Mayors and other groups resulted in a series of compromises. In an effort to save its proposals in the late summer of 1982, the administration offered to continue to pay for most welfare programs. But Congress was unreceptive, so much so that the administration refrained from proposing new legislation. By early 1983, it was obvious that if any form of the New Federalism survived, it would be confined to very few programs.

On February 24, 1983, President Reagan sent to Congress a sharply reduced version of the original proposals. The new plan was designed to return thirty-four federal programs to the states, and to guarantee the same level of federal funding for those programs until 1988. The new version was much cheaper, involving transferring to the states $21 billion worth of programs instead of the $47 billion in programs included in the original New Federalism proposal. But most importantly, from the perspective of state officials, financial abandonment of the federal role was not contemplated, only decentralization. The new proposal included four principal parts. By far the largest were State Block Grants of $21 billion a year to pay for twenty-two health, social service, education, and community development programs. Second, Local Block Grants would combine general revenue sharing and most of the Community Development Block Grant program. Third, Transportation Block Grants of $2 billion were to consolidate six highway programs under the states' control. Finally, Rural Housing Block Grants totaling $850 million would combine four programs for low-income rural housing.

The 1983 version of the New Federalism was greeted with skepticism, even dismay, by state and local officials. The promise that spending for the programs in the proposal would remain constant for five years was hardly reassuring; using 1984 as the base year for future expenditures meant that the deep budget cuts made in the first years of the Reagan administration would be institutionalized for the foreseeable future. In fact, a spending freeze actually translated into future cuts in federal aid, because inflation would take its toll. So while the White House was pointing out that the program would protect states and cities from further cuts, state and local officials were calling the proposed freeze on spending a formula for actual reductions in spending. The U.S. Conference of Mayors, the National Conference of State Legislatures, and the Northeast-Midwest Coalition in Congress immediately announced their opposition to the administration's proposals. Only the Sunbelt Council offered partial support.[116]

The New Federalism proposals were offered against a background of deep cuts in spending for social programs. In his budget for fiscal 1984, President Reagan proposed to reduce all housing subsidies by one-third, to raise rents for public housing tenants by counting food stamps as income, and to eliminate housing rehabilitation loans. Other reductions of importance to state and local leaders included a 68 percent cut in operating subsidies for mass transit, and elimination of all these subsidies in fiscal 1985; the ending of juvenile delinquency programs; cuts in vocational education, energy assistance, and nutrition programs; tougher eligibility requirements for most welfare programs; and reductions of more than 25 percent in grants to state and local governments for air and water pollution control.

Already, states and cities had been forced to reduce expenditures for virtually all services.[117] Human services programs were especially vulnerable. For example, facing a loss of $460 million in federal funds in 1983, New York City cut its education budget by $15 million and reduced or eliminated welfare benefits for 104,000 persons.[118]

Budget cuts had exerted a catastrophic effect on cities with high levels of unemployment and declining populations. Already beset with the most severe economic problems, these cities suffered the steepest declines in federal aid. A 1982 study by the Joint Economic Committee of the Senate showed that these cities were not only losing a larger absolute amount of federal aid because they had formerly received more federal aid, but were also losing a higher percentage of federal aid than the cities that were better off.[119] In effect, cities whose economies were already in trouble before the cuts were being compelled to endure the highest proportional reductions in federal assistance.

Abandoning urban policy made political sense for the Republicans. Party leaders had long sought to capitalize on white suburbanites' disaffection from Democratic civil rights and antipoverty policies. Reagan took advantage of this sentiment in 1980 and 1984. Jimmy Carter and Walter

Mondale carried the vote of large cities by substantial margins, while Reagan won slightly more than a third of the big-city vote in each election. But Reagan carried the suburban and small-city vote by a margin of 53 to 37 percent in 1980, and 57 to 42 percent in 1984. Since only 12 percent of the 1984 vote was cast in large cities, while 55 percent was cast in the suburbs and the small cities, the Republican advantage was devastatingly effective.[120] To illustrate, Mondale carried 65 percent of 173,000 votes in the city of St. Louis in 1984, while Reagan carried 64 percent of 308,000 votes in suburban St. Louis County.[121] Coupled with the antitax core of Reagan support, the administration had strong incentives to abandon forms of urban revitalization that required federal activism or intrusions on suburban autonomy.

City officials are aware of their rapid decline in influence in both political parties. On February 28 and March 1, 1987, the National Municipal League met in Washington, D.C., to try to amplify its influence in the 1988 presidential elections. It established an "Election '88 Task Force," designed to force candidates to promise programs important to local governments.[122]

References

1. U.S. Office of Management and Budget, *Special Analyses, Budget of the United States Government: Fiscal Year 1978* (Washington, D.C.: U.S. Government Printing Office, 1979), p. 276.

2. Donald H. Haider, *When Governments Come to Washington: Governors, Mayors, and Intergovernmental Lobbying* (New York: The Free Press, 1974), p. 109.

3. U.S. Advisory Commission on Intergovernmental Relations, *Eleventh Annual Report*, (Washington, D.C.: U.S. Government Printing Office, 1970), p. 1.

4. Michael Reagan, *The New Federalism*, (New York: Oxford University Press, 1972), p. 97.

5. Quoted in Timothy B. Clark, John K. Iglehart, and William Lilley, III, "New Federalism 1: Return of Power to States and Cities Looms as Theme of Nixon's Second-Term Domestic Policy," *National Journal: The Weekly on Politics and Government*, December 16, 1972, p. 1911.

6. U.S. Congress, House, Committee of the Whole on the State of the Union, *The State of the Union*, Address of the President of the United States, House, 92d Cong., 1st sess., January 1971, pp. 4–5.

7. H. Res. 4185, 92d Cong., 1st sess., 1971.

8. U.S. Office of Management and Budget, *Special Analyses, Budget of the United States Government: Fiscal Year 1972* (Washington, D.C.: U.S. Government Printing Office, 1973), p. 237.

9. W. W. Heller, *New Dimensions in Political Economy* (Cambridge, Mass.: Harvard University Press, 1967), p. 129.

10. Richard E. Thompson, *Revenue Sharing: A New Era in Federalism* (Washington, D.C.: Revenue Sharing Advisory Service, 1973), p. 20.

11. Thompson, pp. 20, 55–57.

12. Duane Lockard, *American Federalism* (New York: McGraw-Hill, 1969), p. 95.

13. Refer to E. E. Schattschneider, *The Semi-Sovereign People: A Realist's View of Democracy in America*, reissued with an introduction by David Adamany (Hinsdale, Ill.: The Dryden Press, 1975), for insights on the significance of the level at which political conflict takes place.

14. Haider, *When Governments Come to Washington*, p. 50.

15. See Thompson, *Revenue Sharing*, pp. 4, 45; refer also to Paul R. Dommel, *The Politics of Revenue Sharing* (Bloomington: Indiana University Press, 1974); and Richard P. Nathan, Allen D. Manvel, Susannah E. Caulkins, et al., *Monitoring Revenue Sharing* (Washington, D.C.: The Brookings Institution, 1975), for discussions of the politics of passing the legislation.

16. U.S. Congress, Joint Committee on Internal Revenue and Taxation, *Summary of Testimony on General Revenue Sharing at Public Hearings, June 2 to June 28, 1971, Held by the Committee on Ways and Means on the Subject of General Revenue Sharing* (committee print), Joint Committee on Internal Revenue and Taxation, 92d Cong., 1st sess., 1971, pp. 2, 14; and Thompson, *Revenue Sharing*, pp. 55–56.

17. Statement of the AFL-CIO Executive Council on Revenue Sharing, Bal Harbour, Florida, February 15, 1971, pp. 2–3; as cited in Thompson, p. 67. Dommel cites this opposition by organized labor as a major contributing factor in Lyndon Johnson's lack of enthusiasm for the revenue-sharing concept (*The Politics of Revenue Sharing*, p. 51).

18. Reagan, *The New Federalism*, p. 117.

19. Reagan, pp. 130–131.

20. U.S. Congress, Joint Committee on Internal Revenue and Taxation, *Summary of Testimony*, p. 8; and Thompson, *Revenue Sharing*, p. 103.

21. U.S. Congress, Joint Committee on Internal Revenue and Taxation, *Summary of Testimony*, p. 11.

22. National League of Cities, United States Conference of Mayors, and International City Management Association, *The Fiscal Plight of American Cities* (excerpts), as reprinted in Appendix A of Thompson, *Revenue Sharing*, p. 145.

23. Robert S. Benson and Harold Wolman, eds., *The National Urban Coalition Counterbudget: A Blueprint for Changing National Priorities, 1971–1976*, foreword by Sol M. Linowitz (New York: Praeger, 1971), p. 129.

24. National League of Cities, United States Conference of Mayors, and the International City Management Association, *The Fiscal Plight of American Cities*, as reprinted in Thompson, *Revenue Sharing*, pp. 130–132.

25. Quoted in Thompson, p. 130.

26. Thompson, p. 130.

27. Refer to the *Washington Post*, March 22, 1971, as cited by Thompson, p. 69.

28. *Newsweek*, May 24, 1971, p. 94.

29. Thompson, *Revenue Sharing*, p. 72.

30. Thompson, pp. 114–116.

31. Thompson, p. 118.

32. Public Law 92-15, 92d Cong. (1972).

33. Haider, *When Governments Come to Washington*, p. 64.

34. Related by Senator Howard Baker (R-Tenn.), and quoted in Thompson, *Revenue Sharing*, p. 120.

35. U.S. Department of the Treasury, Office of Revenue Sharing, *Reported Uses of General Revenue Sharing Funds 1974–1975: A Tabulation and Analysis of Data from Actual Use Report 5* (Washington, D.C.: U.S. Government Printing Office, 1966), p. 5.

36. U.S. Department of the Treasury, Office of Revenue Sharing, *Revenue Sharing: The First Actual Use Reports*, by David A. Caputo and Richard L. Cole (Washington, D.C.: U.S. Government Printing Office, 1974), pp. 10, 12, 29.

37. U.S. Department of the Treasury, Office of Revenue Sharing, *Revenue Sharing*, p. 25.

38. Calculated from data in U.S. Office of Management and Budget, *Special Analyses, Budget of the United States Government: Fiscal Year 1973* (Washington, D.C.: U.S. Government Printing Office, 1973), p. 240; the volume in the same series for *Fiscal Year 1978*, p. 271; and U.S. Department of the Treasury, Office of Revenue Sharing, *Revenue Sharing*, p. 4–5.

39. U.S. Department of the Treasury, Office of Revenue Sharing, *Revenue Sharing*, pp. 4–5.

40. U.S. Department of the Treasury, Office of Revenue Sharing, *Revenue Sharing*, pp. 4–5.

41. U.S. Department of the Treasury, *Renewal of Revenue Sharing* (Washington, D.C.: U.S. Government Printing Office, 1975), p. 11.

42. For a discussion of this topic see Richard P. Nathan, et al., with the assistance of Andre Juneau and James W. Fossett, *Revenue Sharing: The Second Round* (Washington, D.C.: The Brookings Institution, 1977), pp. 1–23.

43. Nathan, et al., p. 2, citing *Congressional Record*, February 20, 1973, p. 746.

44. See e.g., *Congressional Record*, February 22, 1973, p. 987; and *Congressional Record*, March 1, 1973, p. 1160.

45. *Revenue Sharing Bulletin*, June 1973, p. 2.

46. *Revenue Sharing Bulletin*, July 1974, p. 2.

47. Nathan, et al., *Revenue Sharing*, p. 171.

48. U.S. Office of Management and Budget, *Special Analyses: Fiscal Year 1972*, p. 204.

49. See Robert Jacob Kerstein, "The Political Consequences of Federal Intervention: The Economic Opportunity Act and Model Cities in the City of St. Louis" (Ph.D. diss., Washington University, St. Louis, 1975), pp. 23–28; refer also to U.S. Advisory Commission on Intergovernmental Relations, *Grants Management*, pp. 6–7, 17–20.

50. Kerstein, pp. 30–31.

51. U.S. Office of Management and Budget, *Special Analyses: Fiscal Year 1972*, p. 237.

52. Housing and Community Development Act of 1974, sec. 101.

53. Ernest Erber, *The Emergency of the "Housing Density Bonus"* (Washington, D.C.: National Committee against Housing Discrimination, 1974), p. 14.

54. Most of the funds are allocated to entitlement cities with populations of 50,000 or more, SMSA central cities, and certain urban counties. Jurisdictions that participated in the previous categorical programs included in the Housing and Community Development Act also received "hold-harmless" grants under which the level of funding could not decline. About 20% of the monies are distributed without regard to the formulas. These funds represent the competitive portion of the program.

55. Housing and Community Development Act of 1974, sec. 104(a).

56. See the "Community Development Monitor" series, *Housing and Development Reporter* (1976).

57. "New Directions Cited in First Annual Block Grant Reports," *Housing and Development Reporter*, January 12, 1976, p. 761.

58. U.S. Department of Housing and Urban Development, Office of Community Planning and Development, Office of Evaluation, *Housing and Community Development Act of 1974, Community Development Block Grant Program: First Annual Report* (Washington, D.C.: U.S. Government Printing Office, 1975), p. 38.

59. Reported in *Housing and Development Reporter*, January 10, 1977, p. 684.

60. Quoted from the Report of the Southern Regional Council in *Housing and Development Reporter*, April 5, 1976, p. 1051.

61. Citing an interview by SGMP investigator Sharon Cribbs with Nathaniel Hill, Director, Department of Human Resources, Little Rock, Arkansas (Summer 1975), Southern Governmental Monitoring Project, *A Time for Accounting: The Housing and Community Development Act in the South*, A Monitoring Report by Raymond Brown with Ann Coil and Carol Rose (Atlanta: Southern Regional Council, 1976), p. 53.

62. Cribbs interviewing Hill, SGMP, p. 51.

63. For a review of this and other studies, see Carl E. Van Horn, "Decentralized Policy Delivery," presented at the Workshop on Policy Analysis in State and Local Government, State University of New York-Stonybrook, May 22–24, 1977; and Carl E. Van Horn, *Policy Implementation in the Federal System* (Lexington, Mass.: Lexington Books, 1979).

64. "Grants with Strings Attached," *St. Louis Post-Dispatch*, August 6, 1977, p. 4A; reprinted from the *Washington Post*.

65. *St. Louis Post-Dispatch*, August 6, 1977.

66. Dennis R. Judd and Alvin H. Mushkatel, "Inequality of Urban Services: The Impact of the Community Development Act," in *The Politics of Urban Public Services*, ed. Richard Rich (Lexington, Mass.: Lexington Books, 1981).

67. See M. Leanne Lachman, "Planning for Community Development: A Proposed Approach," *Journal of Housing* Vol. 32 No. 2 (February 1975):58.

68. Lachman, p. 58.

69. Roger Starr, "Making New York Smaller," in *Revitalizing the Northeast*, ed. George Sternlieb and James W. Hughes (New Brunswick, N.J.: Rutgers University Press, 1978).

70. Jerome Pratter, "How Cities Can Grow Old Gracefully," *House Committee on Banking, Finance, and Urban Affairs Report* (Washington, D.C.: U.S. Government Printing Office, 1978).

71. Pratter.

72. James L. Greer, "Urban Planning and Redevelopment in Chicago: The Political Economy of the Chicago 21 Plan," presented at the Annual Meeting of the Midwest Political Science Association, Chicago, April 19–21, 1979.

73. Alvin H. Mushkatel and Howard Lasus, "Geographic Targeting of Community Development Funds in Denver: Who Benefits?", paper presented at the Annual Meeting of the Western Social Science Association, Albuquerque, N.M., April 23–26, 1980.

74. Quoted by Robert L. Joller, "HUD Secretary Quiets Critics," *St. Louis Post-Dispatch*, April 18, 1977, p. 38.

75. Reprinted in Roy Bahl, ed., *The Fiscal Outlook for Cities: Implications of a National Urban Policy* (Syracuse, N.Y.: Syracuse University Press, 1978), pp. 111–127.

76. Bahl, p. 112.

77. State of Illinois, Bureau of the Budget, Federal Relations Unit, *Equity in Federal Funding: A First Step* (Springfield: State of Illinois, Bureau of the Budget, December 9, 1976), p. 2.

78. Rochelle L. Stansfield, "Federalism Report: Government Seeks the Right Formula for Community Development Funds," *National Journal: The Weekly on Politics and Government*, February 12, 1977, p. 242.

79. See State of Illinois, Bureau of the Budget, Federal Relations Unit, *Equity in Federal Funding*, p. 32.

80. Refer to Stansfield, "Federalism Report: Government Seeks the Right Formula."

81. Ann R. Markusen, "The Urban Impact Analysis: A Critical Forecast," in *The Urban Impact of Federal Policies*, ed. Norman Glickman (Baltimore: The Johns Hopkins University Press, 1979). Also see discussion by Ann R. Markusen, Annalee Saxenian, and Marc A. Weiss, "Who Benefits from Intergovernmental Transfers?," in *Cities Under Stress: The Fiscal Crises of Urban America*, ed. Robert W. Burchell and David Listokin (New Brunswick, N.J.: The Center for Urban Research, 1981), p. 656. Also see Stansfield, "Federalism Report: Government Seeks the Right Formula.

82. See Stansfield, "Federalism Report: Government Seeks the Right Formula," and Joel Havemann, Rochelle L. Stansfield, Neal R. Pierce, "Federal Spending: The North's Loss is the Sunbelt's Gain," *National Journal: The Weekly on Politics and Government*, June 1976, p. 1031.

83. Robert Reinhold, "More Aid on Way for Older Cities," *St. Louis Post-Dispatch*, May 9, 1977, p. 3C, reprinted from *The New York Times.*

84. Calculated from Richard DeLeon and Richard LeGates, "Beyond Cybernetic Federalism in Community Development," *Urban Law Annual* 15 (1978):31. Also see Paul R. Dommel, "Block Grants for Community Development: Decentralized Decision-making," in *Fiscal Crisis in American Cities: The Federal Response*, ed. L. Kenneth Hubbell (Cambridge, Mass.: Ballinger, 1979), pp. 236–241.

85. Ann Roell Markusen and David Wilmoth, "The Political Economy of

National Urban Policy in the U.S.A.: 1978–81," Working Paper No. 316 (Berkeley, Calif.: Institute of Urban and Regional Development, July 1981); also in *Canadian Journal of Regional Science*, Summer 1982.

86. John P. Ross, "Countercyclical Revenue Sharing," in *Fiscal Crisis in American Cities*, ed. Hubbell, pp. 256–261.

87. Ross, p. 266.

88. Ross, pp. 266–267.

89. U.S. Department of Housing and Urban Development, "The Urban Fiscal Crisis: Fact or Fantasy (A Reply)," in Burchell and Listokin, *Cities Under Stress*, p. 151.

90. Markusen and Wilmoth, "Political Economy of National Urban Policy," p. 15.

91. Markusen and Wilmoth, p. 15.

92. Quoted in Markusen and Wilmoth, p. 19; from President's Commission for a National Agenda for the Eighties, *A National Agenda for the Eighties* (Washington, D.C.: U.S. Government Printing Office, 1980).

93. "Washington Update: Administration Officials, Mayors Have Love Fest," *National Journal: The Weekly on Politics and Government*, January 29, 1977, p. 189.

94. *New York Times*, October 23, 1981.

95. President's Commission for a National Agenda for the Eighties, *A National Agenda*, p. 66.

96. President's Commission for a National Agenda for the Eighties, *A National Agenda*, p. 67.

97. President's Commission for a National Agenda for the Eighties, *A National Agenda*, p. 66.

98. President's Commission for a National Agenda for the Eighties, *A National Agenda*, p. 66.

99. President's Commission for a National Agenda for the Eighties, *Urban America in the Eighties: Perspectives and Prospects* (Washington, D.C.: U.S. Government Printing Office, 1980), p. 4.

100. President's Commission for a National Agenda for the Eighties, *A National Agenda*, p. 69.

101. President's Commission for a National Agenda for the Eighties, *A National Agenda*, p. 69.

102. President's Commission for a National Agenda for the Eighties, *A National Agenda*, p. 70.

103. Timothy K. Barnekov, Daniel Rich, and Robert Warren, "The New Privatism, Federalism, and the Future of Urban Governance: National Urban Policy in the 1980s," *Journal of Urban Affairs 3*, no. 4 (Fall 1981): 3.

104. U.S. Department of Housing and Urban Development, *The President's National Urban Policy Report* (Washington, D.C.: U.S. Government Printing Office, 1982), pp. 2, 23.

105. U.S. Department of Housing and Urban Development, *The President's National Urban Policy Report*, pp. 54, 57.

106. U.S. Department of Housing and Urban Development, *The President's National Urban Policy Report, Ibid.*, p. 14.

107. U.S. Senate, Subcommittee on Housing and Urban Affairs, *Hearings on Housing, Community Development, and Mass Transportation Authorizations* (Washington, D.C.: U.S. Government Printing Office, 1985), p. 863.

108. Henry J. Aaron and associates, "Nondefense Programs," in *Setting National Priorities: The 1983 Budget*, ed. Joseph A. Pechman (Washington, D.C.: The Brookings Institution, 1982), pp. 120–121.

109. Aaron et al., p. 124.

110. "Reagan Unveils His Plan to Aid Depressed Areas," *The Denver Post*, March 23, 1982.

111. White House press release, March 7, 1983.

112. *New York Times*, January 28, 1982, p. 1.

113. *New York Times*, January 21, 1982.

114. *New York Times*, January 21, 1982.

115. Quoted in Rochelle L. Stanfield, "New Federalism: A Neatly Wrapped Package with Explosives Inside," *National Journal: The Weekly on Politics and Government*, February 27, 1982, p. 359.

116. Howard Kurtz, "State, Local Leaders Cry Foul on Budget," *The Washington Post*, February 4, 1983.

117. "Emergency Interim Survey: Fiscal Condition of Forty-eight Large Cities," staff study prepared for the Joint Economic Committee of the U.S. Senate (Washington, D.C.: U.S. Government Printing Office, January 1982), p. 5.

118. *U.S. News and World Report*, January 8, 1982, p. 27.

119. "Emergency Interim Survey," p. 6.

120. Gerald Pomper, "The Presidential Election," in Gerald Pomper (ed.), *The Election of 1984: Reports and Interpretations* (Chatham, N.J.: Chatham House, 1985), pp. 68–69.

121. State of Missouri, *Official Manual, 1985–1986* (Jefferson City: State of Missouri, 1986).

122. "Mayors Plot to Regain Influence," *St. Louis Post-Dispatch*, March 2, 1987, p. 12A.

Chapter 12

THE POLITICS
OF REDEVELOPMENT

The Redevelopment Strategy

The primary issues in contemporary cities revolve around the revitalization of business districts and neighborhoods. Revitalization invariably is described as a process of enticing business and the middle and upper classes to locate in the central cities rather than in the suburbs. In devising strategies to accomplish this goal, cities find themselves participating in an urban sweepstakes that parallels the urban competition of the nineteenth century. During the 1860s and 1870s, cities competed for railroad connections. Those that lost the railroad competition fell into decline. In the 1980s, cities still compete for a share of the nation's economic growth.

According to conventional wisdom, the older cities are disadvantaged as competitors in the urban sweepstakes. It has often been said that the "postindustrial" economy has left the industrial cities behind. Reliance on the automobile and airlines, mass production techniques in sprawling factories, congestion in the central cities, and the relatively low cost of suburban land; all these factors seem important. Added to these "causes" of decline are the social problems of the cities, namely, the movement of minority groups into the cities during and after World War II. According to the urban crisis literature of the 1960s and 1970s, rising crime rates, dilapidated housing, the poor quality of inner-city schools, vandalism, and other social ills pushed business, industry, and middle-class families from the central cities.

In the 1950s, government and business leaders supported policies designed to fight slums and economic decline. Slum clearance was proposed as the way to protect the Central Business District from slums and as the solution to the social ills of inner-city neighborhoods.

A coalition of urban interests in the 1960s fought for more federal assistance to cope with the problems of social control in the inner cities. Local officials were well aware that city budgets were inadequate to attack the social ills of the ghetto. This motivated them to seek such federally funded programs as community action, Model Cities, job training, and rent supplements.

There were three distinct phases in federal urban policy. First, urban renewal helped promote downtown economic redevelopment and slum clearance. Second, the federal government attempted to solve the social problems of American cities. Third, federal programs were designed to alleviate the revenue problems faced by big-city mayors. This was especially the case with revenue sharing and the antirecessionary programs of the 1970s.

The promotion of economic growth and downtown redevelopment attracted support from a broad coalition within all the large cities. The coalition was similar in city after city. It included city politicians working with a "new breed" of bureaucrats, corporations, Central Business District real estate and merchant interests, metropolitan newspapers, and often construction trade unions. This was the coalition that backed urban renewal and highway building in the 1950s.

In the 1960s, the coalition stabilized to such an extent that it was virtually the only unified political interest that spoke for the inner cities. In comparison, neighborhoods were split on the basis of social class, racial, or geographic differences to such an extent that they could rarely come together to articulate an alternative to Central Business District development. The consequence was that the downtown coalition dominated city politics.

By 1960, a coalition of public and private leaders had come together to dominate politics in all the big cities. Examples are numerous. They include Pittsburgh's Allegheny Conference on Community Development, which was formed in 1943 under the leadership of R. K. Mellon to promote revitalization of Pittsburgh's Golden Triangle. Chicago's Mayor Richard J. Daley was able to build the strength of the Chicago machine partly by changing the skyline of Chicago's Loop and lakefront. In Boston, the New Boston Committee helped defeat the machine politician, James Michael Curley, in a 1951 mayoral race.[1] The committee was a business-based reform group that elected Boston's first progrowth mayor. Subsequently, this coalition promoted the Prudential Central project, the urban renewal of Boston's Italian North End, and the construction of a large governmental center. Ultimately, Boston's urban renewal program took 10 percent of the city's land area.[2] In San Francisco, Mayor Joseph Alioto, first elected in 1967, became the leader of a redevelopment coalition composed of big labor, real estate interests, corporations, and the city's metropolitan dailies. Soon, San Francisco's skyline sprouted skyscrapers.

In St. Louis, Mayor Raymond Tucker, first elected in 1953, forged a coalition to push urban renewal and downtown revitalization and to secure social programs for the city. During the 1950s, this group was successful in securing the passage of bond issues to finance urban renewal projects. Urban renewal resulted in the displacement of thousands of black families. In the early 1960s, Tucker called together the members of the coalition to ready St. Louis for the receipt of social programs that might be enacted under the Kennedy administration. St. Louis not only received some of the initial funds allocated by the Ford Foundation under its gray areas program in 1959, but it was also one of the first applicants for antipoverty, Model Cities, and legal services funding.[3]

Writing in 1964, Robert Salisbury referred to this politics as the "new convergence of power" in American cities.[4] The "new convergence" united politicians with business leaders, and it was made possible by the availability of federal programs. In most cases, the urban renewal program had laid the foundation for a permanent coalition of public and private interests. In those cities in which downtown coalitions had not formed to implement urban renewal, the social programs of the 1960s provided the necessary incentive. John Lindsay's successful mayoral campaign of 1965, for example, was built on the idea that New York City should get as much federal aid as possible, and on his promise that as mayor he would work for a "fair shake" for New York in the allocation of federal dollars. Few mayors in the 1960s could afford to forego available federal money, and the best way to secure such money was to enter an alliance with business leaders to support applications for funds.

The Conflicts Inherent in the Growth Strategy

As a result of their successful efforts to secure federal backing for urban renewal, "the pro-growth coalition engineered a massive allocation of private and social resources" for the cities.[5] Through the cooperation between central city mayors and federal bureaucrats, government became an active partner with business in promoting downtown economic growth. Urban renewal required not only public funds but quite obviously invest-ments by private entrepreneurs. By 1968, $35.8 billion had been commit-ted by private institutions in 524 renewal projects.[6] In addition, the huge federal expenditures on interstate highways had provided hundreds of thousands of jobs and considerable profits to construction firms. There was an extraordinarily close connection between governmental policy and private investment.

The revitalization strategy entailed political risks. While business lead-ers talked glibly about the benefits of renewal, it was painfully apparent that poor neighborhoods often were destroyed in the process. Most of the political turbulence in the inner cities was caused by urban renewal, high-way construction, and housing-removal projects. According to one observer, "development issues . . . dominated the neighborhoods" of four cities that were studied in the 1950s and 1960s.[7]

Urban renewal provoked widespread controversy wherever it was initi-ated. As a result, concessions were wrung from the political interests that supported it. In 1959, for example, amendments to the national urban renewal legislation provided funds for moving costs to be paid to residents displaced by urban renewal projects. However, it took another ten years before relocation payments were secured for residents displaced by federal highway construction.

Considering the intensity and frequency of sit-ins, demonstrations, and other forms of mass protest, it may seem surprising that neighbor-hoods were usually unsuccessful in blocking urban renewal projects. The reason for this poor record is that the groups that generally opposed urban renewal were interested primarily in protecting their own geo-graphic turf. The various neighborhoods were so diverse that it was diffi-cult for them to form stable alliances with one another. The only source of centralization in city politics came from the downtown business com-munity and City Hall. As a consequence, the downtown coalition usually outlasted protests originating in the neighborhoods. By astutely selecting renewal and redevelopment sites, this coalition could pursue a politics of divide and conquer: "Neighborhoods have no natural cohesion as politi-cal groups. Particular interests and differences in economic status can 'easily divide a neighborhood.'"[8]

Atlanta provides an excellent example of this process. Beginning in 1952, Atlanta's Metropolitan Planning Commission became concerned that blacks were moving into areas close to the business district. In its report of that year, entitled *Up Ahead*, the commission maintained that "from the viewpoint of planning the wise thing is to find outlying areas to be developed for new colored housing." The commission recommended "public policies to reduce existing densities, wipe out blighted areas, improve the racial pattern of population distribution, and make the best possible use of central planned areas."[9] What all this added up to was a recommendation to locate blacks into areas further from the downtown and to protect the business district area from encroaching slums. Over the next several years, Atlanta Central Business District institutions sought to do just that.

Spearheaded by the Central Atlanta Improvement Association, which was Atlanta's organization of big corporations, the Metropolitan Planning Commission and the white-owned newspapers assiduously promoted urban renewal. In 1955, concerned by the proximity of blighted areas to the Central Business District, downtown businesses began to forge a coalition to support large-scale renewal. Special care was taken to obtain the backing of the chamber of commerce, which represented smaller businesses. The Atlanta Real Estate Board was also coopted by promises that renewal would help maintain segregated housing patterns. Promises were made to business executives and realtors that no public housing would be constructed on urban renewal land. Support from black community leaders was obtained by promises to expand the amount of land available for the construction of black housing subdivisions and by a commitment to build single-family housing for blacks, to be subsidized by federal funds available under section 221 of the 1949 Housing Act.

The coalition was shaky, for its cohesion depended on promises and commitments that could not benefit everyone in every case. The black community, for example, became divided when black areas close to the Central Business District were threatened by clearance, while other areas were left alone. When neighborhoods were threatened with demolition, it was obvious that the "public interest" did not include them. For displaced residents, little or no benefit flowed from Atlanta's revitalization.

Why would a mayor decide to risk the political controversy inherent in renewal projects? Obviously, renewal could set off sustained conflict, which could endanger a mayor's public image. But Mayor Hartsfield had little choice in the matter. In 1957, newspapers began to criticize him for not providing positive leadership on redevelopment proposals. The mayor, who had been lukewarm about the proposals for downtown renewal, soon reversed himself in the face of media criticism and pressure from the business community. After one especially tense meeting with business leaders, he stated that he would "go to the extent of rooting the entire government out if they feel we have been remiss in the face of federal opportunities to make progress."[10] Perceiving that his own future was tied to the renewal issue, Mayor Hartsfield became an avid supporter of Atlanta's redevelopment program.

In 1960, Atlanta elected a new mayor, a well-known businessman named Ivan Allen. He became the center of the business coalition that vigorously promoted the comprehensive renovation of downtown Atlanta. Soon after, Peachtree Street became the location of several million dollars' worth of hotel construction, most notably the Hyatt Regency and the aluminum cylinder that houses the Peachtree Plaza Hotel.

The Rationale for the Politics of Growth

It would be misleading to characterize the progrowth coalition as cynically pursuing its self-interest at the expense of the rest of the city. In fact, members of the coalition usually believe that redevelopment will benefit everyone living in the central city. The downtown coalition is brought together behind the idea that the city's survival depends upon economic vitality. Its members believe that only through private investment can cities raise the taxes necessary to provide quality public services. It is only through business expansion that jobs can be created to raise incomes and reduce poverty. The logic that unifies the growth coalition can be represented in graphic form, as shown in Figure 12–1.

The argument proceeds as follows: investment leads to more jobs and an improved tax base. This, in turn, raises the incomes of city residents and

FIGURE 12–1   The Logic of Capital Investment

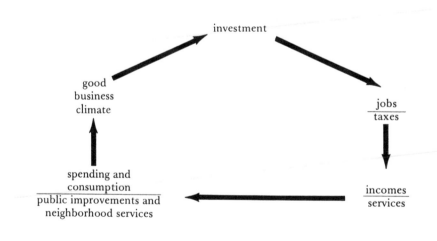

provides more resources to city governments so that they can improve public services. Higher incomes lead to increased spending and consumption by city residents. Better public services are evidenced by good streets, lighting, parks, and public buildings and in better schools, police protection, and public health, all of which improve the quality of neighborhood life. Rising spending and consumption create a favorable business environment, which, of course, encourages investment, and on around the cycle again. The reverse of this process would be declining business investment, a loss of jobs and taxes, lower incomes, fewer services, and so on, so that the city declines in an irreversible spiral. Considering the extent to which business leaders agree with this scenario, it is easy to understand how they equate their own investment decisions with the general public good, and why they become infuriated when "minority factions" challenge their version of civic progress.

Indeed, the growth argument seems compelling, and city officials question it only at their peril. Since local governments lack sufficient resources to remedy the social and economic problems faced by most cities, politicians are forced to support a policy of economic growth in the hope that growth can accomplish what government cannot. The health of the city thus is equated with the business investment that can be attracted. Local political leaders feel that they have no alternative to the growth strategy. If they fail to join forces with business leaders, they are left bereft of the public resources necessary to accomplish any useful policy.

The strength of the renewal coalition, and how far it is willing to go to promote redevelopment, is revealed by the two decades of controversy over the Yerba Buena Center in San Francisco.[11] The major participants in the coalition supporting the building of the Yerba Buena Center were big corporations and financial institutions, hotels and other downtown businesses, the Convention and Visitors Bureau, the Hotel Employers Association, the major labor unions, and the newspapers and other news media.

The idea of a large convention, hotel, and recreational center located in the heart of San Francisco originated in 1953, when the San Francisco board of supervisors approved an area south of Market Street for future redevelopment. Although a redevelopment process failed to materialize for several years, the idea continued to appeal to San Francisco's corporations. San Francisco contains scores of corporate giants, including, for example, Standard Oil of California, Southern Pacific, Transamerica Corporation, Levi Strauss, Crown Zellerbach, Del Monte, Pacific Telephone and Telegraph, Bethlehem Steel, and Pacific Gas and Electric. Among the many financial institutions located in downtown San Francisco are the Bank of America, Wells Fargo, Crocker National Bank, Bank of California, Aetna Life, John Hancock, and Hartford Insurance. During the 1960s, these institutions changed San Francisco's skyline. Between 1960 and 1972, twenty-three high rises were constructed in downtown San Francisco.[12]

In the absence of something like the Yerba Buena Center, corporate expansion would be slowed, for there was virtually no unused vacant land left in the center of San Francisco. Land for corporate expansion would, therefore, have to be created by some kind of urban renewal and clearance process. The importance of a downtown location was stated by one executive in this fashion: "The people who fund the [financial and corporate] centers want all their services and the people they work with—advertisers, attorneys, accountants—around them. It's a complete part of the way we do business in this country."[13]

In late 1955, influential business leaders formed the Blyth-Zellerbach Committee to promote plans for the redevelopment of the wholesale and market area just east and south of the financial district. This area, with its market stalls, narrow passageways, and constant bustling activity, concerned business and political leaders, who worried about its impact on the future of the downtown business district. Motivated by this concern, they formed the San Francisco Planning and Urban Renewal Association in 1959. This was a broader group than the Blyth-Zellerbach committee. Working with the San Francisco Redevelopment Agency, business leaders were able to make detailed input into redevelopment plans through the Association.

The San Francisco Redevelopment Agency assumed a pivotal role in redevelopment beginning in April, 1959, when Mayor George Christopher appointed M. Justin Herman as the agency's executive director. Herman was imbued with a sense of a vital mission: to save downtown San Francisco. He became the "chief architect, major spokesman, and operations commander for the transformation of whole sections of the city."[14] Under his leadership, the redevelopment agency hired several hundred professionals and dozens of consultants and applied for millions of dollars in federal urban renewal subsidies. He was cited in a national publication in 1971 as "one of the men responsible for getting urban renewal" renamed

> "the federal bulldozer and negro removal." He was absolutely confident that he was doing what the power structure wanted in so far as the poor and the minorities were concerned. That's why San Francisco has mostly luxury housing and business district projects—that's what white, middle-class planners and businessmen envision as ideal urban renewal. . . . Also, with Herman in control, San Francisco renewal never got slowed down by all this citizen participation business that tormented other cities.[15]

These sentiments were shared by a HUD official who felt a combination of admiration and distrust for Herman. In 1970, Herman was quoted as saying, "this land is too valuable to permit poor people to park on it."[16] He viciously attacked his critics, and he believed in his mission so completely that he interpreted any criticism of his projects as an attempt by parochial interests to stand in the way of civic progress.

Redevelopment agencies are semiautonomous bodies with vast amounts of independent legal, financial, and technical resources. They are generally independent of municipal government, having their own boards of directors. They also possess the power of eminent domain, which is essential to the redevelopment process because it enables the agencies to assemble large sites by taking land, through compensation, away from individual owners. This land assembly power is absolutely necessary, because business corporations, if attempting land assembly on their own, must buy from "willing" sellers and thus pay a high price for valuable urban real estate.

The professional staffs of redevelopment agencies have far more familiarity with complex urban renewal statutes and regulations than any other agencies or organizations. The result is that this type of agency can spearhead a redevelopment process by coordinating the efforts of other institutions that share an interest in redevelopment. In San Francisco, Justin Herman used the full powers of this agency to mobilize the press, the business community, and the mayor's office behind his plan.

The San Francisco Convention and Visitors Bureau was an important ally of the San Francisco Redevelopment Agency. Its main task was to promote the city and to mobilize public support in favor of downtown investment. As the organization representing the city's tourism industry, the Convention and Visitors Bureau represented hotels, retail stores, transportation and tour agencies, restaurants, athletic teams, banks, hotel and exhibit suppliers, entertainment unions, and the media. The bureau, which employed a staff of forty by the early 1970s, was principally responsible for hotel bookings for groups; for billboard, magazine, and newspaper advertising and brochures describing San Francisco; for group tour promotions, for liaisons with travel agencies; and for the promotion of a great number of special events, such as the Chinese New Year celebration, the Japanese Cherry Blossom Festival, Columbus Day, and St. Patrick's Day. Supported by a hotel tax, the bureau operated on an annual budget of more than $1 million in 1969.

Another important member of the downtown coalition was the Hotel Employers Association, which represented the biggest hotels in San Francisco. The purpose of this group was to promote the full occupancy of hotels through a healthy tourism and convention business.

The Building and Construction Trades Council also joined the redevelopment coalition. At first distrustful of redevelopment, the unions fell in line when it became obvious that construction jobs would be generated by the reconversion of downtown property. In fact, the Building and

Construction Trades Council became an unqualified backer of just about any kind of new construction that would increase employment.

The *San Francisco Chronicle* and *Examiner* were vociferous backers of the Yerba Buena Center. They supplied editorial support and ample space for "information" about renewal plans. Both newspapers were located in the downtown area and each held a substantial economic stake in development. They were owned by influential business leaders who shared the business perspective on downtown development. Radio and television stations likewise were loyal backers. The economic motivation for such support was illustrated in a preamble to an editorial by KPIX television Area Vice-President Louis S. Simon: "Although I am president-elect of the Convention and Visitors Bureau, vitally interested in this subject, I am speaking today solely on behalf of KPIX and our Editorial Board."[17] All of the local television and radio stations aired frequent editorials denouncing opponents of the project and predicting financial disaster for San Francisco if the Yerba Buena Center were not constructed.

Considering the power of the coalition pushing the project, it was surprising that Yerba Buena became embroiled in a heated controversy that lasted for several years. Resistance to the Convention Center came from tenants who lived in the Milner Hotel, which was located in the center of the construction area. Represented by legal services attorneys, the tenants filed a petition with HUD asking for an administrative hearing on the redevelopment agency's "Relocation Plan." HUD denied the request on the ground that no displacement had yet taken place.

During the summer of 1969, the residents of the proposed renewal area held a meeting at the Milner Hotel and formed an association called the Tenants and Owners in Opposition to Redevelopment. Taking their case into federal court, the tenants were able to secure an injunction against the Yerba Buena Center that cut off all federal funds, subject to a revised plan to relocate the area's residents. The judge who heard the case concluded that the secretary of HUD "Had not been provided with any creditable evidence at all" in regard to the redevelopment agency's plan to relocate residents into suitable housing. He indicated that ". . .the record shows that at this point there is no adequate relocation housing in San Francisco that meets the requirements of the 1949 Housing Act and is available for persons yet to be displaced from the project area."[18] Under pressure from the court to revise its relocation plans, the redevelopment agency eventually agreed to increase the hotel tax in San Francisco in order to finance the construction of low-income housing for tenants who would be displaced by the Yerba Buena Center. This construction, however, took several years to accomplish, and was fought bitterly in the courts.

The Yerba Buena Center was "the blockbusting wedge to expand the city's financial district southward across Market Street."[19] Like other developments of its kind, it was promoted on the promise that economic benefits would filter down to all residents of the city through the creation of jobs and taxes. If constructed, however, the Yerba Buena Center would likely have cost the residents of San Francisco several million dollars a year in tax support. Moreover, far fewer jobs would have been provided by the facility than were promised by its backers.[20]

In order to avoid having to place a general revenue bond before the voters of the city, the San Francisco Redevelopment Agency and its backers decided to finance the Yerba Buena Center through a lease revenue bond. Under this arrangement, the Redevelopment Agency would sell the bonds and would lease public facilities in the Yerba Buena Center to the city of San Francisco. In effect, this would commit the city to an open-ended agreement to guarantee the lease revenue bonds for their entire thirty-five–year period. The Yerba Buena Center would, therefore, cost the city nothing only if the activities in it produced annual revenues that exceeded the costs of paying off the interest and the principal on the bonds. Many other cities have made similar arrangements with their convention centers.

It is highly unlikely that the activities in the Yerba Buena Center would have paid for the cost of the facilities. The Exhibition Hall–Convention Center was not anticipated ever to run at a profit. The promise of a revenue surplus came from the anticipation that the new sports arena would attract the basketball team, the Golden State Warriors, and the hockey team, the California Golden Seals. However, neither of these teams had made a commitment to play in the Yerba Buena Center sports arena, and in fact, the California Golden Seals later moved out of the city.

Possibly more serious, the city would have lost revenues that otherwise would finance municipal services. One-third of the city's 5.5 percent hotel tax would have been reserved for the Yerba Buena Center. Obviously, this was money the city could put to other uses. Also, the center would have been supported by the property tax increment in the redevelopment area made possible by the Convention Center and hotel complex. Thus, during the entire thirty-five years of the bond period, there could have been no new property taxes paid to the city by the Yerba Buena Center. This situation was compounded by the fact that businesses that located in the center area from other parts of downtown San Francisco would no longer have been paying their property tax to the city. Their taxes would have been used exclusively to support the center.

The question of whether the Yerba Buena Center ultimately would have paid for itself, and secondarily have benefited the residents of the city of San Francisco, was complicated by the fact that the political groups who promoted it habitually overstated the center's revenue potential and understated its cost. In this respect, the campaign was similar to those organized to promote similar facilities elsewhere. A *Fortune* magazine study found that

> most . . . are financed with bonds issued by state, county, or city governments that are supposed to be paid off by revenues derived from the project, but in practice these revenue bonds almost always turn out to load an open-ended general obligation upon the tax payer. . . .
>
> To drum up public support, the advocates of a stadium generally understate the probable costs, which invariably balloon as construction proceeds. They also overstate the probable revenues by anticipating multiple uses for the structure . . . that in actuality dwindle to a few.[21]

There is little doubt that it serves the financial interests of downtown business and of central city politicians to secure new development. For example, the Eisenhower Convention Center, which was planned for Washington, D.C. in the 1970s, was promoted primarily by large banks, which would have bought the bond issues required to construct the center. The chair of the Riggs Bank headed the nonprofit corporation that would have sold the bonds.[22] In the case of the Yerba Buena Center, the over-building of luxury hotels in San Francisco during the late 1960s and early 1970s made hotel owners nervous about their future profitability. They therefore saw the construction of the Yerba Buena Center as a way to attract tourists and thereby maintain hotel bookings. If banks, hotels, restaurants, bars, and other economic enterprises directly benefit from a convention facility, they will promote it. The fact that others may subsidize their new facility is perfectly acceptable to business and local politicians, especially considering the fact that business leaders believe that their investments benefit the entire city. There is a belief that "what's good for business is good for the city" and also that what's good for the Central Business District is good for the city.

The politics of growth is managed by the economic institutions that invest in the downtown areas of the central cities. A detailed understanding of this politics can be gained by looking at one of the most important facets of central business district economics—the tourism and convention trade.

The Changing Economic Function of Central Cities

Municipal efforts to attract tourist trade reflect the changing economic functions of cities. Central cities, formerly the centers of manufacturing and retailing, have declined in their traditional roles partially as a result of the suburbanization following World War II. As households shifted toward the suburban periphery, the retail establishments that catered to them followed. Central Business Districts rapidly lost jobs in retail trade:

> From 1948 to 1954—while the central cities as a whole were slipping in their relative positions as trade and retail centers—the central business districts were slipping even faster. Whereas thirteen central cities registered a decline of one-tenth in their share of the thirteen metropolitan areas' retail trade employment in which they were located, the thirteen central business districts' share fell by one-quarter. Indeed in seven of these central business districts, there was not only a relative decline in retail sales but an absolute decline, a decline all the more remarkable because it occurred during a period when retail sales in the nation were growing prodigiously.[23]

There were also factors operating to push manufacturing out of the cities. Manufacturing structures in central cities had become obsolete. Rather than face the problems and expenses entailed in site assembly and clearance in a city relocation, many manufacturing establishments chose a suburban location where land was plentiful and relatively cheap.

While manufacturing and retail employment was concentrating in the suburbs, older central cities were becoming centers of service activity. Between 1963 and 1967, nine cities of thirty surveyed in one study experienced declining employment in manufacturing, ten showed a downturn in wholesale employment, eight declined in retailing, but only one showed a loss of jobs in the service sector.[24] Such a transformation was one result of the "life cycle" of older cities:

> As the city ages and becomes more densely populated, central city land becomes more expensive, and manufacturing declines in significance as does retail and wholesale trade. Services, in contrast, appear to thrive on concentration and, through a process of self-selection and survival, emerge as the dominant economic force in the older, large cities. The tendency of central cities to become service centers appears, like rheumatism and decaying teeth, to be a strong function of age.[25]

Increasingly, the jobs in older cities were provided in the service or government sectors. According to a study of eleven large cities,

> The cities entered the postwar era as centers of manufacturing, wholesale and retail trade, principally, and emerged years later as purveyors of government, business, and personal service activities—their predominant and most rapidly expanding activities.[26]

Between 1950 and 1967, these cities lost about 400,000 jobs in manufacturing and trade but gained approximately 1 million jobs in government, finance, and service.[27] As shown in Table 12–1, this trend continued right

TABLE 12–1   Change in Earned Income, by Industry, in the Central City
Counties of the 34 Largest Metropolitan Areas, 1959–1980

	% in each occupational category		% change in share of earned income
	1959	1980	1959–1980
Manufacturing	31	24	–7
Transportation and communication	9	9	0
Wholesale trade	9	9	0
Retail trade	11	9	–2
Finance	7	9	2
Services	15	21	6
Government	12	15	3
Construction	6	6	0

Source: Alexander Ganz, "Where Has the Urban Crisis Gone? How Boston and Other Large Cities Have Stemmed Urban Decline," *Urban Affairs Quarterly,* vol. 20, no. 4 (June 1985), p. 454. Copyright © 1985 by Sage Publications, Inc.

into the 1980s. In the central counties of the thirty-four largest metropolitan areas, manufacturing and retail trade declined in their share of earned income between 1959 and 1980; wholesale trade remained the same. But the share for the service, government, and financial sectors increased.

These economic transformations affected all northern cities. Table 12–2 shows, for example, a steep decline in manufacturing jobs in New York City. In 1969, 22 percent of all of New York City's jobs were in manufacturing. By 1978, however, manufacturing accounted for only 15 percent of New York's jobs. The proportion of jobs in government had grown slightly. By far the biggest job growth had occurred in services, which accounted for 41 percent of all jobs in New York City by 1978.

What had started as an economic transformation affecting old industrial cities soon spread to entire urban areas. Northern metropolitan areas lost jobs to the Sunbelt, and manufacturing employment everywhere in the nation lagged behind other sectors of the economy. As shown in Table 12–3, manufacturing employment declined sharply in seven northeastern and north central metropolitan areas. Jobs in services and the financial sector grew as a proportion of total employment in these same urban areas.

TABLE 12-2 Changing Occupational Structure of New York City

	% employed in each category	
	1969	1978
Manufacturing	22	15
Services, including banking and finance	33	41
Government	14	16
Other	31	28

Source: Adapted from Norman I. Fainstein and Susan S. Fainstein, "Restructuring the City: A Comparative Perspective," in *Urban Policy Under Capitalism*, ed. N. Fainstein and S. Fainstein, Urban Affairs Annual Reviews, vol. 22 (Beverly Hills, Calif.: Sage Publications, 1982), p. 169. Copyright © 1982 by Sage Publications, Inc. Reprinted by permission of Sage Publications, Inc.

Reflecting cutbacks in government spending at all levels in the early 1980s, the percentage of jobs in the government sector declined between 1975 and 1982, after rising from 1970 to 1975.

The losses in the manufacturing sector exceeded the number of new jobs in services and finance. Northern central cities and their metropolitan

TABLE 12-3 Change in Job Categories in Seven Northeastern and North Central Metropolitan Areas,* 1970–1986

	% employed in each category			
	1970	1975	1982	1986
Manufacturing	30.1	25.8	22.4	18.5
Transportation, communications, and public utilities	6.4	6.3	5.9	5.8
Wholesale and retail	20.8	21.6	21.9	22.5
Finance, insurance, and real estate	6.4	6.7	7.4	9.1
Services	18.4	20.6	24.6	27.4
Government	13.6	15.1	14.5	13.4

Source: U.S. Department of Labor, Bureau of Labor Statistics, *Earnings and Employment*, March 1970, 1975, 1982, 1986 (Washington, D.C.: U.S. Government Printing Office). January data are reported in March.
*New York City, Chicago, Boston, St. Louis, Cleveland, Detroit, and Pittsburgh.

areas began to seek economic revitalization through strategies designed to attract businesses associated with the fastest-growing economic sectors. For the central cities the competition to promote tourism heated up. Through the 1970s and 1980s cities built sports arenas and convention centers at a frenetic pace.

Why Cities Seek Tourists

Aside from the direct benefits to downtown interests, cities seek tourists because the convention industry seems uniquely beneficial to all residents, essentially a "free" commodity. It is generally assumed that tourists spend money without taking anything out of the local economy. The convention industry has been described as "the industry without a smokestack." As a consequence, there is keen competition among cities for convention business.

According to the International Association of Convention and Visitors Bureaus, there were approximately 30,000 conventions in the United States in 1975, and that number is expected to double by 1993.[28] In 1975, conventions were a $7-billion-a-year business, and ancillary spending, estimated at up to $18 billion, affected the entire American economy.[29] Conventions are considered a growth industry because of the proliferation of specialized groups and associations that feel the need to pull people together periodically for exchange of information. According to one of the authorities in the field:

> Conventions will increasingly become an important component in the economy. The trend nowadays toward holding conventions is not just a passing fashion, since the countless political, cultural, and especially economic liaisons and unions demand repeated personal contact. This is why conventions are essential and will continue to be so. The tourist industry is particularly interested in conventions. . . . It sees in them an additional market with a relatively high expenditure and a good seasonal distribution.[30]

International conventions are likewise important. A study by the United States Department of Commerce estimated the 1976 international convention market at 2,600 events, with 1.7 million participants.[31] In recent years, the United States Travel Service (USTS) has initiated drives to bring more international conventions to the United States. In 1970, the USTS set up an International Conventions Office in an effort to develop an information data bank on international associations. Its director put the value of the international convention market at $500 million annually and estimated that up to 1,000 international associations have a future potential to meet in the United States.

There are five basic types of conventions. First, the social convention consists of groups who share common hobbies or religious or civic interests. These conventions are likely to proliferate with the reduction of the work week, increased length of paid vacation, and longer life expectancy. Second, there is the professional or managerial convention; for example, groups of lawyers, doctors, academics, or business executives. Third, there is the sales convention, which corporations consider a profitable means of increasing sales of goods or services. Fourth, there are political conventions, both regional and national. Finally, there are trade shows, where manufacturers display their merchandise for wholesale sales. These require more exhibition space than other conventions.

According to a report of the National Tourism Resource Review Commission, the average convention-goer in 1973 was between thirty-five and forty-nine, held a professional or managerial job, had a college education and had an annual income of $15,000 (about $36,000 in 1987 dollars).[33] He or she usually arrived by plane and stayed in a hotel near where the convention was being held. The conventioneer patronized mainly restaurants, night spots, and retail stores.

Table 12–4 provides a breakdown of delegate expenditures in eighty-three convention cities during 1985. From the expenditures on hotels, restaurants, and retail stores it is apparent why these businesses so assiduously promote conventions. Delegates to national or international conventions stayed an average of 4.4 days and spent about $105 each day, for a total of almost $500 for a convention. Most delegates—75 to 80 percent—brought their spouses.[34] Large conventions, such as that of the American Dental Association, bring as many as 15,000 delegates to a city.

The convention industry that has grown up in response to this demand is composed of an amorphous collection of firms, airlines, hotels, restaurants, tourist attractions, travelers' services, and retail trade establishments. Since the early 1970s, a new breed of entrepreneur has emerged —the professional convention planner, who plans events and coordinates activities for organizations that are sponsoring conventions. These agencies, the foremost of which are the Washington-based Associated Services, Inc., and the Jane Condon Corporation of New York, are paid a commission of 5 to 10 percent by the hotels and auditoriums that they book for events.

Steps have been taken to coordinate the activities of this multimillion-dollar industry. In 1972, the First Annual World Meeting Planners Congress and Exposition met in Chicago; 200 members of the industry representing hotels, airlines, and professional planners staged their own

TABLE 12-4   Per-Delegate Personal Expenditures, National and
International Conventions Held in 83 Cities,* 1985

Business	% of total	Daily expenditure, $	Total expenditures, $†
Hotels and motels	46.8	49.35	236.50
Eating establishments	24.1	25.41	121.79
Retail stores	11.0	11.60	55.59
Other (night clubs, sporting events, etc.)	18.1	19.09	91.47
Total average expenditures per delegate		105.45	505.34

Source: International Association of Convention and Visitors Bureaus, 1985. Convention Income Survey as reported in *Successful Meetings* (Champaign, Ill.: IACUB, May 1986), p. 12.
*Based on sample of 14 conventions held in 1985 in 72 U.S. cities and 11 outside U.S.
†Average of 4.4 days.

convention to exchange information and experience.[35] Since this meeting, other convention trade associations have attempted to coordinate the myriad components of the industry.

One indicator of the municipal efforts to attract convention trade is the widespread construction of municipally financed convention centers designed to accommodate larger and more specialized groups. *Aud-Arena Stadium Guide* conducted a survey in 1972 showing that seventy cities ranging in size from Pontiac, Michigan, to New York City had recently opened, had under construction, or had planned multimillion-dollar convention centers, designed to enable them to achieve or maintain competitive positions as convention sites.[36] Another indicator of the intense competition for convention business is the proliferation of municipal convention bureaus. In the 1960s, about sixty-five cities in the United States operated convention bureaus whose primary task was to attract and assist convention groups. By 1977, their number had swollen to approximately 100 and doubled again by 1983.

With the construction of new convention facilities, competitive sales efforts by convention bureaus have been stepped up. Convention bureaus construct lists of national, regional, local, and, in some cases, international associations that are regular sponsors of conventions. The bureaus send them promotional literature and, along with the state governor, the city

mayor, and the county supervisor, send the board responsible for convention site selection an invitation to meet in their city. If the association indicates an interest, the bureau will send sales representatives who describe
the city, its facilities, tourist attractions, and any other features (e.g.,
reduced-rent or rent-free convention facilities) the city has to offer. Representatives often stage promotional presentations, which can be very elaborate, or they may invite group representatives to their city for a
complimentary visit. In November, 1975, for example, the St. Louis Convention and Visitors Bureau hosted representatives of 227 associations for
a weekend tour in an effort to promote its $39 million convention center,
then under construction.[37]

Site selection by the sponsoring association is made two to four
years in advance. According to a study by the National Tourism Review
Commission:

> The key requirements are the availability of specialized facilities such as
> exhibit space, banquet halls, meeting rooms, with sufficient hotel/motel ac-
> commodations at hand, and a site which promises to attract a high level of
> attendance. Attendance relates to ease of access, a locality around which a
> high proportion of attendees live, and the appeal of the city to them. Cost is rel-
> evant absolutely and as a means of bargaining for better terms from those com-
> munities bidding for the conventions.[38]

Tourist appeal is a central consideration in convention site selection.
Although many small and medium-sized cities are competing for a share of
the business, large cities, with their multitude of entertainment, cultural,
and commercial attractions, remain the primary drawing cards for
national and international conventions.

Table 12–5 ranks the top twenty convention cities by their share of the
convention market for the year July, 1978, through June, 1979. Chicago
and New York City, which for two decades have led the nation as magnets
for conventions,[39] drew the largest number of conventions. New York,
despite its high prices, attracted 3 million convention visitors in 1975, who
brought in $403.5 million in direct spending, roughly one-third of the
$1.25 billion spent in the city by all visitors during the year.[40] San
Francisco/Oakland, New Orleans, and metropolitan Washington
attracted the most events after Chicago and New York City, but not necessarily the largest number of conventioneers. Table 12–5 suggests that New
Orleans and Washington attract relatively small conventions, while Dallas,
Los Angeles, and Atlanta draw fewer events but more convention-goers.
Successful Meetings magazine, a publication that monitors convention
trends, identified Atlanta, Houston, and Las Vegas as the fastest-moving
cities in the convention trade in the late 1970s.[41]

TABLE 12–5   Convention Trade, U.S. Cities, 1978–1979*

Top 20 cities for conventions, total events July 1978–June 1979	% share of total events (est. market)	Top 20 cities in total attendance July 1978–June 1979	% share of total attendance (est. market)
1. Chicago/Oakbrook/ Rosemont, Ill.	4.8	1. New York, N.Y.	9.7
2. New York, N.Y.	3.5	2. Chicago/Oakbrook/ Rosemont, Ill.	
3. San Francisco/ Oakland	3.2	3. Dallas, Tex.	5.4
4. New Orleans, La.	3.2	4. Atlanta, Ga.	3.8
5. Metropolitan Washington, D.C.	3.1	5. Los Angeles/ Anaheim	.8
6. Atlanta, Ga.	2.6	6. San Francisco/ Oakland	3.6
7. Los Angeles/ Anaheim	2.4	7. New Orleans, La.	3.4
7. Dallas, Tex.	2.4	8. Denver, Colo.	3.0
9. Miami/Miami Beach /Hollywood, Fla.	2.1	9. Houston, Tex.	2.9
9. Saint Louis, Mo.	2.1	10. Las Vegas, Nev.	2.8
11. Kansas City, Kansas/Mo.	2.0	11. Kansas City, Kansas/Mo.	2.7
12. Houston, Tex.	1.7	12. Detroit/Dearborn, Mich.	2.4
12. Las Vegas, Nev.	1.7	13. Metropolitan Washington, D.C.	2.1
14. Detroit/Dearborn, Mich.	1.6	14. Miami/Miami Beach/ Hollywood, Fla.	1.7
14. San Diego, Cal.	1.6	15. Saint Louis, Mo.	1.6
16. Boston, Mass.	1.5	16. Philadelphia, Pa.	1.4
16. Denver, Colo.	1.5	17. Atlantic City, N.J.	1.4
18. San Antonio, Tex.	1.3	18. Boston, Mass.	1.3
19. Philadelphia, Pa.	1.1	19. San Diego, Cal.	0.8
20. Nashville, Tenn.	1.0	20. Louisville, Ky.	0.8
20. Seattle, Wash.	1.0		

Source: Adapted from *World Convention Dates*, 63, no. 8 (August 1978):3. Reprinted by permission of Hendrickson Publishing Co., Hempstead, N.Y.
*Projected in August, 1978.

Except for the leading cities, each city in Table 12–5 captured only a small percentage of the nation's convention trade. Obviously, the convention trade is highly competitive. The top ten cities for conventions from July, 1978, to June, 1979, accounted for 29 percent of the total events and 48 percent of total attendance. The other cities in the table fought for the remaining share of convention business.

The Impact of the Convention Trade

In soliciting service employment-oriented convention business, cities hold out the promise of supplementing their local economies, which have suffered from the losses of manufacturing and commerce to suburban communities. Cities are beset by high levels of unemployment for unskilled workers. Development of the convention industry, it is argued, provides jobs in hotels and food service for the difficult-to-employ, unskilled segment of the population. Low-skill jobs account for 65 percent of employment in the food service and lodging industries.[42]

In addition to providing service jobs for the low-skilled labor force, convention trade provides professional, managerial, clerical, and sales jobs. Roger Bivus, director of the International Association of Convention Bureaus, estimated in 1972 that for every $20,000 that convention-goers spent in an area, a new job was generated.[43] He claimed that 4 million jobs were supported directly and indirectly by the tourist industry.[44]

Obviously, the impact of tourism and convention money on local economies is difficult to trace, but some estimates have been made. According to Bivus, convention trade pumps "new money" into the local economy, which has the same multiplier effect that any investment does:

> The dollars that a convention-goer spends become income for hotel, restaurant, and other service personnel. Subsequently, these dollars are spent again—on rent, food, and other basic necessities. In the process they generate earnings for real estate investors and other investors who may plow back a portion of their profit into plant expansion and new equipment.[45]

In this way, visitor money may be spent several times, filtering into different sectors of the economy, each time giving rise to new incomes until "leakage" payment for goods and services out of the region takes the money out of circulation. The International Association of Convention and Visitors Bureaus asserts that these funds may change hands as many as ten times before they come to rest.[46]

Convention business also creates tax revenues for cities. It is extremely difficult to pin down exactly how much revenue is generated by visitors. The problems in attempting to estimate tourism revenue result from the fact that tourists and residents often use the same facilities, and it is difficult to apportion the share of sales and revenue attributable to each. In addition, it is nearly impossible to trace tourist expenditures in nontourist businesses. According to a report of the National Tourism Review Commission, "most cities consider the two most obvious revenue sources— taxes and user fees, and then look at the most obvious categories within the two, for example, occupancy taxes and admission receipts."[47]

Even using the roughest of estimates, it is clear that tourist contributions to municipal tax bases are substantial. In most cities hotels and restaurants are subject to special city sales taxes in addition to the regular city or state sales tax. About 75 percent of convention delegates' dollars are spent within city limits.[48] Boston officials have estimated that the city receives 10 percent of its total revenues from visitor-related activities; New Orleans, 10 percent; Washington, D.C., 15 percent; and New York, 15 percent.[49] The United States Travel Service estimated that 7.2 percent of tourism spending in the United States ended up in federal, state, or local treasuries.[50] C. L. Washburn, Assistant Secretary of Commerce for Tourism in the early 1970s, said in an interview with *Commerce Today* that tax revenues brought into cities by visitors generally represented funds given to a community by people who did not stay around to use the schools, roads, and other facilities and services they helped support. He estimated that tourist spending added up to approximately $20 in tax receipts for every man, woman, and child in the nation in 1972.[51]

Urban redevelopment projects in many cities, such as New York, Chicago, St. Louis, Washington, D.C., Indianapolis, and Wichita, to name a few, have centered around the construction of a new convention facility in the Central Business District, which is expected to serve as a catalyst for overall redevelopment. In fact, most central city urban renewal plans include convention centers, hotels, motels, and such related facilities as shops, entertainment establishments, and restaurants, all of which are to be used in part by conventioneers. Convention center sites are carefully selected to provide "anchors" for the flow of vehicular and pedestrian traffic along avenues of hotels, shops, restaurants, and entertainment establishments with cultural or entertainment facilities. The sites are often selected in parts of Central Business Districts marked by blight or slums, which would have little or no market potential for redevelopment outside convention- and hotel-related facilities.[52]

Convention promoters anticipate that the stimulation of retail and entertainment businesses will encourage high-grade residential developments in or near Central Business Districts. New construction and jobs generated in response to the existence of convention facilities are expected to produce property, business-licensing, and earnings-tax revenue for cities and to enable them to preserve capital investments in their infrastructures. The promoters' primary aim is to attract conventions, which will provide good exposure for further tourist trade, but they also hope that entertainment and cultural attractions will draw suburban residents into the city to spend their money.

Potential Social and Economic Liabilities of Convention Trade

Convention bureau literature, reports in trade journals and magazines, and real estate feasibility studies optimistically expound the benefits of the tourist trade. Little or no attention is directed to the potential liabilities of economic dependence on the tourist trade. George Young, in his study, *Tourism: Blessing or Blight?*, explores the other side of the question, which cities and entrepreneurs, in their scramble to get their share of the tourism pie, gloss over or ignore.

Young advances the hypothesis that there is a saturation level for tourism in a given locality and that this level is exceeded when the costs of tourism begin to outweigh the benefits. According to Young:

> These saturation levels may be dictated by the availability of labor, the cost of providing the tourist infrastructure, and the amount of land suitable for hotel and related development. If a national policy is formulated without regard for these saturation levels—and there are signs that this is happening—then that policy must be revised.[53]

Young, a British economist and member of the London Tourist Board and Convention Bureau, maintains that low-wage employment needed to service the tourist and convention industry can be a threat to the local employment structure. He argues that most tourism jobs are low paying, offering only subsistence wages. Hence, these jobs do not increase the overall wage income of a city appreciably or provide much income tax revenue. Because the work is unpleasant, offering little incentive for advancement, the turnover is high and the labor force as a whole never improves its skills. Moreover, because wages are minimal and turnover is high, it is likely that workers will have trouble supporting their families and will require welfare services from government. Thus, he argues, cities may wind up subsidizing tourism and convention-generated jobs. "In this context one can say that saturation levels have been reached when the unfavorable consequences of further growth outweigh the benefits."[54]

Young's second point is that tourism may sometimes cost more in municipal services than it provides in revenue. Convention trade involves costs to the city, because visitors require such services as police and fire protection, airports, transportation, and sewers. An example of residential awareness of this level of saturation was the strenuous opposition mounted by the citizens of San Diego to the Republican Convention Site Selection Committee's designation of their city as host city for the 1972 Republican convention. Taxpayers saw the costs of police protection and city services required during the convention as an excessive revenue drain.[55]

Whether the costs of tourism outweighs the economic benefits for a significant number of cities has never been rigorously calculated. As in the Yerba Buena case, it is likely that downtown economic interests always benefit, but it is also likely that taxpayers sometimes suffer a net loss.

An important cost that has never been calculated concerns the use of land in the central portions of the cities. Land to accommodate tourism replaces land that could be used for housing, schools, and recreation. In redevelopment controversies this issue has caused recurring conflict. In spite of the arguments that increased convention trade will serve as a catalyst for urban economic growth, conflicts arise concerning the benefit of proposed projects to corporate entrepreneurs versus the interests of small business owners and residents, and the justification of subsidizing profits for certain businesses by offering tax incentives to build on redevelopment sites.

A debate in 1972 over the civic and convention center complex proposed as the core of a downtown renewal project in Washington, D.C., illustrates the types of issues that are involved in public investment in convention facilities and renewal projects.[56] The proposed complex was to be built on ten acres of central city land that then was occupied by low-income housing, shops catering to local residents, pleasant open space, and some unique ethnic areas. Officials argued that redevelopment would stimulate overall improvement by bringing jobs, revenue, and business into the area. They asserted that the facility was badly needed, that the city was losing money because of its lack of a convention center to accommodate larger business group functions, and that the center was vital for maintaining the city's competitive position as a tourist destination.

Opponents called the proposed center one more instance of removal of the poor and claimed that there was insufficient information on the future of convention business to gauge whether or not there was a demand for the facility. They recalled similar arguments that a demand existed for a new sports stadium, which subsequently was built and which cost the city $6.7 million in interest subsidies over twelve years—and which failed to keep the city's major league baseball team from moving to Texas. Even admitting the possibility of a demand, opponents claimed that the Convention Center would force residents to move at a time of acute housing shortage, destroy ethnic neighborhoods, and cause many small businesses to close. As land values rose, they asserted, the area would become another enclave for the wealthy. Ada Louise Huxtable raised much the same questions about the Covent Garden plan in central London. Her question logically could be applied concerning all tourist development:

> Is this the place for a convention center? Should this ever be the site for a large-scale building? . . . What will happen to the rich mixture of small enterprises and the cohesive community of elderly residents on small incomes when this construction, with its inevitable inflation of land values, moves in?[57]

Reliable information on convention business and its costs is scarce. Most estimates concerning the extent of the trade and projections of its economic benefits are based on guesswork rather than on hard economic data. Cities are making massive investments in convention centers based on insufficient information, scarce sampling, and sketchy feasibility studies. There is the real possibility that many cities will lose out in the future, since the growing pool of facilities is likely to exceed the demand. As more and more facilities are constructed, and as the competition for business grows more intense, cost is increasingly favorable for convention sponsors and unfavorable for individual cities.

Most convention centers lose money,[58] but city officials are so caught up in the competition for tourism that they cannot refrain from spending taxpayers' dollars. According to New York City Councilwoman Ruth Messinger, "It's exactly like the international arms race."[59] In the decade between 1976 and 1986, 250 convention centers, sports arenas, community centers and performing arts halls were constructed or started, with a price tag of more than $10 billion. In Denver, however, voters rejected bonds for a new center that was pushed hard by downtown business leaders. Expansion of the Moscone Center in San Francisco was the subject of intense political conflict. The final building was constructed mostly underground in order to avoid neighborhood opposition. The Dallas Convention Center makes a profit, but Los Angeles' Convention and Exhibit Center is subsidized by construction bonds backed by the city, though the Center itself makes money. However, San Francisco's center lost $2.5 million in 1985, and Washington, D.C.'s lost $5.9 million.[60]

Competition ensures that all cities cannot be winners in the tourism sweepstakes. If all cities that have 50,000 square feet or more of convention space got an equal share of the trade, each would have less than six bookings each year.[61] Though some cities win, others are bound to lose.

The New Redevelopment Phase

In late March 1977, Detroit dedicated its Renaissance Center, built at a cost of $337 million. The new center was proclaimed the symbol of

Detroit's revitalization by its mayor, who said, "We have here a monumental statement that speaks for itself. The cities are on the upsurge."[62]

The Renaissance Center is impressive. Its seventy-three–story Detroit Plaza Hotel is the cylindrical anchor of a complex of tall, shimmering structures that dominate the Detroit riverfront. Inside, hotel guests eat and drink on overhanging pods, which look down on a huge atrium of ponds and hanging plants.

Partly because of its striking contrast to the rest of Detroit, the Renaissance Center suggests questions about what redevelopment means. As pointed out by the *Newsweek* article that reported the dedication of the new center, critics see "the project as a self-contained white island that will absorb thousands of affluent suburbanites by day, disgorge them to the freeways at night—and do little to pep up a dispirited downtown."[63] The Renaissance Center raises the most basic concern about the politics of growth in contemporary American cities: can revitalization solve the social problems of the central cities?

It seems certain that revitalization—if it is defined as attracting tourists and suburbanites to the central cities—will not solve the problems of poverty, low incomes, or bad housing that historically have plagued the central cities. It seems equally certain that some areas of the central cities will indeed not only become economically viable but also become fully competitive with the suburbs. If the slums of the cities can be securely isolated from the islands of affluence now being constructed, then many political groups—those that have been identified in this chapter as the members of a progrowth coalition—will proclaim that the cities have been saved. The slums will still exist, but they will not seem so bothersome to downtown political and economic leaders, or to the middle-class residents living in their redeveloped enclaves.

Aside from issues of social justice, many people question these developments on their own merits. For example, one critic of the highrise fever that has hit San Francisco noted, "I've only been a resident since 1955; but I've watched a real city turn plastic in that time. The new downtown hotels are structures precisely designed to debauch a metropolis. They are ugly, and they are wasteful of both space and amenity."[64] In a similar vein, writer Calvin Trillin expressed second thoughts about his native Kansas City's redevelopment process: "Now that Kansas City had decided to take on the trappings that will supposedly mark it as what a Crown Center brochure calls 'one of the hot cities of the early '70s' . . . I feel the way I might feel if an old friend, someone who had always been an unassuming and quietly dressed businessman, suddenly turned up in a bushy mustache and bell-bottom hiphuggers and a buckskin jacket; there is a terrible temptation to say, 'Oh, come off it.'"[65] What these two critics fear is that in their rush to attract affluent residents and tourists the cities will lose the cultural uniqueness that has characterized them in the past. Considering the long history of clearance and new construction under urban renewal programs, this fear is not unfounded.

However, the new redevelopment is fundamentally different from the urban renewal of the 1950s and 1960s. First, it usually is designed principally for affluent people, whereas urban renewal projects were statutorily obligated to have other purposes as well. Second, clearance has become less fashionable since the early 1970s and 1980s. Restoration and renovation is the new game in town. Projects that have taken on a historic motif and translated it into a salable package are present in every large city. San Francisco has its Ghirardelli Square and Fishermen's Wharf; Salt Lake City has its Trolley Square; Denver its Laramer Square; Chicago its Navy Pier; Atlanta has Peachtree Plaza; Kansas City has Crown Center; and St. Louis has Laclede's Landing and Union Station. There is Quincy Market in Boston, Harbor Place in Baltimore, and the South Street Seaport in New York. It would be an oversimplification to assert that the revitalization now taking place will do nothing more than create new suburbs downtown or that it will change the downtown areas of the cities into plastic. It depends on the individual city and on the activities of its entrepreneurs.

What seems more likely is that the politics of growth will result in both new construction and an accelerated preservation process, which has been relatively absent in the cities during the past thirty years. Scarcely an American city exists today that is not undergoing large-scale, highly visible rehabilitation of both commercial and residential districts.

Neighborhood Revitalization

There is ample evidence that some degree of neighborhood revival is taking place in cities all across the United States. There are many neighborhood counterparts to the commercial success stories—for example, Society Hill in Philadelphia, the West End neighborhoods in St. Louis, Capitol Hill in Denver. Although the "boosterism" literature inflates the success stories in order to attract readers, there is solid scholarly evidence that neighborhood revitalization is a widespread phenomenon. In 1977, Gregory Lipton published a widely cited study showing that the number of high-status census tracts in several cities had increased between 1960 and 1970. He inferred from these data the existence of a central city migration of high-status residents, especially in cities that provided a high proportion of white-collar and professional jobs.[66] An Urban Land Institute study published in 1975 found that significant renovation activity was occurring in nearly three fourths of all cities of 500,000 or more. About 60 percent of the cities with populations between 100,000, and 500,000 were undergoing renovation in their deteriorated areas.[67] Even stronger evidence became available; comparing data from 1955 to 1960 with data from 1965 to 1970, researchers found that most central cities had improved their ability to attract high-status residents, and that large cities of the northeastern and north central regions had "sharply *increased* [their] ability to attract high-status immigrants compared with large southern and western cities; this difference is especially pronounced for northeastern cities."[68] The authors proposed that large northern cities might have a "much brighter future . . . than many urban analysts have forecasted. . . ."[69]

It would be a serious error to conclude from these studies that an overall reversal of decline is taking place in the older cities. All the old cities still contain large areas that are physically deteriorated. These cities continue to struggle with high crime, deteriorated neighborhoods, poverty, high unemployment, homelessness, and worsening fiscal problems. Even aside from these problems, evidence indicates clearly that throughout the 1970s, old cities were still losing many high-status residents to the suburbs. Between March, 1975, and March, 1977, more than 5.5 million people moved from central cities to the suburbs, while only 3 million people moved in the opposite direction.[70] Between 1968 and 1975, 13.4 million new housing units were constructed in the nation, but only an estimated 50,000 units a year were rehabilitated in central cities in the United States.[71]

Neighborhood revitalization is not a product of a generalized mass appeal, and it does not indicate a significant change in attitudes toward the central cities. Perceptions of large cities are overwhelmingly negative. Of the respondents sampled in a Louis Harris poll conducted in 1977, 90 percent believed that large cities had the most crime, 62 percent felt that large cities had the worst public schools and the worst housing, and 82 percent thought that the large cities were the worst places in which to raise children.[72] A 1979 HUD survey conducted in the metropolitan areas of Houston, Rochester, and Dayton concluded that "the clearest message from tomorrow's neighborhood choices from our 900 respondents is 'not in the city.'" The report further noted that "no more than 20 percent of our sample expressed any interest in ever moving 'back to town.'"[73]

The neighborhood revitalization phenomenon is characteristic of select areas within central cities, not of *all* areas in those cities. Though revitalization is undoubtedly widespread, the total number of people moving into revitalizing or revitalized neighborhoods has not been sufficient to reverse the movement from central cities to the suburbs.[74]

Neighborhood revitalization is sustained by a narrow, though growing, segment of the population. Young singles and newly married childless couples are disproportionately attracted back to the cities.[75] Upper-middle-class levels of education and income also characterize migrants to rehabilitating areas.[76] Changes in the U.S. population profile have resulted in a larger number of people who might prefer living in central cities to living in suburbs.[77] The percentage of individuals between twenty-five and thirty-nine years of age has increased in every census since World War II, and this trend will continue until the turn of the century. A larger proportion of this "baby boom" generation than ever before has either remained single, gotten divorced, or elected to get married but not to have children. The fertility rate dropped to an all-time low of 1.99 births per woman (lifetime) in 1982, and had stayed at about this level since the mid 1970s. It requires 2.1 births for each woman for the population to maintain itself.[78] Households have declined in size from 3.37 in 1950, to 2.72 in 1982.[79]

Demographic trends that increase the pool of potential central city migrants interact with still other factors; an even more stratified profile of potential "neighborhood renovators" emerges. People with higher incomes have the greatest propensity to move,[80] and as shown in a study in New York City, unrelated individuals with high incomes tended to live closer to downtown Manhattan than larger families with either high or low incomes.[81] People in professional and technical occupations are more likely to move than those in any other occupational groups[82]; a large proportion of professional and technical jobs are located in downtown areas[83]; commuting is often an important consideration to people living in central cities.[84] When all of these characteristics are combined with the types of housing and amenities available in many city neighborhoods (relatively small living units, proximity to restaurants, bars, and cultural facilities), what emerges is a profile of a select portion of the population that is potentially interested in redeveloped neighborhoods.[85]

Still, the absolute numbers of the potential "neighborhood renovators" are large. A survey conducted in 1977 found that 10 percent of household respondents felt that big cities were the "best place to live," while 74 percent favored suburbs, small towns, or rural areas. This translates into about 8 million households who might, potentially, move to cities, a big enough market to sustain revitalization, especially when demographic and social trends are also considered.[86]

From the redevelopment literature, it is clear that neighborhood redevelopment affects a small number of the locational choices made each year in urban areas. The people interested in revitalized areas are likely to be from a select group composed of white singles or married childless couples, who are professional, relatively young, and middle-income (the yuppies).

A study of neighborhood revitalization in St. Louis conducted in 1979 showed that even if successful, revitalization might have the effect of increasing social class and racial segregation within the central cities. Potential relocaters to the city's largest redevelopment areas were asked to rate the factors they considered most important in a redevelopment project. Among the most important factors the respondents identified were neighborhood appearance, type of neighbors, distance to work, racial make-up, and school quality. The authors concluded from their study that "many people might be favorably inclined to move back into the city if they felt that they could be segregated from blacks and from poor people, both in their neighborhoods and in their schools."[87]

The consequence of building neighborhoods segregated from the rest of the city would be to heighten economic and social inequality. This kind of neighborhood revitalization takes place at the expense of the minorities, the poor, and the aged. Displacement of neighborhood residents to make room for "higher" land uses is widespread. According to a Congressional report published in 1979, about 370,000 households were displaced each year by such housing conversions as officially-sponsored redevelopment, gentrification, and conversion of apartments to condominiums.[88] Whatever the costs, however, most central cities find that neighborhood revitalization in any form is irresistible: they find it necessary to promote developmental policies "which enhance the economic position of a community in its competition with others."[89] Neighborhood revitalization has developmental, not redistributive, objectives.

The Limits of Revitalization

It is important to note that even if revitalization is successful, measured by economic standards, it does not itself solve the "urban crisis," insofar as that crisis is defined in relation to levels of poverty, unemployment, crime, and slums. It is nearly certain that the poor do not benefit from the revitalization of the central cities. In search of cheap housing near places of employment, the poor will do what they have always done in urban areas: they will move into the housing that has been devalued in the market because it has become undesirable to the middle class. Islands of renewal will float in seas of decay.[90]

References

1. John H. Mollenkopf, "The Post-War Politics of Urban Development," in *Marxism and the Metropolis: New Perspectives in Urban Political Economy*, ed. William K. Tabb and Larry Sawers (New York: Oxford University Press, 1978), pp. 134–139.

2. Mollenkopf, p. 138.

3. See Robert Jacob Kerstein, "The Political Consequences of Federal Intervention: The Economic Opportunity Act and Model Cities in the City of St. Louis" (Ph.D. diss., Washington University, St. Louis, 1975).

4. Robert H. Salisbury, "The New Convergence of Power in Urban Politics," *Journal of Politics* (November 1964):775–797.

5. Mollenkopf, "The Post-War Politics of Urban Development," p. 140.

6. Mollenkopf, p. 138.

7. John H. Mollenkopf, "On the Courses and Consequences of Neighborhood Political Mobilization," paper delivered at the Annual Meeting of the American Political Science Association, New Orleans, September 4–8, 1973.

8. Clarence N. Stone, *Economic Growth and Neighborhood Discontent: System Bias in the Urban Renewal Program of Atlanta* (Chapel Hill: The University of North Carolina Press, 1976), p. 168.

9. Quoted in Stone, pp. 48–49.

10. Stone, p. 66.

11. The following material on the Yerba Buena controversy draws on Chester Hartman's excellent book, *Yerba Buena: Land Grab and Community Resistance in San Francisco* (San Francisco: Glide Publications, 1974). In most cases, citations are limited to quotations or specific data.

12. Hartman, p. 31.

13. Hartman, p. 31.

14. Hartman, p. 48.

15. Hartman, p. 190.

16. Hartman, p. 19.

17. Hartman, p. 73.

18. Hartman, p. 128.

19. Hartman, p. 159.

20. Hartman, p. 179.

21. Charles G. Burck, "It's Promoters vs. Taxpayers in the Superstadium Game," *Fortune*, March 1973, pp. 104–107, 178–182.

22. Hartman, *Yerba Buena*, p. 175.

23. Joseph E. Haring, ed., *Urban and Regional Economics: Perspectives for Public Action* (Boston: Houghton Mifflin, 1972), p. 27.

24. Bennett Harrison, *Urban Economic Development: Suburbanization, Minority Opportunity, and the Condition of the Central City* (Washington, D.C.: The Urban Institute, 1974), p. 18; refer also to Benjamin I. Cohen, "Trends in Negro Employment within Large Metropolitan Areas," *Public Policy* (Winter 1972): Table 1.

25. Quoted in U.S. Congress, Library of Congress Legislative Research Service, *The Central City Problem and Urban Renewal Policy* (Washington, D.C.: Legislative Research Service, 1973), p. 34.

26. Quoted in Legislative Research Service, p. 36.

27. Legislative Research Service, p. 36.

28. Cited in *The New York Times*, February 17, 1976, p. 8.

29. *New York Times*, October 21, 1974, p. 38.

30. Gustav Zedek, *Der Fremdenverkehr in der Osterreichischen Wirtschaft*, quoted in George Young, *Tourism: Blessing or Blight?* (Harmondsworth, England: Penguin, 1973), p. 45.

31. U.S. Department of Commerce, Travel Service, *The Market for International Congresses,* conducted by Karol N. Gess (Washington, D.C.: U.S. Government Printing Office, August 1975), p. 2.

32. "The U.S. Seeks a Bigger Slice of the World's Convention Business," *Commerce Today,* July 10, 1972, p. 11–12.

33. U.S. National Tourism Resources Review Commission, *Destination U.S.A.,* vol. 2 (Washington, D.C.: National Tourism Resources Review Commission, June 1973), p. 41.

34. *New York Times,* January 25, 1976, p. 6.

35. "Convention Business Picks Up a Bit," *Business Week,* February 19, 1972, p. 28.

36. Cited in Governmental Research Unit, "Economic Benefits to St. Louis of the Proposed Convention Hall and Plaza," 1972 (unpublished report), pp. 4–6.

37. *St. Louis Globe-Democrat,* November 9, 1975, Sunday Magazine, p. 8.

38. U.S. National Tourism Resources Review Commission, *Destination U.S.A.,* vol. 2, p. 45.

39. *New York Times,* March 17, 1976, p. 43.

40. *New York Times,* October 8, 1976, p. 45.

41. *New York Times,* October 8, 1976, p. 46.

42. U.S. National Tourism Resources Review Commission, *Destination U.S.A.,* vol. 1, p. 106.

43. "The U.S. Seeks a Bigger Slice of the World's Convention Business," *Commerce Today,* July 10, 1972, p. 12.

44. "The U.S. Seeks a Bigger Slice," p. 14.

45. "The U.S. Seeks a Bigger Slice," p. 12.

46. "The U.S. Seeks a Bigger Slice," p. 13.

47. U.S. National Tourism Resources Review Commission, *Destination U.S.A.,* vol. 2, p. 34.

48. Governmental Research Unit, "Economic Benefits to St. Louis," p. 14.

49. *New York Times,* June 21, 1976, p. 43.

50. "Each Tourist Dollar Found to Be Producing More than 7 Cents in Tax Revenues," *Commerce Today,* March 14, 1974, p. 14.

51. "Each Tourist Dollar," p. 14.

52. Real Estate Research Corporation, "Market Study and Economic Analysis for Proposed Convention Center, Indianapolis, Indiana," 1966 (unpublished report).

53. Young, *Tourism: Blessing or Blight?,* p. 111–112.

54. Young, p. 117.

55. "President Picks a Place: San Diego, California," *Time,* August 2, 1971, pp. 15–16.

56. *Washington Post,* October 4, 1972, p. A1.

57. Quoted in U.S. National Tourism, Resources Review Commission, *Destination U.S.A.,* vol. 2, p. 52.

58. Hartman, *Yerba Buena,* p. 165.

59. "Convention Centers Spark Civic Wars," *U.S. News and World Report*, February 10, 1986, p. 45.

60. *Ibid.*

61. Hartman, *Yerba Buena*, p. 175.

62. *Newsweek*, March 28, 1977, p. 60.

63. *Newsweek*, March 28, 1977, p. 60.

64. Hartman, *Yerba Buena*, p. 177.

65. Calvin Trillin, "U.S. Journal: Kansas City, Missouri—Reflections of Someone Whose Home Town Has Become a Glamour City," *The New Yorker*, April 8, 1974, p. 94.

66. Gregory S. Lipton, "Evidence of Central City Revival," *Journal of the American Institute of Planners* 45 (April 1977):136–147.

67. Thomas J. Black, "Private-Market Housing Renovation in Central Cities: An Urban Land Institute Survey," in *Back to the City: Issues in Neighborhood Renovation*, ed. Shirley Bradway Laska and Daphne Spain (New York: Pergamon Press, 1980), p. 7.

68. Harvey Marshall and Bonnie L. Lewis, "Back to the City: An Analysis of Trends in the Sixties and Seventies," *Journal of Urban Affairs* 4 (Winter 1982):27.

69. Marshall and Lewis, p. 31.

70. George Sternlieb and Kristina Ford, "The Future of the Return-to-the City Movement," in *Revitalizing Cities*, ed. Herrington Bryce (Lexington, Mass.: Lexington Books), pp. 86–87.

71. Black "Private-Market Housing Renovation"; Anthony Downs, *Neighborhoods and Urban Development* (Washington, D.C.: The Brookings Institution, 1981), p. 74.

72. Louis Harris and Associates, Inc., *A Survey of Citizens' Views and Concerns About Urban Life*, conducted for Department of Housing and Urban Development (February 1979), pp. 135, 147, 151, 159.

73. U.S. Department of Housing and Urban Development, *The Behavioral Foundations of Neighborhood Change* (Washington, D.C.: U.S. Government Printing Office, 1979).

74. Larry Long, "Back to the Countryside and Back to the City in the Same Decade," in *Back to the City*, ed. Laska and Spain, pp. 61–76.

75. Gary A. Tobin and Dennis R. Judd, "Moving the Suburbs to the City: Neighborhood Revitalization and the 'Amenities Bundle,'" *Social Science Quarterly* 63 no. 4 (December 1982):771–780; Gary A. Tobin and Dennis R. Judd, "Who Moves into Redevelopment Neighborhoods? Evidence From a St. Louis Study," January 1973 (unpublished paper); Joseph C. Hu, "Who's Moving In and Who's Moving Out—And Why," *Federal National Mortgage Association, Seller/Servicer* 5 (May–June 1978):23; Joseph C. Hu, "The Demographics of Urban Upgrading," *Federal National Mortgage Association, Seller/Servicer* 5 (November–December 1978):30–37; John D. Hutcheson Jr. and Elizabeth T. Beer, "In-Migration and Atlanta's Neighborhoods," *Atlanta Economic Review* 28 (March–April 1978):8; Downs, p. 77.

76. Sternlieb and Ford, p. 103; Tobin and Judd; Gregory Lipton, "Attitudes of Residents toward Returning to the Center of a Growing City: A Case Study of

Eugene, Oregon" (Eugene: University of Oregon, Department of Urban and Regional Planning, 1977); Long, "Back to the Countryside and Back to the City"; Dennis Gale, "Neighborhood Resettlement: Washington, D.C.," in Laska and Spain, pp. 95–115; Phillip L. Clay, "The Rediscovery of City Neighborhoods: Reinvestment by Long-Time Residents and Newcomers," in Laska and Spain, pp. 13–26.

77. Long; Bruce London, "Gentrification as Urban Reinvasion: Some Preliminary Definitional and Theoretical Considerations," in *Back to the City*, ed. Laska and Spain, pp. 77–92.

78. U.S. Bureau of the Census, *Current Population Reports*, Series P-20, No. 379, "Fertility of American Women: June 1982" (Advance Report).

79. U.S. Bureau of the Census, *Current Population Reports*, Series P-20, No. 381, "Household and Family Characteristics: March 1982" (Washington, D.C.: U.S. Government Printing Office, 1983).

80. John M. Goering, "Neighborhood Tipping and Racial Transition: A Review of Social Science Evidence," *Journal of American Institute of Planners* 44 (January 1976):68–70.

81. Clifford R. Kern, "Private Residential Renewal and the Supply of Neighborhoods," in *The Economics of Neighborhood*, ed. David Segal (New York: Academic Press, 1979), pp. 121–146.

82. Karl Taeuber, *Migration in the United States: An Analysis of Residence Histories*, Public Health Monograph no. 77 (Washington, D.C.: U.S. Department of Health, Education, and Welfare, 1968).

83. Alan Kirschenbaum, "City-Suburban Destination Choices among Migrants to Metropolitan Areas," *Demography* 9 (May 1972):321–335.

84. David Goldfield, "The Limits of Suburban Growth: The Washington, D.C., SMSA," *Urban Affairs Quarterly* 12 (September 1976):83–102; John Goodman, "Reasons for Moves out of and into Large Cities," *Journal of the American Planning Association* 45 (October 1979):407–416; Paul Porter, "The Neighborhood Interest in a City's Recovery," *Journal of the American Planning Association* 45 (October 1979):19–32.

85. Goodman, "Reasons for Moves"; Tobin and Judd, "Who Moves Into Redevelopment Neighborhoods."

86. Downs, *Neighborhoods and Urban Development*, p. 77; Paul K. Mancini and Martin D. Abravanel, "Signs of Urban Vitality and of Distress: Citizen Views on the Quality of Urban Life," Department of Housing and Urban Development, *Occasional Papers in Housing and Community Affairs* 4 (1979).

87. Tobin and Judd, p. 778.

88. Office of Policy Development and Research, Department of Housing and Urban Development, *Displacement Report* (Washington, D.C.: U.S. Government Printing Office, 1979), p. 23.

89. Paul E. Peterson, *City Limits* (Chicago: University of Chicago Press, 1981).

90. Brian J. L. Berry, "Islands of Renewal in Seas of Decay," in *The New Urban Reality*, ed. Paul E. Peterson (Washington, D.C.: The Brookings Institution, 1985), pp. 69–96.

Chapter 13

THE ECONOMIC VERSUS POLITICAL LOGIC OF CITY POLITICS

The Conflicting Tasks of Local Governments

The crises of American society have been played out in its cities. Inequality, racism, and class antagonisms have been the principal ingredients in city politics mainly because "American cities have always been the repositories of social problems over which they lack control."[1] Concentration of industry brought millions of foreign immigrants and rural migrants to the cities over a very long period. Thus, the cities became the location for a disproportionate share of the nation's social problems. Cities became peculiar political institutions—virtually foreign countries within the nation. They were different from anywhere else, alien and threatening to the culture within which they were embedded. The twentieth-century political isolation of the central cities is in some ways a logical extension of their political isolation in the nineteenth century by state governments. Certainly the motive for isolating the cities has changed little.

Cities have had little or no choice about whether or not they would participate in these processes. "Neither demographic patterns nor poverty rates are caused in the cities, nor are they susceptible to much manipulation at that level. Urban authorities and citizens can hardly control the characteristics of the national economy."[2] If technological changes, unemployment levels, rates of poverty, profit rates, or other factors resulted in increased migration or inequality in wealth and incomes, the social and political consequences could be severe, but effectively beyond the ability of local governments to solve.

Short of erecting walls with gatekeepers instructed to allow only the affluent to enter, the cities could not avoid becoming the "promised land" for people seeking a better life. This has been their historic problem and function, and it has accounted for their unique place in American history.

Defined as locations for economic activity, cities are bound to use the instruments of government to promote economic growth. As political institutions, however, city governments also must broker among contending groups—in short, they must govern. Often, public officials are pulled in opposite directions—whatever actions they pursue to create economic vitality may exacerbate social tensions, and vice versa. In the 1980s, city officials have neglected the governing task in favor of the economic imperative.

Entrepreneurial strategies constitute the heart of the municipal policy agenda of the 1980s. Virtually all local public leaders consider economic development to be the linchpin that supports every activity undertaken by local government. As an administrative assistant to Denver's Mayor Federico Peña stated in a 1984 interview, "We probably will be criticized by some for focusing too much on downtown. People will ask, 'What does Saks Fifth Avenue have to do with the neighborhoods?' The answer is that downtown retailing has everything to do with the neighborhoods. The city needs the revenue."[3]

Federico Peña is one of the new crop of aggressive, generally young, somewhat unconventional mayors of the 1980s. What makes them unconventional is that many of them engage in populist rhetoric, and they have been elected with the support of new coalitions composed of minority voters, whites who have become disaffected from the two-party system, first-time young voters, traditional liberals and yuppies, and, in some cities, feminists and gays. In most cases, the downtown-oriented business establishment has greeted their election with nervous anticipation or even outright alarm.

What makes these mayors conventional is their acceptance, once elected, of the necessity to subsidize private sector activity in their cities. Coleman Young is as likely as any big city mayor to have pushed for programs of redistribution as well as growth. In the 1950s he was a Marxist labor organizer who was blacklisted by both the United Auto Workers and the auto companies. But since being elected as Detroit's first black mayor in 1973, he has aggressively pursued corporate investment. The

Renaissance Center has been supported with millions of dollars in tax abatements and federal subsidies. In the early 1980s, Detroit engaged in one of the nation's most controversial urban redevelopment projects, involving the clearing of 465 acres of land in a working-class, ethnic, and black area known as Poletown, in an attempt to keep a General Motors Cadillac plant in the city. Young has fully accepted a logic of growth that makes clearance and subsidy projects inevitable:

> Those are rules and I'm going by the goddamn rules. This suicidal outthrust competition . . . has got to stop but until it does, I mean to compete. It's too bad we have a system where dog eats dog and the devil takes the hindmost. But I'm tired of taking the hindmost.[4]

Mayor Young's attitude is hardly unique. Almost every American city is trying to outbid its neighbors in pursuit of its share of national, regional, and economic growth. A complex assortment of weapons is being used in these wars, including (for example) tax abatements and rollbacks, tax increment financing, sales tax exemptions, guaranteed loans, industrial bond financing, free industrial sites. Despite the fact that the Reagan Administration proposal for federal urban enterprise zones has not been passed by Congress, these zones are becoming more widely used year by year. At the beginning of 1984, nine states had enacted zone legislation and there were 180 designated zones.[5]

These policies are based on false premises. The overwhelming scholarly consensus is that tax incentives offered by local governments do not materially influence investment decisions.[6] Taxes are low on the list of business expenses as a factor of production, and there seems to be no relationship between tax levels among states and growth rates in manufacturing or service employment.[7] A study of business location studies conducted since the 1920s concluded that "taxes and fiscal inducements have very little if any effect on industrial location decisions. Thus, state and local policies designed to attract business are generally wasted government resources."[8]

Economic development incentives need not be effective to be favored by urban political leaders. Mayors are caught between opposing forces. They are expected to find solutions to their cities' problems, but they also frequently command diminishing resources with which to implement effective policy responses. "Most cities [find] themselves literally too small to handle their policy problems but politically too weak to resist trying."[9] In such circumstances, public officials find that economic growth policies carry important symbolic value, giving the voting public the impression that aggressive, creative leadership is being applied to the municipality's problems, even if, in the short run, city services and budgetary problems remain largely unchanged.

No big city mayor, however politically conservative, can ignore the fact that local government must manage political conflict. This is especially obvious to those "new-breed" mayors who have put together electoral coalitions that may be impatient for the benefits of growth to trickle down. Thus there are tensions in the current growth strategies. How the conflicts between economic growth and the need for social cohesion will be managed is the most compelling issue for American cities in the 1980s.

The Political Tightrope

Many mayors walk a political tightrope. On the one hand, they feel it necessary to provide tax breaks and other incentives to businesses and affluent residents that may help generate jobs and aid the local economy. On the other hand, poor people and minorities are located disproportionately in cities, and there are pressures to respond to the serious social problems within central city borders. As a consequence, some city officials have searched for economic growth strategies that will keep their *electoral* constituencies satisfied, without alienating their *economic* constituencies.

The politics of big cities is so complicated and contentious that any attempt to focus on "community development" or development of the "local economy" turns to questions about "which community" and "which sector" of the local economy. Cities that contain large numbers of poor people, or large minority populations, are confronted with an economic logic of growth—defined as attempts to attract large corporations, tourists, and affluent residents—that seems at odds with a political logic that mayors are faced with at election time.

By 1985, there were nineteen black mayors in cities with populations over 100,000. In 1987, Baltimore remained the only city of this size with a majority black population that had not elected a black mayor. In the mid-1980s, black mayors governed in four of the ten largest cities—Chicago, Detroit, Los Angeles, and Philadelphia. Three big cities—Denver, San Antonio, and Miami—have elected Hispanic mayors.

Of course, a minority mayor may not necessarily push for a new municipal agenda. Coleman Young and Andrew Young, for example, preside over conventional, old-style, downtown-growth politics in Detroit and Atlanta.[10] Lionel Wilson, the mayor of Oakland, California, has led a fight to cut municipal expenditures and to bring more business investment to that city. Wilson Goode campaigned for the mayoralty of Philadelphia in 1983 on a classic reform platform, promising to streamline city bureaucracies, build a convention center, improve the port, and promote economic development.[11] Indeed, because the coalitions that elect them are usually so tenuous, minority mayors probably feel that it is necessary to be cautious about controversial policy initiatives. A major study, in fact, found that black urban officials expressed attitudes and followed policies not distinctly different from white urban leaders regarding levels of city taxation and indebtedness.[12]

However, it seems certain that pressures on black leaders to advocate progressive policies are accelerating. The Jesse Jackson presidential campaign, with its unprecedented success at mobilizing new voters, played on massive dissatisfaction with the current two-party system and with traditional policy prescriptions.[13] For more than twenty years, public opinion polls have documented a wide gap between black and white attitudes on social welfare spending and government services.[14] The preference by blacks for higher spending levels has remained remarkably stable over time.[15] Possibly because the general preferences of blacks have not changed much for a long period, there is more agreement between the policy views of black public officials and black voters, regardless of social class, than between white officials and the white electorate.[16]

The first blacks elected as mayors of major American cities—Richard Hatcher in Gary, Indiana, and Carl Stokes in Cleveland (both elected in 1967)—successfully pushed for more spending for health, education, housing, and job training programs, and increases in federal grants.[17] Subsequent studies have confirmed that cities with black mayors and black council members have a higher proportion of social welfare expenditures.[18] A study that measured the degree of incorporation of blacks and Hispanics into the politics of ten California cities concluded that political incorporation was associated with policies desired by minorities. Further, in several of the cities "Political incorporation was responsible for dramatic changes in bureaucratic decision rules in many policy areas" such as city hiring and contracting procedures.[19]

The California study also found that federal employment and social programs had the effect of stimulating "demand-protest and electoral mobilization by increasing the resources available to minorities and the cadre of minority leaders committed to mobilization."[20]

Now that the federal government has broken its twenty-year alliance with the civil rights movement and also slashed urban and social programs, a new politics is certain to appear in cities with large minority populations. Voter registration drives have created urban constituencies strongly opposed to federal cutbacks, and have vastly increased black and Hispanic participation in city elections.[21] The mobilization of new voters has sharpened the pressure on local elected officials, as civil rights and community organizations focus attention away from the federal government and toward states and localities. States and cities have, as a result, opposed the federal government on a variety of issues, including the civil rights retreat launched by the Justice Department.[22]

Thus, it seems likely that most minority mayors will either favor progressive policies to begin with or be forced to move in that direction. Nearly all black mayors win office by gaining an overwhelming proportion of black votes, usually more than 95 percent, and a relatively smaller percentage of white votes, typically 10 percent to 20 percent. The key to victory is a combination of huge black majorities and heavier-than-usual turnout. For example, Wilson Goode received 97 percent of the black vote in the Philadelphia primary election held on May 18, 1983, while attracting 23 percent of the vote in white areas.[23] In Chicago's general election of April 12, 1983, Harold Washington received 98 percent of the black vote, 58 percent of the Hispanic vote, and 18 percent of the white vote.[24] When black candidates run for office, voting divides along racial lines.[25] Even in their reelection campaigns, black incumbents rely on racial bloc voting by the black electorate to keep them in office, though turnout and voter interest often decline from the first campaign.[26]

A Populist Agenda?

In cities with racial bloc voting, what is a Populist (or Progressive) agenda? Populist political leaders usually promise increased citizen participation, immediate benefits to neighborhoods, and programs to help underemployed and unemployed people and disadvantaged minority groups. Such programs include home rehabilitation loans, low-interest mortgage loans, small business loans, technical assistance to new businesses, affirmative action hiring standards for women and minorities, health clinics, and more. The experience of two cities, Denver and Chicago, show two different ways this politics is unfolding.

Growth policies in Denver historically have been narrowly targeted toward downtown projects.[27] During the years when Denver's central business district changed from older, red-brick and sandstone commercial buildings to a forest of skyscrapers, William H. McNichols served as mayor.

"Mayor Bill," as many Denverites affectionately called him, was first elected in 1968. McNichols was a cigar-chomping Democrat who applied much of his authority toward encouraging private sector initiative and development downtown. During the 1970s, a new art museum was built, along with a new sports arena, an expanded sports stadium, and a higher education campus next to downtown. McNichols succeeded in getting over $400 million in bonds approved for public improvements, a feat that earned him the nickname, "Bill the bondsman."[28] Through the Skyline Project, the Denver Urban Renewal Authority (DURA) presided over the reconstruction of a twenty-seven–block area in downtown Denver. By the fall of 1984 nearly a billion dollars of public and private funds had been spent on construction in the Skyline Project.[29]

On June 21, 1983, 36-year-old Federico Peña defied the political odds-makers and captured the mayor's office. His campaign manager exulted, "Taking someone with a five percent name recognition who happens to be Hispanic in a city with an 18 percent Hispanic population—that has got to be something of a major political event in the city's history, if not the state and region."[30] Peña's election was, indeed, a unique event, marking the first time that a Hispanic mayor had been elected in a major U.S. city that was not itself predominantly Hispanic.

The coalition that put Peña into office included thousands of liberals who had consistently voted for Representative Patricia Schroeder and Senator Gary Hart but who had never been motivated to vote in large numbers in local elections. The disparate group included blacks and Hispanics, labor, gays, some leading business figures, women's groups, environmentalists, neighborhood activists, the handicapped, and even three of the candidates that Peña had defeated in the primary election.

To build this electoral coalition, Peña ran an issue-oriented campaign with the theme, "Imagine a Great City." In a series of issue papers distributed as part of his campaign literature, he advocated new policies on air pollution, airport expansion, neighborhood planning, economic development and job creation, and planning for and managing the physical development of the city. He promised to open city hall to neighborhood groups, minorities, and others who had previously been shut out of city government. He stressed the need for economic development and long-term planning. Peña charged that McNichols had cut back the city planning staff and almost eliminated neighborhood planning, policies that Peña vowed to reverse.

In contrast to the campaigns in Chicago and Philadelphia that same spring, the campaign and election in Denver were notable for their lack of overt racism. Peña's Hispanic background was seldom mentioned in public. He managed to avoid the topic almost entirely. Peña believed, "When I have a chance to meet people and talk to people the last thing they think of is I'm Hispanic."[31] Peña has persisted in downplaying his minority status while in office. He repeatedly turned down offers to participate in nationwide Hispanic political forums. He also avoided the spotlight during the Hispanic delegates' movement to abstain on the first ballot at the 1984 Democratic National Convention in protest over the Simpson-Mazzoli immigration bill.

Peña consistently maintained that Denver had "gone beyond questions of ethnic background."[32] The election results revealed Peña successfully had brought together a complex electoral coalition. An intensive voter registration failed to achieve its goal of 16,000 new Hispanic voters before the primary. Fewer than one-fourth of that number had registered.[33] It turned out that Peña did not have to rely on new Hispanic voters to win the May 17 primary. Peña finished first in a field of seven candidates. McNichols came in third. Peña's challenger for the general election was former District Attorney Dale Tooley, who attempted throughout the campaign to characterize Peña as too liberal and inexperienced.

On June 21, 1983, a record 71.5 percent of the registered voters went to the polls. Peña won by a narrow margin, 51.4 percent of the total vote to Tooley's 48.6 percent.[34] Peña had sealed the victory by adding more than 5,000 new voters to the rolls in the heavily minority-populated western and northern districts of the city. He won the northeast districts (52 percent black and 21 percent Hispanic) by four to one. New voters, blacks, and Hispanics, together with the other groups in his electoral coalition, put Peña over the top.

Federico Peña captured the mayor's office on the strength of a coalition composed of diverse groups that had never before had much influence in local politics. The new mayor moved immediately to follow through on many of his campaign promises. He pledged to open city governmental leadership positions to women and minorities. With regard to the neighborhoods, Peña had pledged that they would "have a partner, rather than an adversary" in the mayor's office.[35] To gather information from neighborhood groups he initiated "town meetings" in each council district. Peña increased the size of the neighborhood planning staff and ordered a traffic mitigation study of the one-way streets running through the neighborhoods toward downtown.

Denver has enlisted in the competitive race to attract new investment, sales, and jobs. Peña has consolidated the Planning Office, the Zoning Office, and the Community Development Agency under a new director of Planning and Development. An Economic Development Office has been placed within the Planning and Development Department to coordinate the city's economic development initiatives and to oversee such programs as industrial revenue bonds, the city's proposed foreign trade zone, neighborhood business revitalization activities, business information services, and public relations for the city.

Several economic development projects have been proposed. For example, Peña has been working fervently to develop a new convention center as "the major economic development project Denver undertakes in this decade."[36] According to the mayor, the existing convention facilities are inadequate for large national conventions. A new convention center and better marketing of the cultural attractions downtown are considered essential for attracting more visitors.

Another initiative illustrates the Peña administration's economic development priorities. On July 8, 1984, Peña announced that his administration and the downtown business development corporation, the Denver

Partnership, would cooperate in drawing up a new downtown master plan. The plan, to be completed by early 1986, was designed to direct and promote development in and around the central business district. A twenty-seven–member panel served as the steering committee for the project.

Some neighborhood groups were concerned that downtown interests were overrepresented on the committee. Five Denver Partnership members were included, compared to three seats for neighborhood leaders. The Denver Partnership provided 75 percent of the initial funding and two thirds of the staff for the eventual $3 million planning project. William Fleissig, Denver's downtown planner hired in 1984, explained that the Partnership had a dominant voice in the downtown plan because "We just didn't have the core staff or the money to do it ourselves."[37]

Very substantial subsidies are being offered, in the form of below-market rents, to attract a major national retailer downtown. Big-name retailers are considered pivotal to revive the image of downtown and to increase sales tax revenues. According to Mayor Peña, "If in a major city like Denver you have a downtown which is not full of people and where people are literally gone at 5:30 in the afternoon, then you begin to have questions about how exciting that city is."[38]

Soon after his election, Federico Peña attended a symposium for recently elected mayors at Harvard. Peña was surprised to hear the new mayors complain that the main obstacle to governance in their cities was animosity between the central business district and the neighborhoods over development priorities. Most of the new mayors, including Peña, had been elected on platforms advocating more influence for neighborhoods. But following their elections they faced the problem of heightened expectations and inadequate public resources. Peña did not sense this kind of conflict in Denver, and wondered why.[39]

Part of the explanation may be that Peña had successfully invoked the symbols of open and responsive government even though he did not change the substance of development priorities. He promised openness, and proceeded to hold town meetings. He promised representation, and began appointing minority and neighborhood representatives to a variety of posts. Perhaps most important, Peña promised to go to work to improve the city's economic condition and to ensure the vitality of its neighborhoods. It appears that he successfully persuaded most political groups that his downtown-centered development program was the way (eventually) to accomplish both goals.

Some, however, were beginning to feel impatient with the mayor: "He does listen, and we finally have an ear in the mayor's office. But sometimes an ear is not all you need. You still need some implementation. . . . We need to get beyond the listening stage."[40] Perhaps responding to such concerns —and mindful that several candidates have announced an interest in running against him in the next election—Peña emphasized "quality of life" issues over economic development in his State of the City address of July 10, 1985. He announced a $10 million program for low- and middle-income housing near downtown, an $11 million small business loan program, and new park acquisitions and neighborhood improvements.[41] After the address, the mayor's aides complained that the media were responsible for the perception that Peña had neglected the neighborhoods. One of them then went on to explain that the mayor would have to make it a point to persuade city residents that "big ticket" downtown projects such as the convention center were closely tied to city and neighborhood services:

> Even if you never go to the convention center in your entire life, it affects you because it allows us to clean up City Park, tear down a condemned building that's an eyesore in your neighborhood or get quicker response from the police. . . . We can only do these things if we have the money to do them.[42]

When Harold Washington was elected as Chicago's first black mayor on April 12, 1983, a political struggle was initiated over the definition of the municipal priorities. The Washington campaign promised three radical new departures: (1) a redistribution of power and resources away from downtown, (2) the mobilizing of previously inactive groups, and (3) "a substantial downward redistribution of benefits towards the many blacks who occupy the lower rungs of the socioeconomic ladder."[43] These were the central themes of Washington's campaign, summarized by one scholar as the premise that "power and resources had too long been concentrated in City Hall and in the CBD, which has long been seen by many as either the handmaidens of City Hall or as the key component in city government with City Hall as the Handmaiden."[44]

In April, 1983, about two weeks before the mayoral election, the Research and Issues Committee of the Washington campaign released a fifty-two–page document called *The Washington Paper*. These position papers defined city policy priorities in entrepreneurial terms, but populist principles guided the proposed entrepreneurial strategies. *The Washington Papers* constituted the philosophic and strategic underpinning for the lengthy, detailed *Chicago Development Plan* published in May 1984 under the title "Chicago Works Together." The five development goals of the new plan were:

Goal I: Increase job opportunities for Chicagoans
          Targeted business investment in support of job development
          Local preference in buying and hiring
          Skilled labor force development
          Infrastructure investment for job development
          Affirmative action

Goal II: Promote balanced growth
Balanced growth between downtown and neighborhoods
Public and private partnerships
Strengthened tax base
Equitable distribution of the tax burden

Goal III: Assist neighborhoods to develop through partnerships and
coordinated investment
Neighborhood planning
Linked development

Goal IV: Enhance public participation in decision making
Increased citizen access to information
Increased opportunities for citizen involvement

Goal V: Pursue a regional, state, and national legislative agenda

Under the machine, virtually all development money not allocated to downtown projects had been distributed to neighborhood chambers of commerce, in proportion to the powers and electoral successes of the ward committee members.[45] It may have been labeled "development money," but everyone knew it was patronage. Now the money was going to be distributed to neighborhood redevelopment corporations, cooperatives, and private businesses. By 1987, the Economic Development Department planned to create ten to twelve neighborhood corporations through which it would allocate grants.[46]

A successful distribution of money in this manner would undermine the machine's patronage system and at the same time create a new political coalition in the city centered in the neighborhoods. Thus intense battles between the City Council and Mayor Washington were being waged over the new programs.[47]

The *Chicago Development Plan 1984* outlined a formidable number of programs designed to bring recovery to the city's economy.[48] For the year beginning with the plan's publication in May, 1984, the list of job creation "targets" was extremely ambitious:

- Create or retain over 8,000 direct and indirect jobs through financial assistance for business expansion and start-up
- Provide technical assistance to more than 4,000 businesses
- Establish public-private task forces for at least two Chicago industries
- Increase City of Chicago local purchasing from 40 percent of total purchasing to approximately 60 percent or about $480 million; and increase private sector local purchasing by 5 percent or an estimated $2500 million
- Generate 1,500 direct and 2,000 indirect jobs through targeted local purchasing

- Increase City of Chicago purchasing from minority and women-owned firms to 25 percent of total purchasing, or $100 million
- Train 12,000 persons in employment skills, which will result in the placement of 8,000 trainees in jobs
- Enhance the employment skills of 17,000 youth

Neighborhood organizations were encouraged to review all city economic development programs and submit requests for financial assistance. Capital improvement programs were to be reviewed and implemented through the Neighborhood Infrastructure Renewal Task Force. All city contractors and businesses receiving financial assistance from the city were expected to participate in an aggressive affirmative action program. Twenty-five percent of city purchasing was to be targeted to companies owned by minorities and women; this would be overseen by the Purchasing from Minority and Women-Owned Firms program.

Several programs were designed to stimulate citizen participation and neighborhood institution-building. The philosophy guiding these programs was that

> successful neighborhood planning cannot be a "top-down" process. It must be based on an awareness that neighborhood problems and assets are best known to neighborhood residents and the local organizations devoted to the betterment of their neighborhoods.[49]

National news coverage of Chicago politics after 1983 has focused almost exclusively on Harold Washington's clashes with the Board of Aldermen. There were frequent clashes with Edward Vrdolyak, the Cook County Democratic chairman and the real leader in the Chicago City Council, and with Alderman Edward Burke, who chaired the Council's powerful finance committee. There was undeniably a racial component to this conflict, but racial fears were also manipulated as a handy device to organize opposition to the mayor's policies.

There is a common perception that the Washington administration has become bogged down, that the rhetoric of political change has been exceeded only by the ineffectuality of implementing programs. Some writers have noted a common perception that Washington "is disorganized and lackadaisical, an ineffective administrator."[50] A sympathetic observer blames his appointees: "Washington's staff is not organized for a big breakthrough, and its ineptitude sometimes descends to surprising depths: phone calls are not returned, letters go unanswered, the mayor misses meetings."[51]

Even with the best organized staff imaginable, it would be difficult to bring about rapid change. Potential saboteurs work right at the heart of the Washington administration. In every city department a few Washington appointees, often only two or three, occupy the top positions. The vast majority of employees were there long before the latest mayoral election, and they are secure in their jobs. According to the mayor, some of these employees are outright saboteurs: "We get reports of people calling in to ask a question and getting a snotty answer, on purpose. Or they'll say, 'You don't like it? The Mayor did it. You elected him,' and hang up. Or some inspector will harass someone and say it's on orders of the Mayor. We're weeding it out, but we can't control it."[52]

Mayor Washington has been trying to promote a national urban development agenda to other mayors and to the National Democratic party. In June, 1984, just in time for the U.S. Conference of Mayors meeting and the Democratic National Convention, the mayor's office printed 5,000 copies of a slick booklet under the title, "Mayor Harold Washington: A Federal/Urban Partnership to Renew Our Cities." The document outlined a full employment jobs program, a federally assisted effort to build capital infrastructure, and a federally funded housing program. The strategies promoted by Washington are all "entrepreneurial," a concept that provides the unifying theme for the booklet: "We believe that the cities, with the necessary help of the federal government, can become a dynamic entrepreneurial force which can strengthen local and national economies and increase fairness and equity at the same time."[53] The key new programs advocated include the following: a national Production and Jobs Board "that develops industrial policies in coordination with similar local economic development bodies"; a Community Renewal Employment Act; a National Capital Investment Bank to "provide a revolving fund at lower than private interest rates for local capital investment," to be matched by locally raised capital; and a Capital Investment Council to "advise governments on national resource allocation and local investment planning." But the Chicago delegation's efforts to promote these programs at the Democratic National Convention failed. One well-known progressive mayor who attended the Democratic Convention, George Latimer of St. Paul, could not recall any lobbying by the Chicago delegation, and felt that the booklet they distributed had the earmarks of a single politician's pet project.[54]

Whether Chicago's current programs of economic development catch on elsewhere is an interesting and important question. There is much reason to suppose that a constituency exists to support a redefinition of growth as a divisible public good, a set of strategies to promote affirmative action, small business development, neighborhood institution-building, and local job creation.

Mayor Washington says that it will take six years to "change the system" in Chicago enough to institute many programs. Meanwhile, he believes, "The level of awareness in this city has been raised. People are becoming more relaxed with us. The change is slow but perceptible."[55] The new policies he advocates, however, are opposed not only by the Democratic party machine and its local employees but by much of the local business community and by the Reagan Administration's policies. It is doubtful that one city, in isolation, can radically redefine the purposes of municipal government. According to Sidney Lens, it will require a national movement: "To transcend the policy of moderation, [Washington] would have to mobilize poor and disenfranchised Chicagoans for mass activity and join hundreds of other mayors to challenge the American Establishment."[56]

Big city mayors, whether minority or white, cannot escape the contradiction between "trickle-down" policies favored by corporations and business elites and demands from neighborhoods and minority populations that want direct, immediate benefits. City mayors will respond to the contradiction differently.

The New Urban Crisis

Most urban officials and their electoral coalitions have come to believe that growth is the only viable answer to local public problems. The federal government's policies also have exerted an important effect: "The Reagan Administration's cuts in urban aid have stimulated localities to intensify their search for . . . investments. . . .Under desperate conditions, the mere possibility that subsidies may work is apparently enough to prompt politicians to offer them."[57]

But the new methods of stimulating growth by redistributing tax burdens from business to city residents will not remain outside the political arena for long. Growth policies utilized by cities have redistributed tax burdens downward. Urban political leaders and their constituencies have been often reminded that economic decisions carry huge political consequences. Plant closings and the fact or threat of disinvestment by mobile national and international corporations have been the focus of community protest.[58]

Meanwhile, the objective social conditions that spawned the urban rebellions of the 1960s have, on the whole, worsened. As carefully documented by Philip Meranto and others, unemployment levels for minorities—and for whites, too—were far higher in the early 1980s than in the 1960s, and remained at depression levels for young black males.[59] The rate of poverty has increased precipitously since then. These statistics are almost certainly associated with rising suicide and crime rates. Deep cuts in social service programs have exacerbated these problems, so that "it becomes clear that the quality of urban life for millions of Americans is worsening."[60]

The mobilization of new urban constituencies will repoliticize economic development policies. The promises that accompany local versions of supply-side economics will not deter minority electorates from demanding that economic development be directly targeted to providing local jobs, social programs, housing, health facilities, and community physical improvements.

The exclusion of racial minorities from holding important electoral offices in big cities has only recently been ended, beginning with Carl Stokes's election as mayor of Cleveland in 1967. The first generation of black mayors confronted a dilemma: they wanted to implement policies to promote their constituents' material interests, but they faced declining local economies and tax bases, crumbling infrastructures, white flight, and deteriorating neighborhoods.[61] By the late 1970s, and accentuated under the Reagan Administration, all minority mayors must also cope with federal cuts in city programs and social services. In response, many of these mayors capitulated to the demands of the local corporate sector. Of course, these observations may apply equally to Hispanic mayors and to any progressive mayor.

As demonstrated by the Jesse Jackson presidential campaign, a new electoral politics is being created in America, centered in its industrial cities. The Jackson campaign provided an electoral voice for millions of blacks, Hispanics, and progressive whites who reject both the Democrats and Republicans. This new electorate will place new demands upon the second generation of black mayors and upon the first generation of Hispanic mayors. These mayors are caught between "two 'faces' of politics."[62] The one face is the old executive-centered, downtown coalition that has presided over growth politics since World War II. The other utilizes a new electoral coalition that favors policies to redistribute wealth and power broadly throughout the urban community.

> As conditions for blacks continue to worsen, we will see more clearly the two faces of urban politics. While one kind of black politician will seek accommodation with corporate America, other black politicians will become more vociferous *and* sophisticated in their challenges to the powerful. It is the latter face of black and urban politics that will be able to mobilize the masses of blacks and the poor in the electoral arena.[63]

This generation of urban leaders will find it increasingly difficult to pursue the conventional growth politics. Mayors may find it necessary to promise more immediate and visible benefits to their constituencies than in the past. Conflict over the targeting of local economic development efforts is also likely to intensify when national economic growth slows, removing the appearance that virtually all cities and all neighborhoods can simultaneously win from the granting of subsidies to businesses and corporations.

Most of the conflicts within urban culture result from the impact of economic forces on the social make-up of urban areas. The failures of the market to distribute goods and resources equitably to all groups in the urban economy have often brought a violent response in the form of riots, high crime rates, and other types of social disorganization. The task of local government, therefore, has always been to promote urban growth, that is, market processes, and to treat the consequences of that growth. City governments always have been faced with a central question: How are urban governments to solve the social problems that result from the high degree of structural inequality that exists in our society?

Urban politics is so immediately a politics of social class and race and segregation that issues of equity or equality become so divisive they can scarcely be dealt with directly. Even more important, local governments lack the resources and jurisdictions to treat the problems that result from national economic growth and change. But with the withdrawal of the national government from programs that address the problems of cities, political conflicts within cities and metropolitan areas are intensified. And as always, city governments are in the front line when economic growth conflicts with attempts to promote social justice and equality.

References

1. Ira Katznelson, "The Crisis of the Capitalist City: Urban Politics and Social Control," in *Theoretical Perspectives on Urban Politics*, ed. Willis D. Hawley, et al. (Englewood Cliffs, N.J.: Prentice-Hall, 1976), p. 219.

2. Katznelson, p. 219.

3. Interview with Tom Gougeon, administrative assistant to Denver mayor Federico Peña, July 17, 1984. Randy Ready, interviewer.

4. William Greider, "Detroit's streetwise mayor plays key role in city's turn around," *Cleveland Plain Dealer,* July 3, 1978; as cited in Todd Swanstrom, *The Crisis of Growth Politics: Cleveland, Kucinich, and the Challenge of Urban Populism* (Philadelphia: Temple University Press, 1985).

5. Sabre Foundation, *Enterprise Zone Activity in the States: Summary of Survey Findings* (Washington, D.C., 1983).

6. Michael Wasylenko, "The Location of Firms: The Role of Taxes and Fiscal Incentives," in Roy Bahl, ed., *Urban Government Finance: Emerging Trends* (Beverly Hills, Cal.: Sage Publications, 1981); Roger W. Schmenner, "Industrial Location and Urban Public Management," in Arthur P. Solomon, ed., *The Prospective City* (Boston: The M.I.T. Press, 1980), pp. 446–468; Neal R. Peirce, Jerry Hagstrom, and Carol Steinbach, *Economic Development: The Challenges of the 1980s* (Washington, D.C.: Council of State Planning Agencies, 1979); Barry M. Moriarty, et. al., *Industrial Location and Community Development* (Chapel Hill, North Carolina: University of North Carolina, 1980); and Roger J. Vaughan, *State Taxation and*

Economic Development (Washington, D.C.: Council of State Planning Agencies, 1979), p. 98.

7. Swanstrom, pp. 142–145.

8. Wasylenko, "The Location of Firms," p. 155.

9. Theodore J. Lowi, "The State of Cities in the Second Republic," in John P. Blair and David Nachmias, eds., *Fiscal Retrenchment and Urban Policy* (Washington, D.C.: Urban Institute Press, 1979), p. 47.

10. Coleman A. Young, "Detroit: Moving Forward in the Frost Belt," *USA Today* (November 20–22, 1981); and Thulani Davis, "Black Mayors: Can They Make The Cities Work?" *Mother Jones*, vol. 9, no. 6 (July 1984).

11. Dans, "Black Mayors: Can They Make the Cities Work?" p. 36.

12. Terry Nicholls Clark and Lorna Crowley Ferguson, *City Money* (New York: Columbia University Press, 1983), pp. 144–148.

13. H. James, M. Phillips, with D. Hazen, "The New Voter Registration Strategy," *Social Policy* (Winter 1984), pp. 2–9.

14. Albert K. Karnig and Susan Welch, *Black Representatives and Urban Policy* (Chicago: University of Chicago Press, 1980).

15. Susan Welch and Michael W. Combs, "Interracial Differences in Opinion on Public Issues in the 1970s," *Western Journal of Black Studies*, vol. 7, no. 3 (Fall, 1983), pp. 136–41.

16. Karnig and Welch, *Black Representatives and Urban Policy.*

17. William E. Nelson, Jr., and Philip J. Meranto, *Electing Black Mayors: Political Action in the Black Community* (Columbus: Ohio State University Press, 1977); and Charles H. Levine, *Racial Conflict and the American Mayor: Power, Polarization, and Performance* (Lexington, Mass.: D.C. Heath, 1972).

18. Karnig and Welch, *Black Representatives and Urban Policy.*

19. Rufus P. Browning, Dale Rogers Marshall, and David H. Tabb, *Protest Is Not Enough: The Struggle of Blacks and Hispanics for Equality in Urban Politics* (Berkeley: University of California at Berkeley, 1984).

20. Browning et al., p. 252.

21. James and Phillips, "The New Voter Registration Package."

22. Robert Pear, "States are Found More Responsive to Social Issues," the *New York Times*, May 19, 1985.

23. *New York Times*, "Mayoral Nominee Works Hard at Being Goode," May 19, 1983, p. 21A.

24. *New York Times*, "Chicago Election Makes a Dream Come True; "Defection of White Democrats May Hinder Washington," p. 13A, April 13, 1983, p. 13A.

25. Karnig and Welch, *Black Representatives and Urban Policy*; Sharon Watson, "The Second Time Around: A Profile of Black Mayoral Reelection Campaigns," *Phylon* (Fall 1984), pp. 165–178.

26. Watson, pp. 165–178.

27. Dennis R. Judd, "From Cowtown to Sunbelt City: Boosterism and Economic Growth in Denver," in Susan S. Fainstein, Norman I. Fainstein, Richard C. Hill, Dennis Judd, and Michael P. Smith, *Restructuring the City: The Political Economy of Urban Redevelopment* (New York: Longman, 1983), pp. 167–201.

28. George V. Kelly, *The Old Gray Mayors of Denver* (Boulder, Colo.: Pruett Publishing Co., 1974), p. 259.

29. Denver Urban Renewal Authority, *Denver Urban Renewal Authority Skyline Project: Summary of Developments* (Denver, Colo.: DURA, 1984).

30. Gary Delsohn, "Peña's Early Coalition a Winner," *Denver Post*, June 22, 1983, p. 15A.

31. Patrick Yack, "Peña Has Overcome One Issue Political Label," *Denver Post*, April 26, 1983, p. 78.

32. Bill Walker, "Old Guard Joins in Praise for Victor," *Denver Post*, June 22, 1983, p. 15A.

33. Gary Delsohn, "Registration of Hispanics Short of Goal," *Denver Post*, April 26, 1983, p. 1B.

34. Gary Delsohn, "Peña's Early Coalition a Winner," June 22, 1983, p. 15A.

35. Federico Peña, *The Peña Neighborhood Program: Neighborhood Planning, Preservation and Development* (March 19, 1983), p. 3.

36. City and County of Denver, *Economic Development Action Program* (Denver: CCD, 1984), p. 1.

37. Kevin Flynn, "Firms, City to Plan Core Area," *Rocky Mountain News*, July 9, 1984, p. 16.

38. Kevin Flynn, "Downtown Retailers Could Be Costly," *Denver Post*, April 1, 1984, p. 25.

39. Interview with John Parr, Director, Center for Public-Private Cooperation, University of Colorado at Denver, July 19, 1984.

40. Quoted in Gary Delsohn, "Leaders Say Big Problems Not Attacked," *Denver Post*, June 10, 1984, pp. 1, 14A.

41. C. Broderick, "Peña Speech Shifts Focus to 'Quality of Life'," *Rocky Mountain News*, July 12, 1985, p. 8.

42. Quoted in Broderick.

43. William J. Grimshaw, "Is Chicago Ready for Reform? or, A New Agenda for Harold Washington," in Melvin G. Holli and Paul M. Green, eds., *The Making of the Mayor: Chicago 1983* (Grand Rapids, Mich.: William B. Eerdmans Publishing Co., 1984), p. 8.

44. William A. Sampson, "The Politics of Adaption: The First Year of the Washington Administration," in Samuel K. Gove and Louis H. Masotti, eds., *Chicago Politics in Transition* (Urbana: University of Illinois Press, forthcoming 1987).

45. Interview with Kari Moe, assistant commissioner, Policy, Planning and Research, Department of Economic Development, City of Chicago, July 25, 1984.

46. Interview with Robert Mier, commissioner, Department of Economic Development, City of Chicago, July 24, 1984.

47. Sampson, "The Politics of Adaption."

48. City of Chicago, "'Chicago Works Together': 1984 Chicago Development Plan," (Chicago, Illinois: May 1984), p. 5.

49. "Chicago Works Together," p. 14.

50. B. Kelly, "Harold Washington's Balancing Act," *Chicago* Magazine (April 1985), pp. 180–207.

51. Sidney Lens, "A Mayor's Dilemma," *Progressive* (June, 1985), p. 22.

52. Kelly, "Washington's Balancing Act," p. 206.

53. *Mayor Harold Washington, A Federal/Urban Partnership to Renew Our Cities* (Chicago: Office of the Mayor, June, 1984).

54. Interview with Mayor George Latimer, July 27, 1984.

55. Kelly, "Washington's Balancing Act," p. 207.

56. Lens, "A Mayor's Dilemma," p. 22.

57. Harvey Molotch and John Logan, "Tensions in the Growth Machine: Overcoming Resistance to Value-Free Development," *Social Problems* (June, 1984), p. 494.

58. Barry Bluestone and Bennett Harrison, *The Deindustrialization of America: Plant Closings, Community Abandonment, and the Dismantling of Basic Industry* (New York: Basic Books, Inc., 1983).

59. William E. Nelson, Jr., Lawrence Mosqueda, and Philip Meranto, "Reagonomics and the Continuing Crisis in the Black Community," in Mitchell F. Rice and Woodrow Jones, eds., *Contemporary Public Policy Perspectives and Black Americans* (Boulder, Colo.: Greenwood Press, 1984), pp. 15–32; and L. Dunbar, *Minority Report: What Has Happened to Blacks, Hispanics, American Indians, and Other Minorities in the Eighties* (New York: Pantheon, 1984).

60. Nelson, Mosqueda, and Meranto.

61. Rod Bush, *The New Black Vote: Politics and Power in Four American Cities* (San Francisco: Synthesis, 1984), p. 4.

62. J. Jennings, "Blacks and Progressive Politics," in Bush, *The New Black Vote*, p. 290.

63. Jennings, p. 300.

INDEX

425

VA (Veteran's Administration)
loans, 277-279
Vietnam War, 323
Voting registration for blacks, 240
Voting Rights Act (1965), 239, 240,
286
Vrdolyak, Edward, 416

Wagner Labor Act, 139
Wagner, Robert (Mayor, New York
City), 318
Wagner, Robert F. (Senator, New
York), 261, 267
Wagner Steagall Housing Act, 138
Wallace, George, 302
War on Poverty, 302, 307, 312-321,
325
Warner, Sam Bass, 18, 19, 173
Warren, Michigan, 188
Washburn, C.L., 392
Washington, Booker T., 234
Washington D.C., 210, 291, 394
Washington, Harold (Mayor,
Chicago), 410, 414-418
The Washington Post, 414
West Bottoms, 55
West Virginia Turnpike Commission,
222

White, Andrew D., 91
Whitlock, Brand (Mayor, Toledo),
74, 91
Whitney, Eli, 26
Whyte, William H., 165
Wilson, Woodrow (President), 121,
233
Wirtz, Willard, 309
Wobblies, 71
Wood, Robert, 309
Woodcraft Indians, 174
Woolworth, Frank W., 22
Works Progress Administration
(WPA), 234
"Write down" cost of land, 265, 268,
272

Yerba Buena Center, 377-382
Yerkes, Charles, 87
Young, Andrew (Mayor, Atlanta),
408
Young, Coleman (Mayor, Detroit),
406, 407, 408
Young, George, 393
Youngstown, Ohio, 153

Zoning, 183